TRAVELLERS
EUROPE
SURVIVAL KIT

TRAVELLERS
EUROPE
SURVIVAL KIT

edited by
DAVID WOODWORTH

Published by Vacation Work, 9 Park End Street, Oxford

TRAVELLERS SURVIVAL KIT — EUROPE

Copyright © Vacation Work 1990

Sixth Edition

First edition by Roger Brown 1976
Second edition 1978
Third edition 1980
Fourth edition 1982
Fifth edition 1986

ISBN 1 85458 033 7 (softback)
ISBN 1 85458 034 5 (hardback)

All the information in this book has been carefully researched but changes are bound to occur. If you should encounter any inaccuracies or new information on your travels, please write to David Woodworth at Vacation Work, 9 Park End Street, Oxford OX1 1HJ. Those whose contributions are used will earn a free copy of the next edition.

Note: London Telephone Numbers

In this book we have given the telephone dialling prefixes 071 and 081 that will be in use for all London telephone numbers after May 6th 1990. To dial an 071 number from within the 071 area or an 081 number from the 081 area you do not need to dial the prefix and should just dial the last seven digits: in all other circumstances you will need to use these prefixes even if you are dialling an 071 number from the 081 area or vice versa. To dial a London number before May 6th 1990 dial 01- instead of 071 or 081.

Acknowledgements

The revision of this edition has been assisted by too many people to list, but special thanks to Simon Calder, Rebecca Ford, Susan Griffith, Emily Hatchwell and Charles James.

Illustrations by William Swan

Cover design by Miller Craig & Cocking Design Partnership

Printed by Gibbons Barford Print, Wolverhampton, England

Contents

Introduction

The early years of this decade will see great changes for travellers to Europe. The opening of the Channel Tunnel in 1993 will mean that they can travel from the centre of London to Paris or beyond without leaving their seats. The same year will see the beginning of the Single European Market, which will involve not only lower air fares as airlines are free to compete with each other for customers, but also the abolition of duty-free allowances between countries in the European Community.

But for all the talk of European harmonisation, of ambitious plans for unifying time zones and a single European currency, Europe remains an area of great contrasts containing many potential hazards for the unwary traveller. This book will help you to prepare for your trip to Europe and provide you with essential information while you're there — advice that covers the normal traveller's needs: transport, accommodation, eating and drinking and entertainment. And information that will help you deal with disasters like accidents, illness, theft, etc. Although the book might not make you feel at home abroad, all this at your fingertips should at least make your trip go smoothly.

THE PEOPLE

When you go abroad remember that many who have gone before you may have established a reputation that isn't altogether wholesome.

This is particularly true for British people, whose football supporters abroad have branded them with an image as violent troublemakers. You should also bear in mind that many foreigners, particularly in capital cities, suffer from "tourist fatigue" — a condition that happens when citizens trying to go about their daily business find their lives disrupted by tourists who overload the public transport, fill the cafes and restaurants and pester them with questions.

One should always treat local people with respect: remember that it is their country you are visiting.

Language. English is by and large the most popular second language learnt by Europeans, and so it is easy, but rather arrogant, to get by without trying even a few simple phrases in the local language.

You don't have to be fluent to be able to communicate, and all attempts to speak a foreign language are always appreciated. If you want to speak (as opposed to pass "O" Level in) any language, the cheapest casual courses are those arranged locally by technical colleges and adult education institutes. Contact your local education authority for details.

If you want to learn a language at home, there is an extensive range of study courses including Heinemann's *Made Simple* (books and tapes), Reader's Digest (tapes) and Linguaphone audio and video courses. These are expensive to buy, but it's quite possible that your local library may lend them for free. However, there is often a long waiting list for popular courses. An alternative is to follow a language course on television or radio. For details write to BBC Education, London W5 2PA (Tel: 081-991 8031).

Red Tape

PASSPORTS

By and large, you should possess a valid passport when travelling abroad. There may, however, be occasions when you have to travel without one. You do not need a passport to leave the UK. British nationals visiting Eire do not require a passport at all; for stays in Belgium and the Netherlands of 60 hours or less, an identity card (obtainable free at Channel ports on the day of departure in exchange for two photographs) is sufficient. In fact, most Common Market frontiers can be crossed (unofficially at least) with identification such as an expired passport, driving licence, etc, but since your success depends largely on the mood of the border guard this should not be relied upon. The British Excursion Document is valid for visits to France of up to 60 hours. It is available from main post offices, but — unlike the Visitor's Passport — the completed form and identity photograph has to be signed by a "person of standing" (ideally a doctor, lawyer or MP, but in practice anyone with a vaguely professional social standing will suffice). This condition is required also for full passports but not for British Visitor's Passports (see below). The document costs £2 and is valid for one month.

Within groups of countries with Customs Unions (ie Benelux and Scandinavia), there are no significant formalities, and you should rarely, if ever, be asked for identification.

On the basis that international travel is much easier with a valid passport, you should apply for one on a form obtainable from main post offices. Application forms for full passports are classified as follows:

Form A — 10-year passport (£15 for 30 pages; £30 for 94 pages).

Form B — 5-year passport for children under 16 (same price), renewable free for another five years on completion of Form D and two new photos.

Form C — amendment to an existing passport and/or adding children (variable charges).

Forms PD1, PD2, PD3 — post-dating a passport in a woman's future married name (plus form G if you already have a passport).

Young people under 18 from schools and recognised youth organisations may be included together on a collective passport (£30) if travelling together in a group with an approved leader over 21.

Children under 16 can be included on the passport of a parent (or elder brother or sister, except for travel to the Benelux countries) unless Czechoslovakia is your destination, in which case 15 year olds must have passports.

With family passports, only the bearer may go abroad alone. If you're forced to split up with others included on your passport, consult the nearest embassy or consulate immediately.

Apart from the British Excursion Document, only the British Visitor's Passport is available over the counter at main post offices in exchange for a completed form VP, two photos, a birth certificate or similar proof of identity as set out in the form, and £7.50. This can be used for visits of up to three months in Western European countries but for only three months altogether in Scandinavia. It is not valid for employment, nor is it available to children under eight. Applications for other passports must be sent to the appropriate passport office: allow at least four weeks (longer during February-August) for processing. Although Passport Offices are loath to say so, quicker processing may be possible if you make it clear on your application that you need it urgently. Calling in person may speed things up, but there is no guarantee of this; it will almost certainly involve queuing and does not guarantee priority treatment.

New style United Kingdom passports were introduced in 1988 and should be issued by all Passport Offices from 1990. Slightly smaller than the old dark blue passports, they have burgundy covers and share a common format with those issued by other European Community (EC) member states. Old-style passports will, of course, remain valid until their expiry dates.

Take good care of your passport. Keep it with you at all times, as close to your skin as is comfortable. They have a habit of falling out of jacket and trouser pockets, and of being lifted out of handbags. If you lose your passport abroad, report it immediately to the police, then to the nearest embassy or consulate. They in turn will either issue temporary papers to get you home or if necessary, issue a new passport. This will take a week or two to come through, and will probably only have limited validity (extendable when you get home). If you lose your passport in Britain, inform the police and the issuing officer; it is sensible to keep a separate record of your passport number in case of loss.

If you're about to go through the barrier and you realise your passport is out of date, keep cool and say nothing. It's amazing how often immigration officers fail to notice or turn a blind eye. In any case, it's already too late to do anything — but it's safest to check beforehand.

Immigration Act 1971. Freedom from UK immigration control depends on your residence rights. A full United Kingdom passport (but not a British Visitor's Passport) will either have the words British Citizen on page 1 if it was issued after January 1st 1983 or bear the endorsement "Holder has the right of abode in the United Kingdom" if it was issued before that date. Both of these signify that the bearer has the right to reside and work in EC countries (although work permits will be needed to take up employment in Spain and Portugal until January 1993). If your passport has neither of these, obtain form P2 for guidance.

CUSTOMS

Before you leave the UK, consider carefully whether you have any of the following about your person: controlled drugs, firearms, certain endangered species and their derivatives, and certain goods over 50 years old. If not, you should be free from export restrictions.

Your next stage should be to consult the details given under *Customs* for the countries you wish to visit. But, because of a general leniency towards tourists at most customs posts abroad, your most rigorous inspection is likely to be upon your return to Britain. You're allowed to re-import any articles taken out of the

UK duty and tax paid not more than three years previously. To avoid doubt about the legality of such re-imports, take any relevant receipts with you.

Memoranda of foreign customs regulations are obtainable from the Department of Trade and Industry Overseas Trade Division, 1 Victoria Street, London SW1E 0ET (Tel: 071-215 7877); they can also answer specific enquiries.

Duty-free Allowances. Make the most of duty-free allowances: the opening of EC countries to free trade among each other will involve the ending of duty-free allowances in 1993 (and increases in prices, as airlines and ferry companies currently subsidise their fares with the profits they make on duty-free sales).

The table opposite shows the allowances for the United Kingdom: these also apply to most other EC countries. Most EC countries also have restrictions on other items (such as tea and coffee) which are described under each individual country.

You are entitled to either the duty-free allowance or the duty-paid allowance but not both. You can, however mix duty-free and duty-paid provided they are in different categories; for example you can bring in 1 litre of duty-free spirits with five litres of duty-paid still wine. The duty-free column refers to goods obtained from anywhere outside the EC or duty and tax free within the EC e.g.: from a duty-free shop or on an aircraft or ship. The duty-paid column refers to goods obtained duty and tax paid from within the EC.

Import Restrictions. There are prohibitions and restrictions on the import or re-import into Britain of certain goods:

opium, heroin, morphine, cocaine, cannabis, amphetamines and lysergide (LSD); firearms, (including gas pistols, gas sprays, electric shock batons and similar weapons) and ammunition; explosives, including fireworks and amorces (toy caps); animals and birds whether live or dead and/or stuffed (see *Pets* below) and certain articles derived from rare species including furskins, ivory and reptile leather or goods made from them; meat, poultry and their products including bacon, ham, sausage, paté, eggs, milk and cream (but 1 kg per passenger of fully cooked meat or poultry meat products in cans or other hermetically sealed containers of glass or foil is permitted); plants; bulbs, trees, potatoes and certain other vegetables and fruits; flick knives and certain other offensive weapons; radio transmitters (walkie-talkies, citizen's band radios etc) capable of operating on certain frequencies; horror comics, indecent and obscene books, magazines, films, video cassettes and other articles; and counterfeit coins.

Pets. Think twice before taking Rex or Tiddles with you. Britain is one of the few countries in Europe that is still free of rabies, and this is reflected in the procedure for importing mammals — import licence and six months quarantine at your expense. The penalty for smuggling pets is an unlimited fine, often at least £1,000 and up to a year in prison. For details of import of pets, contact The Secretary, Animal Health Division C, Ministry of Agriculture, Fisheries and Food (MAFF), Hook Rise South, Tolworth, Surbiton, Surrey KT6 7NF (Tel: 081-330 4411).

Although no European countries require quarantine for pets coming from Britain, import procedures can still be long and expensive: certificate of health, rabies shots, import permit and a further examination on arrival. Regulations change frequently, so seek information from Embassies or MAFF, Animal Health Division C, Exports Section at the above address.

Duty-free Allowances — European Community

The allowances below are available to travellers entering the United Kingdom (except by land from Eire) if the goods being imported are part of their personal baggage and are broadly the same for Belgium, Denmark, Eire, France, West Germany, Greece, Italy, Luxembourg, the Netherlands, Portugal and Spain (not the Canary Islands) No one under 17 is entitled to the Alcohol or Tobacco allowance.

Alcohol

Alcoholic drink bought at a duty-free shop, on a ship or aircraft, or outside the EC.

1 litre of spirits or 2 litres of fortified, sparkling or still wine

plus
2 litres of still wine

Alcoholic drink bought tax and duty paid (eg from a shop or supermarket) in the EC.

1½ litres of spirits or 3 litres of fortified, sparkling or still wine

plus
5 litres of still wine

Tobacco

Bought duty free or outside the EC

200 cigarettes or 100 cigarillos or cigars or 250 g tobacco

Bought tax paid in the EC

300 cigarettes or 150 cigarillos or 75 cigars or 400 g tobacco

Perfume

Bought duty free or outside the EC

250 cc toilet water

plus
60 cc perfume

Bought tax paid in the EC

375 cc toilet water

plus
90 cc perfume

Other goods

Bought duty free or outside the EC
£32

Bought tax paid in the EC
£250

Most countries outside the EC have similar allowances to those above; variations are given in each chapter under *Red Tape at Entry*.

In addition, all European countries permit travellers to import a reasonable amount of articles for personal use. While this is ultimately left to the discretion of individual customs officers, the guidelines are roughly as follows:

one still camera with five films; one cine camera with two films; one pair of binoculars; one portable musical instrument; one record player and ten records; one tape recorder; one radio; one typewriter; one child's pram; one bicycle; one tent and other camping and sporting equipment (but most countries restrict the import of firearms and ammunition); personal jewellery and clothing.

If you are charged duty on goods you intend to re-export, get a receipt and apply for a refund when you're leaving.

Travellers entering Britain are allowed to import a maximum of 50 litres of beer or 25 mechanical lighters duty free or duty paid: these come under the "Other Goods" allowance.

Because of the state of flux of the world's currencies, our references to prices and exchange rates can only be taken as a rough guide.

Import and Export. In order to protect their currencies on the world market, most countries impose restrictions on monetary imports and exports. At present the UK has no restrictions on the import or export of any currency in any form. Some European countries have very strict regulations; these are listed for each country under *Money*.

Foreign Currency. As a rule of thumb, you will generally get better exchange rates if you change your money when you arrive abroad except in Germany, France and Spain. To change sterling into foreign currency, give the bank or travel agent at least a week's notice. You should, however, be able to obtain reasonable amounts of the more common currencies over the counter at the large branches of the major banks, and at Thomas Cook and American Express. Most building societies now issue foreign currency, but may require four working days to order it from their head office. Commission fees are computed in various ways by various establishments, but overall differences are so slight as to be almost negligible.

The same goes for changing cash or travellers cheques abroad. If one bank displays a more favourable exchange rate than the next, it's probably because they charge higher fees.

Changing Money Abroad. However you carry your money, you'll lose a little each time you change any. Apart from Belgium, where strange bank charges are in force, travellers cheques usually get a better exchange rate than cash. Commission rates are usually lower in banks than in hotels, restaurants and private exchange bureaux, especially those at border points, so plan your budget around banking hours. Remember, too, that low-value coins lose their value once they leave home territory, so if you're counting your pennies, count them before you reach the frontier. Changing money with other travellers cuts out the middlemen. Camp sites close to international borders are good places to exchange currency with travellers heading in the opposite direction.

Travellers Cheques. These are usually chosen as a safe way of carrying money, because they need your countersignature. But treat them with the same respect as cash, and don't countersign until you're actually cashing them. If you lose any, or have them stolen, give immediate notification, by telephone or telegram, to the issuing office or to a local agent or representative. You're responsible for any cheques fraudulently cashed between loss and notification, so speed is of the essence. In claiming refunds, it'll help if you know the cheques' serial numbers, so keep a list of these separate from the cheques. Companies vary a lot in the speed with which they refund lost or stolen travellers cheques; one of the best companies in this respect is American Express, who offer free hand delivery of replacement travellers cheques. In Britain, American Express travellers cheques are marketed under the brand name *Travellers Cheques Associates* (TCA) in conjunction with Lloyds Bank and the Royal Bank of Scotland.

The standard commission charge for travellers cheques is 1% of face value (with a minimum charge of £2 or £3) whether you buy them from a bank or building society. Generally you do not need to have an account with a financial institution in order to buy travellers cheques from it.

Note that the possession of just one American Express cheque (issued, for example, by the Leeds) entitles you to use their free customers' mail service and its *Refund Plus* service in case of crisis, under which American Express will cancel your credit cards, send an emergency message, provide you with temporary identification and help with alternative travel plans.

Uniform Eurocheques. Most British and Irish banks now issue Uniform Eurocheques — and the related card — to account holders. These brightly-coloured cheques and cards are recognised at 200,000 banks throughout Europe and can be used at nearly five million shops, restaurants, hotels and garages. Each cheque is guaranteed up to a maximum of 300 Swiss francs (around £100) *in local currency.* So if you wish to draw cash at a bank in West Germany, you should write the cheque for (say) DM300; if paying a hotel bill in France, you simply enter the amount in francs, up to the maximum of around 1,100 F. If the bill is more, you write extra cheques; there is no limit to the number you may use.

Unlike the previous Eurocheque arrangement, the Uniform Eurocheque system is fairly expensive, both when buying the card (around £6) and when using the cheques (£1.75 per cheque used).

Travellers who receive a personal identification number (PIN) along with the Uniform Eurocheque card can use it to draw money from cash dispensers in many European cities and resorts. There is a charge of £1.65 per cash machine withdrawal.

Postcheques. The National Girobank does not issue Eurocheques. Instead it issues postcheques, which can be cashed at post offices throughout Europe. National Girobank account holders can order postcheques at £6 for a book of ten, each of which can be cashed for the equivalent of £50 in post offices.

Credit Cards. The leading credit cards in the UK (*Visa* and *Access*) can be used in many outlets on the continent, and to draw cash in participating banks. They provide the security of another source of funds, but whether credit card transactions are to your advantage depends on the foreign exchange markets: the exchange rate used for calculations is the one in force on the day your voucher arrives back in Britain. This may be up to three months later, and so if the pound strengthens in the interim then you've made a profit. If you use cash dispensers abroad your account will be debited more quickly. If sterling goes down, however, the cost will increase.

Under the Consumer Credit Act 1974, you may be able to claim compensation from the issuing bank for goods bought using Access or Visa which turn out to be faulty.

The Thomas Cook Credit Card deserves a special mention since it represents the cheapest way to borrow money to finance a holiday (or, indeed, to pay for anything at all, such as buying a car). If your application (on forms available from any branch of Thomas Cook) is successful, you receive a card with which you can pay for travel arrangements through Thomas Cook or draw foreign currency. But most valuably, you can obtain travellers cheques which you need not pay for until up to seven weeks later. Therefore, by careful timing, you can borrow up to your credit limit and pay only the 1% commission charge every seven weeks, withdrawing travellers cheques to pay off your account. The annual interest rate works out at about the same as that of other credit cards.

Charge Cards. Massive advertising over the past few years has resulted in widespread possession and use of charge cards — American Express and Diners

Club — which do not automatically offer extended credit. You cannot easily spread payment over a number of months, but there is no pre-set spending limit. Both require an annual subscription. You can use these cards to guarantee personal cheques (up to £500 in the case of American Express green cards, more for their gold and platinum cards). American Express card holders can use their cards to get advances from cash dispensers on the *Link* network in the UK.

If you lose your credit or charge card, report it immediately to the nearest bank or agent. Any fraudulent use prior to reporting the loss will be charged to your account.

Emergency Cash. If you run out of money abroad, whether through mis-management, loss or theft, the best bet is to contact your bank back home (by telephone or telegram), and ask them to telegraph some money to you. This can only be done through a bank in the town you're in — something you have to arrange with your own bank, so you know where to pick the money up. This method of obtaining money isn't restricted to emergencies, but if you know where you're going to be a week or two in advance, it's much cheaper by mail. If you'll be staying in one place for a long time, ask your bank for an open credit arrangement with a conveniently located bank, which will enable you to draw cash as though you had an account there. Alternatively, simply open an account with a nearby bank in the local currency.

The Western Union, a long-established American company, offers an instant way of transferring cash between its agents (which may include travel agents, chemists, off licences etc). It already has agents in the Netherlands, is currently establishing a network in the UK, and plans to expand the network throughout Europe. For details contact Western Union on 071-251 1577.

Assuming that you have no money in your account at home, and your bank won't give you an overdraft because of your past record, you're in a pretty desperate situation. It sounds very simple and romantic to run out of money abroad and earn extra funds by finding a casual job, but in reality things don't just happen like that. Outside the European Community you aren't allowed to work unless you have a work permit, which usually has to be obtained in Britain. However, provided you have the right stamp in your passport (see under *Passports*, above), you're allowed to look for work in the EC countries, but you still have to get the right paperwork from the local authorities before you're strictly legal. Every Common Market nation has a major unemployment problem, so jobs still aren't easy to find, but seasonal work always provides a demand for the unskilled. Grape-picking in France in September and October is the classic example. Elsewhere, your best bet for finding unofficial work is usually in hotels and restaurants. Casual work is sometimes advertised on college notice boards — here you might find anything from teaching English to shifting pianos. If you have an artistic touch, tourist resorts can be quite profitable for selling even the simplest pen and ink sketches. For many more ideas on finding casual work, consult *Work Your Way Around the World* (Vacation Work, £7.95).

Most other forms of raising cash are also illegal — like begging, busking and street-selling. Even selling your camera is illegal unless you've paid import duty on it (not that anyone's likely to catch you), but no one should mind if you sell your clothes off — so long as you don't go around naked. Blood is a marketable commodity in many European countries (unless you've had jaundice or brucellosis, or carry AIDS antibodies), but you should wait at least four weeks before selling it again. The going rate is anything between £2 and £10 for 600 ml.

Go to your consulate only in the last resort; they aren't very sympathetic, nor are they in a position to dole out cash. The most they can do is cash a £50 cheque drawn on a British bank and supported by a cheque card, or — as a last resort — repatriate you. If this happens, your passport will be impounded upon arrival in the UK until you have paid your fare together with a fee for repatriation. Before they do this, they will try everything else, like contacting friends or relatives who could telegraph money to you. If all else fails and you do have to be repatriated, then all the costs are borne by you upon your return to the UK, together with a fee for the privilege.

Student Discounts. There is an internationally recognised card known as the International Student Identity Card that proves that the bearer is a student, and therefore eligible for student discounts. It is administered by the International Student Travel Confederation of Weinbergstr. 31, 8006 Zurich, Switzerland, an umbrella organisation of student travel offices in 62 countries around the world, in co-operation with the International Union of Students.

The card entitles the bearer to worthwhile discounts on a large number of travel fares, accommodation and restaurant bills, theatre tickets, museum entrance fees, and goods in a variety of shops. With the card comes a booklet giving a country-by-country guide to the discounts available.

The card is only issued to bone fide students and now comes in credit-card sized plastic, which should eliminate fraud. It is available from student travel offices around the world: to get one you will need a passport-sized photograph and proof of student status and you will have to pay a small fee to cover administration. In Britain the card is available from student travel offices (see Youth and Student Travel below for addresses) and costs £5.

Information on crossing to Europe is given under each heading in this section.

Travel Agents. It is usually most convenient to book ferry crossings, flights, hotels and package holidays through a travel agent. However, many individual travellers — and several comprehensive surveys — have found the advice given by agents is frequently inaccurate and incomplete. A good agent should have a good basic knowledge of the industry and rapid access to up-to-date information. However, the knowledgeable traveller who is prepared to undertake a little research can often gain a better grasp of travel options and fares to a particular destination than the local travel agent. It takes a fair amount of work to find the best deal for individual itineraries, and most travel agencies have neither the time nor the inclination to cater for personalised *wanderlust*.

The last years of the 1980s saw a decline in the number of British people going on package holidays, with consequent competition among travel agents for what trade was left. Before booking a holiday shop around your local travel agents for the best deal you can find, as they may be offering incentives to people who book with them. These may include discounts of 5% or more, free tape language courses, free travel insurance, a free set of luggage — and a free beach ball.

W.H. Smith Travel agents to be found within the larger branches of W.H. Smiths, offers an interesting scheme called TravelPlus. In exchange for an annual subscription of around £20 for a single person or £30 for a family you get free holiday insurance for a year (not including winter sports cover), the option of a budget account enabling you to spread the cost of your holiday over a year or more, and a newsletter giving details of special offers and exclusive holidays.

You do not necessarily need to book your holiday through a travel agent. Three credit card companies operate telephone booking services for their cardholders which offer discounts if you spend over a certain amount. With the TSB Trustcard you must spend at least £50 per person travelling in order to get a discount; with the Access Holiday Booking Service you must spend a total of £200; and with the Barclaycard Holiday Club you must spend a total of £350. To take advantage of these you must hold a TSB Trustcard, a Barclaycard, or an Access card (but not those issued by Lloyds Bank or the National Irish Bank) respectively.

Look at the small print carefully; as with some travel agents' special offers, you may have to take out the service's own travel insurance in order to get the discount.

CAR

Channel Crossing. Until the opening of the Channel Tunnel (scheduled for June 1993) taking a ferry remains the only way of taking a car across the channel. Finding the lowest fare requires some investigation: fare scales for each company vary according to season, numbers of passengers and time of sailing (among other factors) and no single operator is consistently cheapest. Competition is fiercest (and hence prices are lowest) on the short sea crossings from Folkestone, Dover and Ramsgate to French and Belgian ports. Longer passages are more expensive, but relaxing, and the ports may be more accessible to drivers from outside the south east of England. Irish drivers may bypass Britain completely by sailing direct from Cork or Rosslare to various French channel ports. Whichever route you choose, obtain quotes from as many operators as possible before paying up. Further details are given in *Sea,* below.

Motoring Organisations. General enquiries should be addressed to the offices below:

Automobile Association (AA), Fanum House, Basingstoke, Hants RG21 2EA (Tel: 0256-20123).
Royal Automobile Club (RAC), RAC House, PO Box 100, 7 Brighton Road, South Croydon, CR2 6XW (Tel: 081-686 2525).

Registration. You need a valid registration document (Form V5) for the vehicle you'll be driving. If, for any reason, this is not in your possession, apply to your local Vehicle Registration Office for a Certificate of Registration (Form V 379). If the registration is not in your name, you also need the registered owner's written permission. Official authorisation forms (obligatory for Portugal, advisable for Eastern Europe) are available from the AA or RAC. For vehicles hired in the UK; the accepted alternative to Form V5 is the Vehicle on Hire Certificate (Form VE 103), also issued by the AA or RAC.

Driving Permits. Within Europe, an International Driving Permit is only obligatory in Spain, if a 'green' UK licence is held, and Finland, if hiring a car or staying for longer than a normal holiday period. The IDP costs £2.50 from the AA or RAC. Elsewhere in Europe a valid UK licence (not provisional) is accepted; but an official translation into Italian is required for visits to Italy if a 'green' UK licence is held. Where the IDP is not obligatory, it may still be useful, for instance to facilitate car hire arrangements. The minimum age for driving in most of Europe is 18. If you are moving abroad permanently, you can exchange your British licence for another EC one subject to a medical check.

Insurance. Motor insurance is obligatory in all European countries, and very few British policies extend unconditionally to driving abroad. Your insurance company will advise you as to the best course to follow, and most will advise investment in a "green card" (International Motor Insurance Certificate) which is evidence in 32 countries abroad that legal motor insurance requirements have been met. Possession of a green card does not necessarily mean that your insurance cover is identical to that you have in the UK; check this with your insurer. Some companies, including the Guardian Royal Exchange, Municipal Mutual, or Municipal General (on their *Motor Plus* policy) issue green cards free to policy holders covering up to 30 days' (or more) holiday motoring. In many countries your own insurance policy is valid without a green card, but, even if it's comprehensive, it will only cover you for the minimum legal requirements in each country. This usually means third party only. So the best advice, still, is to get a green card. The green card should be endorsed if you are towing a caravan or trailer.

It can take days or sometimes weeks to organise a green card through your insurance broker. P&O Ferries sell an instant green card giving cover for 10-17 days for £18.90 at their offices in the channel ports under a scheme known as the Green Card Plus. This will probably be more expensive than organising a green card through your brokers, but is obviously more convenient.

You must show your green card at the frontier when entering a country where it is compulsory (i.e. Greece, Malta, Iceland, Turkey and Yugoslavia); otherwise you will have to buy temporary insurance at the frontier, which usually works out more expensive.

Vehicles with Ten or More Seats. Whether used commercially or not, all vehicles equipped to carry ten or more persons are classed as commercial public service vehicles within the EC, and are therefore subject to stringent rules on international journeys in or through the EC. The driver must be aged 21 or over; detailed log books must be kept; and the hours of driving are limited. These rules are not enforced for journeys solely within the UK, but when you travel abroad, the regulations begin at home. Full details are set out in the booklets *Taking a Minibus Abroad* and *Taking a Coach Abroad* available from the Department of Transport, 2 Marsham Street, London SW1P 3EB (Tel: 071-212 3068).

Other Requirements. Vehicles (and any caravan or trailer) must bear a nationality plate, at least 17.5 cm (7″) by 11.5 cm ($4\frac{1}{2}$″); with black letters at least 8 cm (3.1″) high on a white background.

It is advisable to carry a red warning triangle in all European countries, but this is not usually obligatory for foreign cars fitted with hazard warning lights. In case of breakdown, the triangle must be set up in the road at least 30 metres behind your vehicle. The triangles sold by the AA have a length of red tape to tie to your steering wheel, so you won't drive off without it.

Almost everywhere, headlights must be dipped or deflected to the right. The most effective method is to buy deflectors to fit over the headlamps, but these are expensive and cannot be fitted to halogen headlamps. The alternative is to buy (or make) a masking kit. Don't forget to return your lamps to their normal condition when you return home. A complete set of spare bulbs is compulsory in France, Italy, Spain and Yugoslavia.

Any caravan or trailer being towed abroad must bear a chassis number. If yours has none (or you can't find it) then the AA will supply a suitable numbered plate. Towed vehicles also need an oval registration plate.

Speed Limits in Europe

Limits shown in **bold** are miles per hour (mph); those in normal type represent kilometres per hour (km/h). These limits are for cars and higher-powered motorcycles; limits for commercial vehicles, buses, vehicles towing caravans or trailers and low-powered motorcycles are often lower. In some countries — notably Austria, West Germany and the Netherlands — there is also a minimum speed limit on motorways: vehicles must be capable of travelling at 44 mph/70 km/h on flat stretches.

Lower limits — and occasionally higher limits in urban areas — may be posted locally.

	Urban Areas		Single Carriageways		Dual Carriageways		Motorways	
Austria	**31**	50	**62**	100	**62**	100	**81**	130
Belgium/								
Luxembourg	**37**	60	**56**	90	**75**	120	**75**	120
Eire	**30**	48	**55**	88	**55**	88	**55**	88
France-dry	**37**	60	**56**	90	**68**	110	**81**	130*
-wet	**37**	60	**50**	80	**50**	80	**68**	110*
West Germany	**31**	50	**62**	100	**81**	130**	**81**	130**
Great Britain	**30**	48	**60**	97	**70**	112	**70**	112
Greece	**31**	50	**50**	80	**50**	80	**62**	100
Italy	**31**	50	**68**	110†	**68**	110†	**81**	130†
Netherlands	**31**	50	**50**	80	**62**	100	**74**	120
Portugal	**37**	60	**56**	90	**56**	90	**75**	120
Spain	**37**	60	**56**	90	**62**	100	**62**	100
Switzerland	**31**	50	**56**	90	**56**	90	**74**	120
Turkey	**31**	50	**56**	90	**56**	90	**56**	90
Yugoslavia	**37**	60	**50**	80	**62**	100	**75**	120
Denmark	**37**	60	**50**	80	**50**	80	**68**	110
Finland	**31**	50	**50**	80	**62**	100	**75**	120
Iceland	**28**	45	**44**	70	**44**	70	—	—
Norway	**31**	50	**50**	80	**50**	80	**56**	90
Sweden	**31**	50	**44**	70	**56**	90	**68**	110

Notes

* On toll-free motorways in France, the lower limits for dual carriageways apply. On French toll motorways, there is a minimum speed limit in the outside lane of **50**/80.

** Limits for dual carriageways and motorways are advisory; however, lower limits are being made mandatory on many roads in an effort to reduce air pollution.

† Weekdays. At weekends 56 mph (90 km/h) on dual carriageways and 68 mph (110 km/h) on motorways.

Rules of the Road. Drive on the right, except in Eire, Malta and Cyprus. This takes an hour or two to get used to, and you'll find you want to lapse back to driving on the left when you're starting off, turning and especially coming off roundabouts. So beware, in particular when there's no other traffic about to provide orientation. You may find it helpful, though expensive, to fit an offside wing mirror if your car is not equipped with one. This is obligatory in Italy.

Another thing that's difficult to get used to is the rule that you have to give way to traffic coming from the right, even when you're on what appears to be the main road. On many highways, this priority rule is waived in favour of the main road traffic. The international sign telling you you're on a priority road is a yellow diamond with a white frame. At roundabouts the same rules apply — if you're on the roundabout, give way to traffic coming from the right — except in France, Germany and Poland, where traffic on the roundabout always has priority. In cities with tram services, trams always have priority, and have little hesitation in asserting it.

In all countries except Gibraltar and Portugal and urban areas of Spain, seat belts must be worn by drivers and front seat passengers, with certain exceptions such as pregnant women and dwarfs; under similar legislation, children are banned from the front passenger seat.

Apart from Spain (where only sidelights may be used in towns) it is universally illegal to drive on sidelights alone; and dipped headlights must be used in poor daytime visibility. But be warned that the daytime use of headlights assists police helicopters to track speeding drivers.

Direction indicators must always be used before turning, changing lane or overtaking. Outside built-up areas, it is also customary to show your intention of overtaking either by sounding your horn (by day only), or by flashing your lights. If a foreign driver makes these signals to you, he is only using a recognised code, and not necessarily expressing impatience. Returning the signal indicates acknowledgment of his intention; do not accelerate when being overtaken. Apart from overtaking, horns may only be used in cases of emergency, and this universal law is particularly strictly enforced if a horn is used in a stationary car, at night, or in a built-up area. Incidentally, if an oncoming driver flashes his headlights at you, he may be warning you of a police speed trap further ahead. This practice is widespread but illegal.

Pedestrians have right of way at traffic light controlled crossings and, in most countries, at uncontrolled zebra crossings (where the right of way is established by stepping on to the crossing — exception: someone pushing a pram or push-chair). Do not test your rights unless you're prepared to be martyred for the cause.

Level crossings should always be approached with care — they usually have a barrier on the right hand side of the road only, but some don't have a barrier at all — the only warning is a flashing red light and a bell. When waiting at railway crossings on the continent at night it is usual to switch off the main beam on your car's headlamps.

First aid kits are compulsory in Austria, Greece, Turkey and Yugoslavia, and are advisable elsewhere. Kits may be hired from the motoring organisations.

Carry your driving licence and insurance document at all times.

Petrol. Prices vary widely in Europe — details are given under each country. In general, fuel is cheaper close to refineries and in cities, more expensive in remote areas. Unleaded petrol is available in all European countries except Turkey.

Parking. With parked cars now almost totally blocking the traffic flow in many

European cities (especially Paris), more and more desperate measures are being introduced, which invariably confuse newcomers. Meters and discs are common in the UK and abroad: meters can be used for a certain length of time (so long as you put money in) but over-feeding is usually frowned upon. At night and on Sundays, meter parking is often free. Discs (usually free from tobacconists or local police stations) indicate your time of arrival and latest time of departure. Less common are the systems for limiting parking to one side of the street at a time. Alternate day parking allows parking on the uneven days of the month on the side marked by signs with a Roman I, and/or on the side with uneven numbered houses. Parking on even days is allowed on the side with signs bearing a Roman II. Another common system — alternating twice a month — permits you to park for the first half of the month on the side with signs saying 1-15; for the rest of the month on the side with signs marked 16-31.

Tolls. When planning — and costing — your trip bear in mind that tolls are payable on some motorways in France, Italy, Spain, Portugal, Greece and Yugoslavia, and some roads in Austria. Tourist offices should be able to advise you how much your route will cost in tolls. In addition, vehicles in Switzerland must display a motorway tax sticker showing that motorway tax of 30 Swiss francs has been paid. These stickers are available from motoring organisations and at the border.

Breakdowns. The best way to ensure against breakdowns is to make sure your car is in perfect working order before you set off. Have it thoroughly serviced and take a few spares, as they may be difficult to find abroad. The obvious ones are lights, fan belt, plugs, hoses, ignition key and fuses. Spare kits can be hired from Selectacar Ltd (agents for the RAC), 10 Plaistow Lane, Sundridge Park, Bromley, Kent BR1 3PA (Tel: 081-460 8972) and the AA Hire Service, Snargate Street, Dover, Kent CT17 9XA (Tel: 0304-203655). A list of Lucas agents in Europe is available from Lucas Service Overseas Ltd, Windmill Road, Haddenham, Bucks (Tel: 0844 291681). Unless you're hyper-confident about the condition of your car, invest in one of the continental motoring policies offered by the AA (*Five Star*) and RAC (*Eurocover*) Details from any AA or RAC office. including those at the channel ports. For either policy non-members pay an additional £3.

If you have a breakdown or accident which is so bad that you abandon your vehicle, check that you are not expected to take it with you upon departure; some border officials in southern and eastern countries will otherwise assume that you have sold it illegally, and arrest or detain you accordingly.

Accidents. If you're involved in an accident, and you're still alive and conscious, proceed with great caution. The obvious rules apply: call the police; take names and addresses of other drivers, their insurance companies, and any independent witnesses (give them your version of what happened in case they didn't see). But don't ever admit responsibility. Don't even mutter an apology to anyone else involved. If possible, don't move any of the vehicles, but if you have to because you're obstructing the traffic, mark their wheel positions in the road, and take some pictures if you have a camera. When dealing with the police, don't sign your statement unless you're sure it's been written down accurately. If necessary, insist on having an interpreter there and don't sign unless it's in English.

Winter Driving. Make sure you have enough anti-freeze in the radiator. Try to keep the vehicle somewhere warm overnight. For driving on snow and ice, chains are obligatory on some mountain roads. These can usually be hired locally.

Otherwise studded tyres are advisable, but are only allowed when justified by road conditions. Snow glare can be averted by sunglasses.

Summer Driving. Keep the radiator topped up, using warm, not cold water. If the radiator runs dry, allow to cool before adding any water at all; and don't forget the effect evaporation will have on your anti-freeze ratio. Petrol can also vaporise — leave petrol lines to cool completely before re-starting the engine. Sunglasses are almost essential for driving in the Mediterranean sun. Aerosols can explode at 50°C (122°F).

MOTORCYCLE

Most of the points above apply equally to motorcyclists. Laws on helmet-wearing vary, but to be certain of avoiding the wrath of the authorities — and reducing the risk to your life — wear a helmet at all times.

Brittany Ferries has in the past suffered from a number of unpleasant incidents involving Hells Angels on its Plymouth-Santander route, and so in 1990 announced that it will no longer be accepting reservations for motorcycles over 4 years old (on the principle that Hells Angels do not ride new bikes). But the company has the discretion to relax this rule when they think appropriate, and so serious motorcyclists should check with them before making alternative arrangements.

PUBLIC TRANSPORT

Because of the amazing diversity of services and fare structures in all forms of public transport, particularly air travel and cross-channel ferries, you must be prepared to undertake some research to find the best price and mode of transport for your journey. Things are not quite what reason might dictate in the travel industry. If you're only travelling one way, it is often cheaper to buy a return ticket than a single. Watch the press and travel agents' windows for details of last-minute flight bargains; you may be able to fly for less than the cost of the bus fare. *Business Traveller* magazine (published monthly from 388-396 Oxford Street, London W1N 9HE) will save money for any frequent traveller, and includes a comprehensive air fares guide with each issue.

TRAIN

British Rail International (in conjunction with continental partners) operate services which allow fast international journeys from London and elsewhere. The times to Brussels and Paris have been cut to under six hours, and connections with German *IC* and French *TGV* trains enable you to reach southern France, Switzerland, much of Germany and even Salzburg within a day's travel from London. Dial 071-834 2345 for information and 071-828 0892 for credit card bookings. There are recorded timetables for several destinations: Amsterdam — 071-828 4264; Basel — 071-828 7315; Brussels and Cologne — 071-828 0167; Paris 071-828 8747. Information is available to Prestel subscribers on 5456.

In many countries, supplements are payable for all but the slowest trains and reservations are often essential.

Cheap Deals. Same-day and European Saver five-day returns from the UK offer substantial savings. Night fares to France and leisure fares to most destinations offer the maximum benefit of long stay and low cost.

The age limits for children's reductions vary from country to country, but are standardised for international journeys; children under 4 travel free: children under 12 at half price.

Holders of BR Senior Citizens Railcards qualify for the *Rail Europ Senior Card,* which costs £5 for up to one year. Cardholders benefit from a reduction of 30%-50% on international journeys, and on services on the national railways of Austria, Belgium, Denmark, Eire, France, West Germany, Greece, Hungary, Italy, Luxembourg, the Netherlands, Norway, Portugal, Spain, Sweden, Switzerland and Yugoslavia. Discounts are given on the appropriate standard 1st or 2nd class fare. Supplements must be paid in full. Channel crossings on Sealink, Hoverspeed and the P&O Dover-Ostend route also qualify for a discount.

For details of the Inter-Rail card and other discounts for young people, see *Youth and Student Travel* below. The older reader may be interested to learn that in 1989-1990 Sweden, Norway, Denmark and Finland experimented with issuing an Inter-Rail card to those aged over 26 (normally the maximum age for the card is 25). The experiment will be assessed by all the participating countries in May 1990, and the result may be an Inter-Rail ticket open to all.

Older people from America or Canada are more fortunate; they can buy one of three different types of *Eurailpass,* which give unlimited first class rail travel free of surcharge in Austria, Belgium, Denmark, Germany, Finland, Greece, Hungary, Italy, Luxembourg, the Netherlands, Norway, Portugal, Ireland, Spain, Sweden, and Switzerland. The basic *Eurailpass* is available for 15 days unlimited travel for US $320 (Can $408), 21 days cost US $398 (Can $528), 1 month costs US $498 (Can $660), 2 months cost US $698 (Can $900), or 3 months costs US $860 (Can $1,116).

There is also a 15 day *Eurail Saverpass* that must be issued to at least 3 people in high season (April 1st-September 30th), or 2 people in low season, and costs US $230 (Can $288) for 15 days.

The *Eurail Flexipass* gives 9 days travel in a period of 21 days for US $340 (Can $432).

Americans or Canadians aged under 26 can buy the *Eurail Youth Pass* which gives unlimited rail travel like the above but is valid only for second class travel. The costs are US $360 (Can $456) for one month and US $470 (Can $600) for two months.

Motorail. Allowing the train to take the strain is an expensive option for motorists. However, families who use Motorail can save money compared with the cost of petrol, motorway tolls and hotel accommodation *en route*: it is worth taking the time to sit down and calculate the relative cost of each method. There are year-round services from Calais to Nice and from Paris to Lisbon and Madrid. In summer, there are additional motorail trains from the Channel ports to southwest France and northern Italy and from Brussels to Ljubljana; in winter, from Paris to the French Alps. For details contact a travel agent or motoring organisation. For journeys via France contact French Railways, 179 Piccadilly, London W1V 0BA, and for journeys from Belgium, the Netherlands and Germany contact German Federal Railways, Hudson's Place, Victoria Station, London SW1. Note that roof racks must be removed before boarding. Take a spray demoisturiser to avoid problems with ignition following a long, exposed journey.

Mountain Driving. Descending traffic gives way to ascending. When parking on a hill, use the lowest uphill gear, and either put chocks under the wheels or turn the wheels to the pavement. Engines lose horsepower with altitude — about 10% loss at 3,000 feet (900 m); 20% at 6,000 feet.

Tree-lined Avenues. Beware of driving at a steady speed along straight tree-lined roads, especially with the sun low on the horizon. The rhythm can have a hypnotic effect, and has known to bring on grand mal fits.

Car Hire. In the international world of car hire, there are five giants:

Avis, Trident House, Station Road, Hayes, Middlesex UB3 4DJ (081-848 8733);

Budget, 41 Marlowes, Hemel Hempstead, Herts. HP1 1LD (0800 181181);

EuroDollar Rent-a-Car, Swan National House, 3 Warwick Place, Uxbridge, Middlesex UD8 1PE (0895 33300);

Europcar, High Street, Bushey, Herts WD2 1RE (081-950 5050);

Hertz, Radnor House, 1272 London Road, Norbury SW16 4DQ (081-679 1777).

These are not the cheapest companies by any means, but they are the most versatile — they have offices in large towns and at airports throughout Europe. Rates vary widely from one company to another. Budget, which operates as a network of locally-owned franchises, is usually cheapest; but if you pre-book from Britain, the rates offered by its rivals are more competitive. Each offers a cut-price scheme for vehicles booked and paid for in advance, such as *Super Value* (Avis), *Europe on Wheels* (Hertz) and *Super Sterling* (Budget).

If you just want to rent a car for a day or two, the cheapest deals are offered by the smaller local car rental firms, which advertise in local papers or can be found in the telephone directory. These companies also usually have a lower age limit than the larger companies. If you fly to the continent, ask a travel agent about inclusive Fly and Drive offers.

Britain is the worst place in Europe to hire a care for international journeys. Whether you return the car to Britain or leave it somewhere on the continent, you'll have to pay the car's return passage across the Channel. UK residents may only import a car hired abroad if their own has broken down. It must be declared at importation and should be re-exported or returned to the owner within a fortnight.

BUS

The most comprehensive network of coach services in Europe is operated by *Eurolines*, a consortium of some of the largest coach operators in Europe including National Express in Britain. Their services cover around 190 destinations in Belgium, France, Germany, Greece, Ireland, Italy, the Netherlands, Portugal, Scandinavia, Spain, Switzerland, Turkey and Yugoslavia. Unlike some cheaper coach operators Eurolines adhere strictly to licensing and driver regulations: one hears occasional horror stories about drivers from other companies falling asleep in the middle of Yugoslavia while driving the London-Greece run single handed.

The UK Head Office of Eurolines is 23 Crawley Road, Luton, Beds LU1 1HX (Tel: 0582 404511). In London personal callers can book tickets at 23 Grosvenor Gardens, Victoria, London SW1, or the Coach Travel Centre, 13 Regent Street, London SW1. For information about services dial 071-730 0202: to make credit card bookings call 071-730 8235. Bookings can also be made at any National Express (or Caledonian Express in Scotland) agent. As sample fares, an adult return to Paris would cost £47, or to Frankfurt it would cost £74.

Cheap Deals. Holders of student identity cards can save around 10%: on some routes discounts are also open to people aged under 25. During the winter there may be special "Two for the price of one" deals to certain channel ports in France.

There are two ticket deals open to people who wish to visit more than one European city. *Capital Trippers* permit a circuit from London to Paris and Brussels (or Brussels to Paris) for £57, or to Paris and Amsterdam (or to Amsterdam and Paris) for £58. *Bus Passes* permit a journey from London to Lisbon, Barcelona and Amsterdam for £115.50; to Paris, Lisbon, Barcelona and Amsterdam for £164, and to Amsterdam, Barcelona, Rome and Paris for £165. With both of these tickets you are recommended to reserve a seat for the next leg of your journey as soon as you arrive in a city.

SEA

Consult the *ABC Shipping Guide* for a complete list of operators across the Channel and beyond.

Fares vary according to distance and the amount of competition on a particular route. Offers of interest to both cars and passengers include five-day returns (for about the same price as the one-way journey) and the various winter specials at low prices to fill empty spaces.

Booking is advisable in high summer, but at other times you should be able to turn up and go. Frequent channel crossers may wish to buy shares in P&O Ferries to obtain a discount on certain crossings. You can obtain a full list of concessionary discounts by sending £2.50 to Seymour Pierce Butterfield Ltd, 10 Old Jewry, London EC2R 8EA (Tel: 071-628 4981).

AIR

Your rights as an air traveller are protected by the Air Transport Users' Committee, who will assist with complaints that cannot be settled between the airline and yourself. They are associated with the Civil Aviation Authority (CAA), 45-59 Kingsway, London WC2B 6TE (Tel: 081-379 7311).

To get a cheap air ticket these days there is no longer any need to use back-street bucket shops, as cheap air deals are far more widely available through regular travel agents. For example, Thomas Cook recently installed "Flight Centres" in its stores at a cost of £18 million. In addition to normal high-street travel agents, you should check the deals offered by Campus Travel and STA Travel, which do not restrict themselves to dealing solely with students and those aged under 26. It would also be worth getting quotes from Trailfinders at 46-48 Earl's Court Road, London W8 and 42-48 Kensington High Street, London W8 (Tel: 071-937 5400). For good fares to Paris and Germany try the German Travel Centre Ltd at 8 Earlham Street, London WC2 (Tel: 071-379 5212).

With cheap charter and scheduled flights widely available, there is limited scope for bucket shop tickets within Europe. However, these do exist and can be useful for businessmen and other travellers who need flexibility. There are three kinds: straightforward discounted tickets (such as Barcelona-London on British Airways, sold by Spanish agents for much less than the lowest published fare); "fifth-freedom" flights, where a passenger is carried between two countries by the airline of a third (eg London-Paris on Gulf Air at cut-price rates); and "sixth freedom" tickets for travel via another country (for example flying London-Bucharest-Athens on the Romanian airline *Tarom*).

If all else fails and you have to pay full fare (or if someone else is paying for you) then you might as well use the "maximum permitted mileage" regulation. For instance, you could fly London-Cologne-Vienna-Athens-Rome-London (stopping off in the immediate cities) for the same price as the normal London-Athens return fare. A good travel agent will do the sums for you and tell you of more exotic schemes still.

Couriers. Most companies involved in transporting "time sensitive documents" use full-time employees around Europe, but try Courier Flights on 081-844 2626. Fares are around two-thirds of the lowest official fares. Most trips are for a fixed duration (one or more weeks), and "walk-on couriers" may take only one piece of hand luggage.

Compensation. Once you have checked in on time at the airport, you become the airline's responsibility. This means one of two things, depending on the airline. Most scheduled airlines on international flights in Europe operate a compensation scheme, effective when you are more than four hours late at your destination. This covers costs incurred — meals, phone calls, accommodation etc. and can be as much as half of the air fare.

Charter airlines (or charter flights on scheduled airlines) do not offer anything like the same remuneration. They may or may not offer you food and/or accommodation. They certainly won't give you any money. However, most holiday insurance policies offer compensation for lengthy delays. All bona-fide companies should quote an Air Travel Operator's Licence number (ATOL) in their literature.

Accidents. Despite tales of millions of dollars compensation being paid to survivors and victims' relatives, it's unwise to expect anything, especially if the case is tried in the UK — one of the meanest countries in the world for awarding damages. The Warsaw Convention establishes an upper limit of £11,700 for loss of life, with a condition that more may be paid if wilful misconduct can be proved against the airline or manufacturer. British courts seem to start with the assumption that no price can be put on the grief of bereavement (so no price is).

CYCLING

It is quite feasible to take your bicycle abroad. On international rail journeys from the UK, you are usually required to send the bicycle as registered luggage and pay accordingly. Your machine may or may not arrive at the same time as you. Car ferries accept bicycles for channel crossings; some make no charge, others ask for 50% of the adult fare. You can take bicycles as luggage on most flights (including charters) by removing parts as specified by the airline, so don't forget to take a spanner. A few airlines do not accept bikes, so check before flying. Check also that the bike plus one pannier does not exceed your baggage weight allowance, you can take the other pannier on the plane as hand luggage, so fill it with your heaviest articles. Remember to let down your tyres to avoid explosions at altitude.

For further information on cycling abroad, contact the Cyclist's Touring Club, 68 Meadrow, Godalming, Surrey GU7 3HS (Tel: 04868 7217): they produce information sheets on specific countries for their members. Recommended reading *The Cycle Tourers' Handbook* by Tim Hughes (£9.95).

WALKING

A sign of the increasing concern for health and enjoyment of the Great Outdoors is shown by the growth of hiking trails. Although these cannot be recommended as a sensible means of reaching a faraway destination for a fortnight's holiday there is a network of international long-distance footpaths stretching across Europe.

HITCH-HIKING

Hitching is indisputably the cheapest way of travelling, and if you're lucky it's not necessarily the slowest. If speed is your criterion, remember that you're relying for the most part on sheer luck, so it's unwise to set yourself a deadline. Girls, whether singly or in pairs, always tend to have the shortest waits, but for safety the ideal combination is a man and a girl together. Two men will travel very slowly. Gimmicks are widely used — the Union Jack is reckoned to be a help, and destination signs can be useful when you're just a few miles short of a major junction. But the most constructive way of speeding up your journey is your choice of location. Town centres are as useless as fast stretches of open road in the country. Motorways are illegal (and you can get on the spot fines), but there's nowhere better than a busy slip road or a service area. Service areas are particularly good at night, because they're well lit and you can ask people for lifts.

Part of the art of hitch-hiking is being able to turn down a lift, not merely because the driver looks like a homicidal maniac, but also because of the risk of giving up a good position for the sake of a few kilometres. Don't leave a busy motorway slip road if you risk being dropped at a deserted one, or at an illegal motorway junction. Also, don't be afraid of spending a little cash on bus or train tickets, in order to escape town centres and crowds of hitch-hikers.

The various systems of localised number plates can be extremely useful in identifying the probable origin or destination of each vehicle, and drivers will sometimes stop other cars which look as though they could take you further. Full details of all these systems, plus motorway maps and city guides, appear in *Europe: a Manual for Hitch-hikers* (Vacation Work, £3.95).

YOUTH AND STUDENT TRAVEL

Over the past few years, the criterion for cheap travel for young people has changed from student to youth status. Travellers under 26 are entitled to buy BIJ (*billets internationaux de jeunesse*) international rail tickets at substantial discounts. The only conditions concern the trains you may catch without having to pay a supplement. BIJ tickets contain details of the services which can be used. These are not always the fastest or most comfortable. The biggest operator is Eurotrain. Most BIJ tickets offer a variety of routings and unlimited stopovers.

Within individual countries, as opposed to international journeys, discounts are harder to come by. However, certain nations enable students and/or youths to buy cards which then earn a 50% or so reduction. Details are given under each country.

For travellers under 26 the range of Inter-Rail cards offers unlimited rail travel in 22 countries for one month. Free travel is allowed on the national rail networks of Austria, Belgium, Czechoslovakia, Denmark, Eire, Finland, France, West Germany, Greece, Hungary, Italy, Luxembourg, the Netherlands, Norway, Portugal, Romania, Spain, Sweden, Switzerland, Turkey and Yugoslavia. In addition, holders can use the railways of Morocco. Within the United Kingdom the card entitles you to reduced-rate travel on British Rail and Northern Ireland Railways. Discounts of 30-50% are available on some ferry links to and from Britain. The standard Inter-Rail card costs £155. The Inter-Rail and Boat card at £180 also gives free

travel on certain shipping routes. The Inter-Rail Flexicard, at £145, is valid for any 10 days' travel within a month and offers the same facilities as the Inter-Rail and Boat card. The card also gains the holder free admission to most of the railway museums of Europe. Inter-Rail cards can be purchased from larger British Rail stations and BR appointed travel agents. Upon expiry, cards can be returned to the issuer in exchange for a small refund.

This is to assist with market research and to reduce opportunities for fraud.

In practice, if your travel plans are limited to nearby countries, it may well be cheaper to string together BIJ tickets and national rail passes, most of which offer considerable discounts for youths and students. These are detailed under each country; study the figures carefully before choosing between Inter-Rail and a combination of tickets and passes.

There are two main chains of youth and student travel offices in Britain both of which issue Eurotrain tickets, the ISIC card, Inter-Rail cards, and have information about other travel bargains for young people.

Campus Travel has its main London branch (known as London Student Travel) at 52 Grosvenor Gardens, London SW1W 0AG (Tel: 071-730 3402), with other London branches in the YHA Adventure Store, 14 Southampton Street, London WC2, in the Eurotrain Kiosk in the front concourse at Victoria Station, and in the Students' Union of University College, London, plus regional branches in Birmingham, Bristol, Brighton, Cambridge, Cardiff, Dundee, Glasgow, Liverpool, London, Manchester, Newcastle, Oxford and Sheffield.

STA travel, the other chain, has London branches at 74 and 86 Old Brompton Road, London SW7 3LQ and 117 Euston Road, London NW1 2SX (Tel: 071-937

UNLIMITED TRAVEL IN 22 COUNTRIES

On an Inter-Rail holiday, the nearest you get to a package is your rucksack

If you are under 26, an Inter-Rail ticket will give you one month's unlimited travel in no less than 22 countries across Europe and North Africa, from Morocco to Finland and France to Rumania.

Inter-Railers have an even bigger choice in 1990, with the addition of Czechoslovakia and Asiatic Turkey.

So what are you waiting for? Pick up a leaflet from your nearest BR Travel Centre or appointed travel agents, or phone Teledata on 071-200 0200.

FOR JUST **£155**

≋ **British Rail International**

9921), plus regional branches in Bristol, Cambridge, Manchester and Oxford, and branches in Birmingham, Brunel, Kent and Loughborough Universities.

Another important organisation for youth travel in Wasteels International, which has 190 retail outlets in 16 European countries. Its London address is Wasteels Travel, 121 Wilton Road, London SW1V 1JZ (Tel: 071-834 6744). Wasteels issue their own reduced price rail tickets for travellers under 26 under the name "Route 26". In addition, they issue full price rail tickets for continental rail travel and the rail cards issued by the West German, Dutch, Spanish, Swiss, Belgian, Austrian and Scandinavian rail companies. Anyone travelling on a ticket issued by Wasteels can call in at any of their branches for advice and assistance — a useful perk.

MAPS AND TIMETABLES

The British Rail International timetable and leaflets for individual areas are free. You can consult many countries' timetables in public libraries, either on their own or in the Thomas Cook European Timetable, which also contains information on ferries, visa requirements and other useful tit-bits. In libraries you should also find the *ABC Shipping Guide* (for more detailed ferry timetables) and the *ABC World Airways Guide* (air fares and timetables and car hire directories). The *ABC Air-Rail Guide* contains information on travelling between larger cities in Europe.

For a good free and up to date road map of Europe south of Gothenburg and west of Belgrade write to G. L. Treble Associates, 19 Hampstead Lane, London N6 4BR, enclosing a large stamped addressed envelope bearing a 30p first class or a 24p second class stamp. National Tourist Offices can also come up with a reasonable free map of their country. For specific route planning, try the AA or RAC: European routes are provided free to members of foreign touring services, but a charge is made to regular members. Route planning is not available to non-members, although in the past personal callers have been known to succeed by blatantly lying about leaving their membership card at home.

Abroad, the best deals in maps are usually those put out locally by petrol companies, which tend to be cheap, accurate, but not detailed. The largest collections of maps and guidebooks for sale are at Stanford's, 12-14 Long Acre, London WC2 (Tel: 071-836 1321); the London Map Centre, 22 Caxton Street, London SW1 (Tel: 071-222 4945); the Travel Bookshop, 13 Blenheim Crescent, London W11 2EE (Tel: 071-229 5260); and the Map Shop, 15 High St, Upton-upon-Severn, Worcs WR8 0HJ (Tel: 06846-3146). For transport timetables, the specialists are BAS Overseas Publications, Unit 1c, 159 Mortlake Road, Kew, Surrey TW9 4AW (Tel: 081-876 2131). The specialists in maps, guides and timetables for eastern Europe are Collet's International Bookshop, 129/131 Charing Cross Road, London WC2 (Tel: 071-734 0782).

Further details are given under the *Accommodation* section of each chapter. The notes below apply to certain types that are standard throughout Europe.

Finding and Booking Accommodation. If you're the sort of person who can't plan as far as one day ahead, then follow the advice given under each country. But if you're just going to one town, or you can plan your itinerary so that you know where you'll be each night, it's best to book your accommodation before you set off. You can do this for yourself by getting a list of accommodation from the London offices of the various national tourist offices and writing to a few hotels in your price range. Alternatively, you can book through a travel agent or a local member of an international hotel chain.

Youth Hostels. These provide one of the cheapest ways of having a roof over your head. Membership cost £7.00 for adults; £3.70 for junior members (16-20); and £1.60 for young members (5-15). Membership cards can be bought from the YHA National Office, Trevelyan House, 8 St Stephen's Hill, St Albans, Herts AL1 2DY. In Scotland, contact the SYHA at 7 Glebe Crescent, Stirling FK8 2JA (Tel: 0786 72821); in Northern Ireland, YHANI, 56 Bradbury Place, Belfast BT7 1RU (Tel: 0232 224733). In Eire, An Oige, 39 Mountjoy Square, Dublin 1 (Tel: 0001 363111). To use the card abroad, simply attach a passport sized photograph. There is no upper age limit for youth hostels (except Bavaria — 27 years). The average cost per night is about £3.00, meals are an extra.

The YHA, SYHA, YHANI and AN OIGE cards show the International Youth Hostel Federation (IYHF) triangular symbol. This ensures that the card is valid in hostels throughout the world. In addition, cardholders qualify for benefits such as free admittance to various attractions and discounts on a wide range of goods and services, from restaurant meals to bicycle hire. Full details are shown in Volume 1 of the IYHF Handbook (available from the national YHA's for £4.50 including postage), which covers Europe and the Mediterranean countries.

It is often necessary to book well in advance for popular hostels, particularly in summer (or winter in skiing areas). The Handbook contains information on the International Hostel Reservation Voucher scheme; the basic idea being that you buy vouchers from the National Association in your home country, then post one or more to your chosen hostel as a booking deposit.

Other Hostels. YMCA and YWCA have hostels throughout Europe — not all segregated, and not all strictly religious foundations. The full list of addresses in Europe and the Middle East is given in the booklet *Pack for Europe,* available from the YWCA of Great Britain, Clarendon House, 52 Cornmarket, Street, Oxford OX1 3EJ (Tel: 0865 726110) for £1.50 plus 20p for postage.

Camping. Anyone planning a camping holiday in Europe is advised to buy a camping carnet, which, with a passport photo attached, acts as an identity document and will be accepted as a deposit in place of a passport. In Western Europe it also provides third party and personal accident insurance while camping, and often entitles holders to reductions in campsite charges. The carnet is not obligatory except when camping in French National Forest Parks, and in Portugal and Denmark. It is available from the AA or RAC, or from various camping clubs, including the Camping and Caravan Club, 11 Lower Grosvenor Place, London SW1W 0EY (Tel: 071-828 1012). The Club offers a scheme called the *Carefree Foreign Touring Service* to its members which includes a pitch reservation service for more than 250 campsites throughout Europe.

If you want to try a camping holiday but do not wish to commit yourself to buying expensive equipment there are a growing number of tour operators who operate camping packages to the continent including the cost of the ferry crossing for car and passengers and the use of a ready-assembled tent at the final destination. Below are some of the leading companies in this field:

Canvas Holidays, Bull Plain, Hertford, Herts SG14 1DY (Tel: 0992 53535).
Carefree Camping, 126 Hempstead Road, King's Langley, Herts WD3 8AL (Tel:09177 61311).
Eurocamp, Edmundson House, Tatton Street, Knutsford, Cheshire WA16 6BG (Tel: 0565 3844).
Freedom of France, 2-5 Market Place, Ross-on-Wye, Herefordshire HR9 5LD (Tel: 0989 768168).
Keycamp, 92-96 Lind Road, Sutton, Surrey SM1 4PL (Tel: 081-661 7334).
Sunsites, 22-24 Princes Street, Knutsford, Cheshire WA16 6BN (Tel: 0565 55644).

Home-Swapping. There are a number of agencies that may be able to introduce you to a household abroad who may be willing to swap homes for a few weeks or more. Charges for this service vary from company to company, but many are around the £30 mark. You should telephone the agency first to check that they can help you with the country that interests you.

GlobalHome Exchange, 12 Brookway, London SE3 9BJ (Tel: 081-852 1439).

Homelink International, 2 Westmoreland Avenue, Wyton, Huntingdon, Cambridgeshire PE17 2HS (Tel: 0480 457936).

Intervac, 5 Siddals Lane, Allestree, Derby DE3 2DY (Tel: 0332 558931).

International Living. If you wish to spend a holiday with a private family and increase understanding in the world at the same time, then the British Association of the Experiment in International Living may help you. They arrange for individuals or groups to travel world wide, learning languages, or simply sightseeing. Contact the Association at "Otesaga", Upper Wyche, Malvern, Worcestershire WR14 4EN (Tel: 06845 62577).

Servas International is another organisation devoted to building understanding, which it aims to do by organising exchanges between people of different cultures and backgrounds. It can arrange stays with over 11,000 hosts around the world for serious travellers.

Hosts give their visitors the chance to participate in their daily lives. This scheme should not be looked on as just a way of having a cheap holiday. Servas are based at 47, Edgeley Road, London SW4 6ES.

Holiday Guest Stays. Under the paying guest arrangement a traveller pays a family for the benefit of living among them for two weeks or more: this provides an excellent opportunity for learning or improving a language. These schemes are arranged by Euroyouth Ltd., 301 Westborough Road, Westcliff-on-Sea, Essex SS0 9PJ (Tel: 0702 34 14 34) in most Western European countries; language courses can be arranged with stays in Austria, France, Germany, Italy, Portugal and Spain.

Time Sharing. Buying an annual fixed period of time in a time-sharing development is an increasingly popular method of acquiring a permanent second home. You may stay there every year, or exchange your entitlement for a similar time-share elsewhere. Be warned that not all developers are scrupulously fair: you may find service charges increasing dramatically every year. And it sometimes costs almost as much to buy a fortnight share of an apartment in peak season as to purchase a more modest flat outright.

Communications

Post. If you know where you're going to be, it is usually possible to receive mail abroad. The *Poste Restante* system operates everywhere in Europe: letters addressed care of Poste Restante, town or city should turn up either at the central post office or at a special Poste Restante office (the actual location in capital cities is given under each country). The chances of a letter finding its recipient or vice-versa are increased if *Poste Centrale* is added before the name of the town. All titles and suffixes (eg Mr, Ms, Esq) should be omitted; otherwise, you'll have to try asking under M, E, etc. To make doubly certain of a letter reaching its recipients, senders should use the surname first followed by initials, eg EWING, J. R. If you qualify as an American Express customer (by using their card, travellers cheques or travel agency) then you can pick up mail at their offices — again, addresses are listed under individual countries. Finally,

if you consider yourself to be travelling on business, then you may collect mail addressed to you care of the Commercial Department of the local British Embassy provided that you warn them in advance.

Letter writers who expect a reply from commercial organisations abroad should always enclose an international reply coupon (more than one if sending for booklets or brochures).

When writing to Britain from Europe, prefix the post code with the country code GB-.

Telegrams. You can send telegrams to most countries by dialling 193.

Telex. If you wish to send an urgent message to an organisation abroad which is equipped with a telex machine, then it is much cheaper to use the British Telecom International Telex Bureau service than to send a telegram. Your message can be dictated by dialling 071-836 5432 or one of the regional BTI Bureaufax offices. A sixty-word telex to Spain costs about £2, and you may charge it to your Access or Visa credit card.

Newspapers. One of the most expensive ways of keeping up with the news is to buy English or American newspapers, which cost two to three times as much on the continent as they do at home. Both *the Guardian* and the *Financial Times* print copies in Europe, and these should cost less than imported British papers. Also cheaper are the *International Herald Tribune* (published in Paris and circulated throughout Europe) and *USA Today* (transmitted from North America by satellite and circulated throughout Europe). Wherever language is no problem, local papers are much sounder investments. If you really want to read English papers, the British Council have offices and libraries in all the major cities, although these are not really intended for the use of tourists. British and American embassies also have newspapers in their libraries, and major public libraries will carry a selection.

British radio programmes on the medium wave and long wave can be picked up over most of Europe, but if you're a long way from home you might only get acceptable reception at night. The service you are most likely to be able to receive is Radio 4 198 kHz or 1515m long wave. There is also 'BBC 648', a service carrying World Service programmes in English, French and German on 648 kHz or 463m medium wave and the World Service on various short wavebands. For advice on reception of BBC broadcasts in Europe, contact BBC Engineering Information, Broadcasting House, London W1A 1AA. Telephone: 071-927 5040.

This book does not attempt to list the complexities of short wave transmissions, but English language broadcasts on MW (AM), LW and FM are listed under each country. One short wave station that deserves a mention, however, is 7210 kHz, a frequency loaned to the International Red Cross Committee by the Swiss Short Wave Service, to broadcast two-monthly test transmissions. The IRCC also has use of this and other frequencies as often and as long as required in "times of crisis". The last time this privilege was used was from 1945-1947, to broadcast information on missing persons and prisoners of war from World War II.

Emergency Messages. A close relative in the UK can contact you abroad by calling the BBC (071-580 4468), who will arrange for a message to be transmitted (not necessarily in English) on the appropriate foreign radio or TV station. If you're abroad and need to contact relatives in Britain, get in touch with the motoring organisation of the country you're in, and they will pass on your message.

The BBC only handles messages if: the recipient's address is unknown; the recipient is a close relative of the sender; and the message involves a serious illness or accident in the family. Notification of death in the family will not be handled by the BBC, but will be transmitted by Radio Luxembourg between June and September; dial the international code for Luxembourg City (010 352 from Britain) then 476 61.

TELEPHONE

International. It is possible to dial international calls from most European countries to most others. The procedure follows a fixed pattern. First you dial the international prefix (010 from Britain, other codes shown under individual countries), followed by the country code:

Andorra	330	Gibraltar	350	Netherlands	31
Austria	43	Great Britain	44	Norway	47
Belgium	32	Greece	30	Portugal	351
Cyprus	357	Greenland	299	San Marino	39541
Denmark	45	Iceland	354	Spain	34
Eire	353	Italy	39	Sweden	46
Faroe Islands	298	Liechtenstein	4175	Switzerland	41
Finland	358	Luxembourg	352	Turkey	90
France	33	Malta	356	Yugoslavia	38
West Germany	49	Monaco	33		

The next step is to dial the code for the city area. (These are shown in the British Telecom Everyday Guide to Phoning Abroad, or can be found by calling the international operator on 155). Any initial zero — or 9 in the case of Finland, Romania and Spain — should be disregarded. Finally, the easy part — dialling the subscriber's number.

Thus to call the British Embassy in Vienna from the United Kingdom dial:

010	**43**	**222**	**731575**
international prefix	country code	city code	subscriber's number

Similarly, to call Vacation Work in Oxford from Austria — or Belgium, Cyprus, Czechoslovakia, West Germany, Greece, Hungary, Italy or Switzerland, which also use 00 as the international access code — dial:

00	**44**	**865**	**241978**
international prefix	country code	city code	subscriber's number

Naturally there are exceptions. The most frequent variations are on calls to neighbouring countries, where the international prefix and country code are replaced by a single shorter code. For example, calls from Great Britain to Dublin are prefixed 0001, while to reach northern Yugoslavia from Austria you should dial 030.

Other irregularities concern countries where there is no city code; this stage in the procedure should be omitted. So to call Andorra, Malta, Monaco and San Marino, dial only the international code plus country code plus subscriber's number. The new eight figure numbers in France require no city prefix except for the Paris area, where you must dial 1 before the number. The Vatican City goes one stage further; it has just a single number (part of the Rome exchange), which, from Britain, is 010 39 66982, followed by the subscriber's number. For calls to Andorra, the initial zero of the city code *should* be dialled.

British Telecom (Tel: 0800 272172) can provide you with *Phoning Home from Abroad* leaflets and copies of *The everyday guide to phoning abroad* which give details on international calling for the whole of Europe.

International Operator Services. If you wish to place a collect (reverse-charge) or credit card/BT chargecard call, or call a number which cannot be dialled direct, or if you have problems dialling a call yourself, the local operator will try to place it for you. Within Britain, call the following number:

100: Eire (Republic of Ireland)
155: All other countries

International Direct Dialled calls can be made from over 180 countries to the UK. Collect (reverse charge) and BT Chargecard (formally BT Credit Card) calls may be made from most countries back to the UK by calling the local international operator or by dialling the UK direct number where available, currently available from France, Italy, Sweden, Finland and Netherlands; see info on these countries for further information.

UK direct allows you to make a BT Chargecard call or reverse charge call via the BT operator, thereby avoiding any language or procedural difficulties.

For further information on international calling dial BT free on 0800 272172. (Monday to Friday 8am to 10pm).

International Directory Enquiries. To find a subscriber's number in Europe, when in the UK call the enquiry operator.

192: Eire (Republic of Ireland)
153: All other countries

If you want to consult foreign directories in this country, the best collection open to the public is in the City Business Library, Basinghall Street, London EC2.

Calls within a country. The procedure is normally a simple matter of dialling the city or area code (including any initial zero or 9) plus the subscriber's number. Sophistications such as the French practice of dialling the national access code 16 and waiting for a secondary tone are rare. Most problems arise when you get an unobtainable tone or, worse, an incomprehensible recorded message which may or may not inform you that the number has changed. In either case, call the operator for help.

Tones. The tones that you'll hear on continental telephones are not completely standardised, although steps are being taken in this direction. The commoner tones are listed below. Variations are given under the separate countries.

Ringing tone: beeep (1-2 seconds), pause (2-5 seconds), beeep, etc.
Or (Germany, Denmark, Sweden): beeeeep (2 seconds), pause (10 seconds), beeeeep etc.
Or (France): beeeeeeep (3 seconds), pause (3 seconds), beeeeeeep, etc.

Engaged tone: beep-bip, beep-bip, etc.
Or: beep-beep-beep-beep, etc, (as in Britain).

Out of order/unobtainable: recorded announcement (try again)
Or: beep-beep-beep (ascending pitch), pause, beep-beep-beep, etc.
Or: bip-bip-bip-bip-bip-bip-bip-bip-bip-bip, pause, bip-bip, etc.
Or: (Netherlands): prolonged tone of varying pitch.

Call being put through (hang on): silence for half a minute or more.
Or (France): an extra rapid bip-bip-bip-bip-bip-bip-bip, etc.

Payphones. Most countries have a variety of phone booths. The must primitive can be used only for local calls, others for local regional numbers, or for international calls. Payment systems vary; details are given under individual countries.

There is a trend towards payphones which accept cards rather than cash. Again there is no sign of standardisation. For example, in Britain, Portugal, France and Yugoslavia you buy a prepaid card from Post Office or news stands which you throw away when all the units are etched off by laser. At some international airports, American Express, Access or Visa cards can be used to make calls.

Telephone Bureaux and Post Offices. Given the scope for disaster it is often easier to place your problem in the hands of staff at special telephone bureaux, or failing that at post offices. The usual system is for the caller to dial the number and to pay after the call for the time used.

Hotel Telephones. Calls made through hotel operators are notoriously expensive. It is a better idea to use payphones, which can often be found in hotel lobbies, and if necessary ask your contact to call you back in your room.

Hygiene. In general, the northern European countries are quite safe; you can drink the water and eat whatever's served up without fear of disease.

In the Mediterranean countries, more precautions are necessary, mainly because of the heat, which provides ideal fast breeding conditions for all sorts of bacteria; here, water should be purified either by boiling or by using purifying tablets, which are based on iodine or chlorine and can make the water taste awful. Any alcohol will purify water, so just add a tot of vodka if you prefer the taste. Diseases are also passed by raw vegetables and fruit, and underdone fish and meat. Wash all vegetables and fruit, either in boiling water or in a mild detergent solution, and make sure you cook meat and fish thoroughly. Be wary of reheated foods, and cold pies that might have been prepared a long time earlier. Milk is another danger: either boil it or use powdered or canned milk. Note that freezing is not a purifying method, so ice and ice cream are as suspect as water and milk.

Often soft drinks and ice creams are knocked together in unhygienic conditions, (especially in areas highly infested with tourists), so it is a wise precaution to stick with the major brands.

Some diseases, notably dysentery and hepatitis, are carried in excreta, and the germs can linger in insanitary toilets, especially the hole-in-the-floor type common in Mediterranean countries. To avoid these unpleasant illnesses, follow Lady Macbeth's example and keep washing your hands, especially if you're likely to be handling food.

The main offenders in disease transmission are flies, from which food should be protected. Another insect that might bother you is the louse, certain types of which carry typhus. Even the types that aren't a health hazard, like crab lice, are highly unpleasant if they decide to adopt you. They will nest either in your hair or in the seams of your clothes, and no amount of washing will get them to move. DDT powders are effective on lice (and on most types of insect), as are extremes of heat or cold. Leaving your clothes in the sun, or putting them in the freezer for a few hours is no problem, but when the lice are in your hair, try Gamma Benzine Hexachloride.

Recommended reading: *The Traveller's Health Guide* (£4.95) by Dr Anthony C Turner, published by Roger Lascelles, 47 York Road, Brentford, Middlesex TW8 0QP (Tel: 081-847 0935).

Vaccinations. In northern Europe the chances of catching anything worse than a cold are small. However, southern countries contain a wide range of lurking germs to which travellers sometimes succumb.

Although no antidote has yet been discovered against Legionnaire's Disease, there are precautions you may wish to take against several other hazards. Hepatitis, typhoid, tetanus and poliomyelitis are not unknown, and vaccinations against each are available. The problem is that jabs usually need to be planned several months in advance. Many travellers simply don't bother, taking the attitude that the chance of catching typhoid in a week in Lloret del Mar is little higher than in Llandudno. But if you intend to spend any length of time living in less-than-sanitary conditions (particularly in Greece, Italy, Portugal, Spain and remote rural regions elsewhere), then dosing yourself up against typhoid is recommended. Your doctor or travel agent will provide a form which the doctor should sign after the injection, usually for a fee, and it becomes an international vaccination certificate. In London, the whole operation can be performed by your doctor or by commercial centres such as the Thomas Cook Vaccination Centre, 45 Berkeley Street, London W1 (Tel: 071-408 4157); the British Airways Immunisation Centre, 156 Regent St, London W1 (Tel: 071-439 9584); the Trailfinders Immunisation Centre, 42 Earls Court Road, London W8 6EJ (Tel: 071-937 9631); and the PPP Medical Centre, 99 New Cavendish St, London W1 (Tel: 071-637 8941). Each provides immunisations against a whole range of infections, from rabies to plague, from £5-£25 a shot — depending on the injection.

For further details, including precautions for travel beyond Europe, get leaflets SA40 *Before You Go* and SA41 *While You're Away* from travel agents and local DSS offices. For up-to-date Malaria information by telephone, call the Ross Institute of Tropical Hygiene on 071-636 8636/7921.

Aids. It would be foolish to assume that any part of Europe is entirely clear of Aids, no matter how remote it is. If you can get there it is possible that an infected person has been there before you. You can minimise your chances of getting the disease by not injecting drugs (it is often spread by drug users sharing needles) and only engaging in sexual intercourse, whether homosexual or heterosexual, with strangers when using a condom. British airports sell condoms in packets of eighteen, which should last you over the first few days until you find local supplies.

First Aid and Drugs. The first piece of advice is take any medicines with you that you'll need for continuing or recurrent ailments. Doctors cannot write prescriptions for illnesses that might occur while you're abroad, but may do so for conditions to which you are particularly prone (eg allergies); or for any permanent medication you may be on, including contraceptives. Mechanical contraceptives are now legal and obtainable at chemists throughout Europe (except in the strictest Catholic countries), but the pill is only available on prescription — it's easiest and cheapest to take a supply with you.

Non-prescription drugs should be bought before you go — the most obvious ones are aspirin; kaolin and morphine (for diarrhoea); tablets for vomiting and indigestion; and calamine lotion for sunburn. Add to these a supply of dressings, antiseptic cream and some popular remedies (ammonia or bicarbonate of soda for bee stings, vinegar or lemon juice for wasp stings) and you have a useful first aid kit. The necessary adjunct to any first aid kit is a knowledge of artificial respiration, or at least the instructions readily available at all times.

Sunburn. The most natural way of protecting yourself against sunburn is by tanning yourself gently, an hour or so at a time, to get your skin used to the heat. There are also lotions on the market, which absorb the burning rays of the sun, but most of these will wash off when you bathe. Seawater hastens sunburn, as do perfumes and after-shave. Don't be fooled by the cooling effect of the wind on your skin; you can't blow away the rays of the sun. The tablets that claim to prevent sunburn by increasing your vitamin A intake are considered by medical authorities to be of no value. Aspirin may delay the reddening process, making you unaware of the effects of the sun and hence increasing your suffering. Women on the pill may develop brown patches of skin. If you reach the stage where you need treatment for sunburn, cold compresses can relieve the pain followed by application of calamine lotion. Olive oil is a standard treatment used in Mediterranean countries, and even yoghurt is worth trying.

Heat. The best way to keep cool is to wear loose clothing made out of cotton, which is far better than nylon at absorbing sweat. It will be even more effective if you wear a string vest underneath; try it now, before St. Tropez catches on.

Frostbite. The best way to avoid suffering in cold weather is to eat well, sleep well, and wrap up well, paying particular attention to gloves, headgear, and boots. Alcohol speeds up the onset of frostbite, which is treated by keeping the area warm. Frostbitten hands, for instance, should be placed against the warm skin under your clothing, or, if available, wrapped in warm towels. Do not rub or wet the area, as skin damage might result. Gangrene can result from untreated frostbite, and from re-heating frostbitten areas too quickly.

Prolonged exposure to extreme cold is another danger. It's most important to find shelter from the wind (a wind speed of 25 mph can reduce the effective temperature by 35°F), and keep as dry as possible. Sleeping also lowers your body temperature, so stay awake and move about to keep the circulation going. But over-exertion will merely exhaust you.

Vomiting and Diarrhoea. Both of these are caused by ingestion of viruses or bacteria, and the symptoms are the body's natural means of getting rid of the invading pathogens. It is best to find somewhere quiet to sit it out, and don't worry unless it continues for more than about three days (then see a doctor). The worst side effect is dehydration, so try to keep some water down. Your stomach can send you all kinds of false messages in between the agonizing bouts of stomach cramp, and you may receive cravings for the most disastrous types of food, such as cream cakes or curry. If you must eat, stick to small quantities of plain non-fatty food. If available, the following medications may be of use; kaolin and morphine, Lomotil or codeine phosphate. The latter two are available only on prescription in the UK, and all three may be hard to get abroad.

Toothache. Oil of cloves is a good, cheap local anaesthetic. Dissolving an aspirin on lurking cavities will only give you sore gums.

Creatures to Avoid. In the absence of scorpions, rhinos and grizzly bears, Europe's most feared land animals are snakes. The treatment for snake bites is to apply a tourniquet, keep still and unexcited, and find a doctor fast. Trying to suck out the venom is not advisable as it encourages blood circulation and may help to spread the poison.

Of the land mammals, the wolves, bears and wild boar, though still rare and confined mainly to Eastern Europe, are perhaps the nastiest.

A commoner danger are small mammals — wild and domestic — which are the most frequent carriers of rabies. Rabies is carried in saliva, so the first step after being bitten, scratched or even licked on a scratch by a suspect animal, is to wash the wound — soap and hot water followed by alcohol is the best method. Then seek immediate medical help. Most human cases are contracted from cats and dogs, but deer, foxes, squirrels and bats — indeed any mammals — are suspect, especially if they behave unusually tamely. Diagnosis will be speeded up if you can capture the animal — this will also protect other people and wildlife. If the animal has an owner obtain his address and telephone number, and give him yours. Tell him to contact you if the animal becomes ill or dies within two weeks. In humans, the normal incubation period is 4-8 weeks, but any delay in diagnosis could prove fatal — and it's one the most unpleasant ways of dying.

Never attempt to pull a leech off your skin, because you probably won't be able to remove the business end. Instead try a little friendly persuasion, with a lighted cigarette end, salt or vinegar.

Of the sea creatures that can ruin a holiday, jellyfish are the most painful, and are quite common on southern beaches. The Portuguese Man o' War isn't lethal, but it can cause a painful rash. First remove the tentacle, if it's still in, but cover your hand or you'll sting your fingers. Then apply methylated spirits; if the rash persists, apply antihistamine cream or take antihistamine tablets, both available in Britain without a prescription. See a doctor if you develop a fever.

Another poisonous Mediterranean fish is the weever fish, which has spines that often find their way into bathers' feet. If the spine has broken, remove the remaining section with tweezers or a sterile needle. Bathing the wound in very hot water will eventually kill the poison. The same treatment is good for sea-urchin spines, not all of which are poisonous.

Sharks are an altogether tougher kettle of fish. Although you might see some in the Mediterranean, your chances of being attacked are remote. If you splash about in the water, you'll draw them to you to investigate, but keeping still and shouting might scare them away; if they get uncomfortably close, a sharp kick on the nose should be sufficient to keep them away. The Mediterranean, however, offers no cause for a *Jaws* scale panic.

INSURANCE AND MEDICAL TREATMENT

EC Medical Agreements. Free or reduced medical treatment is available to most EC nationals and their families who are residents of the UK during visits to other EC countries. Treatment is provided on the same terms and conditions as apply to the insured citizens of the countries concerned. In most countries you will need form E111 to obtain treatment. You can get form E111 from any Post Office in the UK. There you will be given leaflet T1 The Travellers Guide to Health, which states who is covered by EC regulations, a blank form E111 (incorporated in the leaflet Health Care for Visitors to EC Countries and form E111G which explains how you should fill in the E111. Once you have filled it in, hand it to the Post Office counter clerk who will, after he has checked that it has been correctly completed, sign, date and stamp it and hand it back to you. Leaflet T1 explains the procedures you must follow in each EC country in order to obtain treatment. The latest information on treatment arrangements abroad is available to Viewdata subscribers on Prestel 50063.

Photocopies of the E111 will prove useful — especially where you intend to travel in more than one EC country.

E111 forms are now issued for an unlimited period and can be used for as long as you continue to live in the UK. If you intend to work or live in another EC country, write to the Overseas Branch of the Department of Social Security, Newcastle NE98 1YX well in advance giving full details about yourself (including your national insurance number), your date of departure from the UK and your employment abroad. They in return will inform you of your social security and pension rights in the EC.

Other arrangements. Certain other European countries have medical agreements concerning British travellers. Details of these are given in the aforementioned leaflet T1.

NHS cards. If you go abroad for more than three months, you should hand in your NHS card to your local Family Practitioner Committee (the address is on the card) or to the Immigration Officer at your point of departure. The idea of this is to ensure that your GP has his income adjusted until your return. But if you're going to Iceland don't hand your NHS card in — you can use your NHS card there to verify your entitlement to health care.

Private Insurance. The reciprocal medical agreements are not usually sufficient for full protection, and travellers going to countries without such agreements are advised to take out at least medical cover for their journeys. Even within the EC, holders of E111 who are visiting France, Belgium and Luxembourg will be expected to pay their medical expenses and then claim back 50-80%. Wherever you go, it's sensible to opt for a full cover policy, including medical and dental treatment; legal liability; loss, theft or damage to your possessions; accidents, cancellations, etc. The cost of bringing a person back to the UK in the event of illness, or death, is never covered by the E111, but should be included in any decent private insurance policy. Insurance is now offered as an optional extra on most package holidays and charter flights. For details of insurance possibilities, send a stamped addressed envelope for the leaflet *Holiday Insurance* to the Association of British Insurers, Aldermary House, 10-15 Queen Street, London EC4N 1TT (Tel: 071-248 4477).

Most insurance companies offer some sort of travel policy; cover for 2 weeks costs £10-£20. Europe Assistance Ltd of 252 High Street, Croydon, Surrey specialises in travel emergency services and controls through its network of agents and offices in over 180 countries worldwide a network of suppliers such as doctors, ambulance airlines, hospitals, hire car companies, garages, etc. who can be called upon to respond to any type of medical or motoring emergencies arising overseas.

There are also companies that specialise in long-term insurance for travel abroad, notably Endsleigh Insurance (Brokers) Ltd, of Endsleigh House, Cheltenham Spa, Gloucs GL50 3NR (Tel: 0242 223300), who are the English representatives of the ISIS (International Student Insurance Service) scheme. American Express cardholders can take out a travel insurance policy that gives one year's cover to the cardholder, spouse and any children aged under 18 for £139. A similar policy called *Travel World* is offered by Marcus Hearn & Co; it should be obtainable from high street insurance brokers.

Credit cards offer automatic free personal accident cover to their cardholders offering reasonable sums in the event of death or permanent disablement: check with your card's issuing company to see what is covered. A more comprehensive package, including medical expenses cover, is offered by the National Westminster Bank's Gold Mastercard provided you used your card to pay for your travel arrangements.

Medical Treatment. The International Association for Medical Assistance to Travellers (IAMAT) co-ordinates doctors and clinics around the world who maintain high medical standards at fixed costs; there are centres in over 125 countries. IAMAT publishes an annual directory of medical centres and provides members with country by country climate and hygiene charts, and very detailed leaflets about malaria and other tropical diseases. Non-members may be treated by IAMAT doctors but cannot expect to pay the rate set for members. There is no set fee for joining IAMAT, but a donation is requested. Unfortunately they cannot be relied upon to answer correspondence but you can try writing to one of the four membership offices all the same: 417 Center Street, Lewiston, New York, NY 14092; 188 Nicklin Road, Guelph, Ontario N1H 7L5, Canada; PO Box 5049, Christchurch 5, New Zealand; Gotthardstrasse 17, CH 6300, Zug, Switzerland.

Death. When you're insuring yourself, don't rule out the possibility that you might die abroad. If this happens, there's not much that you can do about it, except lie down and keep quiet; but if you haven't got an insurance policy that covers the recovery of your body, you'll cause your relatives a lot more grief and expense than is necessary.

To preserve the chance of your body being used to the end, make sure you are carrying your donor card (available from your GP). And, in the hope of saving funeral expenses, carry a statement to the effect that you wish posthumously (make sure you include that!) to donate your body for medical research. There are no special forms, but details are available from HM Inspector of Anatomy, DHSS, Portland Court, 158-176 Great Portland Street, London W1N 5TB.

ACTS OF GOD

Although low on the world table, Europe has its share of geological upheavals. To avoid earthquakes, do not stray into the Alpide zone — a broad band of underground instability stretching from the Azores through the Iberian peninsula, Italy, the Balkan states, and on through Turkey and Asia to the Pacific. Apart from the notorious Lisbon earthquake of 1755, Europe's worst earthquake areas are southern Italy and Yugoslavia. Not coincidentally, southern Italy is also a region with high volcanic activity — Vesuvius is the only active volcano on mainland Europe. Others in the area are: Etna (last erupted 1979), Stromboli (1971) and Vulcano (dormant). Further east in the Aegean is the island volcano of Thira (last erupted 1956). The other danger zone in Europe is the mid-Atlantic fault, which passes through Iceland. Iceland has five active volcanoes and over 100 dormant or inactive; it is also the scene of a rare-geological phenomenon — lava flow without a crater. On a branch line of the mid-Atlantic fault lies northern Europe's only other volcano — Beeren Berg, off the coast of Norway (last erupted 1971).

It is generally agreed that earthquakes and volcanic eruptions happen too fast for you to do anything once you're caught up in them — lava flows faster than you can run, for instance, and your best bet in an earthquake is to get as far as you can from any buildings, especially tall ones. But avoidance is possible by observing the warnings. Before any subterranean activity there are always low rumblings, inaudible to the human ear, that can be picked up by animals (wild animals run directly away from the epicentre; goldfish go berserk) and by seismologists (whose predictions are still taken as something akin to witchcraft). Earthquake prediction is based largely on study of past records, so geodetic survey stations have been set up in the suspect areas. They cannot give much advance warning, but whatever reports they put out should be treated with respect.

Avalanches can be avoided by keeping away from snowy mountainous areas, especially in the spring when the snow is thawing (or during a hot spell in winter). If you do get caught in one, you're least likely to be hurt if you lie face down and cover your head with your arms. Best advice is to hold your breath, if possible until it's all over — as the commonest cause of death in avalanches is from inhaling snow particles.

Embassies and Consulates. These are invaluable if you lose your passport or a war breaks out where you're staying. In emergencies like this, they're always ready to spring into action.

In other emergencies, they usually show a mild apathy bordering on total uninterest. If you lose your money or get arrested you should in theory contact them, but don't expect a lot of positive help. If you need to contact them in a hurry, the telegraphic address of all British embassies is PRODROME; and of all British consulates BRITAIN. Any policeman should be able to give you the address of the nearest. Note that embassies and consulates close on public holidays of both their home country and the host nation.

Legal Aid. Public lawyers are available at little or no cost in all western European countries, but in some places, particularly in the southern countries, a free lawyer will invariably be less helpful than one you pay.

Travel Clubs. The main benefit of joining a travel club is the interchange of up to date travel information, but there are also advantages if you are looking for travelling companies or friends to meet along the way. Try the worldwide Globetrotters Club, BCM/Roving, London WC1V 6XX. One year's subscription costs £7 or US$14, which includes regular newsletters: members can buy lists of members in Europe who may be able to help you for £1/US$2.

Recorded Information. Pre-recorded holiday information on over 300 destinations, and on current special offers by tour operators, is offered by a Birmingham-based company named *Telephone Information Marketing*. To choose a particular destination you can use the inter-active recorded message on 0839-800 800, or you can get a free card listing the choices available by calling 021-554 3361.

But be warned that this is not a free service: you are incurring phone charges of 5p per 8 seconds at peak time, or 5p for 12 seconds off-peak.

The Sunday Times operates a similar scheme at the same charges under the name Guidelines. For a pre-recorded message lasting around three minutes dial 0898 336 followed by the number given below:
388 for climates; 390 for Passports; 391 for ten pre-holiday tips; 393 for vaccinations; 394 for visas; 377 for France; 381 for Greek Islands; 378 for Italy; 380 for Portugal; 379 for Spain; 383 for Turkey and 386 for Yugoslavia.

Naturism. It is indicated in the individual country chapters where nudity is, and is not, acceptable. For more specific information about where you can strip off there are two books available from bookshops or from the author, Phil Vallack at 16 Viewbank, Hastings, Sussex TN35 5HB for £6 each. *Free-Sun Beaches* covers coastal areas, and *Inland Free-Sun* covers other areas. For information about naturism, contact the Central Council for British Naturism at Assurance House, 35-41 Hazlewood Road, Northampton NN1 1LL (Tel: 0604 20361): the Council is affiliated to clubs and holiday centres all over the world. There is also a company, Peng Travel, that organises holidays for naturists in France, Yugoslavia, Spain, Greece and Turkey: their address is 86 Station Road, Gidea Park, Essex RM2 6DB (Tel: 04024 71832).

Disabled Travellers. The Royal Association for Disability and Rehabilitation (RADAR) publish the book *Holidays and Travel Abroad*. It has a special supplement of holidays abroad, giving useful addresses and a selection of hostels suitable for the disabled; it costs £2 from bookshops or £3 by post. At their headquarters (25 Mortimer Street, London W1, Tel: 071-637 5400) there is a holidays officer who is able to answer individual queries.

Mobility International, of 228 Borough High Street, London SE1 1JX (Tel: 071-403 5688) exists to promote international travel for the disabled. It produces *Mobility International News* (£4 per annum), a newsletter which provides hints on travel and facilities, and will answer individual enquiries.

Pauline Hethaistos Survey Projects, of 39 Bradley Gardens, West Ealing, London W13 8HE, publish detailed guides to the Channel ports, Paris, London, and Jersey. Known as Access guides, they are free, but a contribution of around £4 per guide is appreciated.

On completion of appropriate advance bookings, special fare concessions are available on most cross-channel ferries for the vehicles of disabled members of the Disabled Drivers' Association, Ashwellthorpe, Norwich (Tel: Fundenhall 449).

Special Needs. The Holiday Care Service, a registered charity, provides free advice and information for those with special holiday needs, such as the disabled, the elderly, and single parent families. It can advise on specialist tour operators, accommodation, etc. and can provide a helper for those who would otherwise be unable to take a holiday. Its address is 2, Old Bank Chambers, Station Road, Horley, Surrey RH6 9HW.

Churches. Whether you're religiously minded or not, churches are useful contacts. A directory of English speaking churches in Europe, the Middle East and North Africa is available from the Intercontinental Church Society, 175 Tower Bridge Road, London SE1 2AQ (Tel: 071-407 4588).

An excellent series of *Pilgrims' Guides* to various countries is available from the Secretary, St Basil's House, 52 Ladbroke Grove, London W11.

War Graves. If you're searching for your roots, information about war graves from the two world wars is obtainable from the Commonwealth War Graves Commission, 2 Marlow Road, Maidenhead, Berkshire SL6 7DX (Tel: 0628 34221). Please send them as much information as you can about the casualty you are interested in before setting off.

Vegetarianism. The Vegetarian Society of the United Kingdom produce a book entitled *The International Vegetarian Travel Guide* (£3.95 from bookshops) which, among other things, lists restaurants all over the world that serve vegetarian food and tour operators who organise holidays for vegetarians. The society also produces free leaflets giving translations of useful phrases for vegetarians: send a stamped addressed envelope, with a note stating which language(s) you are interested in, to the Vegetarian Society of the United Kingdom (Translations), Parkdale, Dunham Road, Altrincham, Cheshire WA14 4QG (Tel: 061-928 0793).

Complaints. If you have any cause for complaint about anything, start complaining immediately — to the manager of the shop, hotel or restaurant, for instance — then back it up in writing either to the same person or to a superior or central head office. If at a later date you wish to take up a case for damages, it will hardly even be considered if there is no record of an immediate complaint. It is to be hoped that most complaints can be resolved without fuss, but don't hesitate to pursue complaints until you are personally satisfied. Be warned, though, that most complaints machinery is designed to protect the defendant, rather than to vindicate the plaintiff.

Complaints about package holidays booked in the UK should first be taken up on the spot with the company's nearest representative, then the company (either directly or through your travel agency), and finally (if the company is a member) with the Association of British Travel Agents (ABTA), 55 Newman Street, London W1 (Tel: 071-637 2444). Collect as much documentary proof as possible about your complaint, such as signed statements from fellow holidaymakers, and/or photographs if your complaint is about shoddy accommodation or non-existent views. The Office of Fair Trading publishes a useful leaflet called *Package Holidays* which can be obtained from most travel agents.

The Simple Man's Guide to Metrication and other useful conversions

We all know about decimal currency, and some of us are young enough to have learnt nothing but the metric system at school. For the older ones, who'll just have to get used to metric units when they're on the continent, here are a few simple guidelines and approximate conversions to make ready reckoning a bit easier.

Distance. One centimetre (cm) is about two-fifths of an inch. There are about $2\frac{1}{2}$ cm to an inch, 30 cm to a foot. One metre (m) is just over 39 inches, not much more than a yard for rough calculations; more accurately, 9 metres are ten yards. One kilometre (km) is $\frac{5}{8}$ of a mile, so 8 km = 5 miles. If it's easier for you, reckon 5 km = 3 miles.

Weight. The kilogram (kg or kilo) is about 2 lb 3 oz. Roughly, $\frac{1}{2}$ kilo (500 grams) = 1 lb. For smaller things, 28 (reckon 30) grams (g) make an ounce. At the other end of the scale, the tonne, or metric ton, is 1,000 kilos, slightly less than the imperial ton. 50 kilos are very close to 1 cwt.

Capacity and Volume. The standard unit for liquids is the litre (l), approximately $1\frac{3}{4}$ pints. There are about $4\frac{1}{2}$l to a UK gallon, about $3\frac{3}{4}$ to a US gallon. In a bar, you buy spirits in millilitres (the standard English measure of one-sixth gill is about 25 ml); wine by the decilitre; and beer in fractions of a litre — $\frac{1}{2}$l is about a pint. You may think that 0.2l is a ridiculous size for a standard glass of beer in a German bar — until you hear the price.

How it's Written. The first warning concerns the use of commas and full stops. Where we use a full stop for a decimal point, the Europeans use a comma; 2,5 cm means $2\frac{1}{2}$ centimetres. Conversely, they use the full stop to denote thousands 5,000 in Britain is written 5.000 on the continent.

Secondly, there are several ways of expressing the same thing, by clever use of the decimal point and prefixes. The basic units (metre, gram and litre) can be changed by adding the prefixes: milli- (one-thousandth), centi- (one hundredth), deci- (one-tenth) and kilo- (multiply by 1,000); the other prefixes, deka- (multiply by ten) and hecta- (multiply by 100) are rarely used. Thus, for instance, 1½ litres can be written as 1,5 1, 15 dl, 150 cl, or 1.500 ml. On road signs, one kilometre may be written: 1.000 m.

Two numbers that are often confused are 1 and 7. On the continent, 1 is usually written with a pronounced tail at the top, thus looking like a 7. To avoid confusion, 7 is normally written with a horizontal bar across the upright stroke.

Petrol Consumption. Continentals are likely to reckon in term of the number of litres they use to travel 100 kilometres.

miles per gallon:	16	20	23	26	28½	31½	35	39	42	46
litres per 100 km:	19	14	12.5	11	10	9	8	7	6.5	6

Temperature. Temperatures are expressed in degrees Celsius or Centigrade, the system being based on water freezing at 0° (32° Fahrenheit) and boiling at 100° (212°F). Normal body temperature is 36.9° (98.4°F); an average room temperature (68°F) would be 20°; and you know it's hot outside when it's up to 27° (80°F). To convert Centigrade into Fahrenheit, multiply by 9, divide by 5, then add 32. For a rougher figure, multiply by 2, then add 32. To convert Fahrenheit into Centigrade, first subtract 32, then multiply by 5 and divide by 9 (or subtract 32, then divide by 2).

Clothing. Continental sizes can't be converted exactly into British sizes, but these tables are a close enough guide.

Shoes	Women				Men				Children				
Britain	3	5	7	9	6	8	10	12	2	4	6	8	10
Europe	36	38	40	42	40	42	44	46	18	20	23	25	27

	Men's Suits					Shirts				Hats			
Britain	36	38	40	42	44	14	15	16	17	6½	6¾	7	7¼	7½
Europe	46	48	50	52	54	36	38	40	42	53	55	57	59	61

Sizes for women's coats, suits and dresses are nowhere near standardisation, but the table below provides a rough guide. Since sizes may be graded by bust, waist or hip measurements or a combination of all three, the only real advice is to try everything on before buying.

UK	34/8	36/10	38/12	40/14	42/16
France/Belgium	38/34N	40/36N	42/38N	44/40N	46/42N
Denmark/Norway	36	38	40	42	44
West Germany/Finland	34	36	38	40	42
Switzerland	35	37	40	42	44

Reading Timetables. The 24-hour clock is used in timetables: instead of recounting the hours from midday, it continues to midnight being 24 hours, written 24.00 or (more usually) 0.00.

International timetables use local time throughout. Most European countries now employ Energy Saving Time, whereby one hour is added to local time during the summer. Clocks in most countries go forward at the end of March and back at the end of September. There are as yet no definite plans to harmonise Britain's clocks with those of most western Europe. Variances from Greenwich Mean Time (GMT — Winter Time in Britain) are shown in the table below.

	Winter	Summer		Winter	Summer		Winter	Summer
Albania	+2	+3	Germany	+1	+2	Netherlands	+1	+2
Andorra	+1	+2	Gibraltar	+1	+2	Portugal	GMT	+1
Austria	+1	+2	Greece	+2	+3	Spain	+1	+2
Belgium	+1	+2	Greenland	-3	-3	Sweden	+1	+2
Cyprus	+2	+3	Iceland	GMT	GMT	Switzerland	+1	+2
Denmark	+1	+2	Italy	+1	+2	Turkey	+2	+3
Finland	+2	+3	Luxembourg	+1	+2	UK	GMT	+1
France	+1	+2	Malta	+1	+2	Yugoslavia	+1+	+2

Tuning the Radio. Apart from VHF, the traditional British method of tuning a radio by wavelength, measured in metres (m) is being phased out in favour of the continental method which is by frequency, measured in kilocycles (1,000 cycles) or megacycles (1,000,000 cycles) per second — also known as kilohertz (kHz) and Megahertz (MHz). Radio waves all travel at 300,000 kilometres per second, but in waves of varying lengths. It follows that:

wavelength (in metres) × frequency (in kHz) = 300,000. Therefore:

$$\text{frequency (kHz)} = \frac{300,000}{\text{wavelength (m)}} \qquad \text{wavelength (m)} = \frac{300,000}{\text{frequency (kHz)}}$$

Electricity. The supply in Europe is now almost universally 220 or 230 volts, alternating at 50 cycles per second, therefore effectively the same as in Britain. But there are some rural areas — particularly in France, Italy, Portugal and Spain — where they still use around 110 volts. If you plug a 220 volt appliance into a 110 volt socket, you won't damage anything but you will get a poor performance: a light will be dim, an iron will produce only a quarter of its proper heat and so on. But if you have any 110 volt appliances — or dual-voltage items switched to the lower setting — they could go up in smoke should you plug them into a 220 volt socket. A good way to check the local voltage is to look at the markings on light bulbs.

Plugs are a major problem. British plugs should work in Cyprus, Eire, Gibraltar and Malta, but elsewhere you'll have to buy an adaptor or a new plug to replace the British one. The most common continental plug is the *Schuko*, with two round pins and earth contacts on either side. However, these are not used in Belgium, Denmark, France and Switzerland, which each have their own versions. Strange plugs can also be found in Greece, Yugoslavia and the Soviet Union. Buying adaptors abroad can be risky, since electrical standards are not always adhered to scrupulously. Those sold in Britain which adhere to the appropriate British Standard should be reliable.

Addresses in London

Austria
Austrian Embassy, 18 Belgrave Mews West SW1X 8HU (071-235 3731).
Austrian National Tourist Office/Federal Railways, 30 St. George St, W1R 0AL (071-629 0461).

Belgium/Luxembourg
Belgian Embassy, 103 Eaton Square, SW1W 9AB (071-235 5422).
Belgian National Tourist Office, 2 Gayton Rd, HA1 2XU (081-861 3300).
Belgian National Railways, 10 Greycoat Place, London SW1P 1SB (071-233 0360).

Luxembourg Embassy, 27 Wilton Crescent, SW1X 8SD (071-235 6961).
Luxembourg National Tourist Office, 36 Piccadilly, W1V 9PA (071-434 2800).

Eire
Irish Embassy, 17 Grosvenor Place, SW1X 7HR (071-235 2171).
Irish Tourist Board, 150 New Bond St, W1Y 0AQ (071-493 3201).

France/Monaco/Andorra
French Consulate General, 21 Cromwell Rd, London SW7 6EW (071-823 9550).
French Government Tourist Office, 178 Piccadilly, W1V 0AL (071-499 6911).
French Railways, 179 Piccadilly, W1V 0BA.

Monaco Consulate, 4 Audley Square, W1Y 5DR (071-629 0734).
Monaco, 50 Upper Brook St, W1Y 5DR (071-629 4712).

Andorran Delegation, 63 Westover Road, SW18 2RS (081-874 4806).

West Germany
German Consulate, 21-23 Belgrave Square, SW1X 8PZ (071-235 5033).
German National Tourist Office, 65 Curzon Street, London W1Y 7PE (071-495 3990).
German Federal Railways, Suite 118, Hudson's Place, Victoria Station SW1V 1JL. (071-233 6559).

Great Britain
British Tourist Authority, Thames Tower, Black's Road, Hammersmith, W6 9EL (Tel: 081-846 9000).

Greece/Cyprus
Greek Embassy, 1a Holland Park, W11 3TP (071-727 8040).
Greek National Tourist Office, 4 Conduit St, W1R 0DJ (071-734 5997).

Cyprus High Commission, 93 Park St, W1Y 4ET (071-499 8272).
Cyprus Tourist Office, 213 Regent St, W1R 8DA (071-734 9822).

Italy/Malta
Italian Consulate, 38 Eaton Place, London SW1 (071-235 9371).
Italian State Tourist Office, 1 Princes St, W1 (071-434 3844).
Italian State Railways (CIT), 50-51 Conduit Street, London W1R 9FB (071-434 3844).

Malta National Tourist Office, Suite 300, 4 Winsley St, W1R 7AR (071-323 0506).

Netherlands
Royal Netherlands Embassy, 38 Hyde Park Gate, SW7 5DP (071-584 5040).
Netherlands Board of Tourism, 25-28 Buckingham Gate, London SW1E 6LD (Tel: 071-630 0451).
Netherlands Railways, 25-28 Buckingham Gate, London SW1E 6LD (071-630 1735).

Portugal
Portuguese Consulate-General, 62 Brompton Road, London SW3 1BJ (071-581 8722).
Portuguese Tourist Office, 1-5 New Bond St, W1Y 0NP (071-493 3873).

Spain/Gibraltar
Spanish Consulate, 24 Belgrave Square, SW1 80A (071-235 5555).
Spanish National Tourist Office, 57 St. James St, SW1 (071-499 0901).

Gibraltar Tourist Office, 179 Strand, WC2R 1EH (071-836 0777).

Switzerland
Swiss Embassy, 16-18 Montagu Place, W1H 2BQ (071-723 0701).
Swiss National Tourist Office/Swiss Railways, New Coventry St, W1V 8EE (071-734 1921).

Turkey
Turkish Consulate, Rutland Lodge, Rutland Gardens, Knightsbridge, London SW7 1BW (071-589 0360).
Turkish Information Office, 170-173 Piccadilly, London W1V 9DD (071-734 8681).

Yugoslavia
Yugoslav Consulate General, 5 Lexham Gardens, W8 5JU (071-370 6105).
Yugoslav National Tourist Office, 143 Regent St, W1R 8AE (071-734 5243).

Scandinavia
Royal Danish Embassy, 55 Sloane St, SW1X 9SR (071-235 1255).
Danish Tourist Board, Sceptre House, 169 Regent St, W1R 8PY (071-734 2637).

Finnish Embassy, 38 Chesham Place, SW1X 8HW (071-235 9531).
Finnish Tourist Board, Greener House, 66 Haymarket, SW1Y 4RF (071-839 4048).

Icelandic Embassy, 1 Eaton Terrace, London SW1W 8EY (071-730 5131).
Icelandic Tourist Office, 3rd Floor, 172 Tottenham Court Road, London W1P 9LS (071-388 5599).

Royal Norwegian Embassy, 25 Belgrave Square, SW1X 8QD (071-235 7151).
Norwegian National Tourist Office, 5-11 Lower Regent St, SW1Y 4LR (071-839 6255).
Norwegian State Railway, 21 Cockspur St, SW1Y 5DA (071-930 6666).

Swedish Embassy, 11 Montagu Place, W1H 2AL (071-724 2101).
Swedish National Tourist Office, 29-31 Oxford St, W1R 1RE (071-437 5816).

Austria

KAPRUN, SALTZBERGERLAND   W.S.

Area. 32,375 square miles   **Population.** 7,600,000

Capital. Vienna (population: 1,550,000)

Weather. The Alps create a strange weather pattern that gives Austria a lot of rain throughout the year, and very cold winters with good ski conditions. Summers can be hot, but don't go far without a raincoat; you'll also need warm clothes for the evenings.

THE PEOPLE

Despite statistics that indicate a lower standard of living than most of the other western European countries, the Austrians are fond of the good life. In their social life, they are very carefree and love good food, which is why so many of them tend to obesity. *Gemütlichkeit* is a key word to define the Austrians' philosophy — homely comfort and relaxation.

Politics. Austria is a federal republic consisting of nine provinces. Since full independence was restored ten years after the war, her studious neutrality and proximity to seven Eastern bloc and Western nations has resulted in popularity among both refugees and international organisations.

Religion. Seven-eighths of the population are Roman Catholic. Take care what you wear in churches and what you do on Sundays.

Language. The official language is German, but it's spoken with a heavy accent, so even if you speak German, you may find it difficult to understand. In the south and east, there's a small Slovene minority. English is quite widely spoken.

Making Friends. The old Austro-Hungarian Empire, although a thing of the past, lives on both in the architecture (Schönbrunn Palace, near Vienna, is a magnificent example), and in the character of the people, who are absolute examples of courtesy and gallantry. In fact they are polite to the point of grotesque formality: they not only shake your hand when greeting you, the older generation are also likely to bow, or a man might kiss a woman's hand. Professional people (and sometimes even their spouses) should be addressed by their title — eg *Herr Doktor* or *Frau Direktor*. This formality is, in true Germanic tradition, also transferred to the world of officialdom. Kafka knew what he was talking about.

If any Austrians invite you to their home for a meal, you should arrive a few minutes late, bring flowers for the hostess and express great admiration for the meal and more than a mild interest in the wine.

See the introduction for details of passports, customs regulations, duty free allowances, vaccinations and importing pets.

Passport and Visas. Visitors with a full British passport are allowed to stay six months; holders of US, Canadian and British Visitor's Passports only three months. For extensions, apply to the police. All foreigners should register with the police within three days of arrival: hotels and campsites will do this for you. No one usually bothers, but it can be used as a reason for expulsion.

Customs. Variations on the duty free allowances given in the introduction in the lower column include a reasonable amount of articles for personal use, plus gifts to a value of AS 400; allowances apply only to persons over 17. 1 litre of spirits and 2 litres of sparkling wine or 2.25 litres of still wine may be brought in. Art objects need an export permit, available from the shop of purchase or from the Austrian National Bank in Vienna.

100 Groschen (Gr.) = 1 Schilling (AS)
£1 = AS 20   AS 1 = £0.05
$1 = AS 12   AS 1 = $0.08

For general information on handling, exchanging and earning money, see the introduction.

Coins. 2 Gr, 5 Gr, 10 Gr, 50 Gr, AS 1, AS 5, AS 10, AS 20; AS 25, AS 50, AS 100, AS 500 and AS 1,000 coins are issued as collectors' items.

Notes. AS 20 (brown), AS 50 (violet), AS 100 (olive green), AS 500 (red-brown), AS 1,000 (blue-grey).

Banking Hours. Monday-Friday, 8 am-12.30 pm and 1.30 pm-3.30 pm (5.30 pm on Thursdays). Bank head offices in central Vienna remain open at lunchtime. Outside these hours, you can change money at main stations (daily), and at some travel agents (Saturday mornings only). The exchange bureau at Schwechat is open 6 am-11 pm daily.

Shopping Hours. 8 am-6 pm, Monday-Friday (optional lunch break from 12.30 or 1 pm for up to three hours); 9 am-noon or 1 pm Saturday (until 6 pm on the four Saturdays before Christmas). Food shops often stay open later in the evening (until 10 pm at stores in large rail stations), and all day Saturday and Sunday. In Vienna, there is a 24-hour supermarket in Ausstellungsstr, near the Nordbahn.

Import and Export. No restrictions on imports; export limit of AS 100,000 without special permission.

Tipping. Hotels — 10-15% service charge always included (*einschliesslich Bedienung*) but a tip is also expected. Restaurants, Cafés, Bars — 10-15% service charge in addition. Taxis — 10-15%. Station Porters — flat rate of AS10 per item, but they expect a tip (AS 3-4 per item) as well.

Emergency Cash. Employers are only allowed to employ foreigners if they can prove that no available Austrian national can do the job, and work permits are not issued to travellers already in Austria. Unofficial work prospects are worsening as the authorities clamp down, but you might strike lucky with a tourist-related job in a hotel or restaurant in the Tyrol. Street selling is illegal without a licence, but if you have something to sell or pawn try the Saturday flea market in Vienna (near Kettenbrückengasse U-bahn).

Taxes. Sales tax (*Mehrwertsteuer*) runs at 32% on luxury items, 10% on food and 20% on just about everything else. Foreigners can claim exemption on items costing over AS 1,000, by asking the shopkeeper for the special form U34. Sign it there and then, and have the copy signed by customs when you leave the country. This procedure is not possible for those travelling by train: they should send their purchases as registered luggage, and the baggage clerk at the railway station will sign the customs declaration. When leaving by plane the validation should be applied for before checking in. Post this back to the shop to obtain your refund. If you buy from a shop with the sign *Tax Free Shop* (German for tax free shop) you can usually get a cash refund from Austrian Automobile Club (OAMTC) frontier offices, on production of the signed U34.

Getting Around

The information in this section is complementary to that given in the corresponding section in the introduction.

CAR

For information on road conditions, dial the Vienna number 1590. If you want the information in English, dial 72 21 01, extension 7 or 85 35 35, extension 7.

For winter driving you can rent chains from the OAMTC and ARBO. Studded tyres are permitted from November until April. Some passes close for several months, but can be circumnavigated by tunnels, as well as the car transport trains which operate on the lines from Vienna to Innsbruck, Salzburg and Villach, and through the Tauern tunnel. Tolls are levied on roads over several passes — Grossglockner Tauern, Felbertauern and Brenner.

Rules and Requirements. In addition to the points raised in the introduction, all vehicles must carry a first aid kit and a red warning triangle. In cars fitted with rear seat belts, these must be worn by passengers; children under 12 are banned from the front seat. The green card is not obligatory for British drivers. Horns must not be sounded within Vienna. In towns with tram services, the trams have absolute priority, and will assume that you are aware of this. The police can impose spot fines for motoring offences. Exceeding the drink-driving level of 0.8% results in a minimum fine of AS 8,000 and confiscation of licence.

Parking. A major rule in Vienna, which if broken involves heavy fines, is that parking is banned on streets with tram lines between 8 pm and 5 am from December to March: this is to permit the streets to be cleared of snow. On some streets there are short term parking zones marked *Kurzparkzone* on street signs that allow a maximum parking period of between 30 minutes and three hours, as marked on the sign: if no time limit is marked, the maximum permissible stay is three hours. These zones are known as blue zones and are often marked by blue lines in the road. The use of them is subject to payment in Vienna, Graz, Klagenfurt, St. Veit/Glan, Volkermarkt and Salzburg; this is signified by the word *Gebuhrenpflichtig* either on the *Kurzparkzone* sign or on a separate sign.

Parking tickets (*Parkscheine*) must be bought from tobacconists, banks, or the OAMTC in the above towns: the arrival time should be written on them and they should be clearly displayed behind the windscreen. In Vienna tickets come in three shades and cost AS6 for a red ticket ($\frac{1}{2}$ hour), AS 12 for one hour (blue) and AS18 for $1\frac{1}{2}$ hours (green). In other towns short term parking is governed by parking clocks on which both the arrival time and estimated departure time should be set: these are available free from tobacconists and police stations.

Petrol. A litre of *super* (about 97 octane) costs about AS9 per litre (around £2.00 per UK gallon, £1.70 per US gallon). *Eurosuper* (95 octane lead-free) costs AS8.6 per litre and regular lead-free (91 octane) costs AS 8.20 per litre. Lead-free petrol is available at all Austrian filling stations.

Touring Clubs. OAMTC, Schubertring 1-3 1010 Vienna (Tel: 72 99 0). (They provide a translation of British driving licences that may simplify matters if you get stopped by the police.) ARBO, Mariahilferstrasse 180, 1150 Vienna (Tel: 85 35 35-0).

Breakdowns. Both organisations operate a touring breakdown service on all motorways and main roads. For help, dial 120 (OAMTC) or 123 (ARBO) or, on motorways, ask the operator for them at one of the emergency telephones.

Accidents. The police must be informed if anyone is injured, or a road is likely to be obstructed. Either dial 133 (144 for ambulance) or use the emergency motorway telephones.

TRAIN

The *Osterreichische Bundesbahn* (OBB) has its head office at Elisabethstrasse 9, Vienna (Tel: 5650). For timetable information, dial 1717. Complaints to Nordbahnstrasse 50, Vienna (Tel: 5650, ext 3999). Showers are available for use by travellers at the railway stations in Vienna and Salzburg.

Trains have two classes, first costing 50% more than second, just under AS 2 per km (£1 or $1.60 for 10 miles). All lines are now electrified, and trains are graded by speed: the *Personenzug* (P in the timetable) and *Eilzug* (E) are both painfully slow. Seat reservations (AS 30) are advisable on faster *Schnellzug* (D), *Triebwagen* (TS) and *Express* (Ex) services which require a supplement of AS 40, except for tickets issued outside Austria. The best expresses are the *Städte*

Schnellzug — the Austrian version of Inter City trains — which run hourly between Salzburg, Vienna and Graz, and every two hours between Innsbruck, Vienna and Klagenfurt. TEE trains also require a special supplement of AS 50-250, according to the distance travelled; advance reservation are necessary. Telephones are available on most expresses. Trains which traverse Germany or Italy to reach another part of Austria are known as *Korridorzuge*.

Cheap Deals. Children under 6 travel free; 6-15 at half price.

Nationwide area tickets (*Bundes-Netzkarte*) offer unlimited travel over 9 or 16 days or a month over the whole Austrian rail network. Second class costs AS 1,440, 1,960 or 3,100; the return of five used tickets to the issuing office earns one free ticket. *Regional-Netzkarte* giving unlimited travel for between 4 and 10 days within one of 18 different regions are also available for between AS 400 and AS 760.

BUS

There are two kinds of long-distance bus services; one run by the OBB (often parallel to rail lines — tickets from stations) and KWB; the other by the postal service (tickets on the bus).

BICYCLE

Cycles can be hired between April 1 and November 2 at around a hundred main stations for AS 85 a day; 50% reduction if you hold a valid train ticket. Cycles can be returned to any station.

AIR

For flight information at Schwechat Airport, dial 22277. Buses operate from the Vienna City Air Terminal at the Hilton Hotel via the Westbahnhof and Südbahnhof to Schwechat between 5 am and 9 pm and cost AS 50. For taxi rides from Vienna to the airport AS 100 is added to the fare to cover the return journey.

HITCH-HIKING

Young people under 16 are forbidden to hitch-hike in the provinces of Vorarlberg and Styria (Steiermark). Motorway hitching is also strictly *verboten*. Generally, hitch-hiking can be very slow, but a neat appearance should help.

To get onto the West-Autobahn leading out of Vienna, take the U-bahn line 4 to Hutteldorf and walk a few hundred yards south. To hitch south, try tram 67 to the Altes Landgut roundabout four miles south of the city centre. For Prague, tram 32 will take you along Prager Strasse to the Nord-Autobahn junction. For a pre-arranged lift, call *Mitfahrzentrale* in Vienna on 564174 or Innsbruck on 32343.

BOAT

Most inland boat services (including those on the Danube) are run in conjunction with the OBB, are listed in railway timetables, and can be booked as part of a rail journey. The Vienna booking office for Danube steamers is at Mexikoplatz 8 (Tel: 26 25 93). Enquiries and complaints to Hintere Zollamtsstrasse 1 (Tel: 72 51 41).

CITY TRANSPORT

Taxis. Taxis don't cruise, but there are plenty of taxi ranks, or look up *Auto-Ruf* or *Taxiruf* in the directory. The numbers in Vienna for radio taxis are: 3130; 4369; 6282; 9101. Fares work out around AS 40 per km (£3.30 or $5.50 a mile), with a basic charge of AS 26. All taxis are metered, but fares for journeys outside the city should be negotiated in advance. There is a supplement charge for luggage carried in the boot.

Horse drawn fiacre cabs (fares negotiable, but higher than taxis) can be hired in Vienna at the stands in Stephansplatz, Heldenplatz, or Albertinaplatz.

Bus/Tram/Underground. All Vienna public transport is run by the *Wiener Verkehrsbetriebe*, Favoritenstrasse 9 (Tel: 65 9 30).

All forms of transport — bus, tram, U-bahn (underground) and Schnellbahn (rapid metropolitan railway) — are operated on a flat fare system. A single ticket costs AS 20 (AS 7 for children) from ticket machines at U-bahn or Schnellbahn stations or from the few remaining conductors (who sit just inside the door marked *ein*) or, on trams without conductors (marked *schaffnerloser Zug*), from machines behind the driver (enter by the front door). Some trams have cars marked *schaffnerloser Beiwagen* with neither conductor nor machine — so avoid these if you need to buy a ticket: the fine for travelling without a ticket is AS 350.

It is more usual to buy tickets in advance in multiples of 4 for AS 56 from ticket machines, city transport offices (*vorverkaufstellen*) or most tobacconists (marked tabak-trafic). For short journeys of up to 4 stages (around 1 mile) short-distance tickets are obtainable at AS 28 for 4.

This fare structure extends beyond the city limits on services run by the Verkehrsverbund Ost-Region (VOR) on a zone system. Journeys inside Vienna cost one ticket: outside the capital, zone network maps show the boundaries, each of which increase the fare by one ticket.

If you are planning to do a lot of travelling it makes sense to buy a one or three day travel pass. The 24 Stunden-Netzkarte costs AS 40, and the 72 Stunden-Netzkarte cost AS 102.

See the introduction for information on youth hostels, other hostels, camping and advance booking of accommodation.

Hotels. The official categories are one-star (modest) to five stars (deluxe) for hotels; for pensions and seasonal hotels (*saisonhotels*), one to four stars. Prices for a double room in a one-star hotel (equivalent to a two star pension) start around AS 200 a night (£10 or $16) in a cheap area. Vienna and Salzburg lead the list of expensive hotels, followed closely by resorts such as Kitzbühel. Many towns charge a local or spa tax of up to AS 10 per night.

Castles. Around 30 genuine castles and mansions have been converted into luxury hotels. Prices are high, but cut-price weekend breaks are available in spring and autumn. For further information and bookings, contact the Central Bookings Office, Hotel Schloss Lebenberg, 6370 Kitzbühel (Tel: 053 56-4301).

Hostels. The Austrian Youth Hostel Association HQ is at Schottenring 28, 1010 Vienna (Tel: 222/53 35 353). Prices range from AS 80-130 per night.

A number of student hostels are available for use by travellers during the summer vacation; ask at local tourist offices for details.

Mountain Huts. For climbers and walkers, there's a network of Alpine huts and refuges, with just the basic facilities. Beds cost AS 60-180 per night, with priority booking and 50% reductions for Alpine Club members. For details, contact the Austrian Alpine Club, Getreidemarkt 3, 1060 Vienna (Tel: 5638673).

Camping. Campsites charge anything between AS 20 and AS 60 per person per night, but you're still allowed to camp wherever you like, provided you have the permission of the landowner or the local *Bürgermeister*. Open fires are banned in or near woodland.

In recent years, the Austrians have been encouraging hikers in summer. There is a complex numbering system for many hiking paths, rather like road numbers. Many Alpine resorts offer free bus rides to the mountains, guided hikes and badges for even the gentlest of strolls. Local tourist offices will provide full details. After 15 hours of hiking within one year, you qualify for the Austrian Hiking Boot medal. Even the less enthusiastic might consider joining the Austrian Alpine Club (Getreidemarkt 3, 1060 Vienna; 56 38 673) to qualify for discounts on accommodation and travel. Their United Kingdom branch is at Longcroft House, Fretherne Road, Welwyn Garden City, Herts AL8 6PQ (Tel: 0707-324835).

Communications

See the introduction for general information on Telephones and English language newspapers and radio broadcasts.

Post. Post offices (look up *Post* in the directory) open 8 am-6 pm (small branches close 12-2 pm), Monday-Friday. Larger branches also open Saturday, 8-10 am. 24-hour service at Vienna's three main railway stations and at the central post office in Postgasse. Main post offices have a free poste restante service, and philatelic counters. For information on postal services, dial 83 21 01. Stamps can also be bought at tobacconists and from vending machines outside most post offices. Mail boxes are yellow; the blue ones are for airmail only.

The correct way to address mail is: name, city (in capitals); street (name, then number). Cities are preceded by a four-figure zip code (Vienna zips all begin with 1); if writing from abroad, the zip code is preceded by the prefix A-.

Telephone. Automatic system within Austria and connected to several European countries. The code for Vienna is 1; the international prefix is 00, except for neighbouring countries: dial 030 for Northen Yugoslavia, 040 for Italy, 050 for Switzerland and 060 for West Germany.

Public telephones take some combination of AS 1, AS 5, AS 10 and AS 20 coins. Those with three or four coin slots can be used for international calls, as can cardphones — buy a *Telefon-Wertkarte* from post offices or tobacconists, these are to the value of either AS 50 or AS 100. To make a call, lift the receiver, insert your card or money (minimum AS 10), dial, then press the red button to make your connection; if there's no reply don't press the red button but replace the receiver to get your money back or retrieve your card. An audible tone will warn you of time running out. Calls are one-third cheaper from 7 pm-8 am and at weekends. Many public telephones have instructions printed in English. For international collect and BT Chargecards calls through the operator dial 09.

Directories are divided into two sections-alphabetical and commercial (yellow pages). The alphabetical section is first sub-divided into communities, starting with the principal town in the region, then proceeding alphabetically. Unlike the German directories the letters A, O, U are treated as A, O, U (not AE, OE, UE). Emergency numbers (*Notrufe*) and other important numbers are given on the outside cover of the alphabetical section. The first pages of the directory give codes, charges and services.

Directory information: 08 (international/long distance); 16 (local).
Operator: 09 (international/long distance); 16 (local).
Emergency: 133 (police); 144 (ambulance); 122 (fire).
Weather: 15 66.

Telegrams. Can be sent from post offices — 24 hour service at Borseplatz 1, Vienna; or by telephone — dial 10 for inland, 119 overseas.

Broadcasting. Radio Austria (520, 584 or 1024 kHz AM) gives news, weather and road information in English daily from 8.05-8.15am. Blue Danube Radio (102.5 MHz FM) broadcasts in English, Spanish and French from 7am-10am, noon-2pm and 6pm-7.55pm to Vienna and the surrounding area. The Austrian short wave service broadcasts to Europe in English at 8.30am, 12.30pm and 6.30pm daily on the 49 metre band.

Health and Hygiene

See the introduction for general information on first aid, hygiene, medical treatment, and insurance.

Hygiene. Austria is among the healthiest countries in Europe. There's no danger from tap water, in fact it's probably Europe's freshest and coolest.

Reciprocal Agreements. British visitors should go to the Viennese District Health Insurance Office (*Wiener Gebietskrankenkasse*), 1060 Vienna, Mariahilferstrasse 85-87, Room 325, for a health insurance form which will enable them to visit a doctor. The general hospital in Vienna is at Alserstrasse 4, 1090 Vienna. British subjects receive free in-patient treatment at Austrian public hospitals upon production of a passport; charges for other medical services are reduced.

Treatment. If you want English-speaking doctors, contact the American Medical Society, Lazarettgasse 13, Vienna 1090 (Tel: 42 45 68).

Emergencies. The telephone number for medical emergencies is 144. Chemists (*Apotheken*) have a weekend and evening rota, displayed in all chemists' windows, or dial 1725. Doctors have a similar rota — look up *Arztenotdienst* at the front of the directory (in Vienna, 57 75 20). For Vienna's anti-poison centre, dial 43 43 43.

If you're planning anything tricky in the mountains, inform the nearest rescue service (*Bergrettungsdienst* — there's one in all mountain resorts) of your intentions, so they'll be more able to get you out of any difficulties: if you're in distress, the recognised signal is six signals a minute, evenly spaced, a gap of one minute, then repeat. Any audible or visible signal will do, but most mountaineers carry whistles. Acknowledgement at a rate of three signals a minute means help is on its way.

Entertainment

Sport. Austria is mainly known for winter sports. The main season is December-March, but the higher slopes are open November-May. Eight glaciers — Mölltaler, Kaprun, Kaunertaler, Pitztaler, Stubaier, Tuxertaler, Otztaler and Ramsauer — are open all year round.

Soccer is very popular; the leading teams are the Vienna sides *Austria* and *Rapid*.

Nightlife. Whether it's the Vienna Boys' Choir, the Vienna State Opera or the Vienna Philharmonic Orchestra, classical music is the focal point of Austria's nightlife. For formal concerts, opera and theatre, evening dress is still obligatory. You'd be advised to book in advance; several months in advance for the two major festivals in Salzburg and Vienna. Students usually get reductions. Most films are dubbed into German. When Austrians want an informal evening out, they usually just sit in a café or wine garden.

Casinos. Baccarat, blackjack and roulette can be played at casinos in Vienna, Graz, Linz, Salzburg, Bregenz and six Alpine resorts. The rules are explained each Monday and Friday between 8 pm-9 pm. Entrance costs AS 170, but you are given chips worth AS 200 once you get inside.

Spanish Riding School. The world famous Lipizzaner horses, and displays of horsemanship can be seen twice a week at the Winter Palace in Vienna from April to the end of June and from September to mid December. Seats cost AS 200 upwards, but standing room only costs AS 135. Tickets are available from the Vienna Tourist Office or from the Spanish Riding School office in the Hofburg. On most days between 10 am and noon (except Mondays, and throughout January and July), you can pay AS 50 to watch the horses training. Go to Gate 2 on Josefplatz.

Vienna Boys' Choir. Masses are staged by the Vienna Boys' Choir every Sunday morning at 9.15 am (except in July, August and early September) at the Imperial Chapel of the Hofburg. Seats cost AS 50-180, but standing room is free.

Museums. There is no set pattern to opening hours, although most museums are closed on public holidays. Most national museums charge an AS 15 admission fee, except to children under 14 and students, and at weekends from September to April. Municipal museums in Vienna are free throughout the year. The booklet *Museums — Vienna* gives full information on opening hours; it is available free from tourist offices.

Eating out. The Austrians seem to spend the whole day eating in large quantities; the food is predominantly rich and heavy with plenty of meat. Meals are always slow, long drawn out affairs, so if you can't stand waiting, take a book into the restaurant with you.

The cheapest restaurants are the *Wienerwald* and *WIGAST* chains. Be prepared for long waits between courses. If you want something quick, cheap and filling, just order the soup. The daily *spezial* served in bars and small restaurants from noon-2 pm is usually good value. Or buy a sausage and some bread at a street stand. For evening meals, most restaurants (except in cities) stop serving by 9 pm. Reckon on at least AS 100 for a reasonable meal (£5 or $8): a quarter litre of wine to go with your food will set you back around AS 30.

Drinking. The Austrian wine industry is still reeling from the effects of the 1985 wine scandal, when potentially lethal quantities of diethylene glycol (an ingredient of anti-freeze) were found to have been added to wine as a sweetener. As a result, Austria now has the strictest wine control laws in Europe.

For beer drinking, go to a *Bierkeller*, where you buy it straight out of the barrel. They are often self-service places — take a mug (one-litre), wash it, fill it from the barrel, then pay at the till, it should cost around AS 42. They always provide a beer warmer, in case the beer's too cold. For wine, there are *weinlokale*, which serve food as well as wine. Or go to a *Heuriger* (or *Buschenschenke*), where the new wine is usually served in a garden. They serve food, too, but no one will be offended if you bring your own sandwiches. The control of the sale and consumption of alcohol is very lax — most eating places (even McDonalds) also serve alcohol. Special licences are not necessary.

Although both wine and beer are domestically produced and consumed in great quantities, more time seems to be spent drinking coffee. All Austrians are coffee connoisseurs, and use cafés as second homes, meeting places or excuses to sample the luxurious Austrian pastries (with the almost obligatory *Schlagobers* — whipped cream).

Smoking. Austrian cigarettes come in two types — light and dark. The most popular light brand is *Milde Sorte*. You can find yourself paying anything between AS 25 and AS 35 for a packet of cigarettes, depending on their quality and country of origin.

Police. The Austrian police, like other Austrians, are extremely polite, and unlikely to bother you. The fact that you're a foreigner carries a lot of weight, so claim ignorance when approached.

Drugs. For simple possession, expect to be sent away for medical treatment, fined up to £1,000 and jailed for up to six months. The maximum for supply is ten years plus £15,000 fine. If you get caught with a very small amount of cannabis for personal use and the judge is in a very good mood, you may stand a chance of dismissal — but the chances are against you.

Legal Aid. Embassies and consulates can help you, and you should have no trouble getting in touch with them if you're arrested. Some of the organisations in the *Help and Information* section might prove helpful.

Nude Bathing. The Austrians are not as easy going about nudity as the Germans. The Austrian Tourist Office can provide addresses for naturists.

Embassies and Consulates.
British Embassy, Jauresgasse 12, 1030 Vienna (Tel: 713 1575)
British Honorary Consulate, Alter Markt 4, 5020 Salzburg (Tel: 8 48 133).
British Honorary Consulate, Mathias-SchmidStrasse 12, 6021 Innsbruck (Tel: 58 83 20).
British Honorary Consulate, Schmiedgasse 8-12, 8010 Graz (Tel: 82 61 05).
American Embassy, Boltzmanngasse 16, 1091 Vienna (Tel: 31 55 11).
Canadian Embassy, Dr. Karl Lueger-Ring 10, 1010 Vienna (Tel: 533 36 91).

Lost Property. The term for lost property office is *Fundamt* or *Fundbüro*. If you lose something in any form of transport, apply to the company concerned. Things lost on trains should eventually end up at the lost property office at Westbahnhof in Vienna. Otherwise, go to the police; the central lost property office in Vienna is at Wasagasse 22 (Tel: 313 44). Be patient; it may take several days for lost property to make its way there.

Guides/Baby-sitting. Should be easy to find, especially in towns with a lot of students. In Vienna, there's an *Austrian Visitors Service* for tourists, providing guides, secretaries, translators and baby-sitters, at Mühlgasse 20 (Tel: 587 35 25). There's also a *Babysitter-Zentrale* at Herbstrasse 6 (Tel: 95 11 35).

Information. The commonest terms for tourist office are *Verkehrsverein*, *Verkehrsamt* or *Verkehrsverband*. In Vienna, it's in the Kärntnerstrasse 38 (Tel: 513 8892). In Salzburg, at Mozartplatz 5 (Tel: 84 75 68); in Innsbruck, at Burggraben 3 (Tel: 53 56). In many towns there are information offices in stations; and this is usually where the room reservations service is located. Approaching Vienna, there are also information offices on the South and West Autobahns and at the Reichsbrücke landing stage on the Danube (open only between May and September).

Osterreich-Information at Margaretenstr 1, 1040 Vienna (Tel: 58 72 000) provides free literature and information, but cannot book rooms. For a tape recorded summary of coming events in Vienna dial 15 15.

Help. The Vienna Social Services Department has an advice and help centre at Prarnergasse 12 (Tel: 34 73 53).

Disabled Travellers. For the price of return postage, you can obtain (in German only) a national Hotel Guide (*Hotelführer*) and Vienna city guide (*Stadtführer*) for the disabled, from the Verband der Querschnittgelähmten Osterreichs, Liechtensteinstrasse 57, Vienna (Tel: 34 01 21).

Austria's major travel and holiday service for the physically handicapped is Mobility Tours, Piaristengasse 60, Vienna, (Tel: 43 97 32).

Student Organisations. OKISTA, Türkenstrasse 4, 1090 Vienna (Tel: 34 75 26), for information on courses and exchanges.

Youth Information Centres. Vienna has a Youth Information Centre at Bellaria passage 3, 1010 Vienna, (Tel: 96 46 37).

English Language Churches. The most significant is Christ Church (Anglican), Jauresgasse 17-19, 1030 Vienna (Tel: 712 33 96)

American Express. Kärntnerstrasse 21/23, 1015 Vienna (Tel: 52 05 44); and offices in Innsbruck, Linz, Salzburg and Graz.

Calendar of Events

Public Holidays are shown in **bold**

January 1	**New Year's Day**
January 6	**Epiphany**
February	Carnivals throughout Austria, especially in the cities
March	Vienna Trade Fair
March/April	**Easter Monday**
May 1	**Labour Day**
May/June	**Ascension Day, Whit Monday**
June/July	**Corpus Christi**
June	Vienna Music Festival: brochure published January, available from Austrian National Tourist Offices; book with the theatres direct
June-August	Summer Theatre Festival at Friesach
June-September	Marionette Theatre at Salzburg
July	Youth and Music Festival in Vienna
July-August	Bregenz Festival
	Salzburg Festival — programmes published in December, booked up in January. Information from the Salzburg Festival Director, Festspielhaus, Salzburg
August 15	**Assumption Day:** folklore processions in many Tyrolean towns
August	Wine festivals in Hollabrunn, Eisenstadt and Leibnitz
September	Vienna Trade Fair
	Bruckner Festival at Linz
	Theatre and opera season begins (until June)
October	Concert season begins (until June)
October 26	**National Day**
November 1	**All Saints**
December 8	**Conception Day**
December 25, 26	**Christmas Day, Boxing Day**

Belgium

BRUGES

Area. 11,781 square miles   **Population.** 9,800,000

Capital. Brussels (population: 1,000,000)

Weather. The climate is temperate — warm summers and cool winters, with no extremes of temperature. The further inland you go, the more stable the climate. But always have a coat or jacket handy, even in summer.

THE PEOPLE

Belgium is the meeting point of the Latin and the Teutonic, and this is seen both in the natives' physical characteristics (a mixture of dark and blonde), and in their personalities. On the one hand, they are a hard-working, well-ordered people; but at the same time they love to sit around and drink the evenings away, and they have a long-lived disrespect for authority — when Julius Caesar said: "Of all the Gauls, the Belgians are the bravest," he probably meant they were the most stubborn. In general they are very sociable and like foreigners, being particularly Anglophile for historical reasons.

Politics. Belgium is a constitutional monarchy, with the capital and seat of government at Brussels. King Baudouin is the nominal Head of State, but the real power lies with the Parliament, divided into two chambers: Representatives and Senate, whose members are elected every four years.

Belgian politics belie the nation's image as staid and unexceptional. There have been over 30 governments since the war, most of them fragile coalitions between the centre and right. The Socialists have rapidly been gaining in influence, and the next few years could witness the consolidation of their support.

Religion. Very strongly Catholic. At the last count there were over 20,000 nuns in the country. It's advisable to wear respectful clothing in church; and not to criticise the church in conversation.

Language. For linguistic purposes Belgium must be divided into the two regions of Wallonia (south and east) and Flanders (north and west). In Wallonia French is spoken; but the majority (58% of the population) come from Flanders and speak a variety of Dutch which they call Flemish. In 1971 Brussels was declared bi-lingual, a linguistically neutral territory. A fourth sector — German-speaking — exists in the Eupen and Malmédy areas along the German frontier. English is widely spoken in Flanders and in Brussels, which is a very international community. French is spoken throughout Flanders as well as Wallonia.

Making Friends. Belgians are traditionally very formal, and it may take a long time to get on Christian name terms with them. They shake hands a lot, but a firm handshake is considered unrefined; visitors are advised to cultivate a light 'wet fish' shake. Women might kiss you three times on the cheeks when you get to know them well. Young people are less formal, particularly in the cosmopolitan atmosphere of Brussels, and relationships should be easy to strike up. Attitudes towards sex are reasonably open, without going to the extremes shown in neighbouring Holland.

Red Tape

See the introduction for details of passports, customs regulations, duty free allowances, vaccinations and importing pets.

Passports and Visas. Holders of British, US and Canadian passports may stay three months. Technically, you should inform the local *maison communale* of your address within one week of arrival. For extensions, apply to the local *maison communale.*

Customs. In addition to the duty free allowances listed in the introduction, there are limits on coffee and tea (figures in brackets for goods bought and taxed in the EC):
500g (1,000g) coffee or 200g (400g) coffee extract or essence — including instant coffee.
100g (200g) tea or 40g (80g) tea extract or essence.

Travellers under 17 are not entitled to allowances on tobacco, alcohol or coffee and may only import 800 BF worth of other goods (2,000 BF of goods bought and taxed within the EC). Adults can bring in other goods to the value of 2,000 BF, or 15,800 if they were bought in the EC.

Money

100 centimes = 1 Belgian franc (BF)
£1 = 60 BF   10 BF = £0.16
$1 = 38 BF   10 BF = $0.26

For general information on handling, exchanging and raising money, see the introduction.

Coins. 50c, 1 BF. 5 BF, 20 BF, 50 BF.

Notes. 100 BF (pink), 500 BF (blue), 1,000 BF (grey), 5,000 BF (green/brown).

Banking hours. Monday-Friday, 9 am-noon and 2-4 pm. Larger banks may remain open through lunchtimes. To change money at weekends, the best rate is given at the exchange bureaux at main railway stations and airports. The bureau at the Gare du Midi is open daily from 10 am to 11.30 pm, and the one at the Gare du Nord from 7 am to 11 pm. Hotels will change at a lower rate. When changing small amounts of money, travellers cheques are bad news, because a high minimum charge is imposed. Either change a lot at a time, or stick to cash. Exchange rates are better at banks inside Belgium than in airport exchange offices.

Shopping Hours. 9 am-6 pm, with an optional lunch break (say, 12-2 pm), Monday-Saturday. Food shops may open as early as 7 am, and many large stores stay open till 9 pm on Fridays; shopping centres and hypermarkets may stay open until 8 or 9pm, Monday-Saturday.

Import and Export. No restrictions.

Tipping. The Belgians feel very strongly about their tips; if you don't give one when they think you should, they'll let you know in no uncertain terms. Restaurants, cafés and hotels — usually include 16% on the bill. Theatres and cinemas — 20 BF for the usher(ette). Porters and bell-boys — 40 BF per item, slightly more at night and on Sundays. Taxis include the 20% tip on the meter. Don't give them more.

Emergency Cash. Begging and street-selling are illegal. If you're British, you're allowed to work, provided you have the right of abode in the UK. A division of the *Office Nationale de l'Emploi* known as *T-Service* specialises in temporary work; it has offices in Antwerp, Brussels, Charleroi, Ghent and Liege.

Taxes. For goods shipped directly out of the country, ie by the shop, you can apply for exemption from sales tax (TVA in French, BTW in Dutch — 6%, 16% or 25% depending on the type of goods).

The information in this section is complementary to that given in the corresponding section in the introduction.

CAR

Road conditions in Belgium are good, thanks to short distances between towns and a comprehensive and expanding toll-free motorway network. There are, however, cobbled and potholed streets in towns, not to mention one of Europe's highest accident rates: many drivers on the roads have never taken a driving test. For information on Belgian and international road conditions, dial 02 642 66 66. For international road conditions, dial 513 82 40. Between November and March motorists can call 511 66 67 for a pre-recorded message about road conditions.

Rules and Requirements. All vehicles must carry a fire extinguisher, and a red warning triangle is obligatory. Seat belts must be fitted to all vehicles, and drivers and front seat passengers are required to wear them at all times; children under

12 (under 10 in Luxembourg) are banned from the front seat. Trams have absolute priority, and will assert it.

Place Names. The following are among the towns that have separate names in French and Dutch. Apart from Brussels, for which both names are official, the official name is given first:

Aalst/Alost	Antwerpen/Anvers	Brugge/Bruges
Brussels/Bruxelles	De Panne/La Panne	Gent/Gand
Ieper/Ypres	Kortrijk/Courtrai	Leuven/Louvain
Liege/Luik	Mechelen/Malines	Mons/Bergen
Namur/Namen	Roeselaere/Roulers	Ronse/Renaix
St. Truiden/St. Trond	Tienen/Tirlemont	Tournai/Doornik

Parking. No Parking is *Stationnement interdit* in French, *Parkeren verboden* in Dutch. There are two widely used systems of controlling short-term parking in Belgian towns and cities. Some towns have streets which contain parking zones for which you must buy a ticket from a machine. Or a town may contain blue zones (*zone bleue/blauwe zone*): to park in these you must display a parking disc, which can be obtained from garages, motor accessory shops, bookstores or police stations. Brussels and some other large towns possess a number of meters that take 5 BF coins: the rate is 25 BF for one hour. The alternate day and half-monthly systems are also in operation (see the introduction).

Petrol. Since June 1989 leaded petrol has not been available in Belgium. Normal unleaded (92 octane) costs 25.10 BF per litre: super unleaded (95 octane) costs 25.80 per litre (£1.94 per UK gallon, $2.54 per US gallon). Prices increase the further you get from the refineries at Antwerp, but are lower in Luxembourg.

Touring Clubs. *Royal Automobile Club de Belgique* (RACB), 53 rue d'Arlon, Brussels (Tel: 230 08 10). *Touring Club Royal de Belgique* (TCB), 44 rue de la Loi, Brussels (Tel: 233 22 11).

Breakdowns. Motorways have emergency telephones, and, along with other main roads, are patrolled by the TCB *Touring Secours* and RACB vehicles. The number for the TCB service varies from place to place (233 22 11 in Brussels): the national breakdown number for the RACB is 02 736 59 59.

Accidents. If anyone is injured the police must be informed: dial 101 which also calls the ambulance: for ambulance only dial 100.

TRAIN/BUS

Belgian Railways, are run by the *Société nationale des Chemins de Fer Belges* (SNCB), 85 rue de France, 1070 Brussels (Tel: 219 28 80 for information). Unlike many cities, Brussels has no terminal stations — so there's no need to transfer from one station to another if you're travelling through.

The Inter-City (IC) concept is used on Belgian railways to describe expresses on main internal routes. Complementing the 13 IC lines, 16 others are designated Inter-Regional (IR). Most main lines are served by trains at hourly intervals or more frequently.

On international routes there are EC (EuroCity) trains, which are fast trains between the main European cities. Reservations are advisable, and obligatory on some trains. An EC supplement is payable on some routes (including those to Germany); this includes a reservation fee.

Single tickets are valid only on the day of issue; the return half of a return ticket (no reduction in price) must be used on the same day. Second class fares are about 3.50 BF per km (£0.60 or $0.92 for 10 miles); first class costs 50% more.

Cheap Deals. Children under 6 travel free; 6-11 — half fare.

Weekend return tickets are available that offer a 40% discount on the cost of the fare for between the 5th and the 150th km of a journey inside Belgium (the maximum journey you are charged for in any case is 150 km). The discount improves for groups of up to 6 people: the first member of the group gets the 40% discount and the others get a 60% reduction. The outward journey must be made between Friday noon and Sunday noon, and the return journey should be made between Saturday noon and Monday noon.

The Tourrail card gives unlimited travel on any 5 days in 17; second class tickets cost 1,700 BF for an adult, or 1,300 BF for those aged between 6 and 25.

The TTB card is valid on all train, tram and bus services in Belgium; a second class ticket costs 2,200 BF for an adult, or 1,700 BF for those aged between 6 and 26. It is valid for any 5 days in 17.

A season ticket offering unlimited rail travel for 16 days is available for 3,050 BF.

The *Benelux Tourrail* card gives unlimited travel in all three Benelux countries on any five days in 17 for 2,490 BF or 1,790 BF for those aged 25 or under.

Benelux Weekend tickets are designed to encourage travel for groups of up to six people. If a minimum of two people travel together, then the first adult pays 75% of the fare. The second to sixth adults pay 50%, and up to five children under 12 pay 25% of the normal adult fare. As the name suggests, these tickets are available only at weekends: the away journey must be between 16.00 on Thursday and 24.00 on Sunday, and the return journey between 00.00 on Saturday and 24.00 on Monday.

AIR

Brussels National Airport is at Zaventem, 12 km from the town centre, and linked by a regular train shuttle service (fare 120 BF) to the Gare du Nord and the Gare Centrale, adjoining the Sabena Air Terminus at 37 rue Cardinal Mercier. There are also bus connections to Antwerp, Ghent and Liège. For airport information, dial 751 80 80. A departure tax of 300 BF is payable by international passengers leaving from Brussels, 115 BF from Antwerp, Liège or Ostend.

BICYCLE

Bikes can be hired from 58 railway stations and returned to any one of the 89 handling stations. The cost per day is 105 BF for a bicycle, or 350 BF for a tandem, if you hold a valid rail ticket.

HITCH-HIKING

You can expect a lot of attention from the police, but enlightened drivers have been known to wait patiently for the law to drive away before picking you up.

From Brussels heading west to Ostend, take tram 62 to the terminus at Berchem St. Agathe, where the A10 motorway starts. North to Antwerp — tram 52 or 92 to the start of the A12 at Gros Tilleul; east to Aachen — underground line 5 to Diamant; south to Luxembourg — underground line 1 to Beaulieu.

The *Taxi-Stop* organisation will arrange lifts for you, in exchange for a small fee. Their offices are at Onderbergen 51, Gent (Tel: 23 80 73); 6 place des Brabaçons, 1340 Louvain-la-Neuve (Tel: 41 81 99); and 31 rue de Bruxelles, 1300 Wavre (Tel: 22 75 75).

WALKING

It is quite possible to walk right across Belgium on a network of footpaths. For details, contact the *Comité Belge des Sentiers de Grandes Radonnées,* BP 10, 4000 Liège (Tel: 041-23 99 60) or GR — Paden, Van Stralenstraat 40, 2008 Antwerp.

CITY TRANSPORT

Taxis. Taxis don't cruise; the way to get one is either by phone (*Taxi* in the directory), or by hunting out a taxi-stand — outside stations, large hotels, theatres and cinemas. Meters start with a flag-down rate of 80 BF, plus 31 BF per km (£1 or $1.60 per mile), increasing to 62 BF per km for out-of-town journeys. The 20% tip is included.

Belgian Railways offer the chance of reserving a taxi upon arrival at Brussels Midi station. Reservations can be made on the train by the ticket-collector, for a down-payment of 100 BF (of which 76 BF count against the fare). The taxi-stand is on avenue Fonsny.

Bus/Tram/Underground. Brussels has 14 tram routes, 38 bus routes, and two underground lines. The system is run by the *Société des Transports Intercommunaux de Bruxelles* (STIB), 15 Avenue de la Toison d'Or (Tel: 515 30 64), in conjunction with the suburban lines, where certain STIB tickets are also valid. Most public transport runs until about midnight.

Métro tickets are bought at the desk or from automatic machines, and must be franked by placing them, arrow first, in the slot in the automatic turnstiles. Your ticket is then valid until you return to the surface.

All buses and trams are one-man operated — board at the front, exit at the rear. Fares are collected, and tickets issued, by machines. Single tickets (for métro or bus/tram journeys) cost 35 BF; this can include two changes (only one of which may be suburban). Ten trip tickets cost 250 BF.

Season tickets cost 300 BF for a week (Monday-Sunday); 935 BF for a calendar month; 9,350 BF for a year. These allow unlimited travel on urban and suburban bus, tram and métro routes, but also require a validation card, obtainable, like the tickets, from the information offices at the Midi/Zuid, Rogier and Porte de Namur métro stations. Unlimited travel for one day is offered by the *Tourist Ticket*, available for 140 BF from the BBB (61 rue du Marché aux Herbes), or from métro information offices in Brussels, or from organisations abroad such as British Rail and London Regional Transport. This *Tourist Ticket* is valid in 25 Belgian cities.

Local transport in other Belgian towns also works on a set fare basis with reductions on period tickets and multiple ride tickets. Apart from the STIB, Belgian local transport systems (including services around Brussels) are run by the *Société Nationale des Chemins de Fer Vicinaux* (SNCV), 14 rue de la Science, 1040 Brussels (Tel: 526 28 28).

Accommodation

Unmarried couples of which one or both partners are under 21 are not allowed to share a hotel room or tent, on pain of three years imprisonment.

Hotels/Pensions/Boarding Houses. Approved hotels display a shield issued by the National Tourist Office. There is no official classification system. Prices normally include breakfast; at some pensions and boarding houses, either lunch or dinner may be included in the price. You usually pay per person; so a double room will not be much less than twice the single cost. In Brussels, double rooms (with breakfast) will rarely cost less than 800 BF (£13), the cheapest areas being the Place Rogier and the Gare du Midi. By law, prices should be posted in all rooms. VAT (6%) and local *taxes de séjour* are normally included.

Camping. There are over 500 camping sites in Belgium, ranging from one to four stars in quality. The average price for an overnight stay is 50 BF per adult.

Youth Hostels. Belgium has two national head offices — *Auberges de la Jeunesse* (CWAJ) 52 rue van Oost, 1030 Brussels (Tel: 215 31 00) for the French speaking area, and *Vlaamse Jeugdherbergcentrale,* Van Stralenstraat 40, 2008 Antwerpen (Tel: 232 7218) for the Dutch area. Expect to pay around 300 BF for bed and breakfast, except in Brussels and Ostend where charges are 50-100% higher.

Friends of Nature hostels. Dial 04-52 28 75 for *Amis de la Nature;* 03-36 18 62 for *Natuurvrieden.*

Sleeping out. Not the warmest country for sleeping out, but the police can only do you for vagrancy if you're broke.

Finding and Booking Accommodation. the National Tourist Office publishes free lists of campsites, vacation homes and youth hostels, and the *Official Hotel, Motel and Pension Guide.* Bookings can be made direct with the hotels or through travel agents; in Brussels, try the TIB booking service (Tel: 513 89 40 extn 244) which charges a 75 BF booking fee for making reservations.

Communications

General information on telephones and English language newspapers and radio broadcasts is given in the introduction.

Post. Post offices are open Monday-Friday 9 am-6 pm in large towns, to 5 pm elsewhere. Small offices might have a lunch break (12-2 pm), and will close by 4 pm. For permanent 24-hour service, go to the office in the Gare du Midi (48 A avenue Fonsny). Mail boxes are red. There are philatelic and free poste restante services at all main post offices.

The Central Post Office in Brussels (where letters addressed to *Poste Restante, Poste Centrale* should arrive) is at the Place de la Monnaie.

The correct ways to address mail are as given under France (for French addresses) and the Netherlands (for Flemish). Towns are preceded by a four-figure code (Brussels codes begin with 1, starting at 1,000 in central Brussels). If you're writing from abroad, precede this code with the country code B-. Confusion often arises with Brussels streets, most of which have both French and Dutch names. Thus rue de Marché aux Herbes is Grasmarkt.

Telephone. The system is all automatic, however for international calls from Belgium use payphones marked with European flags and cardphones. Most Belgian and Luxembourg phones take only 5 BF coins (the price of a local call in Luxemborough, 10 BF minimum in Belgium); newer telephones take 20 BF coins as well. Cardphones are gradually becoming available in Belgium. The procedure is to lift the receiver, insert the money, then dial; unused money will be returned when you replace the receiver. For calls to the UK dial 0044 followed by UK area code (minus initial 0) and local number. There are various time expiry warnings-audible or visible. Calls are cheaper from 7pm to 8am and at weekends. BT Chargecard and collect calls can be made from Belgium and Luxembourg. In Luxembourg, dial 0010 and ask the local operator to connect you to the number you wish to call. BT Chargecard calls can only be made from Post Offices. For the code to dial the local operator in Belgium check locally. International calls can also be made at special booths in the RTT offices; the most central in Brussels is at 17 blvd de l'Imperatrice.

Brussels area code is 02; Antwerp — 03. The international prefix is 00, then wait for the second dialling tone before continuing. Directories list different codes for frontier areas of France, Germany and Holland; and codes for all localities within Belgium.

Directories come in the usual two parts — alphabetical list of subscribers and yellow pages. The yellow pages have an English index at the front; other information (including current postal, telephone and telegraph charges) is in French and Dutch.

Subscriber information: Brussels — 1207; Belgium — 1208; Europe — 1204; intercontinental — 1222; difficulties with international calls — 1224; and 1222. Fire/ambulance/police — 100; operator — 1224, international operator — 1224; complaints — 128; time — 1200; weather — 1702.

Telegrams. Telegrams can be sent in person at any RTT office or post office. There is a 24-hour telegram service at the Gare du Midi post office in Brussels. They can also be sent by telephone by dialling 1225. For information, dial 1215.

Newspapers. The *Bulletin,* published every Friday, contains *What's on in Belgium.* In the entertainment sections of Belgian papers, films shown in the original language are marked *VO* (*Angl* = English, *AM* = American).

Broadcasting. Most British TV and radio services can be picked up near the coast. Details of British programmes are published in many daily newspapers. The American Forces Network has radio stations at Brussels, Klein Brogel and SHAPE, which broadcast around 100 MHz VHF/FM.

Emergency messages will be passed on to the relevant radio company or station by the Touring Club de Belgique in Brussels. Dial 513 82 40 or 512 78 90 any day before 3 pm.

Health and Hygiene

For general information on hygiene, first aid, insurance and medical treatment, see the introduction.

Hygiene. No problem. Tap water is drinkable.

Reciprocal Agreements. For subsidised treatment, British travellers with Form E111 should proceed as follows. For hospital treatment, first take the E111 to the local *Caisse auxiliaire d'Assurance Maladie-Invalidité* (sickness insurance fund), who will direct you to a participating hospital and authorise part payment of costs. In an emergency, the hospital can make the arrangements if you show your Elll. If you visit a doctor or dentist, show your Elll, pay the full cost of treatment, and take the receipt to the local insurance fund for around 75% refund. This procedure also applies to prescriptions, but in addition to the receipt you must take a stamped copy of the prescription. Further information: Caisse auxiliaire, 12 blvd St. Lazare, 1210 Brussels.

Pharmacies. Close on Saturday afternoons and all day Sunday.

Emergencies. The duty rotas (*services de garde*) for pharmacies, doctors, dentist and vets are listed in the weekend editions of local papers. Pharmacy rotas are also posted in pharmacy windows. Or, for the doctors' rota, dial 479 18 18. Other useful Brussels numbers include: 648 80 80 — 24-hour medical and dental treatment; 426 10 26 — dental emergencies (Saturday afternoons, Sundays and holidays); 478 58 50 — burns; 345 45 45 or 649 29 29 — anti-poison. The universal emergency number for ambulances — 900 — also calls the police.

Nightlife. Belgium shuts down pretty early, most restaurants being closed by 10 or 11 pm, but private clubs, cabarets, strip clubs and discotheques stay open till the early hours.

Eating out. Restaurants are obliged to display their menu outside. The price for a three-course meal starts at about 300 BF (£5 or $8). The places for cheap snacks are *fritures* and *snackbars*. Brussels is full of foreign restaurants, including Italian, Greek, Yugoslav, Chinese and Indian. At lunchtime, the cheapest deal is the *plat du jour;* at dinner, *ménu* means an inclusive three-course meal, considerably cheaper than eating à la carte. The leading hamburger chain is Quick, and McDonalds is also well-represented.

Drinking. The Belgians are the world's number two beer drinkers. Expect to pay around 30 BF for a glass of beer. As well as making at least 50 different beers, including the highly potent Trappist brew, they also make liqueurs, like *Elixir d'Anvers, Péquet de Liège,* and *Elixir de Spa.* Most of the wine is imported, but it's frequently drunk with meals. Spirits are not sold in Cafés, but only in night clubs, hotels, and private clubs. These private clubs tend to have very low temporary membership fees, and are otherwise like regular bars.

Smoking. Belgian cigarettes such as *Bastos* cost about 79 BF for 20, British and American brands about 86 BF. Pipe smokers can try the native tobaccos from the Roisin and Harelbeke regions. Smoking is prohibited in many public places.

Police. The police force has two branches — local police deal with municipal matters, thefts and so on, while the *Gendarmerie (Rijkswacht)* is used for traffic control and major crimes. To call the police in an emergency dial 101.

Drugs. On paper there is no distinction between hard and soft drugs, and prison sentences are not unusual for possessing small amounts of marijuana.

Driving Offences. Immediate fines range from 750 BF for a light traffic violation to 6,000 for a dangerous offence. A law introduced in 1985 states that when a foreign motorist commits an offence, he or she must pay the fine immediately or suffer more severe consequences. Fines must be paid on the spot in Belgian Francs or foreign notes; if not, the vehicle may be removed (at your expense) and, as a last resort, sold to pay the fine. If you're suspected of drunken driving and asked to breathe into the breathalyser, you're allowed to claim a 30-minute sobering period before doing so.

Nude Bathing. Topless sunbathing is permitted, but no beaches are set aside for nude bathing/sunbathing.

Legal Aid. Embassies can supply lists of lawyers. An all-round help organisation that can help people with limited funds with legal advice is *Télé-Service*, 24 rue du Boulet, 1000 Brussels (Tel:511 91 55). Other contacts are given in *Help and Information*.

For general information on useful contracts, churches, and complaints procedures, see the introduction.

Embassies and Consulates.
British Embassy, Britannia House, 28 rue Joseph II, 1040 Brussels (217 90 00).
British Consulate General, 24 Klarenstraat, 2000 Antwerp (232 69 40).

Also honorary consultates in Ghent and Liège.

American Embassy, 1 Square Bastion, 1050 Brussels (513 38 30).
American Consulate General, Nationalestraat 5, Antwerp (225 00 71).

Canadian Embassy, 6 rue de Loxum, 1000 Brussels (513 79 40).

Lost Property. On trains, ask at your destination, then at the Gare du Luxembourg (Tel: 218 60 50). On buses, trams, métro — go to the company concerned; in Brussels, telephone 512 67 90. Otherwise, go to the nearest police station.

Baby-sitting. Look up *Baby-sitting* in the Yellow Pages. In Brussels, try the University Placement Office (Tel: 647 23 85).

Information. The BBB Tourist House, 61 rue du Marché aux Herbes, 1000 Brussels (Tel: 519 90 90) provides information on Brussels, Brabant and Belgium as a whole. Tourist offices elsewhere are known as *Syndicats d'Initiative* in Wallonia, *Dienst voor Toerisme* in Flanders.

Free Maps. Road map with street plans from tourist offices abroad; Brussels transport map from the BBB.

Help. In emotional crises, contact *Télé-Acceuil* (Tel: 538 28 08). Sympathy in English on Tuesdays and Thursdays.
   For help with any kind of problem, contact *Help Line,* 302 Chaussée de Vleurgat, Brussels (Tel: 648 40 14), a service manned 24 hours a day by volunteers from IF (the Interested Few).
   Another all-round service is *Acotra,* 38-40 rue Montagne, Brussels (Tel: 518 44 89; 518 44 80 for the accommodation service).

A counselling service for women only (in English, again, on Tuesdays and Thursdays), is *Infor-Femmes:* dial 511 38 38 or 513 17 29.

In cases of intoxication, dial 345 45 45 in Brussels.

Disabled Travellers. The Belgian Red Cross can give advice to disabled people hoping to visit Belgium. Contact the Croix-Rouge de Belgique, Comité Provincial de Namur, Service du "Car de l'Evasion", rue de l'Industrie 124, B5002 Saint-Servais (Namur) (Tel: 081-73 02 24).

Student Travel. Sytour — TEJ, 33 Chaussée de Hoecht, 1030 Brussels (Tel: 217 33 44); Acotra, 38 rue de la Montagne, 1000 Brussels (Tel: 512 86 07).

Youth Information Centres. Contact Jongeren Informative en Adviescentrum-Tilt VZW, St. Katelijneplein 19 (Tel: 218 11 80) or Infor-J, rue du Marché aux Herbes 27 (Tel: 512 3274).

English Bookshop. W. H. Smith, Boulevard A Max 71-75, 1000 Brussels.

English Language Churches. In Brussels: Holy Trinity (Anglican), 29 rue Capitaine Crespel (Tel: 511 71 83); St. Andrews (Scottish Presbyterian), 181 Chaussée de Vleurgat (Tel: 649 02 19); and the International Baptist Church, 17 rue Hoton (Tel: 537 59 28).

American Express. 2 place Louise, 1000 Brussels (Tel: 512 17 4) and in Antwerp.

Calendar of Events

Public Holidays are shown in **bold**

January 1	**New Year's Day**
February	Shrovetide carnivals at Aalst, Eupen and Malmedy
March	Festivals at Geraardsbergen and Stavelot, including bun-throwing and goldfish swallowing
March/April	Procession of the Entombment at Lessines (on Good Friday)
	Easter Monday
April	European Youth Music Festival at Neerpelt
April/June	Festival of Flanders (spring section): Music at Antwerp, Kortrijk, Tongeren and St-Truiden
May 1	**Labour Day**
May	**Ascension Day** — Procession of the Holy Blood in Bruges
May (second Sunday)	Cat throwing at Ypres (Ieper): procession featuring various cat legends; then toy cats are thrown from the belfry
May (Trinity Sunday)	Battle of the Lumecon at Mons
May/June	**Whit Monday** — March of Ste Rolande at Gerpinnes
June	Blessing the sea at Ostend
	Adrian Brouwer Beer Festival at Oudenaarde
July	Ommegang and Midi Fair, both in Brussels
	Shrimp Festival at Oostduinkerke
	Procession of the Penitents at Veurne
July 21	**Independence Day**
August	Festival at Ath, with giants.
August 15	**Assumption Day**
August/September	Festival of Flanders (summer section) in Bruges and Mechelen

September	Breughel Festival at Wingene
	'September Nights' Music Festival at Liége
November 1	**All Saints' Day**
November 11	**Armistice Day**
December 25, 26	**Christmas**

Luxembourg

Area. 999 square miles   **Population.** 400,000
Capital. Luxembourg City (Population: 80,000)

Luxembourg is an independent Grand Duchy, ruled by the Grand Duke Jean. The official language is Letzeburgesch (the vernacular) but French, German and English are widely spoken. Much of what has been said about Belgium is also true for Luxembourg — customs, laws, traffic regulations and so on.

Money. Taxes are lower than in neighbouring countries, so prices are too. The official currency is the Luxembourg franc, on a par with the Belgian franc. Notes and coins of both currencies circulate freely, but Luxembourg francs are difficult to offload abroad. Shops open 8 am-noon and 2 pm-6 pm Tuesdays to Saturday, and 2-pm-6 pm on Mondays. Banks open 9 am-noon and 1.30 pm-4.30 pm.

Telephone Numbers. Emergencies — 012; ambulance and fire — 44 22 44; Luxembourg information/pharmacy duty rota — 017: difficulties in making calls — 17; time — 10; weather — 18; train information — 49 24 24; international enquiries — 016; operator 018; international prefix — 0010.

Useful Addresses.
British Embassy, 28 boulevard Royal (Tel: 298 64).
American Embassy, 22 boulevard Emmanuel Servais (Tel: 46 01 23).
Visitor and Convention Bureau (tourist office), place d'Armes, PO Box 181 (Tel: 228 09).
Main Post Office, 8 avenue Monterey (Tel: 476 51).
Police Headquarters, rue Glesener (Tel: 49 49 49).
Automobile Club de Luxembourg, 13 route de Longwy (Tel: 31 10 31 — 24 hours).
Sotour (student travel), 15, Place du Theatre (Tel: 46 15 14).
Anglican Church, 5 avenue Marie-Thérèse (Tel: 47 66 64).
Centrale des Auberges de Jeunesse, 18A place d'Armes (Tel: 255 88).
Luxair Termainal, place de la Gare: buses to Findel airport cost BF 120.

Eire

THE FOUR COURTS, DUBLIN

W.S.

Area. 26,600 square miles   **Population.** 3,550,000

Capital. Dublin (population 1,100,000)

Weather. Wet, but healthy and never too cold. The west winds sweep rain in from the Atlantic winter and summer, but snow is rare except in mountainous areas. The air is cleaner than elsewhere in Northern Europe, and many rich Europeans are buying up property in the extreme south west of the Republic for use in the event of nuclear war.

THE PEOPLE

The last few hundred years have been traumatic for the Irish. Unwelcome domination by the British was punctuated by the potato famine and subsequent mass emigration, which halved the population of Ireland during the 19th century. Following growing pressure for independence and the Easter Rising of 1916, the provinces of Leinster, Munster and Connaught together with three counties of Ulster formed the Republic of Ireland. The other six counties of Ulster remained in British control. The border has caused ill feeling and violence between the Protestant 'loyalists' and mainly Catholic 'republicans' in the north. This has occasionally spread to Great Britain, but has had little physical effect on the Republic. Visitors should be wary of offending the strong national pride of the Irish.

Politics. A Republic, with a 'figurehead' President. The Irish Parliament (*Oireachtas*) enshrines a conventional western European democracy. The two main parties are *Fianna Fail* and *Fine Gael*, with the Labour Party a distinct minority.

Religion. 95% Roman Catholic. This is reflected in the conservative laws on divorce and abortion, but religion is not as politically significant as in the north — two of the six Presidents have been Protestants.

Language. English is spoken everywhere, but as a second language in the *Gaeltachtai* — Irish speaking areas, mostly in the far west. Irish (a Celtic language) is compulsory in schools and making something of a comeback.

Making Friends. The best way to make a friend is to buy him or her a drink, and to accept all the drinks you are offered. The best way to keep a friend is to avoid politics and religion as topics of conversation.

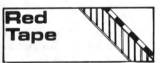

See the introduction for details of passports, customs regulations, duty free allowances, vaccinations and importing pets.

Passports and Visas. British citizens born in the UK and travelling from Britain or Northern Ireland do not require passports to enter Eire, but some form of identification (driving licence, student card etc) is needed to satisfy the security forces both in Eire and UK. Others (including British travellers entering from the Continent or North America) must hold valid passports.

Customs. Duty free allowances are as shown in the introduction. These allowances are only for travellers arriving by air or sea, not for those crossing the land border from the north. Eire is the only feasible destination for British cats and dogs wishing to holiday abroad — so long as the animal arrives direct from the UK and has been a British resident for six months, there are no quarantine restrictions. However, meat, poultry and dairy products are prohibited, as are caged birds and anything resembling a weapon.

100 pence (p) = 1 punt (IR£)
£1 = IR£1.10   IR£1 = £0.91
$1 = IR£0.69   IR£1 = $1.45

For general information on handling, exchanging or raising money, see the introduction.

Coins. 1p, 2p, 5p, 10p, 20p, 50p. All coins are the same size as their British equivalents.

Notes. IR£1, IR£5, IR£10, IR£20, IR£50, IR£100.

Shopkeepers and publicans are happy to accept British currency at face value — not surprisingly, since they effectively gain a 10% premium on such a transaction.

Banking Hours. 10 am-12.30 pm and 1.30 pm-3 pm (5 pm in some banks on Thursday), Monday to Friday. In outlying areas, banks may open only on certain days of the week. Irish banks are prone to industrial action and several prolonged strikes have shown that commerce is largely unaffected. However, if you are relying on banking services then an alternative course of action should be prepared well in advance.

The exchange office at Dublin airport opens every day except Christmas Day. From Easter to the end of October, the hours are 7.15 am-11.30 pm; from November to Easter, 8.15 am-9.00 pm.

Shopping Hours. Monday to Saturday, 9 or 9.30 am-5.30 pm. Each town has an early closing day where shops close at 1 pm; it may be taken on any day from Wednesday to Saturday. Lunch hours are usually 1 pm-2.15 or 2.30 pm.

Import and Export. No more than IR£100 (in denominations of IR£20 or less) may be exported, plus foreign currency up to IR£500; to export over £500 in foreign currency you must have declared it on arrival.

Tipping. Taxi drivers and waiters expect gratuities in about the same volume as their counterparts. Never attempt to tip a bartender — buy him a drink instead.

Emergency Cash. Britons and other citizens of the EC are allowed to seek work without a permit, either directly or through offices of the National Manpower Service. For Canadians and Americans it's harder, but if you can strum a guitar and know Bob Dylan's greatest hits then work in a tourist bar — or simply busking — is possible. For the unmusical, then the Irish Hospitals' Sweepstake (drawn every month or two, tickets IR£2) is the best hope apart from hotel and bar work at cut-price wages. North American students can take part in Summer Work in Ireland schemes — details from student offices in the USA or Canada.

Taxes. There are no less than seven rates of Value Added Tax: nil, 2%, 5%, 8%, 18%, 23%, and 35%. The most common rate is 18%, but the 8% rate is used for tourist services such as hotel accommodation and car hire. VAT is almost always included in quoted prices.

Getting Around

The information in this section is complementary to that given in the corresponding section in the introduction.

CAR

There are few stretches of dual-carriageway roads, but many trunk roads have wide shoulders which slow vehicles can use to allow faster traffic to overtake. The main hazards are from agricultural vehicles and animals.

Rules and Requirements. Drive on the left, as in the UK. A British, US or Canadian licence will suffice. Seat belts are compulsory for drivers and front seat passengers, and children under 12 must sit in the rear.

Road signs. As in Britain, newer signs are standardised with the rest of Europe, but even the older ones are unambiguous. The road numbering system has changed (from "T" and "L" roads to "N") and old numbers may appear on some signs. Direction signs usually bear both the English and Irish place names: Dublin = Baile Atha Cliath; Cork = Corcaigh. Dun Laoghaire is pronounced Dunleary. Distances may be quoted in either miles or kilometres or both. Newer signposts use only kilometres.

Parking. Similar regulations to Britain, with single and double yellow lines. Meters (in Dublin, Cork, Galway and Limerick) cost up to 60p for an hour.

Petrol. Three grades "lower" — 90 octane; "middle" — 94 octane; "top" — 98 octane. A litre of "top" costs around IR£0.59 (£2.42 per UK gallon, $3.20 per US gallon). Unleaded petrol is slightly cheaper.

Motoring Organisation. The Automobile Association, 23 Suffolk St, Dublin (Tel: 779481) provides a free breakdown service for members of foreign motoring clubs between 7am and 1am daily. Non-members can use (and pay for) the 24 hour radio-controlled service of National Garages Ltd, Long Mile Road, Dublin 12 (Tel: 508930: after 5.30 pm and at weekends dial 694800, ext. 20).

AIR

Internal flights are operated by Aer Lingus, 40 Upper O'Connell St, Dublin 1 (Tel: 377777) and Aer Arann, Galway Airport (Tel: 091 55437). Dublin airport is seven miles north at Collinstown, reached by bus 41A from Lower Abbey St, price IR£0.90.

TRAIN/BUS

All rail services are run by Iarnrod Eireann-Irish Rail, Connolly Street Dublin 1 (Tel: 366222 for passenger enquiries). Most rail lines radiate from Dublin; only the Rosslare-Limerick line runs cross-country. There are two classes: Standard, which corresponds to second class, and Inter City 1st, which is available only on selected services. Fares are high, the 130 miles from Dublin to Limerick costing IR£21 (£19 or $30) in standard class, 20% more in 1st class. Main line trains from Dublin for the west and southwest run from Heuston Station just south of the River Liffey and west of the city centre; trains for the south, north and north-west operate from Connolly. Suburban trains run from Connolly, Tara Street and Pearse Stations.

All bus services except those in Dublin city centre are run by Bus Eireann, a subsidiary company of Irish Rail; for information about services contract the Travel Centre at the Busarus (Central Bus Station), Store Street, Dublin 1. Its services include Expressway inter-urban coach services, local bus services and city services in Cork, Galway, Limerick and Waterford.

Cheap Deals. Children under 5 travel free, those aged 5-15 at half price (maximum fare IR£9).

Rambler Pass: Eight or 15 days unlimited travel on trains and BE buses, IR£66 or IR£95.

Overlander Pass: the all-Ireland version of the Rambler Pass, valid additionally on Ulsterbus and Northern Ireland Railways (IR£109 for 15 days).

Family Tickets: one or two parents with up to four children are entitled to substantial reductions on return journeys.

Holders of ISIC cards who are also under 36 may pay IR£6 for a Travelsave stamp permitting half price travel on IE-IR trains and BE and Dublin Bus buses; these stamps may also be obtained from student travel offices abroad.

BICYCLE

With relatively short distances between towns, little motorised traffic and less-than-perfect public transport, Eire is ideal cycling territory. Information sheets on cycling are free from Tourist Offices. Bicycles can be hired in most towns for around IR£4.50 per day. Raleigh Rent-a-bike are the biggest operator with around 70 dealers around the country; their Dublin address is 8 Hanover Quay, 2 (Tel: 774395).

HITCH-HIKING

In the absence of a complex motorway system, there are no problems with the law. Everyone in Ireland hitch-hikes, from priests to grandmothers. However, traffic is very light and rarely going far, and combined with the thousands of continental hitchers taking their summer break, means that progress is slow. The only recourse is to take your place in line and wait for a ride to the next town. Even when you get a lift, don't expect high speed — rides may well be punctuated with visits to friends, scenic detours and drinks in bars. Heading north from Dublin, take the airport bus to the gates of the airport and hitch along the N1. For the south and south-west, a bus (from the Busarus) 20 miles out to Naas costs IR£2.80 but may save half a day. Similarly, for Galway and Sligo, take bus 66 about 15 miles out to Maynooth.

HORSE DRAWN CARAVAN

If you're content to travel ten miles a day, then horse drawn caravans are ideal. You are given a short lesson on handling the beast and must pay attention to your animals' needs for water and grazing. The largest operators are Shannon Horse Caravans, Adare, Co. Limerick (Tel: 061-43844); and Connemara Horse Caravans, Westport, Co. Mayo (Tel: Westport 130), each with 50 caravans.

CITY TRANSPORT

Taxis. The only metered taxis are found in Dublin, Cork and Galway. Rates are standardized: IR£1.80 for the first mile, then IR£0.80 per mile. There are extra charges for telephone pick ups, additional passengers, luggage and night journeys. Outside these cities, fares are run by negotiation — agree a price before you start. To get a taxi in Dublin, dial 76 66 66 or 76 11 11.

Bus. Bus services in the city of Dublin and surrounding area are operated by Bus Atha Cliath — Dublin Bus, of 59 Upper O'Connell Street, Dublin 1 (Tel: 720000). Urban fares vary according to distance; a three mile journey would be roughly IR£0.65 (IR£0.25 for those aged under 16). In Dublin destination boards often appear in Irish — An Lar is city centre. A timetable is available for IR£2 from the above address that gives details of bus routes, times and fares.

Travel ticket bargains available include unlimited travel tickets valid for one day, one week, or one month (IR£2.20, £8.80 and £39 respectively).

Unlimited travel for one month on Dublin's buses and suburban trains is available with a Commuter Card — price IR£39.

Hotels. The grading system runs from A-star (luxury) through A, B-star and B to C (basic). In remote areas hotel rooms are hard to find; beds and breakfast or rooms in inns are a better prospect. A double room with breakfast in a C-class hotel in one of the cities is likely to cost a minimum of IR40 (£36 or $57) per night in summer, but cheaper deals can be found off-season.

Bed and Breakfast. In some parts of Ireland, every house in the main street of town and village seems to offer B & B. Given the large size of Irish breakfasts, IR£10 is a reasonable sum to pay per night. Prior booking is advisable in summer. Farms and country houses provide other possibilities, but again advance booking is recommended. Approved establishments are listed in *Irish homes accommodation in town and country and on the farm,* from Tourist Offices.

Youth Hostels. Eire's 46 hostels are run by *An Oige,* 39 Mountjoy Square, Dublin 1 (Tel: 363111): these include a new 400 bedded hostel in Mountjoy Street, close to the centre of Dublin. Cost per night depends on age, season and location: someone aged 18 or older staying in Dublin in July or August might pay up to IR£7.50, while elsewhere in the off season costs begin at £2.50 for someone aged under 16.

Camping. List of approved sites in *Caravan and Camping Parks,* IR£1.50 from the Irish Tourist Board. Expect to pay IR£4 per tent, car or caravan per night. You can rent-a-tent from O'Meara Camping at Ossary Business Park, Ossary Road, Dublin 3 (Tel: 363233).

Sleeping Out. Possible, but likely to be damp. If the land looks as though it has an owner, ask for his permission.

Finding and Booking Accommodation. The Irish Tourist Board produces an annual *Official Guide to Hotels and Guest-houses.* Reservations can be made for almost any form of accommodation — hotels, guest houses, bed and breakfast, horse drawn caravans etc — through their Central Reservations Service at 14 Upper O'Connell Street, Dublin 1 (Tel: 747733). The usual charge for reservations is about IR£1.

Post. It is usual, particularly in rural areas, for a post office (*oifig an phoist*) to be part of a shop and to keep the same hours. Main post offices generally open 9 am-1 pm, and 2.15 pm-5.30 pm, Monday to Friday.

In Dublin, the main post office lies at the centre of O'Connell St. It is open from 8 am (9 am Sundays) to 8 pm daily for stamps, telegrams, registered and express letters; 8 am-7 pm on weekdays for parcels; 8 am-8 pm on weekdays for all other services including Poste Restante.

Telephone. Booths are green and labelled Telefon. Coin boxes accept 10p coins with 10p the minimum charge for local calls. Most places in Ireland can be dialled direct as can many international calls. The international prefix is 010, but calls to the UK should use the prefix 03, followed by the STD code (with the initial zero), followed by the number. However, different codes should be used to dial the following cities: Belfast — 084; Birmingham — 032; Edinburgh — 033; Glasgow — 034; Liverpool — 035; London 031; and Manchester — 036.

Useful numbers: Fire/Police/Ambulance — 999 or, in some areas, call the operator; directory enquiries — 190; tourist information — 747733; operator — 100.

The commercial section of the telephone directory is known as the *Golden Pages*.

Newspapers. All major Irish newspapers are in English; British newspapers are sold everywhere.

Broadcasting. The authority responsible for both Radio and TV is *Radio Telefis Eirann* (RTE), and the majority of programmes are in English. In the north and east of the Republic, it is possible to receive many British and Northern Irish broadcasts. Dublin has at least ten pirate radio stations and even an illegal TV station.

Hygiene. Tap water is soft and drinkable everywhere. Ireland, like Britain, is a rabies-free zone. St. Patrick is alleged to have rid Ireland of snakes, and you are unlikely to find any outside Dublin Zoo.

Medical Treatment. British citizens can get free treatment by contacting the local Health Board, who will arrange help from a doctor, dentist or hospital within the public health service. Make it clear to all concerned that you wish to be treated under EC social security regulations.

Emergencies. Dial 999 for an ambulance. Every town of any size has a 24 hour casualty department at the local hospital, and any police station will tell you its location. In Dublin, the 24 hour medical service is at 15 Zion Road (Tel: 776644).

Sport. The most popular sports (apart from drinking) revolve around the lush turf and sparkling waters, as featured in tourist literature. Horse racing takes place in Phoenix Park, at Leopardstown and the Curragh (all close to Dublin) and on many other courses. Greyhound racing is equally popular. On-course betting is tax-free; off-track gambling is subject to a tax of 10%. Golf is extremely well provided for, and clubs can be hired on public courses. Gaelic football and hurling are the traditional sports, and well worth sampling (as a spectator); hurling in particular is an unusual combination of hockey, rugby football and all-in wrestling. Soccer and rugby union international matches are staged at the Lansdown Road stadium in Dublin.

Coarse fishing and sea angling are free almost everywhere; game fishing usually requires a licence, obtainable from tackle shops.

Nightlife. Despite the resurgence of Irish culture, all serious nightlife still revolves around drinking. The staple beverage is stout, Guinness being the most popular (tours of the brewery at St. James's Gate in Dublin are richly rewarded). Bitter ale and lager are both available but usually more expensive. To drink like a native, follow each pint with a whisky chaser. Expect to pay around IR£1.60 for a pint of Guinness.

Licensing hours are theoretically 10.30 am to 11 pm (winter) or 11.30 pm (summer) on weekdays, 12.30 pm-2 pm and 4 pm-10 pm Sundays. Pubs are expected to close for an hour or two during the day (in Dublin and Cork, 2.30 pm-3.30 pm). However, practice does not always coincide with these regulations: in remote areas, a question like "when do the pubs close?" has been known to get the reply "October".

Some of the finest 20th Century writers have been irish, but good theatre is not abundant. The government is trying to encourage drama; VAT is no longer charged on theatre tickets. Music is easier to find, whether authentic Celtic folk (try the Pipers Club at 15 Henrietta Street, Dublin 2) or rock bands following in the footsteps of U2.

Eating. The range of food available is much as is in Britain, but slightly more expensive. A large breakfast is usually followed by a sizeable lunch and a light supper.

Museums and Galleries. Mostly free and closed on some combination of Sundays, Mondays and Tuesdays.

Smoking. Good quality Virginia tobacco is used, at good quality prices. *Major* cigarettes (about IR£2 for 20) are popular, tasty and lethal. For something a little safer, British and American brands are available.

Police. Your friendly neighbourhood policeman is called a *garda* (plural *gardai*), but is not a common sight except in larger towns and along the border. Tourists are largely ignored unless they commit an outrageously unlawful act. However, any activity remotely connected with illegal weapons and the like will lead to instant arrest. Contraceptives are now legal.

Crime. Car theft by joyriding teenagers is rife in Dublin. Some drivers own a personal Denver Shoe (wheel clamp) with which they immobilise their vehicle.

Driving Offences. The attitude to speeding seems to be astonishment that anyone ever need travel faster than the blanket limit, and fines are commensurate with such outrage. Driving after drinking beyond the limit is dealt with severely.

Drugs. Possession of small amounts for personal use is usually punished by a fine, but jail is another possibility open to the judge. Visitors from Britain are reminded that although passports are not required, they still face a customs search upon entry to the Republic; the penalties for importation of narcotics are heavy.

Nude bathing. Technically illegal, but find an empty beach and no-one need ever know.

For information on useful contacts and complaints procedures, see the introduction.

Embassies.
British Embassy, 33 Merrion Road, Dublin 4 (Tel: 695211).
US Embassy, 42 Elgin Road, Ballsbridge, Dublin 4 (Tel: 688777).
Canadian Embassy, 65/68 St. Stephen's Green, Dublin 2 (Tel: 781988).

Help. For suicide or emotional problems, contact the Samaritans, 112 Marlborough Street, Dublin (Tel: 727700), any time day or night. They also have offices in 15 other large towns.

Information
Irish Tourist Board (*Bord Failte Eireann*), 14 Upper O'Connell St, Dublin (Tel: 747733) open 8.30 am-6 pm, Monday-Saturday. Branches at Dun Laoghaire (in the summer only) pier and Dublin Airport.

Free Maps. Given away by tourist offices and car hire companies.

Youth and Student Travel. *USIT,* Aston Quay, Dublin 2 (Tel: 798833).

Disabled Travellers. Tourist offices can provide lists of hotels recommended by Mobility International as suitable for visitors in wheelchairs. Disabled motorists, vehicles can be carried free from Britain to Eire on B & I and Sealink ferries. Parking is free at meters for vehicles displaying a disabled drivers' certificate.

American Express. 116 Grafton St, Dublin 2 (Tel: 772874).

Calendar of Events

Public Holidays are shown in **bold**

January 1	**New Year's Day**
March 17	**St. Patrick's Day:** Week of celebrations and parade in Dublin
March/April	**Good Friday, Easter Monday**
	Carling Country Music Festival, Cork
	Cork City Marathon
May 1	**Labour Day**
June	**First Monday**
June, second week	Festival of Music in great Irish Houses, Dublin region
late June	Paddy Whiskey World Road-Bowling Championships, Co. Cork
late July-early Aug	Shannon Boat Rally, Athlone, Co. Westmeath
	Galway Races.
August	**First Monday**
August, second week	Dublin Horse Show
mid August	Puck Fair, Killorglin, Co. Kerry
early September	All-Ireland Hurling Finals
mid September	All-Ireland Gaelic Football Finals
mid Sept-early Oct	Waterford International Festival of Light Opera
	Dublin Theatre Festival
	Great October Horse Fair, Ballinasloe, Co. Galway
late September	Galway Oyster Festival
early October	Castlebar International Song Contest, Co. Mayo
	Kinsale Gourmet Festival
	Cork Film Festival
late October	Wexford Festival of Opera
	Guinness Jazz Festival, Cork
	Dublin City Marathon
October	**Last Monday**
early December	Lakes of Killarney Car Rally
December 25	**Christmas Day**
December 26	**Boxing Day**

France

THE LOUVRE/PONT ROYAL, PARIS   W.S.

Area. 211,208 square miles   **Population** 56,000,000

Capital. Paris (population: 2,150,000)

Weather. France covers an area that includes all three European climatic divisions — maritime (in the north and west), continental (inland), and Mediterranean (in the south). The Côte d'Azur has very hot summers and mild winters, although the northerly Mistral blows from November to April; the north has cold winters and mild summers. Good ski conditions can be found in the Massif Central, the Pyrenees and the Alps, where the skiing season extends year-round.

THE PEOPLE

Typical of the cartoonists' view of them, the majority of Frenchmen are short and dark. In line with their Latin origins, they have a fiery temperament and are easily aroused, and just as easily placated. In speech they use their arms as much as their tongues, and one of their main pleasures in life seems to be eating.

Politics. Republic. There is minority group unrest in Brittany, Alsace, and particularly Corsica, where bombing is not infrequent. The Socialist government also faces problems from the extreme right wing National Front movement.

Religion. 90% Roman Catholic. Dress carefully in churches — bare arms, legs, and even heads are frowned on.

Language. The official language is French, but three separate regional languages are spoken — Breton in Brittany, Basque in the south west, and Catalan in Roussillon (Eastern Pyrenees). In remote border areas, German, Flemish and Italian are spoken near the respective frontiers. The first foreign language taught in schools is English, but few people are willing to speak it, except in tourist resorts.

Even if you don't speak French, you will soon become aware that the French language has absorbed a wide English vocabulary, known as *Franglais*. For reasons of patriotic pride, such words are now banned by law from being used in official documents.

Making Friends. The French are very fond of shaking hands at every meeting and when you reach the "good friend" stage, you should expect women to kiss you on each cheek as a greeting. In keeping with their Latin neighbours, the French are easy to make friends with, but the men are not so attentive of foreign women as their Latin or Spanish counterparts are; however, many female visitors still find them over-attentive. If you want to get on with French women, make out you are Irish or Scots — they find this much more chic than English or American.

See the introduction for details of passports, customs regulations, duty free allowances, vaccinations and importing pets.

Passports and Visas. Holders of British, US and Canadian passports are allowed to stay three months. Should you wish to stay longer, you must obtain a *carte de séjour* (residence permit) from the local police station, *mairie* (town hall) or, in Paris, the *Département des Etrangers* (aliens' department) at the *Préfecture*, 9 blvd. du Palais, Paris 4.

Customs. The EC list of duty free allowances in the introduction applies to France, but restrictions on tea and coffee are the same as described under *Belgium*.

100 centimes (c) = 1 franc (F).
£1 = 10 F   1 F = £0.10
$1 = 6.25 F   1 F = $0.16

For general information on handling, exchanging and raising money, see the introduction.

Coins. 5 c, 10 c, 20 c, 50 c, 1 F, 2 F, 5 F, 10 F.

Notes. 10 F (brown), 20 F (pinkish), 50 F (blue), 100 F (multicoloured), 200 F (multicoloured), 500 F (brown-green).

Banking hours. Most banks open 9 am-noon and 2 pm-4 pm, Monday to Friday or Tuesday to Saturday, according to local habit. They usually close at noon on the day before a public holiday. Outside banking hours, money can be changed at a lower rate at hotels; or at the "official rate" at airports, air terminals, main railway stations and tourist offices. Beware of the so-called "official rate"; the rates of two banks in the same street can vary by as much as 5%. Rates of exchange tend to be worse at French airports than in French banks.

Shopping Hours. Monday-Saturday, 9-12 am and 2-6 pm; some shops close on

Monday; some shops don't close at lunchtime. Bakeries, dairies and some groceries open very early (7-7.30 am) but close for 3 or 4 hours at midday. You will always find some shops open on Sunday mornings. Large department stores and hypermarkets (on the outskirts of large towns) stay open until 9 or 10 several nights a week. Hypermarkets often close on Monday mornings.

Import and Export. No restriction on imports. Exports are limited to 5,000 F in French or foreign banknotes. However, you may export more in foreign banknotes if you can prove you are re-exporting no more than you imported — do this by filling in a customs declaration at you point of entry.

Tipping. Restaurants and hotels — service is usually included (*service compris*), if not (*service non compris*), give 10-15%. Cafés — as for restaurants if you have your drink at a table. If you drink at the bar, service is not normally included, so leave a few coins of your change in the saucer (no more than 15%). Porters — rates fixed and indicated on posters at the station; usually about 2.50 F per item. Taxis — 15%.

Emergency Cash. EC citizens can legally look for work through offices of the *Agence National pour l'Emploi* (ANPE). Jobs are available picking fruit (especially grapes, in September and October), working in hotels and restaurants and even catching snails. Street selling and busking are usually illegal, but many practitioners avoid trouble simply by moving on when they see the police. The world's largest flea market, *Marché aux Puces,* takes place in the north of Paris and is at its best on Saturday mornings. A customary way of raising cash in Paris is to buy carnet of métro tickets and to sell them off individually to people entering the station at busy times. There is a wide margin for profit.

Gamblers can bet on horses from 8.30 am-1 pm on the day of a race, in all cafés marked PMU (*Pari Mutuel Urbain*), or at the course. Whole or one-tenth (*dixième*) tickets for the national lottery can be bought at tobacconists; results in the national press each Wednesday or Friday. The largest prize — over ten million francs — is drawn on January 1st each year. In 1985 it was won by a 14-year-old girl.

Young Person's Discount Card. The *Carte Jeunes* is a government-sponsored scheme allowing discounts for young people over a wide range of goods and services. It should not be confused with the French Railways *Carte Jeune* and *Carré Jeune* (see *Train: Cheap Deals),* although it does qualify holders for a 10% reduction on these railcards. Other benefits include discounts on such things as hotel and campsite prices, museum entrance fees, campsite charges and meals at some fast food chains.

The *Carte Jeunes* was launched in the summer of 1985 and is still evolving. the general principle is that it may be bought in France by anyone who will be under 26 at the end or the current year. It is sold by *Centres d'Information Jeunesse* (usually found in town halls and tourist offices), Post Offices, Caisse d'Epargne branches (National Savings Offices) and youth hostels.

The cost is 70 F, which includes a local regional guide. In the early stages of the scheme, some foreigners were refused the card. The French Ministry of Youth and Sport insist it is available to all foreigners under 26; show any recalcitrant issuer this page if you think it might help.

Taxes. TVA, the French version of VAT, is charged on most goods and services. On "luxury" items (including car hire) it is 33%.

Nationals of EC countries are entitled TVA exemption on goods over 1,800 F that are exported. To claim the refund, obtain duplicate copies of the sale slip, present them to British customs for endorsement on your return, and send them to the Bureau des Douanes de Paris — La Chapelle, BP 24, 75018 Paris. Residents outside the EC are allowed exemption on goods over 400 F: obtain duplicate sales slips and an SAE from the shop; hand these in to French customs when leaving the country. In either case, the article(s) concerned should be carried in your hand luggage, available for customs inspection if required.

Getting Around

The information given in this section is complementary to that given in the corresponding section in the introduction.

CAR

French roads are usually very crowded in summer — especially those going from Paris to the Mediterranean and Atlantic coasts. Driving in Paris can be worrying for foreigners, since French drivers are so aggressive. Be prepared for the special bus and taxi lanes in Paris (they are marked by a continuous yellow line); the traffic in them may travel against the stream. Outside the cities, the French are Europe's finest exponents of "the shunt" — ie they drive nose to tail until the first car stops, then they all run into each other. Rush hours are about 8-10 am and 5-7 pm.

The motorway (*autoroute*) network is around 4,500 miles and is still being extended. The longest continuous stretch is from Calais to the Spanish border near Perpignan. There are emergency telephones at 2 km intervals; repairs are charged according to a fixed scale. Rest areas with toilets and picnic areas are provided every 10 km. Full service areas occur at intervals of about 35 km. For motorway information, contact *Autoroutes Informations,* 7 bis rue Dupont des Loges, 75007 Paris or call (1) 47 05 9001 between 9 am-6 pm. At weekends in summer there is a welcome point for British motorists at the St. Omer junction on the A26.

The *Bison Futé* (Clever Buffalo) route system was introduced to combat the congestion on through routes at times of peak holiday traffic. A special map (available from French Government Tourist Offices abroad, or upon arrival in France) shows major roads in red with yellow sections for bottlenecks and circles around black spots; alternative routes are shown in green. Information tents can be found alongside main roads, identifiable by a large Red Indian cartoon character. Another useful source of information is the 24 hour service run by the Centre National d'Information Routiere: call (1) 48 58 33 33.

Rules of the Road. All cars must carry a red warning triangle (unless they are fitted with flashing hazard warning lights) and a complete set of spare bulbs. French cars are required to use amber headlights, and, although this rule is relaxed for foreign cars, it is still advisable, as white headlamps seem inexplicably to annoy the natives.

On the *autoroutes,* beware of speed traps on the last few miles before a toll booth. The police often wait on the other side to fine you. Sometimes the police check the time shown on the ticket you receive on joining an *autoroute,* and use it as evidence if it shows you have exceeded the limit by arriving at the toll booth earlier than you could have done by observing the limit.

Children under 10 are banned from the front seats. Seat belts must be worn at all times.

Insurance. Insurance claims are processed through the *Bureau Central Français des Sociétés d'Assurances contre les Accidents Automobiles;* Tour Gallieni, 2-36 Gallieni, 93175 Bagnolet cedex (Tel: 43 60 37 37).

Road Signs. The most significant are *priorité a droite* (usually found in urban areas, meaning traffic entering from the right has priority) and its converse *passage protége,* indicating that you are on a priority road and need not give way to traffic from the right. *Gravillons* — loose chippings; *rappel* — "reminder", eg continuation of 60 km/hr speed limit; *chaussée déformée* — uneven surface.

Place Names. Lille is Rijsel in Dutch.

Parking. Be warned that the French park absolutely bumper to bumper. Paris is permanently clogged up with parked cars; the city has 50,000 meters (present rate is 4F-6F an hour). Other parking controls currently operating include: blue zones (indicated by a blue circle on posts supporting other road signs and blue markings for parking places), for free parking for 1 hour from 9 am-12.30 pm and 2.30-7 pm and for two hours from 12.30-2.30 pm. Discs available from police stations, newsagents, tobacconists and tourist offices. Alternative days — *Coté du stationnement jours pairs* (even days) or *jours impairs* (odd days); and half-monthly — *stationnement alterné semi-mensuel* with either 1-15 or 16-31 on the sign. Red axe signs threaten impoundment for cars parked there. *Stationnement inderdit* = No Parking; the end of prohibited parking zones = *fin d'interdiction de stationner.*

Petrol. There are three grades of leaded petrol: *super-super* (97 octane), *super* (95 octane) and *ordinaire* (90 octane) (which is gradually being phased out). Unleaded comes either in regular *sans plomb* (95 octane) or *super-super sans plomb* (97 octane). A litre of super costs 6F per litre (£2.45 per UK gallon, $3.60 per US gallon); unleaded petrol is 6% cheaper. Petrol is 10% cheaper at Hypermarkets.

Tolls. Apart from a few miles in and around large cities, all motorways carry tolls. Tickets are given on entry, and paid for on exit. The toll from Calais to Menton (1,259 km) costs around £34 ($54). If you're desperate to save time it's obviously worth it, but the old roads make for more pleasant driving. Many toll booths accept credit cards.

Touring Clubs. *Automobile Club de France* (ACF), 6 place de la Concorde, Paris 8 (Tel: 42 65 34 70). *Automobile Club de I'le de France* (ACIF), 14 avenue de le Grande Armee, 75018 Paris.

Breakdowns. ACIF operates an *Automobile Secours Service:* the free 24 hour number is 05 05 05 24. On motorways, there are orange emergency telephones every 2.4 km, to contact the police or breakdown services.

Accidents. If anyone is injured, the police must be informed — either through the emergency motorway telephones, or by dialling 17. If you're involved in an accident that might present legal difficulties, it's worth hiring a *hussier* (court assessor) for around 1,000 F to make an independent report. His word will carry a lot of weight in court.

TRAIN

French railways are run by the *Société Nationale des Chemins de Fer* (SNCF), For train information, dial (1) 45 82 50 50, for reservations dial (1) 45 65 60 60.

Trains have two classes, first class costing 50% more than second. On most main lines, coaches are of the *Corail* walk-through variety. Second class costs about 0.50 F per km (approx £1.50 or $2.20 per ten miles); supplements are payable on TEE expresses (first class only), Intercité trains and peak hour services of *Trains á Grande Vitesse* (TGV) on the 168 mph Paris-Brittany line (which is even faster than Japan's famous Bullet Train). Reservations (13 F) are compulsory for the latter. They can be obtained at any time from two months to a few minutes before departure. There are coin-operated *Réservation Rapide* machines at TGV stations. These do not allow you to select smoking or non-smoking areas; if bookings are heavy, however, they will ask if you are willing to up or down-grade to first or second class; and if your choice of train is full, they offer other alternatives and indicate any supplement payable.

Tickets must be validated in one of the automatic date-stamping machines at the platform entrance before boarding the train; otherwise, you are considered to be travelling without a valid ticket, and will be asked to pay a surcharge of 20% of the ticket's cost with a minimum of 52 F.

Paris has six main line termini. The cheapest way from one to another is by métro, but there are special SNCF buses, which have a fixed fare, inclusive of baggage.

Cheap Deals. The *France Vacances Special* rail rover pass offers unlimited travel throughout France on any 4 days in 15 days, or any 9 days during a period of one month. It is sold only outside France and costs either £75 or £127 second class, and either £103 or £185 first, for the 15 day and 1 month tickets respectively. (40% less for children under 12). Seat reservation fees on TEE and TGV services cost extra, but supplements for these trains are waived. A bonus for travellers is that overnight journeys which commence after 8 pm are counted only as travel on the following day. Additional benefits include free travel to the city centre from Paris airports if you arrive by air, travel concessions on the Paris metro and buses, reduced fares on the narrow guage *Chemins de Fer de Provence* line from Nice to Digne, and a number of discounts on car hire rates, entrance fees to historic buildings and monuments, channel crossings by Hoverspeed, and river trips on the Seine.

Children aged 4-11 years pay half the adult fare. Those under four travel free, but are not entitled to a separate seat. On family trains (see *Special Trains,* below) under fours are allowed to occupy a seat for 25% of the adult fare.

The main basis for other cheap deals is the red/white/blue calendar system. This calendar — copies of which are shown at ticket offices and given away — classifies travel according to the time in which the journey started:

Red (peak) — particularly busy days during summer and at public holidays.

White (standard) — weekend travel peaks, generally 3 pm Friday to noon on Saturday, plus 3 pm Sunday to noon on Monday. These may vary due to public holidays.

Blue — all other times.

None of the reductions below are available on "red" days, and there are restrictions on "white" days.

Carte Vermeil — for men and women over 60; the card costs 125 F and gives 50% reduction for one year during "blue" periods.

Carte Couple — free to married couples or those *vivant en concubinage,* allowing half-price travel for one partner when both travel together. Valid for five years for travel during "blue" periods.

French Railways offer several cheap deals for under-26s, under the general heading of *Voyages Jeunes.* The most useful are the two rail cards described below, which are valid in 1st or 2nd class on all SNCF routes except Paris suburban lines.

Carré Jeune — valid for one year, price 160 F; passport photograph required. Four coupons allowing half-price travel on one-way journeys during blue periods, 20% reduction during white periods. After four journeys you can buy another Carré Jeune.

Carte Jeune — valid from 1 June-30 September, price 160 F; passport photograph required. Half-price travel and one free couchette and cut-price travel on the Newhaven-Dieppe ferry during blue periods. Note that the *Carte Jeune* should not be confused with the French Government *Carte Jeunes* which is a more general discount card. Holders of this card get a 20% reduction on both the *Carte* and *Carré Jeune.*

A third alternative is to buy a domestic BIJ youth ticket (saving 25%), valid on specified services and available from student travel offices. This option is best for single journeys when it would be uneconomic to buy a *Carré or Carte Jeune.*

Special Trains. Some "family trains" are equipped with a nursery compartment, games carriage and restaurant car with a special children's menu. The *Jeune Voyageur Service* (JVS) provides hostesses to escort unaccompanied children aged 4-13 on journeys between 150 main stations; a supplement of 150-250 F is payable in addition to the child's ticket.

Train plus Accommodation Deals. French Railways has recently introduced a scheme known as Liberte for independent travellers that gives unlimited travel on any four days within a fifteen day period together with ten night's flexible accommodation at any of over 150 family hotels around France. The package costs £299 and should be booked from offices of French Railways outside France. It is possible to extend the holiday by purchasing extra accommodation vouchers.

BUS

Long-distance bus travel is difficult, since there's no domestic network. Country buses operate from all towns, usually run by French Railways, who also operate day trips and longer tours. Smoking is not allowed on buses.

BICYCLE

Hire shops for both cycles and mopeds can be found in many cities, university towns and Mediterranean resorts. In Paris, Try *Paris-Vélo,* at rue de Fer-à-Moulin, 75005 Paris (Tel: 43 37 59 22). French Railways operates a *Train + Vélo* cycle hire scheme from 283 stations. Sports machines cost about 45 F per day, "traditional" bikes about 40 F. These prices are reduced for hire periods of three or more days. A returnable deposit of 500 F is required, except by holders of Access/Mastercard, Visa or French rail cards.

The town of La Rochelle on the west coast has a collection of bright yellow municipal bicycles. They are to be found at various places around the port area and can be used, free of charge, within the town boundaries.

Bicycles can be taken free on many trains which operate over shorter routes (up to 200 km). These are designated in timetables by a cycle symbol at the head of the table. Long-distance trains are a more difficult proposition as the bike is carried only as registered baggage. On some trains it can travel on the same train as you providing it is checked in 30 minutes before departure. On others, it travels separately and may arrive anything up to five days later. A fee of around 30 F is charged for registering and carrying the cycle. Many cyclists choose either to hire a bicycle or to travel long distances by stringing together trips on local trains, rather than to consign their machine to the mercies of French Railways' baggage handlers.

AIR

Internal flights are operated by Air France, its subsidiary Air Inter, Air-Alpes, Air Alsace, Brit Air, Rousseau Aviation and Tourraine Air Transport. Regular travellers can purchase a *Cart d'Abonnement* which entitles the holder to 30% reductions on specific routes.

Paris has three airports, of which Roissy-Charles de Gaulle is the busiest. Air France flights operate from terminal 1, all others from terminal 2. Both terminals are linked by a free shuttle bus to the RER (suburban railway) station at Roissy.

Air France and French Railways have combined to offer bargain air and rail tickets from one of 16 airports in Great Britain to any of the 3,000 stations in France: prices start at £77 return.

The Paris Airport Authority, 291 boulevard Raspail, 75675 Paris 14 (Tel: 43 26 10 00) issues (in English) guides to Orly and Charles de Gaulle Airports; *Passport to Paris (guide to the city and facilities at the airports);* and *Assistance to Disabled Persons at Charles de Gaulle and Orly.*

HITCH-HIKING

Legal but discouraged, and not very reliable. For long trips don't count on more than 500 km a day. For some reason, France is surprisingly good for hitching at night. Hitch-hikers under the age of 18 should carry a letter signed by a parent or guardian, permitting them to hitch-hike.

France has a number of agencies that arrange lifts for a small registration fee. These are listed in full in *Europe — a Manual for Hitch-hikers;* the central office in Paris is *Allostop* at 84 passage Brady 75010 (Tel: 42 46 00 66). They also fix up rides in private aircraft.

Hitching out of Paris, the most popular (and most crowded) points are the motorway entrances — Porte de la Chapelle going north; Porte d'Orléans going south. It often pays to get a bit further out of town (just to avoid the crowds) eg going north, take bus 152 from Porte de la Villette to the autoroute slip road at Le Bourget; heading South out of Paris, relatively few *autostoppeurs* seem to have heard of Place de la Porte d'Italie, which is on the métro and infinitely preferable to Porte d'Orléans.

Lyon is quite possibly the worst place to hitch in Europe and therefore to be avoided.

BOAT

Car ferries to Corsica, often with connecting rail services, sail from Marseille,

Nice and Toulon. Drivers may get reductions of 10% on through bookings from Britain with British shipping operators.

CITY TRANSPORT

Taxis. Taxis are recognisable by the sign on the roof, and are all metered. You'll find one either at a taxi-rank (*tête de station*) or in the yellow pages (under *Taxis*).

Taxis in Paris have a pick-up charge of about 9 F, with waiting-time priced at 80 F per hour. There are three tariffs depending on location and time of day: A (2.55 F per kilometre), B (3.97 F) and C (5.33 F). The first applies to journeys within Central Paris (inside the Boulevard Peripherique) from 6.30 am to 10.00 pm. Tariff B is used in the Centre at night, and in the rest of Paris and the three adjoining *départements* by day. The most expensive applies for one-way journeys in the suburbs at night, and at all times outside the suburban zone. When you add the 15% tip, you might feel that overcharging was somewhat unnecessary; however, it has been known. If you think you have been overcharged, ask for a receipt (*quittance*), and make a note of his number (just to scare him). If he doesn't flinch, he's probably honest. Taxis are slightly more expensive in the provinces.

Bus/Métro. All Paris transport — métro, RER and buses — is run by the *Régie Autonome des Transports Parisiens* (RATP), which has a sales and information office at 53 ter, quai des Grands Augustins, Paris 6. For information phone 43 46 14 14: for bus information in English call 40 46 42 12.

Paris, Lyon and Marseille all possess métos, and Lille is building. The Paris métro is divided into two sections — *métro urbain,* with a fixed fare regardless of the length of the journey (except to extreme stations) and number of changes; and suburban (RER) lines, with their own fare structures. However, métro tickets are valid on urban sections of the RER. Lines are numbered, but are more frequently identified by the names of their terminal stations. Smoking is not allowed. Doors close automatically, but you must raise the handle or push a button to open them. Trains run from 5.30 am to 1.15 am.

Paris buses are one-man operated: so board at the front, get out at the rear. There is a flat fare per ticket, but longer journeys may require more than one ticket. Smoking is not allowed. Buses run from 7 am to 9 pm with some continuing until after midnight. There is a skeleton service of night buses, all running outwards from Châtelet (Avenue Victoria): the fare is two normal tickets, or you can use the above travel passes. For a cheap sightseeing tour, take bus 69 from Place Gambetta to the Eiffel Tower.

Single tickets for buses and métro cost 5 F, available from bus drivers, from ticket desks and/or machines at station entrances and from some tobacconists. First class métro compartments (in the middle of the train) are less crowded but cost 7.20 F. Children aged under 4 travel free: those aged 4-10 travel at half price. There's a 50 F fine for travelling first class on a second class ticket.

Cheaper than single tickets are the *carnets* of 10 tickets — 46 F first class (métro and RER) 30 F second class (métro, RER and buses) — available from métro and RER ticket desks and from shops and tobacconists with the RATP sign (not from bus drivers).

All tickets must be validated in order to be valid. This is done by passing the ticket through the electronic machines at the entrances to stations, or showing them to the driver on buses.

Other cheap deals include the *carte hebdomadaire* — two journeys a day over a six day period — aimed, obviously, at commuters. Yearly or monthly *carte orange* — allowing unlimited RATP and SNCF travel in Paris and the surrounding region: prices depend on the extent of validity, but one month for Paris and the inner suburbs costs 255 F. *Billet de Tourisme* 60 F for two days, 90 F for four days, 150 F for a week — unlimited travel on buses the RATP network and first class métro and RER lines A and B south of Gare du Nord. These tickets are available from the RATP offices, over 50 métro and RER stations, certain banks, the six main Paris railway stations, many provincial stations and SNCF offices abroad.

In towns other than Paris, bus services are run on a flat fare basis, sometimes with very high fares. Fares are collected by the driver, who can usually give change. Tickets must then be cancelled in the machine by the door.

Helicopter. A trip round Paris by helicopter could make your stay in Paris unforgettable. M. Balard of 4, avenue de la Porte-de-Sevres (Tel: 45 57 53 67) will take parties of at least 4 people up for 225 F-850 F per person.

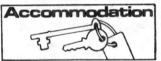

See the introduction for information on youth hostels, other hostels, and advance booking of accommodation.

Hotels. Hotels are officially graded by the French Ministry of Tourism. There are five main categories: one to four stars and four stars L (de luxe). In a rock-bottom one-star hotel in Paris a single room might cost 150 F (£15 or $24), a double 210 F. For this you won't have a private bath, in fact you might not even have hot water in your room, and there may be one smelly lavatory to each floor, which may well be of the stand-up-over-a-hole variety. Cockroaches are not unknown as fellow residents. In two-star hotels you are likely to find rooms with a telephone and private bathroom. In Paris, there are often cheap hotels around the railway stations; also in the 5th, 6th, 14th, 17th and 18th *arrondissements*.

Prices are strictly controlled and the maximum price must be posted on the door of each room. The cost of breakfast is not normally included in the price of a room; it will cost an additional 15 F-25 F in a cheapish hotel. Common practice is to round this maximum price up (in case you don't leave a tip). In holiday resorts, many hotels open only during the season. Other hotels offer 30-50% reductions in the off-season.

Holiday Villages/Holiday Clubs. Cheap accommodation in flats or bungalows in very quiet areas (with sporting facilities); list of villages and clubs can be obtained from *Villages Vacances Famille*, 38 boulevard Edgar Quinet, 75015 Paris (Tel: 43 90 12 88).

Logis de France. These are Government sponsored tourist inns offering accommodation in the one to two-star categories. There are around 4,000 of them, and they are normally off the usual tourist track. *Auberges* (smaller and ungraded) are included in the scheme. A free guide to both is available from French Government Tourist Offices or from Logis de France at 83 avenue d'Italie, 75013 Paris (Tel: 45 84 83 84).

Gîtes. An association of French families offering self-catering accommodation at very low prices — always in the countryside; you can buy a list of *Gîtes* from the *Fédération Nationale des Gîtes de France*, 34 rue Godot de Mauroy, 75019 Paris (Tel: 47 42 25 43) or French Government Tourist Offices abroad.

Youth Hostels. *Ligue Française pour les Auberges de la Jeunesse*, 38 boulevard Raspail, 75007 Paris (Tel: 45 48 69 84) — for a free map and list of hostels. Fees vary from 20 F-90 F according to the grade of the hostel.

Another national youth organisation, *Accueil des Jeunes en France*, offers a budget accommodation service for young people (in youth centres or small hotels). Their head office is at 12 rue des Barres, 75004 Paris (Tel: 42 72 72 09) but they also have a kiosk at the arrivals hall of the Gare du Nord — and a large office opposite the Georges Pompidou Center at 119 rue St. Martin (Tel: 62 77 87 80).

Camping. France has over 7,000 camping sites, classified from one to four stars. The charge per person is between 5 and 18 F depending on the category of the site, plus 3 F-15 F for a car. Many coastal sites are ludicrously overcrowded in summer, so advance booking (or avoidance) is recommended. The situation is so bad that a special leaflet has been issued (*Memento du Campeur Averti*) with details of the 11 regional information posts, 21 telephone information centres and 59 local reception centres set up to deal with the crush. Radio Monte Carlo (214 kHz LF) broadcasts up-to-date camping information (in French) at 1pm and 7pm daily during the summer.

Sleeping out. Not illegal, and usually warm enough, except in the north.

Finding and Booking Accommodation. Apart from the lists of specialised chains (*gîtes, logis,* etc) mentioned above, lists of hotels and their facilities are available free from regional tourist offices. When writing to hotels, be sure to ask for the prices to be stated precisely — *demi-pension* = bed and breakfast plus one meal; *pension complète* = bed and breakfast plus 2 meals; *prix tout compris or prix net* = service and taxes included.

The *Accueil de France* offices, situated in tourist offices (*Syndicats d'Initiative* or *Offices de Tourisme*) in the larger towns, will also book accommodation for you, for a small commission fee. Advance booking is strongly recommended everywhere for July and August, and for ski resorts at Christmas and Easter.

General information on telephones and English language newspapers and radio broadcasts is given in the introduction.

Post. Post offices (*PTT's*) are open 8 am-6 or 7 pm, Monday-Friday, sometimes with a 2-3 hour lunch break, and 9 am-noon on Saturdays. The main post office in Paris is at 52 rue du Louvre, Paris 1 (24 hour service). Main post offices in larger cities operate a skeleton service on Sunday mornings. Postal information — dial 42 80 67 89 in Paris.

Large post offices have different counters for different services — Poste Restante, for instance (for which there's a 2 F charge); *Vente Philatélique* (philatelic sales); or, for ordinary stamps, *Vente (de Timbres) au Détail*. Stamps are also sold at tobacconists (sign: *Tabac* and a big red cigar). Mail boxes are yellow, but at large post offices there are separate boxes for inland and foreign mail. In Paris boxes marked *Pneumatique* are for express deliveries within Paris and the suburbs.

The correct way to address mail is: name, street (number then name; words like rue, avenue, boulevard can go in lower case); town, preceded by a five figure zip code, the first two digits of which are the departmental code (75 for Paris). When writing from abroad, precede the code by the country code F-.

Telephone. Public pay phones are still rare in France, and are often ridiculously situated (eg at open bus stops on busy streets), but the newer ones may even have doors. Cash telephones take 50c, 1 F, 5 F or 10 F coins, which should be inserted before dialling (minimum 50c for a four minute local call). If there is no reply, replace the receiver to return money. Increasingly, public telephones operate with phone cards (*télécartes*) which are available for 40 F or 96 F from post offices or tobacconists. Calls are more expensive in cafés and hotels. The cheap rate is 8 pm-8 am.

The French telephone network was changed late in 1985 and even the natives have trouble understanding the new system. For the purposes of the network, France is divided into two areas: Paris plus the Ile de France (described below as *Paris*); and everywhere else (described below as *provinces*). All city or area codes have been abolished, with exception of Paris which retains the area code 1; numbers within Paris have, however, been changed by adding a digit to the front. Numbers outside Paris have changed simply by adding the old area code at the front. The following combinations are possible:

From *Paris* to *Paris:* dial the eight-figure number only. Example — to call SNCF enquiries from a Paris payphone, dial 45 82 50 50.

From *provinces* to *provinces:* dial the eight-figure number only. Example — to call the *Maison du Vin* in Bordeaux from Calais, dial 56 52 82 82.

From *Paris* to *provinces:* dial 16, wait for the secondary dialling tone, then dial the eight-figure number. Example — to call the *Office du Tourisme* in Lille from Paris, dial 16...20 57 96 69.

From *provinces* to *Paris:* dial 16, wait for the secondary dialling tone, then dial 1 followed by the eight-figure number. Example — to call the British Consulate in Paris from Marseilles, dial 16...1 42 60 91 42.

The international prefix is 19; you must wait up to 30 seconds for a second tone before dialling further. To make international calls through the operator, dial 19, wait for the tone, the dial the code for the country. For UK Direct calls insert 1 F, dial 19, wait for the second tone then dial 0044. Check the green pages of the directory for unexpected country codes, expecially in border areas. It it is too complicated, go to the telegraph office (attached to large post offices) and place your problems in their hands.

Useful numbers in Paris: directory enquiries — 112; speaking clock — 44 63 84 00; stock exchange — 42 60 84 00; alarm calls — 44 63 71 11.

Directories come in two parts: alphabetical and commercial. Outside Paris, the subscriber section is first divided into communities. Important numbers and information (in French), and lists of government and official departments are contained in the green pages at the beginning of the directory.

Telegrams. Either go to a post office or dial the number shown in the local directory — 44 44 11 11 in Paris. From Paris, telegrams can be telephoned in English — dial 42 33 21 11.

Broadcasting. There are four national television networks including *Canal-Plus*, a cable channel for subscribers. Two more commercial stations are planned. On or near the northern coast, British TV stations can be picked up. In summer, Radio France Inter (738kHz MW) broadcasts news, weather and road conditions in English between 6 and 7pm. This network also broadcasts emergency messages. You should be able to pick up the BBC's Radio 4 on 198 kHz long wave throughout much of France.

Health and Hygiene

For general information on hygiene, first aid, insurance and medical treatment, see the introduction.

Hygiene. Tap water is theoretically drinkable unless the sign *eau non potable* is displayed. Bottled mineral water is easily available for the prudent. Although not necessarily a health hazard, France seems plagued with beetles and cockroaches. One villa rental firm has a standard clause in their contracts disclaiming liability for invasion by insects. French lavatories can be very insanitary, and the hole in the ground type are still common. Public lavatories are rare, particularly with the demise of the *pissoir* — only one remains in Paris. The new "Superloos" (sophisticated unisex cabins, complete with background music) cost 1 F but the experience is recommended. If you can't find a public lavatory, you're allowed to use a cafés without buying a drink.

Reciprocal Agreements. British travellers with Form E111 should take the form to the local insurance office (*Caisse Primaire d'Assurance-Maladie*) to obtain a sickness certificate and a list of participating doctors. On production of the sickness certificate, the doctor will treat you, but you must pay the full fee, and have the doctor enter the fee on the certificate. The same procedure applies for dental treatment. In emergencies, any participating doctor or dentist should issue the necessary certificate, without reference to the insurance office. The sickness certificate must be produced again if medicines are prescribed, and the chemist should enter the amount on the prescription and give you a copy to attach to your sickness certificate. There is also a space on the certificate for you to attach the seal from the medicine bottle — giving the name and cost of the medicine. Finally, sign the certificate and return it to the insurance office to claim your refund of about 75% of the doctor's or dentist's fee; 40-70% of prescription charges. 80% of hospital expenses will be paid directly by the sickness insurance office if you inform the local insurance office before entering hospital, and show Form E111 to the hospital authorities. The refund will (eventually) be sent to your home address. Only public or "approved" private hospitals participate in the scheme.

For information, contact the *Service des Relations internationales de la Sécurité Sociale,* 84 rue Charles Michels, 93 St. Denis.

Treatment. In the Parisian suburbs there are two private hospitals with English speaking staff: American Hospital of Paris, 63 boulevard. Victor Hugo, Neuilly (Tel: 46 37 72 00); French-British Hospital, 30, rue Baribés (Tel: 47 58 13 12).

Emergencies. Pharmacies (recognisable by the green cross used as a shop sign) are open six days a week (9-12 am and 2-7 pm). Sunday and evening duty rotas are posted in all chemists' windows. The duty chemist is also officially on call at night — you'll find a bell (*sonnette de nuit*) by his door. In Paris, the Pharmacie Dhéry, 84 Champs-Elysées (Tel: 45 62 02 41) is open all night. Doctors also have night and weekend rotas. They, and chemists, are listed in local newspapers — look for the headings *pharmaciens de garde* and *médecins de garde.* In Paris, dial 43 37 77 77 for the night doctor (*SOS médécin*) service. The Paris number for the ambulance service is 48 87 27 50; the anti-poison centre is at 200 rue du Faubourg St. Denis, Paris 10 (Tel: 42 05 63 29).

Entertainment

Sport. A uniquely French game is *boules* or *pétanques*, which you can watch, or join in if invited, in parks and village squares. It is played rather like the British game of bowls, only the balls are smaller and metallic, and they're thrown, not rolled. The south-west offers both types of rugby; and the obvious Spanish influence is seen in bull fighting and pelote. Despite good performances by the national soccer team, the domestic game leaves little to be desired.

Nightlife. Paris is brimming over with nightlife — theatres, opera, cinemas, discos, and the naughty revues and striptease of the Pigalle. Full details are given in the weekly glossies *L'Officiel des Spectacles* and *Pariscope,* the English language magazine *Paris Passion,* and in the free booklet *Allo Paris.* Films are usually dubbed into French. If not, the letters *VO* will appear by the listings in these papers and upon posters. Dial 47 20 94 94 for entertainment information in English.

Museums and Galleries. Paris has some of the most outstanding art galleries in the world, including the Louvre, Orsay, Orangerie and Centre Georges Pompidou. Opening times vary, but 10 am-5 pm is average. The national museums close on Tuesdays apart from Versailles, the Trianon Palace and the Musee d'Orsay which close on Mondays. Free or 50% reduced admission on Sundays (the Louvre is free) and reductions for holders of the *Carte Jeunes* either daily or only on certain days.

The full price for entrance to museums is 10 F-25 F. If you are planning to absorb a lot of culture it will pay to invest in the *Carte Musée* issued by the RATP, which grants free admission to 65 museums and monuments, including the Louvre and the Pompidou Centre, in the Paris region. The pass costs 55 F for one day, 100 F for two days, and 150 F for five days. It can be purchased from museums and metro stations in Paris.

Municipal museums offer free admission to their permanent collections, but not special exhibitions, and are closed on Mondays.

Family Attractions. In 1992 Europe's first *Disney World* will open, just 38 miles from Paris. Until then the *Parc Asterix* should keep the children entertained. It is sited off the A1 motorway north of the Roissy-Paris airport, or can be got to by special shuttle buses from the metro station at Fort d'Aubervilliers or the RER station at Charles de Gaulle. Adult admission costs 120 F, children aged 2-12 are charged 90 F.

Eating out. It is still true to say that food is one of the French people's main concerns. There's no such thing, for instance, as a quick lunch, and you may find it difficult to get a cheap one; people usually stop work from 12 noon-2 pm, and have time to get a good meal in a restaurant or at home. The most important meal is dinner, served any time from 7 pm.

Don't expect to pay less than 20 F for a meal. If you just want a snack, go into a café for a *sandwich*, or *casse-croûte*. Most large towns also have Quick and McDonalds hamburger bars. A lot or restaurants serve a special *ménu touristique*, with prices beginning at 50 F (£5 or $8) for a three-course meal. In the country, you can get cheap, substantial meals in the *relais routiers* — the transport cafés used by lorry drivers. These are not to be confused with the *relais gourmands*, which are very exclusive (and expensive) country restaurants. Snack bars in hypermarkets usually offer good value. Some Paris supermarkets provide baskets of cut-price food to people who can prove they are short of cash. The Hare Krishna organisation is sent surplus food by the government, and gives away free vegetarian meals on the boulevard Sebastopol.

Dégustation. If you want a free nibble or sip of whatever is being produced locally look for the sign *Dégustation* which means tasting. Depending on your locality and the time of year, you might be able to get a free taste of wine, nougat (around Montélimar), chocolates, fresh fruit or honey. This method of attracting custom is particularly popular in the wine growing regions (and there are many of them), where special *caveaux de dégustation* are set up for the purpose. In Bordeaux, the Maison du Vin at 1 cours du XXX Juillet (Tel: 56 52 82 82) provides free tastings and information.

Drinking. The French do all their serious drinking in cafés (or *bistros*). The first cafes are open by 7 am and normal closing time is between midnight and 1 am, though some close a lot earlier. There are no laws governing opening hours, but the minimum drinking age is 18.

Cafés serve all kinds of drinks, hot and cold, alcoholic and non-alcoholic. Many of them also serve sandwiches or *casse-croûtes* (snacks). Café prices depend on the type of place and where you take your drinks. Cheapest is to buy your drink at the bar — but you will be unpopular if you then take it and sit at a table. Alternatively, sit at a table and wait for the *garçon* to serve you — this will cost 30-50% more than drinking at the bar. Be warned against the exorbitant surcharges on sitting on the *terrasse* (usually the pavement) in cafés along the Champs Elysées and blvd. St Germain. These are, in any case, the priciest cafés in France.

Wine is the cheapest drink, and it's served at any time of day. Three broad classifications: *appelation controlleé, vin delimité qualité superieure* and plain *vin de table.* The cheapest wine is also known as *vin de pays* or *vin ordinaire;* in restaurants, it's cheapest if you ask for *une carafe.* Many wine growing areas have local co-operatives where good wine is sold at giveaway prices if you bring your own container. Aperitifs are another national institution, served before either of the two main meals; the most common is probably *pastis* (also called *Ricard* or *Pernod* after brand names) which is made of aniseed. Port when it is served at all, is taken chilled as an aperitif.

Smoking. The French government has control over tobacco, which means that French cigarettes are much cheaper than foreign ones. Unfortunately, French cigarettes (*Gauloises* and *Gitanes* — about 6 F per pack of 20) are dark tobacco and may be too rough for the uninitiated. Foreign cigarettes are readily available but cost at least 10 F a packet. Tobacconists (*tabacs*) are easily recognised by the long red cigar-shaped signs outside. Cafés sell cigarettes, but are allowed to raise prices by 10%.

The Law

Crime. France (along with Spain) has the highest incidence of personal assault in Europe. Theft is also prevalent, particularly on the Paris métro.

Police. Local police matters are dealt with by the *commissariat de police* or, in rural areas, the *gendarmerie* (actually a branch of the army). The CRS (*Compagnie Républicaine de Sécurité*) are a much tougher branch of the police force whose main duty nowadays is controlling riots and demonstrations. To call the police in an emergency, dial 17; otherwise, look up

Police or *Gendarmerie* in the directory. The police headquarters in Paris are at 9 boulevard du Palais (Tel: 42 60 33 22).

Laws. Always carry your passport. The police can take you in if you don't have satisfactory identification with you. Also, you must always have at least 10 F on you, to avoid a vagrancy charge. In any case, if the police take a dislike to you, they have the right to hold you for 24 hours (this is known as *garde à vue*). Demonstrations should be avoided unless you're deeply involved in the cause. Innocent bystanders have been hurt in the past.

Nude Bathing. Still officially illegal in public, but tolerated and á la mode on the Côte d'Azur; less so on Corsica, where topless bathers have had paint thrown over them by the local citizenry. In Paris the Piscine Deligny (Quai Anatole France) allows topless bathing and sunbathing.

Driving Offences. Not treated lightly, fines of up to 2,500 F may be imposed for traffic violations. Random breath tests are made, and a driver with more than 0.4% alcohol in his blood is automatically subject to a penalty. A little-known law forbids carrying more than three litres of wine and two litres of spirits in a vehicle without a permit (which can be obtained from the shop which sells you the drink).

Motoring fines are normally paid on the spot, though you may be given a card to which special stamps (sold in licensed tobacconists) must be stuck; payment is equivalent to a plea of guilty (keep the receipt). You have the right to refuse to pay and take the matter to court, but this is inadvisable due to high court costs and you will still have to pay a deposit (amende forfaiture). For serious offences you must leave a cash deposit (or your vehicle) with the police pending prosecution.

Drugs. Up to 10 years for possession, a maximum of 20 for supply. If you're caught importing, you can expect ludicrous customs fines. However, these are to some extent negotiable, since if you can't pay then the customs authorities must finance your stay in prison between arrest and sentencing.

Legal Aid. Embassies and consulates can be quite influential. If you need a lawyer, the court will appoint one, but you'll have to show you're broke if you don't want to pay his fee.

For general information on contacts and complaints procedures, see the introduction.

Embassies and Consulates.

British Embassy, 2 Cité du Retiro, 75008 Paris; postal address 35 rue du Faubourg St. Honoré, 75008 Paris (42 66 91 42).
British Consulate, 16 Rue d'Anjou, 75008, Paris (42 66 91 42).
British Consulates General in Bordeaux, Lille, Lyon and Marseille; a Consulate in Le Havre; Honorary Consulates in Boulogne, Calais, Cherbourg, Dunkirk, Le Havre, Nantes, Nice, Perpignan and Toulouse.

American Embassy, 2 avenue Gabriel, 75382 Paris (42 96 12 02).
American Consulates General in Bordeaux, Lyon, Marseille and Strasbourg.

Canadian Embassy, 35 avenue Montaigne, 75008 Paris (47 23 01 01).
Canadian Consulates General in Bordeaux, Marseille and Strasbourg.

Lost Property. The central lost property office in Paris is: *Prefecture de Police Bureau des Objets Trouvés,* 36 rue de Morillons, Paris 75 (Tel: 45 31 14 80), open 8.30 am-5 pm, Monday-Friday.

Baby-sitting. Look up *Baby-sitting* in the directory. In Paris apply to: CROUS 39 avenue George Bernanos, 75005 Paris (Tel: 40 51 37 50) who also provide guides, secretaries and translators; or try Kid Service (42 96 04 16), Allo Maman Poule (47 47 78 78) or Baby Sitting Service (42 37 51 24).

Information. Tourist offices are known as *Offices de Tourisme* or *Syndicats d'Initiative.* The central tourist office in Paris is at 127 Champs Elysées, Paris 8 (Tel: 47 23 61 72), with branch offices at the Gare de l'Est, Gare de Lyon, Gare du Nord and Gare d'Austerlitz. For information on Paris and the surrounding region write to the *Comité Regional des Tourisme et des Loisirs,* 73-75 rue Canbronne, Paris 75015 (Tel: 45 67 89 41).

Free Maps. Road maps of France from French Government Tourist Offices, or from local tourist offices. Street plans of Paris from any of the Paris Tourist offices; métro and bus maps from RATP offices (see *City Transport).* You'll usually find a basic Paris street plan and métro map in your hotel lobby — or in someone else's hotel lobby. You have little chance of getting lost in a French town because of the quantity of maps that decorate railway stations, main streets, squares and bus stops. The highly useful *Guides Blay* to most large French towns are obtainable in Britain from Roger lascelles, 47 York Road, Brentford, Middlesex TW8 0QP (Tel: 081-847 0935).

Disabled Travellers. A special guide to Paris entitled *Access in Paris* is available from Pauline Hethaistos Survey Projects, 39 Bradley Gardens, West Ealing W13 8HE. It is free, but a contribution of £4 towards costs would be appreciated.

Detailed wheelchair guides to either Paris or the whole of France are published (in French) by the *Comite National Francais de Liaison pour la Readaptation des Handicapes* at 38, blvd. Raspail, 75007 Paris (Tel: 45 48 90 13). They are called *Touristes quand même! Promenades en France pour voyageures Handicapés* and *Touristes quand même! Paris.*

Gay Information. Sos Homosexualité operates an information and advice service for gay men and women from 10 am to midnight every day on 46 27 49 36.

Student Travel. OTU, 6 rue Jean Calvin, 75005 Paris (Tel: 43 36 80 27); Council Travel, 31 rue St. Augustin, 75002 Paris (Tel: 42 66 20 87) and also at 51 rue Dauphine (Tel: 43 25 09 86), 16, rue Vaugirard (Tel: 46 34 02 90) and 49 rue Pierre Charron (Tel: 45 63 19 87), plus offices in Nice, Lyon, Montpelier and Aix-en-Provence.

Student Organisations. Students facing problems such as finding cheap accommodation and food should contact their nearest *Centre regional des oeuvres universitaires et scolaires* (CROUS); the Paris office is at 39 avenue Georges Bernanos, Paris 5 (Tel: 40 51 36 00 or 40 51 37 10). There are CROUS offices in 28 towns and local centres (CLOUS) in twelve others.

Youth Information Centres. The *Centre d'Information et de documentation pour la jeunesse* (Cidj), 101 quai Branly, Paris 15 (Tel: 45 66 40 20) will try to solve most problems — accommodation, work, medical and legal problems. They have provincial offices throughout the country.

English Bookshops. W H Smith, 248 rue de Rivoli, 75001 Paris; Shakespeare and Company, 37 rue de la Boucherie, 75005 Paris.

English Language Churches. The American Cathedral, 23, rue George V, Paris 8 (Tel: 47 20 17 92); St. Michael's (Anglican), 5 rue d'Aguesseau, Paris 8 (Tel: 45 53 71 52); St. George's (Anglican), 7 rue Auguste Vacquérie, Paris 16 (Tel: 47 20 22 51); Church of Scotland, 17 rue Bayard, Paris 8 (Tel: 48 25 30 67); St. Joseph's (Catholic), 50 avenue Hoche, Paris 8.

American Express. Paris offices at 11 rue Scribe, 75009 Paris (Tel: 42 66 09 99); 83 bis rue de Courcelles, 75017 (Tel: 47 66 03 00); avenue de Wagram 75008 Paris (Tel: 42 27 58 80). Other offices in Cannes, Le Havre, Lourdes, Lyon, Nice, Rouen and St. Jean de Luz.

Calendar of Events

	Public Holidays are shown in **bold**
January 1	**New Year's Day**
late January	Monte Carlo Rally
February	Nice Carnival
March/April	**Easter Monday**
late April	Evian Classical Music Festival
May 1	**Labour Day**
May 8	**VE Day**
mid May	Paris Marathon
late May	Cannes International Film Festival
May	**Ascension Day**
May/June	**Whit Monday**
late May/early June	Monaco Grand Prix
early June — odd years	Paris Air show
mid June	Le Mans 24 hour race
late June/mid July	Tour de France (cycling)
July	Jazz Festivals: Antibes, Nice, Nimes
July 14	**Bastille Day**
early August	Cannes Fireworks Fiestas
early August	Lorient Celtic Festival
August 15	**Assumption Day**
September-November	Paris Dance Festival
early Oct-even years	Paris Motor Show
early October	Grand Prix de l'Arc de Triomphe: horse race at Longchamp, Paris
November 1	**All Saints' Day**
November 11	**Remembrance Day**
December 25	**Christmas Day**
December 26	**St Stephen's Day (Alsace-Lorraine only)**

When a public holiday falls on a Tuesday or Thursday, it is common practice to take off the preceding or following day (*faire la pont*, literally "to make the bridge") in order to obtain a four-day long weekend.

Monaco

Area. $\frac{3}{4}$ square mile   **Population.** 27,000

The principality of Monaco lies on the Côte d'Azur between Nice and Menton. It covers a strip of land about $2\frac{1}{2}$ miles long and is nowhere more than a mile wide. There are no formal frontiers with France. French currency is used alongside Monégasque coins, which are not valid outside Monaco. Along with tourism, banking is a major industry: over 30 banks serve the population, an average of one bank for every 850 inhabitants. Philately is another important source of revenue, and only Monégasque stamps are permitted. The Central Post Office is at Square Beaumarchais (Tel: 93 50 69 87). Monaco is part of the French telephone network.

Although to all intents and purposes it may appear to be a merely a *département* of France, Monaco is an independent sovereign state headed by His Serene Highness Prince Rainier Grimaldi. A treaty signed in 1918 provides that Monaco will be turned over to France should the dynasty end. However this is highly unlikely since the line can be continued by adoption. The changing of the guard at the Prince's Palace takes place daily at 11.55 am, and the royal apartments are open from 9.30 am-6.30 pm every day.

Getting Around. For taxis, phone 93 50 56 28, 93 50 47 26. Four bus routes adequately cover the state. Bicycles may be hired from Auto-Motos Garage, 7 rue de la Colle (Tel: 93 30 24 61). Monaco/Monte-Carlo station is on the main Marseille-Nice line; in summer, the SNCF Métrazur service runs every 30 minutes. Buses to Nice and Menton operate half-hourly from 6 am-9 pm. For a faster getaway, Héli-Air-Monaco (Tel: 93 30 80 88) flys a dozen times daily from Fontvielle heliport to Nice airport. The one-way fare is 250 F.

Help and Information. In emergencies dial 17.
Tourist Office: 2a boulevard des Moulins (93 30 87 01).
Police and Lost Property: rue Suffren Reymond (93 30 42 46).
American Express: 35 boulevard Princesse Charlotte (93 30 96 52).
English-language Church: St. Paul's, avenue de Grande-Bretagne 993 30 71 06).
Consulates: British and US — Nice; Canadian — Marseille.

West Germany

SCHLOSS PFALZ KAUB   W.S

Area. 96,010 square miles **Population.** 61,200,000

Capital. Bonn (population: 292,000).

Weather. In general, the climate is continental — but of course the weather on the North Sea coast is very different from the alps. In winter there is heavy snow and good winter sports conditions everywhere, north and south; in summer, the chance of rain — whether a shower or a Wagnerian storm — should not be excluded, and rainwear is advisable.

THE PEOPLE

The Germans are very neat and tidy people, and very hard-working — hence the country's strong economic position today. Their love of order is often annoying, especially when you come face to face with officialdom.

Politics. After the last war, Germany was divided into four occupied zones (British, French, American and Russian), and the troops from these countries are still there. The Russian zone because East Germany (German Democratic Republic); the allied

102

zones became West German (German Federal Republic). The division between East and West was a bitter point, particularly since a lot of families were still split which is why the opening of the Berlin Wall in 1989 was such a momentous event for Germans. At the time of going to press the prospect of the re-unification of Germany seems more of a probability than a possibility.

Religion. There is an equal division between Catholics and Protestants; the strongest Protestant church being Lutheran. The times of church services are posted on the roads entering a town. Sunday observance is still an issue, especially in strongly Catholic areas. In 1975 a man was acquitted of washing his car on a Sunday, but only after the case reached the State Supreme Court. He was acquitted on the grounds that "the quiet of fellow-citizens had only slightly been impaired". You're unlikely to fall foul of the law in this way, but you could upset or offend.

Language. German is spoken throughout the country, the most difficult accents being in the south. High German, as she is learnt in schools in Britain, is spoken widely in business and public life, but not by the average citizen. English is the first foreign language taught: French is widely spoken along the French frontier.

Making Friends. Friendliness varies from region to region: southerners are known for friendliness; Rhinelanders are extremely hospitable, but the northerners are very reserved — a man who says Hello and Goodbye is reckoned to be a brilliant conversationalist. In Lower Saxony, a barman with only ten tables is in trouble when his 11th customer walks in.

If you do get into a conversation with a German, don't expect to get away with a few trite comments on the weather: he'll want to know your views on politics, whether you're Protestant or Catholic (no other alternatives), and all about your views on the life in general. Among some of the older inhabitants you'll find traces of guilt feeling from the last world war.

If you are invited into their homes for a meal, it's customary to arrive punctually and to take flowers for the hostess. Or, if there's no hostess, a bottle of wine for the host.

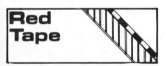

Red Tape

See the introduction for details of passports, customs regulations, duty free allowances, vaccinations and importing pets.

Passports and Visas. Holders of British, US and Canadian passports are allowed to stay three months. For extensions, apply to the Aliens' Authority at the local *Ordnungsamt*.

Customs. The EC list of duty free allowances in the introduction applies to Germany.

Restricted or prohibited items include firearms, flick-knives, narcotics, saccharin, pure alcohol, raw meats, parrots, parakeets or subversive literature.

Money

100 Pfennig (Pf.) = 1 Deutschmark (DM).
£1 = 2.85 DM   1 DM = £0.35
$1 = 1.78 DM   1 DM = $0.56

For general information on handling, exchanging and raising money, see the introduction.

Coins. 1 Pf, 2 Pf, 5 Pf, 10 Pf, 50 Pf, 1 DM, 2 DM, 5 DM. The 10 Pf coin is known as a *Groschen*.

Notes. 5 DM (green), 10 DM (blue), 20 DM (green), 50 DM (brown), 100 DM (blue), 500 DM (brown-red), 1,000 DM (brown).

Banking Hours. At least 9 am-12.30 pm, Monday-Friday, but hours vary from city to city — other possibilities are 9 am-4 pm; or 9 am-1 pm, then 2 or 2.30 pm-4 or 4.30 pm; with late opening (until 5.30 or 6 pm) on Thursdays. You can change money at airports, stations and frontier posts every day, 24-hour service only at very busy stations and airports.

Shopping Hours. 9 am-6 or 6.30 pm, Monday-Friday; 9 am-noon or 2.00 pm on Saturdays. Many small shops observe the siesta and close from 1-2.30 pm. Saturday afternoons are absolutely dead, except the first Saturday in the month, when most shops are open till 5 or 6 pm.

Import and Export. There are no restrictions for travellers, only upon large sums for investment.

Tipping. Hotels — service charges always included (*einschliesslich Bedienung*). Testaurants — likewise, but it's customary to leave some loose change (up to about 5%). Bars — no tip is necessary. Taxis — no tip obligatory, but round the fare up to the next DM. Porters — have fixed charges and expect a small tip in addition. Public toilets — attendants can get very piqued if you don't throw a couple of Groschen in their little saucer.

Emergency Cash. British citizens are allowed to work, provided you have the right paperwork (see the introduction). The *Manpower* organisation has offices in some large cities; also look for the *Adia* and *Interim* chains throughout Germany, or you can apply to the local *Arbeitsamter* (labour exchange) or *Service-Vermittlung* (mobile exchanges for temporary work). American military bases are also good territory. The best chances of work are in hotels, restaurants, building sites and farms. You can sell your blood in most large hospitals, but street-selling and busking are illegal. There is a national lottery with a monthly draw; tickets are sold at shops bearing the *Lotto-Toto* sign, and are sold in whole units, in halves, quarters or eighths.

Some less sophisticated slot machines will accept British 5p (the old, pre August 1990 version) or Belgian 5 F pieces instead of 1 DM coins. However, investors who see this method as the ideal opportunity to improve exchange rates in their favour, are warned that some slots activate alarms in the local *Polizei* station and premature departure from Germany may ensue.

Taxes. The German version of value added tax is called *mehrwertsteuer* (MWST) and currently 14%. Foreigners can claim refunds on single expensive items by having receipts stamped at customs, then sending them back to the shop.

Getting Around

The information given in this section is complementary to that given in the corresponding section in the introduction.

CAR

The German Autobahn system is the most extensive in Europe — but some of them feel as if they haven't been touched since Hitler had them built. There are no tolls. Roads are kept clear in winter, but tyres are recommended. Chains can be hired and fitted at 88 ADAC offices in mountain areas.
A leaflet entitled *Autobahn Service* is available free at most motorway service stations. It gives the wavelengths of the nearest local radio stations that broadcast traffic information, and lists the facilities available to motorists on Autobahns. Wavelengths of local radio stations are also posted alongside autobahns.

Rules and Requirements. The red warning triangle is obligatory. Seat belts must be worn at all times by driver and front seat passengers and, if fitted, by rear seat passengers; children under 12 are banned from the front seat.
   Unlike most of Europe, traffic already on roundabouts takes priority over vehicles waiting to enter.

Road Signs. Worth noting are: *Umleitung* — Detour; *Fahrbahnschäden* or *Strassenschäden* — Damaged road surface; *Kreuzung* — Crossroads; *Strasse gesperrt* — Road closed; *Steinschlag* — Falling rocks; *Hupverbot* — One way street.
   If you are diverted from an autobahn, the diversion sign will bear a number, say 24. You should then follow blue/white signs saying *U24* (*Umleitung* number 24) which will eventually take you back to your route. The Germans seem to have signposted every conceivable diversion, and so the blue/white signs are to be relied upon.

Place Names. Brunswick = Braunschweig; Cologne = Köln; Munich = München; Nuremburg = Nürnberg. Cities with French names include: Aachen = Aix-la-Chapelle; Trier = Tréves. Munich = Monaco in Italian.

Parking. Cities have meters, which take 10 Pf, 50 Pf, or 1 DM coins at varying rates. *Halten Verboten* or *Halteverbot* = No Waiting.

Petrol. Leaded petrol (verbleit) is only available in super (98 octane); the cost is 1.25 DM per litre (£2 per imperial gallon or $3.10 per US gallon). Unleaded petrol (*bleifrei*) is available as normal (92 octane) at 1.10 DM per litre, or as super (98 octane) at 1.18 DM per litre. Self service stations are slightly cheaper and Autobahn filling stations are slightly more expensive.

Touring Clubs. ADAC, Am Westpark 8, 8000 München 70 (Tel: 7 67 60); AvD, Lyonerstrasse 16, 6000 Frankfurt 71 (Tel: 66 06 300); DTC, Amalienburgstrasse 23, 8000 München 60 (Tel: 811 10 48).

Accidents and Breakndowns. ADAC runs a breakdown service (*Strassenwacht*) on all motorways and main roads (Tel: 1 92 11). Police (dial 110) must be informed if anyone is hurt in an accident. They or the ADAC can also be called by the automatic telephones on the motorways.

TRAIN

The rail network is operated by Deutsche Bundesbahn (DB), who provide information centres with multi-lingual staff at all main stations. Inter-City trains are staffed with hostesses who serve refreshments and advise on rail services. most expresses have coin-operated telephones on board.

Buying a ticket can be a daunting, almost Kafka-like experience due to the massively complex system of train types and fares.

The fastest trains in Germany are known as IC (InterCity); these connect major cities, and a supplement of 7 DM is payable. They are known as EC (EuroCity) if the train crosses a national border: again, a supplement is payable, the cost of which depends on the journey made. Almost as fast are the new IR (InterRegio) trains which connect medium size towns with each other and the IC network. A supplement of around 3 DM is payable as long as the journey is under 50 km. D-Trains are basically the same as IR trains, but with older rolling stock: they will have been replaced by them by 1992. The other types of train are E-Trains, which are semi-fast trains over short and medium distances and the S-Bahn, fast suburban train services for major cities.

Second class fares cost around 20 DM for 100 km (£12/$19 for 100 miles); first class is 50-70% more expensive.

Journeys of up to 50 km require you to buy a ticket from an orange and white ticket machine (marked *Fahrausweise*). Stations are listed alphabetically on the front, with a number alongside each which denotes its zone from 1 (nearest) to 7 (farthest). There are two columns of buttons, the left-hand column for full-fare tickets, the right for half-price. Select the appropriate ticket type and zone number, and push the button. The display should show the fare. If, however, you require a return ticket, push the button marked *Rf.* For travel on IC trains, push *IC-ZU*. The final fare should be shown. Insert coins and DM 10 or 20 notes to at least the figure shown, and a ticket (plus any change due) should emerge. The "X" button can safely be ignored; it is for tickets to a major station over 50 km away, the identity of which can be inferred from the list alongside; this button is used only by hardened devotees of the system.

It is worth spending some time watching expert natives operating the machine before using it yourself. Unless you are absolutely confident of you ability to buy the right ticket, you may prefer to board a train without a ticket. So long as you seek out the guard or ticket inspector immediately, you pay a surcharge of only DM 3 for having him write the ticket for you. The exception to this is the S-Bahn, a ticket for which must be bought before boarding. If you wait to be found, however, you pay twice the cost of your ticket with a minimum of DM 40. These surcharges apply equally to journeys of over 50 km. However, the procedure for buying a ticket is far easier for journeys over 50 km; you simply go to the ticket office, state your destination and whether you require a one way (*einfache Fahrt*) or return (*Hin-und Rückfahrt*) ticket, and hand over the cash. You can pay the supplement for TEE and IC trains at the same time. One-way tickets are valid four days, return for two months. If the ticket office is closed when you wish to buy your ticket, you should follow the procedure above to buy a ticket, preferably for zone 7, from the machine and buy an additional ticket on the train. No surcharge is payable so long as you buy some sort of ticket from the machine before boarding.

Cheap Deals. Children under 4 travel free; 4-11 at half price. 15% reduction on Holiday Return Tickets (*Vorzugkarte*) — minimum 201 km, return journey no earlier than the Sunday after the outward journey.

Ther German Rail Pass and the German Rail Youth Pass allow unlimited travel on any 4, 9, or 16 days within a period of 21 days. They can only be purchased from German Railways in Britain by people not resident in Germany. The four day Pass costs £80 (£45 for those aged under 25); the 9 day Pass costs £120 (£70); and the 16 day Pass costs £170 (£95) (fares quoted are for second class travel).

The regional *Tourenkarte* (fares vary; available for one person, two travelling together, or a family) allows ten days unlimited travel within its area, and 50% reductions on DB and postal buses.

BUS

The rail network is supplemented and overlapped by buses run by DB (red), the postal service (yellow) and independent operators.

BICYCLE

Cycles can be hired from most rail stations or look up *Fahrradverleih* in the Yellow Pages. Rates are about 5 DM a day for rail ticket holders, double for everyone else. Bicycles may be carried on trains with a luggage van (except IC and TEE) if you buy a *fahrradkarte,* price 6.50 DM one way.

AIR

Internal flights (except to Berlin) are operated by Lufthansa, their domestic subsidiary DLT and Regionalflug GmbH (RFG). The hub of the Lufthansa network is Frankfurt airport, linked by rail to the city centre (journey time 11 minutes, six trains hourly from 5 am-8 pm, three hourly until 1 am). Trains from Munich, Nürnberg, Mainz, Bonn, Köln and Düsseldorf also run direct to and from the airport. Some of these services are Lufthansa Airport Expresses, operated by the airline exclusively for passengers connecting with flights at Frankfurt.

Frankfurt Airport (60 01 for information) has all the facilities you'd expect, plus several others you might not: a bowling alley, discotheque and a cinema showing pornographic films.

Connections between other main cities and their airports include:

Dusseldorf — train from hauptbahnhof (15 minutes).
Hamburg — S-bahn to Ohlsdorf then bus 110 (50 minutes).
Munich (information: 9 21 21) — bus from Starnberger Station (25 minutes).
Hannover — bus 609 from Hauptbahnhof.

HITCH-HIKING

Legal except on motorways. Motorway rest areas and the larger entries to motorways are good territory, but minor roads can be pretty dismal. The area codes on number plates can help a great deal on longer journeys — your driver may well flag down another motorist who, judging from his registration, can take you further. It is thus possible to travel right through Germany in several lifts while hitching only the first. See *Europe — a Manual for Hitch-hikers* for a complete list of codes by regions. If you prefer to plan and pay for your ride, contact *Mitfahrzentrale* who have offices in 40 cities.

BOAT

In some cases, parts of a train journey can be replaced by boat travel on the KD (Köln-Düsseldorfer) Line, whose head office is at Frankenwerft 15,5000 Köln 1 (Tel: 2088 318/319). State this intention when buying the rail ticket; a transfer ticket will be issued on payment of the required surcharge at the landing stage office.

CITY TRANSPORT

Taxis. Charges vary from town to town, but the standing charge is about 4 DM, then about 2 DM per km (£1.12 or $1.80 a mile). All taxis are metered. They can be hailed or telephoned.

Bus/Tram/Underground. Germany is the pioneer in efficient, automated transport, and the process of evolution has resulted in a confusing number of different systems existing side by side. The advance of automation confounds even the most hard-headed Germans. The guidelines below merely scratch at the surface, and only practice will give you the necessary confidence.

Tickets are now mostly issued by machines, located in underground (*U-Bahn*) station entrances (in Berlin, Cologne, Düsseldorf, Frankfurt, Hamburg, Hanover, Munich and Stuttgart); or at bus or tram stops; or inside trams or buses. Many towns still have conductors or fare-collecting drivers on trams and buses, but the tickets they issue will probably be for single journeys only, whereas machines issue a frightening variety — single journeys (*Einzelfahrkarten*), several rides (*Mehrfahrtenkarten*) and period tickets, all with reduced rates for children (*Kindertarif*), and, in larger towns, complex fares structures.

Machines in Frankfurt and Munich (and new machines in other towns) take any coins and will give you the right change, but rely on you to press the button you want. More old-fashioned machines issue tickets of one fare, will only take certain coins to the right amount, and still might not release your ticket until you've pulled a lever or turned a handle.

The fares structure varies considerably from town to town. Small towns have a flat fare, usually allowing you any number of changes within a given time limit (1 hour on average) and in one direction. Larger cities (like Munich, Hamburg and Frankfurt) divide their areas into zones, and grade fares by the number of zones you pass through (there are always maps by the ticket machines). Some towns also divide routes into fare stages (also marked on the maps) — in Munich, for instance, you may use a children's ticket if you cross no more than two fare stage boundaries. In cities with integrated transport systems, the same tickets are valid on all forms of transport, and are usually valid for changes (*Umsteigen*) from one form of transport to another. Fares range from 1-5 DM.

Having bought the correct ticket, your troubles are just beginning. A feature common to nearly all forms of transport in nearly all towns is the necessity to cancel tickets, generally in machines (at platform entrances or inside buses or trams) marked E (for *Entwertung* = cancellation). These machines mark the ticket with the date, time, route and direction. Put your ticket in the machine arrow first, and the side to be cancelled upwards. The machine will usually ring or click when it's done its job. If you have a multi-ride ticket, you usually have to bend it back the appropriate number of strips (depending on the number of zones — minimum of two in Munich) before cancelling.

Riding on an uncancelled ticket is as illegal as riding without a ticket and merits an on-the-spot fine (50-100 DM is the norm). If you're planning several changes, some towns have systems whereby you must cancel your ticket (or the separate coupons) at each change; other towns let you get away with cancelling only at the start of the journey.

In general, multi-ride tickets are a better bargain than singles, but period tickets are better still. In Hamburg a day ticket costs about 8 DM, or 12 Dm including first class travel on city trains and express buses. Munich and Frankfurt have two types of 24-hour ticket (inner zones 10 DM; 20 DM all zones); in Frankfurt these come out of the machines with the date stamped on; in Munich, they must be signed and cancelled before starting your first journey. Season tickets and longer period tickets, if available, must normally be obtained from the city's

Verkehrsverbund (VV), who also issue maps and apologias. The Munich VV is at Thierschstr. 2; and the Hamburg VV at Hamburgestr. 11 (Tel: 2 20 11 31).

See the introduction for information on youth hostels, other hostels, and advance booking of accommodation.

Hotels. If you think the public transport systems are complicated, then abandon all hope of comprehending German hotel classifications. Firstly, a letter indicates whether there is a restaurant open to the public (R), or meals are served to guests only (P), or breakfast only is served (G). The general quality of accommodation is assessed from I down to III, and the "characteristics" of each hotel are designated "comfortable", "standard" or "economy". Finally, individual rooms are graded according to facilities: type 1 rooms have a WC and bath or shower; type 2, bath or shower, type 3, running water only. Thus, there are theoretically 81 different classes, ranging from a type 3 room in a GIII "economy" establishment to a type 1 room in an RI "comfortable" hotel.

However, whether you stay in a Hilton or a country inn, you can be sure that your room will be clean and tidy. Prices are usually computed per room; double rooms are less than twice as much as single rooms. Breakfast, taxes (including the spa tax payable in many inland resorts) and service charges are normally included. The lowest price for a single room and breakfast is about 40 DM (£14 or $22). Rooms in private houses cost 20-40 DM. There are motels on all major autobahns. Many cities hold annual trade fairs during which rooms are very difficult to find; unless you book in advance you may find that accommodation is only available in a town 30 miles away. During fairs rates are normally higher.

Youth Hostels. *Deutsches Jugendherbergswerk,* Bismarckstr, 8, 4930 Detmold (Tel: 05231 7401-0); will send you an official list in exchange for five international reply coupons; alternatively, tourist offices have free maps showing hostels. The maximum age limit in Bavaria is 27.

Friends of Nature Hostels. Simple accommodation in mountain regions. Details from *Naturfreundejugend,* Grossglockner Str. 28, 7000 Stuttgart 60.

Farms. Many farms open their doors to visitors in the summer. A list of addresses which costs 10 DM plus postage, is available from *Landschriften Verlag GmbH, Kurfürstenstr. 53, 5300 Bonn-Bad Godesberg.*

Camping. There are over 2,100 sites, many of them shown on free maps from tourist offices; about 400 stay open in winter. You might pay 4-6 DM a night; extra for tents, cares and caravans. It is not normally possible to reserve places in advance.

Sleeping out. Not illegal, but permission is required from the landowner and/or the local police. If the police find you in parks or town centres, they'll move you on and tell you it's *verboten*. All large stations have a *Bahnhofsmission*, a church-run organisation which provides travellers with beds at 5 DM per night. If you're absolutely penniless, you won't be thrown out. In Munich, ask for the *Tent*, a municipal circus tent which provides shelter in July and August for a few DM per night.

Finding and Booking Accommodation. The German National Tourist Office will send you regional hotel guides, or a map listing camping sites free on request. Similar lists are available from local tourist offices, or *Zimmernachweis* offices at stations and airports, where reservations can also be made. There is a central advance reservations agency: *Allgemeine Deutsche Zimmerreservierung* (ADZ), Corneliusstrasse 34, 6000 Frankfurt/Main 1 (Tel: 069-74 07 67). For on-the-spot room hunting, look for the sign *Zimmer frei.*

For general information about telephones and English language newspapers and radio broadcasts, see the introduction.

Post. Post offices are open 8 am-6 pm Monday-Friday and 8 am-1 pm on Saturdays. The railway station post offices in the major cities stay open till midnight or later. Post boxes are yellow and bear the post horn symbol. Large towns also have special airmail boxes (blue). There are stamp machines outside most post offices and at stations. Large post offices have many different counters for different things. The counters for stamps only are marked *Wertzeichen;* special philatelic counters are marked *Sammlerschalter.* Mail to neighbouring countries is charged at inland rates.

Poste Restante: the service is free at all main post offices.

The correct way to address mail is: name; street (name, then number); town (preceded by a four figure code, which, if writing from abroad, is preceded by the country code D-). Large cities also have zone numbers, which follow the town's name.

Telephone. The system is all automatic. Codes for the main cities include: Berlin — 030; Bonn — 0229; Düsseldorf — 0211; Frankfurt — 069; Hamburg — 040; Munich -089. The international prefix is 00.

Public call boxes take some combination of 10 Pf. 1 DM and 5 DM coins. Local calls cost a minimum of 50 Pf. To operate, lift the receiver, insert the money, then dial. The yellow light will be replaced by a red one as the cut-off warning. Unused coins will be returned when you replace the receiver. Calls are cheapest from 6 pm-6 am Monday to Friday, after 2 pm on Saturdays and all day on Sundays. International calls can be dialled direct from booths marked Inland and Ausland or National International.

Directories come in two sections — subscribers (*Amtliches Fernsprechbuch*) and commercial (*Branchen-Fernsprechbuch*). The subscriber directory is first divided into communities listed on the cover, then proceeds alphabetically. At the head of each community listing are a selection of useful number like recipes, cinema programmes, sports information and consumer advice.

Emergency (*Notruf*) numbers are printed on the outside front cover, below the map. Information in all directories includes postal, telephone and telegram rates, and how to use the telephone. Beyond this, some directories are more informative than others — giving emergency numbers and information sources. Hamburg's directory even prints a plan of the underground and suburban railways. All directories are alphabetically ordered according to DIN (German Standard) 5007; thus, for instance, the letter ä, ö, ü are placed as if they were ae, oe, ue. The letter ß represents ss.

Useful numbers: operator — 010; international operator — 0010; information — 0118; international information — 00118; complaints — 0114; other numbers vary from place to place, but police — 010 — and fire/ambulance — 112 — are almost universal.

Telegrams. The post office is the best place to send telegrams, but you can do it from a private (not public) phone by dialling 0113.

Broadcasting. English programmes on German radio include news and weather at 9 am daily on Bayrischer Rundfunk (Bavaria) — VHF stations only. Allied Forces' radio stations include BFBS (in the British sector in the north) — 87.8, 93, 95.4, 96.5, 97.6 and 99.8 MHz VHF; CFN (in the Canadian section in the south-west) — 101.125, 101.25 and 102.5 MHz VHF; and American Forces Network (AFN) — 200 215, 230, 263, 271, 290, 321, 344 and 491 m MW; and, on VHF — 101.4 MHz in Bonn, 100.7, 101, 101.75 MHz in the south; plus 24-hour stereo on 98.7 MHz (Frankfurt), 100.4 MHz (Heidelburg) and 102.4 MHz (Stuttgart). Another American station broadcasting from Germany (Munich) is Voice of America on 259 M MW, which has programmes in English at 3-4 am, 6-7 and 5-5.30 pm.

AFN also transmits television from three stations — Wiesbaden (Channel 22), Spangdahlem (Channel 27) and Kaiserslautern (Channel 30).

Radios and televisions require licences, obtainable from post offices.

For radio and TV stations in Berlin, see under *West Berlin*.

Emergency Messages. The ADAC (see *Getting Around*) runs an emergency message service for motorists. Messages to be handed in to ADAC offices or police stations. Emergency messages received from abroad will be broadcast nationally; if you hear a message that might concern you, contact the Hessischer Rundfunk (069-15 51) for details.

Health and Hygiene

For general information on hygiene, first aid, insurance and medical treatment, see the introduction.

Hygiene. Germany is a very clean country; tap water is all drinkable. Public conveniences can be found in most towns, and especially at railway stations; keep some change with you, because they normally charge 0.50 DM. Some gents' urinals flush automatically when a photo-electric beam is activated.

Reciprocal Agreements. British visitors with Form E111 should take it to the local sickness insurance office (*Allgemeine Ortskrankenkassen,* or AOK, usually open only during the morning from Monday to Fridays) who will issue a sickness certificate (*Krankenschein*) and a list of doctors and dentists who will give free treatment. Surgery hours are usually 10-12 am and 2.30-4.00 pm (closed Wednesday afternoons). In emergencies, find a doctor with *Alle Kassen* on his name plate, pay him for his treatment, and take his receipt to the AOK; the AOK will give you the *Krankenschein*, which you then take to the doctor for a refund. If you need hospitalisation, the doctor will give you a certificate (*Notwendigkeitsbescheinigung*), which you take the AOK, who will give you another certificate (*Kostenübernahmeschein*) entitling you to treatment on a public ward. You must pay a small charge per day from the start of hospital treatment for a maximum of 14 days. If necessary, the hospital can obtain this certificate direct. There is a nominal charge for prescribed medicines.

Emergencies. Each town has its duty rotas (*Notdienst*), for pharmacies (*Apotheken*), doctors (*Arztlicher*), dentists (*Zahnärztlicher*) and anti-poison (*Gift-Informations*). These are given in local papers; or look up the enquiry numbers at the head of the town listings in the telephone directory. The almost universal number for the ambulance service is 112.

Nightlife. Germany is the home of classical music, which still plays a major role — in the form of concerts, opera and ballet — in the country's nightlife. There's also cinema, theatre and pop concerts; reductions for students in many places, but not on Saturday nights. Films are nearly always dubbed into German.

Every large town has its discos and nightclubs, whether they offer music, cabaret or strip-tease. The most notorious area for the latter is St. Pauli in Hamburg, where life goes on until dawn. If you're still up that late, visit Hamburg's fish market, which comes to life about 6 am.

Museums and Galleries. The best museums and galleries are in Berlin and Munich. There's nearly always an entrance charge of 3-8 DM, often with reductions for students.

Eating out. Three-courses set lunches in restaurants start at about 16 DM (£5.60 or $9), but a simple *Bratwurst* or *Currywurst* and chips, in an inn or cafe, should keep you going for 6 or 8 DM. Greek, Italian, Turkish and Yugoslav restaurants are cheaper than their domestic counterparts. Department stores like *Hertie* and *Karstadt* usually have cheap restaurants on the top floor; station canteens are good value but often seedy and hang-outs for drunks. The cheapest of all is a *Schnellimbiß* or *Imbißstuß*, where you often have to stand or sit up at the bar. In large towns, try eating at the university or college canteen — known as *Mensa* — where no identity is required; they're all self-service and cheap. *Wienerwald* and the ubiquitous *McDonalds* offer reasonably cheap and standardized fare all over West Germany.

Drinking. Both beer and wine are drunk with meals; *Schnaps* before dinner; and quite often a liqueur after. Many Germans tend to drink in their homes rather than go out. Unless you drink in one of the *Imbißstuben,* where you almost always have to drink at the bar, you normally sit at a table and wait for service. A small glass of beer (0.2 litre) costs around 3 DM; the same measure of wine, about 4 DM. Some bars (*gasthof* or *kneipe*) close at 1 am, but others are open (and noisy) till the early hours of the morning.

Smoking. There are many different German brands of cigarettes, which are comparable to American and English cigarettes. They cost about 4 DM for a packet of 20. The cheapest cigarettes are the own-label brands sold by supermarkets. Supermarkets are also the best place to look for cheap disposable lighters, sometimes as cheaply as 2 for 1 DM. Germany is a good place to buy English cigarette rolling tobacco: a 50 g packet of Old Holborn will be about will be about half the UK price. American brands are available but slightly more expensive. If you want some in the middle of the night, you should have no trouble finding machines in the streets, with a wide selection. They take 1, 2 and 5 DM coins.

Police. The police are polite and helpful, apparently because they have such an easy life keeping an eye on a nation of law-abiding citizens. However, if you do break the law, don't expect to get away with it, even if the policeman seems very friendly and jovial about it. With memories of the Baader-Meinhof activities, it's wisest to avoid any sort of demonstration.

Rights and Responsibilities. Under German law, all liabilities are apportioned to the people involved, and nothing can be written off as an accident. This applies not only to road accidents, but to any series of events that result in damage. Parents are deemed responsible for their children, teachers for their charges, etc. To be on the safe side, take out an all risk liability insurance policy — most Germans do.

If you do get taken in by the police, you are not obliged to say anything or make a statement. The police must provide an interpreter if there's a language barrier. They also have to tell you the specific charge against you.

Nude Bathing. Permitted in specially marked zones on certain North Sea and Baltic beaches and on the shores of many lakes. Public baths often have hours set aside for nude bathing.

Driving Offences. Expect on-the-spot fines for speeding, minor offences, and things like hitching on motorways and sleeping on motorway verges. Although even the sanest looking citizen will call you a maniac for crossing the road against a red light (even with no traffic in sight), it is very rare for the police to take any action apart from a strict admonition. The permitted alcohol level for driving is 80 mg/100 ml. Serious cases are likely to involve imprisonment and confiscation of licence.

Drugs. Two years for possession, ten years for supply. Foreigners are not allowed bail, and cases may take six months to come to trial. In theory, a small (unspecified) amount of cannabis for personal use is permissible, but you are not advised to test this particular legal loophole.

Legal Aid. If you can't afford a lawyer, the court is obliged to appoint one for you — although these lawyers are likely to be inexperienced. Embassies and consulates, and liaison officers at British, American or Canadian army bases, may be able to help.

For general information on contacts and complaints procedures, see the introduction.

Embassies and Consulates.
British Embassy, Friedrich-Ebert-Allee 77, 5300 Bonn 1 (0228-23 40 61).
British Consulates General in Düsseldorf, Frankfurt am main, Hamburg and Munich; Honorary Consulates in Bremen, Freiburg and Stuttgart.

American Embassy, Deichmanns Ave, 5300 Bonn (0228 33 91).
American Consulates General in Bremen, Düsselforf, Frankfurt am Main, Hamburg, Munich and Stuttgart.

Canadian Embassy, Friedrich-Wihelmstr. 18, 5300 Bonn 1 (0228-23 10 61). Canadian Consulates General in Düsseldorf, Hamburg and Stuttgart.

Lost Property. For articles lost in any form of transport, apply to the appropriate office or station. Otherwise, go to the police. Some large cities have a special lost property office (*Fundamt* or *Fundbüro*). Anything lost on motorways, or at motorway rest areas, should find its way to the ADAC, Am Westpark 8, Munich (Tel: 089-76 76 0).

Baby-sitting. Ask at your hotel, or look in the local paper under *Nebenbeschäftigung*. In university towns, try the university notice boards.

Information. The head office of the German National Tourist Office is: *Deutsche Zentrale für Tourismus* (DZT), 6 Frankfurt, Beethovenstr. 69. Each town and region has its own tourist office (*Verkehrsamt*) often in or near the railway station. Some addresses are: 1, Bieberhaus, Hamburg; Ernst August-Platz 8, Hanover; Sandlingn Str. 1, Munich; Am Hauptbahnhof, Frankfurt.

Free Maps. From tourist offices. For smaller scale road maps those on sale at *Aral* garages (about 3 DM each) are probably the best deal. A free leaflet *Autobahn Service,* with maps, is available at all Autobahn service areas, or from the *Gesellschaft für Nebenbetriebe der Bundesautobahnen m.b.H.,* Poppelsdofer Allee 24, 5300 Bonn 1 (Tel: 0228-70 91).

Help. If you're feeling suicidal, you'll get sympathy looking up *Telefonseelsorge* in the directory. Release have offices in several towns, including: Sielwall 7, Bremen (Tel: 0421-78 52 8); and karolinenstr. 7-9 Hamburg (Tel: 040-43 45 41).

Disabled Travellers. The German association *Hilfe für Behinderte,* Kirchfeldstrasse 149, 4000 Düsseldorf produces a hotel guide and a holiday guide for the handicapped (both in German).

Student Travel. The German Student Travel Service (*RDS*) main offices are: Maximilianstrasse 22/V, Bonn (Tel: 65 29 77); Von-Melle-Park 5, Hamburg 13 (Tel: 44 23 63); Karlstrasse 39, Karlsruhe 1 (Tel: 2 07 42); and Dachauer Strasse 149, Munich 19 (Tel: 19 53 53). *ARTU Studenten Reisen,* Schulterstr. 22, 2000 Hamburg 13; *Studiosus Reisen,* Luisenstr. 43,8000 München 2 (Tel:500 600).

English Bookshop. The British Book Shop, Borsenstr 17, 6000 Frankfurt 1.

English Language Churches. Tourists are welcome at services on the British Canadian and American bases. Civilian churches include the Church of Christ the King (American Episcopal), Sebastian-Rinz Strasse 22, Frankfurt (Tel: 55 01 84); St. Thomas á Becket (Anglican), Zeughausmarkt, Hamburg (Tel: 31 28 05); Church of the Ascension (American Episcopal), Clemensstr. 58, Munich (Tel: 64 81 85).

American Express. Steinweg 5, Frankfurt-am-Main (Tel: 21051); Promenadplatz 6, Munich (21990); and offices in Berlin, Bonn, Bremen, Cologne, Düsseldorf, Hamburg, Hannover, Heidelburg, Stuttgart and Wiesbaden.

Calendar of Events

Public Holidays are shown in **bold**; those marked * are not observed in all *Länder*

January 1	**New Year's Day**
January 6	**Epiphany**
March/April	**Good Friday, Easter Monday**
May 1	**Labour Day**
May	**Axcension Day**
May/June	**Whit Monday**
May/June	**Corpus Christi***
June 17	**Day of Unity**
June	Mozart Festival at Würzburg
late June	International Film Festival at Berlin
	Sailing Regattas at Kiel
July	*Kinderzeche,* Children's Festival at Dinkelsbühl
July-August	Opera Festival at Munich
	Richard Wagner Festival at Bayreuth
August	Motor Racing Grand Prix at Nürburgring
mid August	Fireworks display at Koblenz
August 15	**Assumption Day***
late August	Horse Racing Week at Baden-Baden
	Wine Festival at Rüdesheim, Winningen and Mainz
September	Berlin Festival
	Wine Festivals at Bernkastel-Kues and Bad Durckheimk
September/October	*Oktoberfest* Beer Festival at Munich
	Beer Festival and Folk Festival at Stuttgart
	Heidelberg Autumn Fair
October	Wine Harvest Festival at Neustadt/Weinstrasse
	Freimarkt Folk Festival at Bremen
November 1	**All Saints' Day**
early November	Berlin Jazz Festival
November/December	Hamburg Folk Festival
late November	**Day of Prayer and Repentance***
to December 24	*Christkindlsmarkt* Christmas Fair at Nürnberg
December 24, 25	**Christmas Day, St Stephen's Day**

West Berlin

Although fully integrated economically into West Germany, West Berlin is not politically part of the Federal Republic. Unlike West Germany, it is nominally controlled by the Allied powers, and its representatives in Bonn have no voting rights. However, much of what has been said for West Germany also goes for West Berlin.

City Transport. Buses, the S-Bahn (suburban elevated railway) and the U-Bahn (underground railway) are run by BVG, Potsdamer Strasse 188 (Tel: 2 16 50 88 for information). Tickets are interchangeable and allow transfers between all three modes of transport within a two-hour period: this can include the return journey. Both the U-Bahn and S-Bahn extend into East Berlin, and tickets bought in one sector are valid in the other. Multi-ride tickets, tourist passes and monthly cards are available at Kleistpark and Zoo stations.

Broadcasting. BFBS — 98.75 MHz VHF; AFN — 87.85 MHz VHF (24-hour stereo); AFN-Television — Channel 29. BFBS broadcasts some BBC material including *The Archers*.

Useful Addresses and Numbers. ADAC breakdown service — 86 86 86.
British Consulate, Uhlandstrasse 7-8 (Tel: 3 09 52 92).
US Mission, Clay-Allee 170 (Tel: 8 32 40 87).
Canadian Consulate, Europa-Center (Tel: 2 61 11 61).

Tourist Office, Europa-Centre, Budapester Str. (Tel: 030 212 34). Open from 07.30-22.30. Offices can also be found at the airport, Zoo, Station and at the Dreilinden frontierpost: all are open from 08.00-23.00.
German Student Travel Service (RDS), Hardenberg Strasse 9 (Tel: 3 12 10 42).
Release, Albrechtstrasse 41 (Tel: 7 92 37 42).
American Express, Kurfürstendamm 11 (Tel: 8 82 75 75).

TRANSIT FROM WEST GERMANY

Please check the chapter on *East Germany* for currency controls, etc.

Air. No visas are necessary (since flights from West Germany are effectively internal), therefore flying is the only means of reaching West Berlin for holders of British Visitors Passports and Irish Visitors Cards. Flights are run by British Airways, Pan Am and various British, French and American charter operators (but not, for political reasons, by Lufthansa). For destinations outside West Germany, a departure tax of 11 Dm is payable by passengers aged 12 and over. The 8 km from Tegel Airport to Berlin takes 20 minutes by bus to the zoo at Hardenbergplatz. The Tegel number for flight information and enquiries is 41 01. Foreigners may also use Schönefeld Airport in East Berlin, reached by bus (at least two hours before flight departure) from the Funkturn terminal at Messedam 8 (Tel: 302 52 67).

Rail. There are five routes open, using border crossings at: Büchen (from Kiel and Hamburg); Helmstedt (from Cologne and Hanover); Bebra (from Frankfurt); Ludwigsstadt (from Stuttgart); and Hof (from Munich). Other lines may not be used for travel to West Berlin. Visas are issued free on trains. Do not get out in East Germany.

Bus. Buses leave from about 100 points in West Germany, and use, from south to north, the roads E6 (crossing at Rudolphstein); E70 (Herleshausen); E8 (Helmstedt); and E15 (Gudow). Free group visas are issued.

Car. West German cars may use the four roads listed above, but foreign vehicles may only use the E6 and E8. Non-Germans pay 5 DM for a one-way transit visa; 10 DM return (either route). for rules of the road, see under *East Germany*. Other hints: stop only at the specified service areas (where DM may be used), but not at those marked for buses only. Do not stray from the main road. Do not disseminate literature (this includes giving away, leaving or even throwing away newspapers or magazines). Do not pick up passengers in East Germany, or otherwise give the impression of helping East Germans to escape (this includes chatting to them at service areas).

Hitch-Hiking. Note the above regulations, and make sure you get a lift going all the way. The best routes are the E6 and E8. Try the Helmstedt (E8) or Münchberg (E6) service areas. A *Berlin* sign will help. A sign is also necessary for hitching out of Berlin. Try the Dreilinden frontier post (U-Bahn to Oskar-Helene-Heim, then bus 18), reckoned to be the best hitching spot in Europe.

DAY TRIPS TO EAST BERLIN

Despite the dramatic changes which took place in the German Democratic Republic in December 1989 the regulations concerning day trips to East Berlin have not been greatly affected at the time of going to press. Changes are anticipated, however, so before planning a trip check with Berolina Travel, the GDR's tourist representative (22a Conduit Street, London W1 (Tel: 071-629 1664). There are differences in regulations for West Germans and foreigners, so take care if you're travelling with West Germans. Note that day visas are valid for East Berlin only; for areas outside the city, a full visa or a transit visa is required.

Points of Entry. Friedrichstrasse Station for entry by U-Bahn. On foot or by car, non-Germans must use Checkpoint Charlie on Friedrichstrasse. By bus, Germans and foreigners can travel together — the three authorised bus tour operators are Berliner Bären (Tel: 883 60 02), Berolina (Tel: 213 40 77) and Severin & Kühn (Tel: 883 10 15), all on Kurfürstendamm.

Time Limits. Visitors can cross into East Berlin between 6 am and 8 pm, but must return via the same crossing by midnight. A day visa can be extended at offices of the Reisebüro der DDR, provided you book accommodation at the same time (normal minimum £40 ($64). Friedrichstrasse station is open 7 am-midnight; Checkpoint Charlie is open 24 hours.

Costs and Currency Regulations. The permit itself costs 5 DM. You no longer have to change a minimum amount of money per day from West to East German currency. The two currencies were once officially of equal value, but you can now change West German Deutschmarks for three times their value in Ost-marks in, East German banks. It is illegal to import or export Ost-marks. No limit on imports of western currencies, but it must all be declared; make sure you can account for it all when you leave.

Great Britain

Area. 34,195 square miles

Population. 57,100,000

Capital. London (population 6,767,500).

Weather. British weather is a constant theme of idle speculation among meteorologists and laymen alike — such a constant theme, in fact, that it accounts for a high proportion of all conversations. Platitudes like "Nice day today" or "Looks like rain" have become virtually synonymous with "Hello". The reason for this perpetual interest in the weather is undoubtedly its unpredictability. While there are no extremes of temperature in winter or summer, the chances of rain, snow or fog cannot be ruled out even in summer. Warm clothing is therefore recommended for most of the year.

THE PEOPLE

The British should not be judged by the thuggish behaviour of their drunken football hooligans abroad. More usually they are polite and reserved, often to the point of shyness. Although many British people would deny it, they also tend to be conservative: the main features of the British character and way of life have survived since the days of the Empire. The monarchy and the aristocracy, for instance,and the class system in general: the House of Lords is the embodiment of the medieval principle that the ruling class is hereditary. The sense of fair play that is at the core of the British character is instilled at an early age through such phenomena as cricket and the overwhelming habit of waiting one's turn, even if it means missing the bus, or not getting a seat in the theatre. The British love the underdog which is possibly why they so seldom win and why Eddie "The Eagle" Edwards became a national sporting hero.

Politics. Britain is a constitutional monarchy, with Queen Elizabeth II as nominal head of state. But the real power lies with the House of Commons, the lower chamber of Parliament, whose members are elected by universal suffrage. Great Britain is a nation made up of four countries — England, Scotland, Wales and Northern Ireland — so be wary of generalising and calling all the British "English". The four countries have never lived really peacefully together, and today is no exception. While devolution is a purely political issue in Wales, Scotland, the Channel Islands and the Isle of Man, the situation in Northern Ireland frequently is violent and has spread to spasmodic bombings in England, theoretically against military targets but often involving civilian casualties.

Religion. The majority of Britons are Protestant, although there is complete freedom of religion. The state church is Anglican (Church of England), but others are well represented.

Language. English is universally spoken. Queen's English or Oxford English is a class distinction rather than a geographical one. The hardest accents to understand are probably those in Wales, Cornwall, Scotland and the North of England. Welsh — one of Europe's oldest languages — is still the native language in parts of Wales, but Cornish, Gaelic and Manx are no longer much in use. Irish is undergoing a revival.

Making Friends. The British are, in general, very reserved, so don't be too keen to plunge into an intense conversation. Although some members of the older generation cling to strict formality, the younger generation is ensuring that most social barriers and taboos are breaking down. Unlike other Europeans, the British have never gone in much for shaking hands — except at first meetings, or after a long absence.

See the introduction for details of passports, customs regulations, duty free allowances, vaccinations and importing pets.

Passports and Visas. A valid US or Canadian passport entitles you to a stay of up to three months but the immigration authorities can refuse entry if they are not convinced that you will be able to support yourself during your stay. Extensions are dealt with by the Immigration and Nationality Department of the Home Office, Lunar House, Wellesley Road, Croydon, Surrey (Tel: 081-686 0688), who again will require proof that you can continue to support yourself.

Customs. Customs halls are divided into red lanes (goods to declare) and green lanes (nothing to declare). If you have nothing beyond the duty-free allowances, saunter through the green lane with a clear conscience.

£1 = 100 pence (p)
£1 = $1.60 $1 = £0.62

For information on handling, raising and exchanging money, see the introduction.

Coins. 1p, 2p, 5p, 10p, 20p, 50p, £1.

Notes. £5 (blue), £10 (brown), £20 (purple), £50 (green).

Britain converted to a decimal currency in 1971, but a number of the old one and two shilling coins are still in circulation alongside the 5p and 10p coins that replaced them. This will change with the introduction of new smaller 5p coins in June 1990 and 10p coins in June 1992.

Not listed above are the crown (a 25p coin) and the £2 coin which are issued on a commemorative basis; they are legal tender but are not in general circulation.

Although English money can be used anywhere in the United Kingdom, there are separate coins minted in the Channel Islands, the Isle of Man and Northern Ireland. These can only be used on their territory. Scotland issues its own banknotes, which are used alongside English ones. These are usually accepted in shops outside Scotland, but if there is any problem they can be exchanged for English notes in any bank.

Banking hours. All banks are open from 9.30 am to 3.30 pm Mondays-Fridays, and in larger towns some branches may be found open until 4.30 pm on weekdays and from 9.30 am to 12.30 pm on Saturdays. Some are even experimenting with opening on Saturday afternoons, until 3.30 or 4.30. Outside these hours it should be possible to obtain a cash advance with a Visa or Mastercard credit card through the ubiquitous cash dispensers. Changing money at weekends is a particular problem (outside London, where there are many commercial exchange bureaus open on Sundays) since hotels are increasingly reluctant to empty out their tills. Airports have exchange bureaux open every day, and there's a seven-day bureau at Victoria Station in London. Thomas Cook have shops in many towns and are open on Saturdays: some are also open on Sundays. In Scotland and Northern Ireland banks close 12.30-1.30 pm for lunch.

Shopping Hours. Variable but approximately 9 am-5.30 pm Monday-Saturday, with some shops in smaller towns closing from 1 to 2 pm at lunch time. Smaller towns may also have an early closing day, when many shops will close at 1 pm. Many large stores and supermarkets stay open late on Thursdays and/or Fridays especially in London.

Import and Export. There are no restrictions on the import or export of foreign currency.

Tipping. Restaurants and hotels — often included in the bill, otherwise 15%. Pubs — don't tip at all, but if you want to show appreciation to the barman (or barmaid), offer him (or her) a drink. Porter — not so common any more: they have no fixed charges, but usually accept a tip of about 50p per item. Taxis — 10%. Hairdressers — at your discretion; give 10% if you think they have deserved it.

Emergency Cash. Street-selling and busking are illegal without a licence, although buskers are often seen in underground stations and around theatre queues. Blood is donated, not sold. You aren't allowed to work without a work permit, and unofficial job prospects are not good except in London hotels at cut-price wages.

Taxes. Value added tax (VAT) of 15% on most goods and services.

The information in this section is complementary to that given in the corresponding section in the introduction.

CAR

British roads are fairly crowded, having more cars per mile than most European countries. Driving in London should be avoided unless absolutely necessary, especially at rush hour when it has been estimated that traffic moves at an average of 11 miles per hour. London now has the M25, an orbital ring-road, but even that can get congested at peak hours. The motorway network links all the major towns and is being constantly extended. There are no toll roads, except on certain strategic bridges and the Dartford Tunnel. You can obtain a free windscreen sticker saying *Visitor to Britain* from the AA or RAC; it doesn't give you any special privileges, but it does warn other drivers to expect the unexpected.

Requirements. National or international driving licence; green card insurance; log book and any relevant registration documents. Headlamps must be dipped to the left.

Rules of the road. Drive on the left, overtake on the right. This takes a while to get used to, and, if you don't concentrate, you're likely to find yourself on the wrong side when you're coming off junctions and roundabouts, especially if there's no other traffic around. At roundabouts, priority is given to vehicles already on the roundabout. Headlamps must be used in fog or poor daylight conditions. It is compulsory to wear seat belts in the front seats of a car and children aged under 14 must wear seat belts in the back seats where they are fitted.

Speed Limits. 70 mph on motorways; 70 mph on divided roads; 60 mph on other roads; 30 mph in built up areas with street lighting, unless 40 (mph) signs are posted.

Parking. Meters are in operation in London and most other cities; there are no standard rates, but expect to pay at least 50p an hour (or £1 in London). Meters may take 10p, 20p, 50p or £1 coins, depending on their age. It is illegal to "feed" a meter — ie to go back and put more money in when the time has almost expired. Meters have maximum time limits of one hour, two hours or four hours. Many towns have disc parking, usually free, with time limits — discs available from police stations, information offices, hotels or traffic wardens. Cars parked illegally in London risk being clamped — temporarily immobilised, with a fine to pay before you are released.

Petrol. Petrol in Britain in now sold by the litre, although most British drivers think in terms of gallons. Leaded petrol is only available at 98 octane, known as four star, and sells for about 42p a litre (£1.89 per UK gallon, $2.52 per US gallon).

Regular unleaded petrol (95 octane) is almost universally available, and costs about 5% less than four star; the recently introduced super unleaded (98 octane) costs somewhere between the two. You can save 5%-10% by shopping around for the cheapest petrol.

Touring Clubs. AA (Automobile Association), Fanum House, Basing View, Basingstoke, Hampshire RG21 2EA (Tel: 0256-20123). RAC (Royal Automobile Club), RAC House, M1 Cross, Brent Terrace, London NW2 1LT (Tel: 081-452 8000). Both of these offer many of their services free to members of foreign motoring organisations.

Accidents and Breakdowns. Motorways have emergency telephones every mile to contact the police for assistance. The police must be contacted in case of accidents. Elsewhere, dial the emergency number — 999 — for police, an ambulance or the fire brigade.

TRAIN

All train services are run by British Rail, which is currently state-owned but which the government plans to privatise (which may lead to severe price increases in the interests of profitability). Information about services can be found and bookings made at the main London stations (the telephone number for Victoria is 071-928 5100) or at the British Travel Centre, 12 Regent Street, London SW1 (Tel: 071-730 3400 between 9 am and 6.30 pm Mondays-Saturdays). Reservations are not usually necessary but are recommended for longer journeys unless you are prepared to stand. Trains are divided into two classes: First costs 50% more than Standard. Standard fares per mile vary according to the distance travelled but average out at 14p (22c) per mile.

London has a number of main line termini, each serving a different part of the country — Liverpool Street for East Anglia; Kings Cross for the North East and Scotland; St Pancras for the East Midlands; Euston for the West Midlands, the North-West, North Wales and Scotland; Paddington for the West and South Wales, and Victoria, Charing Cross and Waterloo for the south. If you have to change from one of these to another allow yourself enough time to cross London by public transport.

Cheap Deals. Day returns are available for journeys of up to 50 miles and cost little more than a single. For longer distances, or if you want to return on a different day, Saver tickets save up to 40%. Higher rates are charged for Saver tickets on busier days, such as Fridays and Saturdays in summer.

For unlimited rail travel in England, Scotland and Wales, the All Line Railrover is valid for 7 or 14 days; the cost is £150 for 7 days or £240 for 14 days (standard class). Similar regional Railrover tickets are available with a validity of 7 days at costs varying from £20-£46 depending on the region.

There are a number of passes offering a better deal than the above that must be bought in your own country before you arrive in Britain. The Britrail Pass and the Britrail Youth Pass (for those aged between 16 and 26) give unlimited travel throughout Britain. The prices are: $189 for 8 days (or $169 for the Youth Pass), $285 (or $239) for 15 days, $359 (or $309) for 22 days, or $415 (or $359) for 1 month. The similar Britrail Flexipass allows travel on odd days during a set period, enabling stopovers to be made. For travel on 4 days in 8 it costs $159 (or $139 for a Youth Pass); $229 (or $199) for 8 days in 15; or $359 (or $289) for 15 days in one month. Just introduced is the BritFrance Railpass, which gives unlimited rail travel in both Britain and France and includes one round trip between the two by hovercraft. The cost is $199 for travel on 5 days in 15 or $299 for travel on 10 days in one month; children aged between 4 and 11 travel at half rate, but there is no youth equivalent for those over 11.

A Young Person's Railcard offering reductions of around 30% on fares is available to anyone under 24 and full time students: it costs £15.

BUS

When the British mention buses they are normally referring to local services: for long distance travel they use the word coach. Coach services linking 1,500 destinations in England, Scotland and Wales are operated by National Express, whose London terminal is at Victoria Coach Station, Buckingham Palace Road, London SW1. Information can be obtained and bookings made also at the Coach Travel Centre, 13 Regent Street, London SW1, the Coach Travel Centre opposite terminal 2 at Heathrow, or any of the 3,000 National Express agents throughout the UK. The main telephone number for information is 071-730 0202.

Coach fares are usually around half the equivalent train fare, but the journeys may take up to twice as long. Day return and period return tickets are available: the savings they offer vary from route to route. You are recommended to book in advance (for which there is an extra charge of £1.20) to be sure of a seat but if you turn up on spec you will probably get on. Most coaches now carry toilet facilities and most long-distance coaches offer refreshments.

Cheap Deals. Anyone aged between 16 and 23 can buy a Young Person's Discount Card which gives $\frac{1}{3}$ discount off standard fares. Two other passes are only open to visitors to Britain: both are obtainable from National Express agents in the UK. The *Britexpress Pass* cost £10 and gives $\frac{1}{3}$ off coach fares for a 30 day period.

The other pass, the *Tourist Trail Pass*, gives unlimited travel on coach services and is available for periods of 5, 8, 15, 22 or 30 days. Prices range from £50 for the 5 day pass to £145 for the 30 day pass.

CYCLE

Cycles can be hired in most large towns: bike dealers who hire out bikes will normally state so in their entry under Cycle Shops in the Yellow Pages. Expect to pay around £5 a day or £10 per week; the longer you hire a bike for the cheaper it should be.

The Cyclists Touring Club at 69, Meadrow, Godalming, Surrey GU7 3HS (Tel: 04868 7217) produce various publications about cycling in Britain and will give free information to members of affiliated cycling clubs abroad.

HITCH-HIKING

The pace is good but certain strategic points, like exits from London, can get choked with hitch-hikers. Hitching on motorways is illegal.

Recommended reading: Simon Calder's *Hitch-hikers Manual Britain,* which contains motorway maps and guides to around 200 towns, as well as general advice on how to set about hitching. The book costs £3.95 and is published by Vacation Work, 9 Park End Street, Oxford OX1 1HJ (Tel: 0865 241978).

CITY TRANSPORT

Taxis. Taxis come in two varieties: licensed and unlicensed — not that the unlicensed ones are in any way illegal. The practical differences between them are that licensed taxis carry standardised meters and can be hailed on the street. Unlicensed cabs (known as mini-cabs) can only be hired by telephone and their meters may vary from company to company. In London, bulbous taxis, the majority of which are black, are licensed by the Metropolitan Police Office and others aren't. London taxis base their charges on a combination of the distance travelled and the time it takes, with a minimum fare of £1.00 (which would take you around 1152 yards) and a subsequent rate of circa 20p per every 384 yards until the fare exceeds £6.00, thereafter charging 20p per 256 yards. They are legally allowed to refuse to take you if you wish to travel over six miles or for a destination outside the Metropolitan Police District. Taxis at Heathrow Airport must accept hirings of up to 20 miles within the Metropolitan Police District. In this case, if you wish to travel outside the Metropolitan Police District and the driver agrees, you must negotiate the fare with the driver before entering the cab, as fares charged outside the Metropolitan Police District do not run on the meter. Within Greater London the fare indicated on the meter remains in force whether you travel six or over six miles.

Bus/Underground. In London both bus and underground (known as the tube) services are run by London Regional Transport, whose central office is at 55 Broadway, London SW1. A 24 hour information service is available on 071-222 1234; for recorded details of how services are actually running phone London Travelcheck on 071-222 1200.

There are information centres in the underground stations at Piccadilly Circus, King's Cross and Heathrow Central Terminals 1, 2 and 3. These centres hand out a free map and guide to both underground and bus routes which will prove invaluable in making sense of the system.

Fares are calculated by dividing London into five concentric zones, the middle zone (1) covering central London. Both bus and underground services in central London are full to capacity, and so fares for journeys including travel inside the central zone are higher than those for journeys of equal length outside it to encourage people to use alternative routes. Bus fares for a journey including the central zone start at 70p for one zone, rising to £1.50 for a journey through five zones. There is a cheaper fare of 50p for a journey of up to three quarters of a mile. Underground fares from the central zone begin at 70p for one zone and rise to £2.10 for five zones.

Bus tickets are bought from the conductor, or driver on a one-man operated bus. For underground tickets most stations now have self-service ticket machines, although there will normally also be a manned ticket window. Ticket machines take coins ranging from 5p to £1, and will issue change with the ticket if necessary.

Some large ticket machines will also take £5 notes. To enter and leave the tube system you put your ticket into the slot next to the automatic gates, magnetic side down.

Regular bus and tube services in London run from 5.30 or 6 am until 11.30 pm or 12.30 am; the last tube services leave central London at around midnight (boards at tube stations state at what time the last trains leave). There are a number of special night bus services running from Trafalgar Square and the West End across London into the suburbs between midnight and 6 am.

Cheap Deals. There are special passes for visitors from abroad called Visitors Travelcards that offer almost unlimited travel by bus and tube and come with discount vouchers to attractions such as London Zoo and Madame Tussauds. They can only be bought from British Tourist Offices and travel agents abroad, and cost $15 for 3 days, $21 for 4 days or $35 for 7 days.

People already in England can buy a range of daily, weekly, monthly or annual Travelcards that give free travel by bus and underground. Those travelling after 9.30 am can buy a one day Travelcard valid for all 5 zones for £2.60, or just 3 zones for £2.30. Weekly, monthly and annual Travelcards can be bought to cover from 1 to 5 zones: a card covering all 5 zones for one week costs £19.70.

Those not interested in using the underground can choose from a range of different bus passes but not, unfortunately, a one day pass that covers bus travel only including travel in the central zone. A seven day bus pass covering all zones costs £12.50.

See the introduction for information on youth hostels, other hostels, and advance booking of accommodation.

The national tourist boards for England, Scotland and Wales grade hotels — and accommodation offered by inns, motels, guesthouses, farmhouses and bed and breakfasts — by a system known as the Crown Scheme according to the facilities and services offered. There are six levels, from Listed to 5 Crown. A further grading system to indicate the quality of what is offered has just been introduced: the categories are Approved, Commended and Highly Commended.

Hotel accommodation varies enormously in price and costs more in big cities. You have a good deal if you find a single room for £15 ($24) or a double for £20 ($32). In central London you may find prices at that level around Russell Square or near Victoria Station, or slightly further out in Bayswater or Earls Court: advertisements for cheap hotels can be found in the "what's on" weekly *Time Out,* available on any news stand, or in the giveaway magazine *TNT* that can be picked up in pubs around Earls Court.

Room prices almost always include breakfast — in the more expensive hotels this usually means a light continental breakfast, but in cheaper establishments, including pubs and guest houses, you'll get a full English breakfast — bacon and eggs, sausages, tomatoes, and piles of toast and marmalade, washed down with as much tea as you can drink.

Pubs. British pubs are a unique institution, whose main function is to serve drinks. A wide range of pubs now offer accommodation at prices from about £15 for a double room, although they can be much higher in tourist areas. For a real taste of England try rooting out a small pub in an out-of-the-way village. You'll be given a warm welcome, and sent on your way with one of the best breakfasts you can remember.

Guest Houses/Boarding Houses. The choice of other accommodation includes farms, guest houses and boarding houses — basically private houses which offer accommodation for from about £8.50 per person per night, including an English breakfast. All advertise their accommodation with a large Bed and Breakfast sign: before you ring the bell, look for a Vacancies (or No Vacancies) sign in the window.

Youth Hostels. There are over three hundred Youth Hostels around Britain, with prices for an adult varying from £3.20 to £9.00 per night depending on the standard of the Hostel. The YHA head office for England and Wales is at Trevelyan House, 8 St Stephen's Hill, St Albans, Herts (Tel: 0727 45047); for Scotland contact the Scottish Youth Hostels Association, 76, Glebe Crescent, Stirling FK8 2JA (Tel: 0786 51181); for Northern Ireland contact the Youth Hostel Association of Northern Ireland, 56 Bradbury Place, Belfast BT7 1RU.

Camping. Prices on camp sites begin at around £5 per night for a tent, with a further charge for a car, on a site with reasonable facilities. Details of over 750 sites can be found in the British Tourist Office publication "Where to stay — Camping and Caravan Parks in Britain" (£3.95 from bookshops or tourist offices). Information on camping in Britain can be obtained from the Camping and Caravan Club, 11 Lower Grosvenor Place, London SW1W 0EY (Tel: 071-828 1012). In the country you may find a farmer who is willing to let you camp in a corner of a field for a couple of pounds a night. London's most famous camping ground is *Tent City,* Old Oak Common Lane, East Acton, London W3 7DF (Tel: 081-743 5708) with over 450 bunks in 14 marquees (£4 per night).

Sleeping out. Can be cold and wet, but is not illegal unless you do not have any money in which case you can be arrested for vagrancy. Local bye-laws may prohibit sleeping out in public places: the police do nightly round-ups in the major London parks.

Finding & Booking Accommodation. Lists of accommodation are available from the British Tourist Authority Offices overseas or from national and regional tourist boards in Britain. (These are usually in the form of saleable guides). The 800 or so tourist information centres in Britain also have accommodation lists, including caravan and camping parks and these are usually free. Tourist information centres will often book accommodation locally or at your next stop for you for a small fee as will the British Travel Centre in 12 Regent Street, London SW1 Tel: 071-730 3400. The tourist information office at Victoria Station will also book accommodation in London. Alternatively, you could use an agency, listed in the Yellow Pages under *Hotel Booking Agents.* If you want to make your own reservations, the appropriate headings in the Yellow Pages are *Guesthouses, Hotels, Inns* and *Motels.* Don't bother with the long list of *Public Houses* — the ones that have rooms will also be listed under *Inns* or *Hotels.*

General information on telephones and English language newspapers and radio broadcasts is given in the introduction.

Post. Mail boxes are red and either stand on the kerb or are built into a wall. Stamps are sold at post offices. Opening hours may vary but are generally Monday-Friday 9 am-5.30 pm and 9-12 am on Saturdays. In central London, the Trafalgar Square post office at 24/28 William IV Street, London WC2N 4DL is open from 8 am-8 pm Monday-Saturday. Stamps are also available from shops displaying the "Royal Mail Stamps Sold here" stickers and from stamp machines outside some post offices.

For certain denominations there are separate country issues in Wales, Scotland and Northern Ireland. These are valid, alongside English issues, in all parts of the United Kingdom. But the Channel Island and the Isle of Man are quite independent postally, and have no such mutual arrangements.

Poste Restante. Free service at main post offices. Letters addressed simply Post Restante, London, will go to the King Edward Street post office just north of St Paul's Churchyard.

Philately. Special philatelic counters at main post offices in most large towns. Commemorative stamp issues come out about eight times a year (usually on a Tuesday). Full details from the British Philatelic Bureau, 20 Brandon Street, Edinburgh EH3 5TT.

Telephone. There are a few telephone kiosks run by Mercury, a private telecommunications company, but most are run by British Telecom. Most British Telecom kiosks are red and will take either coins or a pre-bought phonecard (available in denominations of £1, £2, £4, £10 and £20 from post offices and newsagents). Booths taking cash will accept any coin except the 1p. There are three rates: peak rate (9 am-1 pm Monday to Friday), standard rate (8 am-9am and 1 pm-6 pm Monday to Friday) and cheap rate (all other times). Calls are more expensive if, for any reason, you have to go through the operator. Also, if you have a telephone in your hotel room, be warned that they are allowed to charge up to 100% extra for the calls you make.

To make a call from a public telephone, first insert money (at least 10p) then dial. If there is no reply your coins will be refunded when you replace the handset. When you are speaking on the phone a meter will show you how much credit you have left, and so you can see when to insert more money. If you have any credit left when you finish your call the machine will refund any unused coins, but only if you have given it small enough change to begin with: if you have paid for a 10p call with a 50p coin you will not get any change.

Essential numbers: operator — 100; directory enquiries — 192 (or 142 if you want a London number and you're calling from London); emergency — 999 and ask for police, fire or ambulance (if you ask for fire or ambulance, the police will be informed anyway); complaints — 152.

Area codes for the main cities include: London — 071 or 081; Birmingham — 021; Edinburgh — 031; Glasgow — 041; Liverpool — 051; Manchester — 061; Belfast — 0232. The international prefix is 010; for international calls through the operator, dial 100, ask for the international service, and state which country.

Directories come in two parts — white pages are the alphabetical list of subscribers, yellow pages the commercial section (usually in a separate volume). Area codes are listed in the introductory section of the white pages.

Telegrams. You can no longer send telegrams to an address inside Britain, but you can dictate a *telemessage* (dial 100) over the telephone which will be delivered to the desired address by first post the following day. Dial 100 to send a telegram abroad.

Newspapers. National dailies are broadly divided into 2 basic categories — the popular tabloids and full size "quality" newspapers. The former are generally cheaper and less news-orientated. Sunday papers are produced quite separately from their weekday counterparts and tend to be bigger and more expensive.

Broadcasting. All radio and TV programmes are run either by the BBC (funded by a licence fee: no commercials) or the IBA (independent: with commercials). There are two national BBC channels and two independent (ITV) channels in any area, one of which has its programmes produced by different companies in each region. Cable television is available in some regions, but has never really taken off. Britain has one satellite television network, Sky, which will soon be joined by another, BSB. Each of these has several channels and they should serve to widen the choice of viewing for those whose hotels have invested in receiving equipment.

The BBC has 4 national radio channels all of which broadcast on stereo fm. Radio 1 (97.7-99.5 MHz) is for pop music; Radio 2 (88-90.2 MHz) is for light entertainment including pop music for the older listener (more like muzak than adult orientated rock); Radio 3 (90.2-92.4 MHz) is for classical music and serious drama; and Radio 4 (92.4-94.6 MHz) is for news, current affairs and drama (including the Archers, the world's longest running soap opera). In August 1990 the BBC will gain a fifth national radio network covering sport and education. Independent radio does not at present have any national channels, although it will gain at least two during the 1990's. Like the BBC it does, however, have a number of local radio stations in most large towns (frequencies and programme details can be found in local papers). There will soon also be smaller community stations in cities.

Britain also has a number of illegal radio stations, known as pirates; it is technically an offence to listen to them, but prosecutions for doing so are almost unknown. Once pirate radio involved stations broadcasting from boats in the North Sea but now it more often involves small stations that spring up in cities to broadcast to particular communities, such as the Greek-Cypriot immigrant community in London. These stations are frequently tracked down and have their equipment confiscated, but normally soon spring up again as soon as they can obtain new equipment.

Health and Hygiene

For general information on hygiene, first aid, insurance and medical treatement, see the introduction.

Medical Treatment. The National Health Service provides free treatment (although some services, such as dental treatment, prescriptions and eye tests must be paid for) to all British residents and aliens from countries with reciprocal agreements, which include Australia and New Zealand. Other foreigners who have been in the country for less than six months will have to pay for treatment, although occasionally doctors will waive the charges, especially outside London. To find the address of the nearest doctor look under *Doctors* in the Yellow Pages. Accident and emergency cases are treated free for as long as the patient remains in the accident and emergency department, but if they are moved to another ward charges may be payable.

Emergencies. Chemists keep normal shop hours; in London there's a branch of *Boots* open until 8pm daily at Piccadilly Circus. Elsewhere, chemists work on a weekly duty rota, staying open each evening and for an hour or two on Sundays. The list is posted in all chemists' windows, or ask at the local police station. A second duty rota (ask the police about this one) puts one chemist in each locality on permanent 24-hour-call — but only for prescriptions marked "Urgent". For the ambulance service dial 999.

In London, 24-hour casualty services are operated at the following hospitals: University College Hospital, Gower St., London W1; St., Mary's Hospital, Praed Street, W2; and Westminster Hospital, Horseferry Road, SW1.

Entertainment

Sport. Soccer is the most popular spectator sport — played on Saturdays, September-April. The other major winter sport is rugby (in some ways similar to American football), which comes in two varieties — rugby union: an amateur game with 15 men to a side; and rugby league, the professional version, with 13 men to a side, played only in the north of England. The dominant summer sport is cricket, a slow game that outsiders find difficult to follow. County matches last three days, test matches (international) five days. The best introduction is through one of the one-day tournament matches, played on Sundays. London's two main cricket grounds are Lord's (St. John's Wood) and the Oval (Kennington).

Nightlife. The West End of London (around Leicester Square and Piccadilly Circus) probably has a higher concentration of theatres and cinemas than any other city in Europe. Prices are low and the standard is high. A few blocks further north, Soho is filled with restaurants and still has some strip clubs, despite a clean-up. To know what's on in London, try the weekly *Time Out* magazine. Advance booking is recommended for theatres if you want one of the cheaper seats. The Society of West End Theatres opens a ticket booth in Leicester Square from 2.30-6.30 Mondays-Saturdays that sells unsold theatre tickets for the same day at half price, plus a service charge of £1 or £1.24. It is not on the telephone. There are a number of ticket booking agencies that may be able to come up with a theatre ticket when the theatre box office has sold out, but you will have to pay commission on top of the face value of the ticket. Three of the largest are: First Call (Tel: 071-240 7200) for theatre and cinema; Keith Prowse for theatre tickets (Tel: 081-741 9999); and Premier Box for concerts and sport (Tel: 071-240 2245).

Museums and Galleries. Opening hours vary, so always check before you make a special trip. Nor is there any definite policy about charges. At present entrance to the British Museum (Great Russell Street), the Tate Gallery (Millbank) and the National Gallery (Trafalgar Square) is free. Entrance to the Victoria and Albert Museum in South Kensington is nominally free, but visitors are strongly encouraged to make a voluntary donation of £2. Some other national museums, such as the Imperial War Museum, the National Maritime Museum, The National Railway Museum, the National History Museum and the Science Museum do have compulsory charges; expect to pay around £2. You will normally have to pay to see special exhibitions at any museum or gallery.

Popular Music. Live music of all types from rockabilly to reggae can be found in Britain. The weekly magazine *Time Out* contains the best day to day guide to what's on in London, including thumb-nail sketches of artists who are performing. Consult the music weekly *NME* to find out who is playing where around the country.

The booking agents Keith Prowse have a special bookings number for pop music (081-741 8989) and should be able to advise you what is coming up in London. Every summer there are a number of large outdoor events, some of which have become annual events — for example the Reading Festival takes place in Berkshire every August bank holiday, for rock fans, or the Cambridge Folk Festival takes place every July. Cognescenti of folk-rock head for Fairport Convention's annual event in Cropredy in the second weekend of August every year (details from PO Box 37, Banbury, Oxfordshire).

Eating Habits. English food is notoriously plain and the subject of much mirth among the more cuisine-oriented European nations. However, three cooked meals a day are the standard fare: bacon and eggs for breakfast, a hot snack for lunch at about 12-2 p.m., and the main meal in the evening any time after six. To supplement these meals, the English are constantly drinking tea, although tea-time is officially at 4 p.m.

Eating Out. You are more likely to find Indian, Chinese, Italian, French or American style restaurants in the average British high street than a British one. For a decent standard of British cooking, such as a traditional Sunday lunch of roast beef, Yorkshire pudding, roast potatoes, your best bet will probably be the dining rooms of middle grade hotels. But these are not cheap: you can expect to pay at least around £20 ($32) for a three course meal for two with wine. For something cheaper and closer to home cooking you should look to pubs, many of which serve hot food at lunchtime and in the early evening. You can expect to pay between £2 and £4 ($3.20-$6.40) for either traditional dishes such as bangers and mash (sausages and mashed potato), a ploughman's lunch (bread, cheese, pickles and perhaps some salad), or steak and kidney pie, or more exotic fare such as chile con carne and lasagne.

Traditional English cafes, with steamy windows, and plain wooden tables and chairs have tended to get pushed out of town centres and into cheaper neighbourhoods by both high rents and competition from fast food chains. When you do come across them they should provide unadventurous but cheap and filling snacks and hot meals, or you can just linger over a tea or coffee for 50p or less (they are not licensed to serve alcohol). For good value in more exotic food many Chinese and Indian restaurants offer "businessmen's lunches" on weekdays: these are 3 course lunches with a limited menu for about £3.50.

Take-away Food. The standard British take-away is fish and chips (about £1.50) wrapped in newspaper, but Chinese establishments (£1.50-£2.00 for a main course) are providing tough competition, with Indian restaurants following suit. The growing American influence is seen in hamburger stands, McDonalds, Colonel Sanders' Kentucky Fried Chicken, Burger King, Wendy Burger and take-away pizza joints.

Drinking. For over 50 years England and Wales suffered from licensing laws which stated that pubs could only open at lunchtime and in the evening. This has now been relaxed, and pubs can now choose their own opening hours provided they fall between 11am and 11pm Mondays-Saturdays and 12am — 3pm and 7pm — 10.30pm on Sundays. At first many pubs experimented with staying open all day but once the novelty wore off many found that they were not getting enough business to justify staying open all afternoon. Now roughly one pub in four will stay open all day and the others will stick roughly to opening between 11am and 2.30 or 3pm and from 5.30 or 6pm to 11pm (or 10.30pm in some rural areas) on Mondays-Saturdays.

There is one area in Wales, the Lleyn Peninsula, that has voted to keep its pubs closed on Sundays. The situation in Scotland is even more liberal than in England and Wales, as pubs can open all day every day if they choose. Perhaps half the pubs in Scotland stick roughly to opening from 11am to 3pm and from 5pm to 11pm: some of the rest may not only stay open all day, but also remain open until the small hours. The exception to this total freedom exists in the outer islands of Scotland, where pubs are closed on Sundays for religious reasons.

Beers, wines and spirits can also be bought in many supermarkets and in special shops known as off-licences. On Sundays off-licences can only open during pub opening hours. Restaurants need a licence before they can serve alcohol; once they have obtained one they are allowed to serve drinks outside licensing hours, as long as the customer is eating a meal.

All serious drinking is done in pubs, which also double as social clubs, sometimes with live entertainment, almost always with a juke box or piped music. Pubs have at least two bars — the public bar being rude and bare and often crowded; the saloon bar (slightly more expensive) will have a bit more decor and possibly a carpet and clean upholstery. There is no such thing as waiter service. Order your drink at the bar and pay straightaway. No need to tip either.

When deciding what to drink, most Englishmen drink beer, which comes in many varieties. The British drink by the pint (a very large glass) or half pint (a normal sized glass): expect to pay around £1.20 for a pint of beer (or more or less depending on the brand and the locality — London prices are the highest in the country). English beers are served somewhat warmer than is normal in other countries. The most popular type is bitter (rather watery), but you could try brown ale (darker and sweeter) or stout (even darker and thicker, usually ordered by brand names such as Guinness or Mackeson). Or try mixtures like shandy (bitter and lemonade), black panther (Guinness and cider) or black velvet (Guinness and champagne — rather expensive!) Continental and American types of beer are lumped together under the title of lager, often with a dash of lime. Most beers are available on draught — sometimes cider as well. The British feel very strongly about their beer, and support the small breweries, which are threatened with extinction as the larger and more powerful breweries take over the market.

Smoking. Entering the Common Market has involved a change in the taxation of cigarettes; they are now taxed a standard rate per cigarette, not in proportion to their size, and so there is very little price difference between small and king size cigarettes. Packs of 20 cost around £1.50-£1.85 for a well known brand; you can save around 10p a packet by buying from supermarkets. Wherever you buy from, scan the shelves for cheaper, if less well known brands; these can be found for £1.20-£1.30 for 20.

Police. The police are generally very civilised, and you're unlikely to ever come into contact with them, apart, perhaps from asking the way. The regular "bobby" wears a tall, rounded helmet; higher ranks and traffic police wear peaked caps with a black and white checked band. Traffic wardens (who only handle parking) wear black caps with yellow bands. With the instruction of the Sex Discrimination Act of 1975, policewomen — formerly an auxiliary branch of the force — now have the same duties as men. The British police do not carry guns, only truncheons. The emergency number of the police is 999. If you look like being in a bit of trouble always promote the officer concerned. Thus you call constables "sergeant", sergeants "inspector" etc. Flattery can sometimes get you anywhere.

Laws. There is little in British law that will take you by surprise. Driving laws are fair but strictly enforced: police do not have the right to fine you on the spot — everything must go through the courts. If you are charged with an offence, the policeman has to go through a complicated ritual, including warning you that anything you say will be taken down and may be used in evidence. You don't, of course, have to say anything, nor do you have to go along to the police station unless a charge has been read against you. The police often play on people's ignorance, so it helps to know your rights.

There is still quite an active drug scene in Britain and aliens who get caught are likely to be deported. But you could get up to 14 years for pushing.

Legal Aid. If you are arrested, you're allowed to telephone a solicitor or a friend. There is a state legal aid system, whereby the court will appoint a lawyer for you if you can't afford one. For legal advice, go to the local Citizens' Advice Bureau; local community centres also offer free legal advice at weekly evening sessions — details also from Citizens' Advice Bureaux. More concrete legal assistance (as opposed to advice) can be obtained from some of the organisations listed under *Help and Information.*

Help and Information

For general information on useful contacts, churches, and complaints procedures, see the introduction.

Embassies and Consulates.

American Embassy, 24/31 Grosvenor Square, London W1 (071-499 9000).
American Consulate General, 3 Regent Terrace, Edinburgh 7 (1556 8315).
American Consulate General, Queens House, Queen Street, Belfast, (28239).

Canadian High Commission, Grosvenor Square, London W1 (071-629 9492).
Canadian Consulate, 2 St. Phillips Place, Birmingham 3 (233 2127).
Canadian Consulate, 195 W. George Street, Glasgow 2 (248 3026).
Canadian Consulate, Canada House, North Street, Belfast 1 (27365).

Lost Property. Property lost on London Transport — bus or tube — will probably end up at the lost property office at 200 Baker Street, London W1; you must apply in person. For things left in taxis, telephone the taxi company — for the black London taxis dial 071-278 1744 (the Public Carriage Office). It helps to know the taxi's number, which is printed on a disc facing the back seat. Local taxi companies, bus companies and the larger British Rail mainline stations all have their own lost property department, as do all police stations.

Baby-sitting. Almost every town has at least one agency for casual baby-sitters (look up Babysitting in the Yellow Pages). In London, one of the largest is Universal Aunts, 250 King's Road, Chelsea, London SW3 5UE (Tel: 071-351 5767). If you want someone to look after your children for long periods, or on a regular basis for a few weeks, ask at the local Social Services Department (in the council offices) for their list of registered childminders.

Information. Top of the information network is the British Tourist Authority, Thames Tower, Black's Road, Hammersmith, London W6 9EL (Tel: 081-846 9000). The four national tourists boards are: England — 24 Grosvenor Gardens, London SW1W 0ET (Tel: 081-846 9000); Scotland — 23 Ravelston Crescent, Edinburgh EH4 3EU (Tel: 031-332 2433); Wales — Brunel House, 2 Fitzaian Road, Cardiff CG2 1UY (Tel: 0222 227281); Northern Ireland — River House, 48 High Street, Belfast BT1 2DS (Tel: 0232 235906). Every large town and tourist resort has its own information centre — London has several. For information about anywhere in Britain visit the British Travel Centre, 12 Regent Street, London SW1 (Tel: 071-730 3400): it is open from 9am — 6.30pm Mondays-Fridays, and from 10am — 4pm on Saturdays and Sundays. For information about London only there are tourist information centres in the forecourt of Victoria Station, in Harrods and Selfridges department stores, Heathrow Airport underground station (Terminals 1, 2 and 3), and inside Heathrow Terminal 2.

Free Maps. Maps are available — free and otherwise — from the Tourist Boards and Information Offices. London Transport maps free from London Transport travel enquiry offices (see Getting Around). Free road maps of the whole country from Little Chef restaurants, or from Trust Houses Forte hotels or offices.

Help. If you are feeling desperate you can telephone the Samaritans for sympathy and advice. The 24 hour number for London is 071-439 2224: elsewhere consult a telephone directory.

For free advice on almost any subject, and especially on legal matters, you will find a branch of the Citizens' Advice Bureau in most towns (consult a telephone directory for addresses and telephone numbers). There are over 100 of these Bureaux in London.

The Capital Helpline is a confidential advice and information service operated by Capital Radio in London on 071-388 7575 during working hours. They attempt to answer any query, no matter how trivial or serious, or will refer you to a more appropriate organisation.

Alcoholics Anonymous (in London telephone 071-352 3001, elsewhere consult a telephone directory): a self help group for people with a drink problem.

Narcotics Anonymous: a similar organisation for people with drug problems. Their London number is 071-351 6794 during working hours in the week: they can refer callers from outside London to the nearest branch that can help.

Lesbian and Gay Switchboard (Tel: 071-837 7324) offer 24 hour help with problems and more general advice for gay and lesbian people.

The National Aids Helpline (Tel: 0800 567123) offers 24 hour advice and information on Aids.

Disabled Drivers. The AA publishes *The AA Guide for the Disabled Traveller* that lists details of suitable accommodation, adapted lavatories, etc. in England and Wales. Send an international money order for £2.95 to the AA, Fanum House, Basingstoke, Hampshire, RG21 2EA.

RADAR publish and/or distribute a wide range of material for the disabled in Britain; send an international reply coupon to them at 25 Mortimer Street, London W1 for a list of publications and prices.

Student Travel. There are two main chains of student travel offices in Britain.

Campus Travel has its main London branch (known as London Student Travel) at 52 Grosvenor Gardens, London SW1W 0AG (Tel: 071-730 0AG), with other London branches in the YHA Adventure Store, 14 Southampton Street, London WC2, in the Eurotrain Kiosk in the front concourse at Victoria Station, and in the Students' Union of University College, London, plus regional branches in Birmingham, Bristol, Brighton, Cambridge, Cardiff, Dundee, Glasgow, Liverpool, London, Manchester, Newcastle, Oxford and Sheffield.

STA Travel, the other chain, has London branches at 74 and 86 Old Brompton Road, London SW7 3LQ and 117 Euston Road, London NW1 2SX (Tel: 071-937 9921), plus regional branches in Bristol, Cambridge, Manchester and Oxford, and branches in Birmingham, Brunel, Kent and Loughborough Universities.

American Express. 6 Haymarket, London SW1 (Tel: 071-930 4411).

Consumer Rights. The law protects you against being sold goods that are unsatisfactory or wrongly described. Any complaints should first be addressed to the manager of the shop concerned. But if he takes no action, go to the local Citizens' Advice Bureau or Trading Standards Department.

Public Holidays

New Year's Day	(also January 2 in Scotland)
March 17	(St Patrick's Day: N. Ireland only)
Good Friday	Easter Monday
May Day	nearest Monday to May 1st
Spring Bank Holiday	last Monday in May (first Monday in Scotland)
Summer Bank Holiday	last Monday in August (first Monday in Scotland)
Christmas Day	
Boxing Day	

Greece

THE ACROPOLIS   W.S.

Area. 50,534 square miles   **Population.** 9,895,000

Capital. Athens (population including Piraeus: 3,100,000).

Weather. Greece boasts a seven-month summer; and sunburn is a very real danger. But it should be remembered that winter can be cold. Snow is far from unknown in the mountains, Athens suffers occasional blizzards and rain is common from the end of November to February. Skiing is popular on Mounts Olympus and Parnassus from December to April.

THE PEOPLE

Greece is the first step to the orient, and the way of life is much more leisurely than in the rest of Europe; despite joining the European Community in 1981, many Greeks don't think of themselves as Europeans. They are very easy-going people, and easy to make friends with. In country areas, a man with a regular job is the exception, rather than the rule: work is considered either as a privilege or as a curse. While the women slave away fetching water, cooking and so on, the men will be seen sitting in cafés and playing with their worry beads, ostensibly waiting for the olives or grapes to ripen. This means, of course, that there is considerable poverty, but since most of their food is home produced, it doesn't worry them too much.

Politics. Greece has been independent since 1830, when the Turkish rule was overthrown. Since then politics have been unstable, characterised by assassinations and coups. The kingdom lasted till 1967, and was finally abolished by law in 1974.

The junta, which ruled from 1967-1974, left a bitter legacy of torture, treason and murder. Since the election of Andreas Papandreou's Panhellenic Socialist party (PASOK), the political scene seems more stable; but politics is still not a safe subject for conversation, and the issue of Cyprus should be avoided.

Religion. 97% Greek Orthodox. Services are held in New Testament Greek; even if you don't understand, you're welcome to attend. Non-orthodoxes are not allowed to take part in holy communion, but you may take a piece of *antidoron,* the consecrated bread produced in coffers at the end of the liturgy. If your interest in churches is architectural, the best examples of Byzantine churches are north of the Pinios River, in Macedonia, Epirus and Thrace. There are also Muslim mosques in Thrace and Rhodes.

For such a religiously-minded community, the Greeks are also extremely superstitious, particularly in rural areas. Tuesdays are unlucky; it's also unlucky to praise someone too highly. Certain ceremonies still survive from pagan times to ward off evil spirits particularly at special events like births, marriages and deaths. The most important religious festivity is Easter (not Christmas), which is possibly a tradition dating from the pagan rites of spring.

Language. Greeks are surprised at foreigners who speak their language fluently, but they greatly appreciate stumbling attempts at it. Knowledge of Classical Greek won't mean you can converse, but it'll help you with reading. English is the most common foreign language — even in tiny villages you'll find a student on vacation, or an ex-sailor, or a one-time New York waiter, who'll speak English. French is quite widely spoken in Athens, and Italian in the once Venetian-occupied Ionian Islands and Rhodes. Many official notices are accompanied by a French translation. In any case, the Greeks are always willing to try and break the communication barrier, and won't hesitate to use sign language.

Making Friends. Some Greeks have reacted strongly against the tourist boom: a new Orthodox prayer asks for protection against "these contemporary western invaders." But most Greeks are very easy to get to know; their natural curiosity will probably break the ice. They are very proud of their hospitality, and you must be careful not to offend or patronise them. Conversations are seen as verbal duels — don't expect to change their views, and remember that the quickest way to a Greek's heart is a calculated word of abuse against the Turks.

Female tourists should be warned against Greek men, who try to shower their affections on almost any woman. Tell them you're married and waiting for your husband. Men will have little luck with Greek girls, who have an ugly brother waiting in the background ready to defend the family honour (on the other hand, many girls may invent an ugly brother to put you off). City girls, particularly students, are more emancipated in their outlook.

Red Tape

See the introduction for details of passports, customs regulations, duty free allowances, vaccinations and importing pets.

Passports and Visas. EC and North American passport holders are entitled to stay in Greece for three months. For extensions, apply, at least 20 days before the original visa expires, to the Police Authorities, or, in Athens, to the Aliens Department, 173 Alexandras Avenue, 11522

Athens (Tel: 6468 103). At the time of going to press, Greece was refusing to admit anyone whose passport indicates that they have visited the Turkish-occupied north of Cyprus since November 1984. If you arrive on a cheap charter flight, make sure you have vouchers for genuine, registered accommodation (these should be issued with your ticket). If not, you may be refused admission. Note that if you arrive on a charter flight and, during your stay, spend a night outside Greece (for example in Turkey), you will be deemed to have broken the strict conditions for charter tickets and may be refused permission to join the return flight: in other words, contrary to popular belief you are permitted to make day trips to Turkey. The important exception to this is that charter flight passengers may not take day trips from Kos to Turkey.

Customs. Some airports have adopted the red-green channel system. Otherwise, be prepared for a complete search of baggage, particularly if you enter via the Turkish border. No duty is payable on the EC alcohol and tobacco allowances given in the introduction. In addition, you may import up to 10kg of cooked food and non-alcoholic drink, five boxes of matches and two packs of playing cards. Import of firearms, cigarette papers, ammunition and parrots is restricted as is export (or even purchase) of antiquities. Import regulations for drugs (including prescribed medicines) are very strict and may require the prior permission of the Greek authorities. One unusual ruling is that it is illegal to take any medicine including codeine into Greece.

Frontier Posts. Five road frontier posts (Niki, Evzoni, Promachon, Kastania and Kipi) are open at all times, but the border with Albania at Kakavia keeps erratic opening hours.

Departure Tax. All travellers must pay a tax of around £2/$3 on leaving Greece.

100 lepta (l) = 1 drachma (dr)

£1 = 265 dr	10 dr = £0.04
$1 = 165 dr	10 dr = $0.06

For general information on handling, exchanging and raising money, see the introduction.

Coins. 1 dr, 2 dr, 5 dr, 10 dr, 20 dr, 50 dr.

Notes. 50 dr, 100 dr (red-brown), 500 dr (green), 1,000 dr (brown), 5,000 dr (multi-coloured).

Rapid political changes have produced a formidable array of coins, with the royal issues alongside the republican. Most of the older coins are now out of circulation, but watch your change carefully. There is a permanent shortage of small change, particularly in villages, so don't be alarmed to find sweets and chewing-gum as part of your change.

Banking Hours. 8am-2pm, Monday-Friday with some larger banks opening on Saturday mornings. In tourist areas, exchange desks may stay open 8am-8pm. Airports and major rail stations have pretty permanent exchange offices. The safest place outside these hours are hotels or the local office of the Tourist Police. Taxi-drivers and bar-tenders are to be avoided, because it's theoretically illegal, so there's nothing you can do if they cheat you.

Shopping Hours. Highly variable, but roughly as follows: Non-food shops are open from 9am to 5pm on Mondays and Wednesdays, from 10am to 7pm on Tuesdays, Thursdays and Fridays, and from 8.30am-3.30pm on Saturdays. Food shops are open from 9am to 2.30pm on Mondays, from 9am to 6.30pm on Tuesdays, Wednesdays, Thursdays and Fridays, and from 9am to 3.30pm on Saturdays. There may be longer afternoon opening hours in winter (on certain days of the week, varying from place to place). Newspaper kiosks (*peripteroi*) keep longer hours, mostly seven days a week, and sometimes stay open all night; they sell absolutely anything.

Import and Export. The limit on import of drachma notes is 100,000 dr in 50, 100 or 500 dr notes: the limit on export is 20,000. Money may not be mailed out of Greece in any form. No limit on import of foreign notes or travellers cheques, but a declaration must be made on entry if you plan to re-export more than $1,000; exports naturally limited to the amount imported.

Tipping. Hotels — 15-20% service included in the bill. Restaurants, cafés and bars — 15-20% included, but this doesn't go to the waiter, so leave about 10% on the table. Taxis — up to 15%, but they don't mind if you just round off the fare. Porters — 30 dr an item at stations, 50 dr per item over 50 kilos (110lbs). Cloakroom attendants: about 50 dr. Hairdressers: about 10%.

Emergency Cash. Now that Greece is a member of the EC, citizens of Common Market countries do not require work permits but others will need them. These are not granted to anyone who enters Greece and then finds a job. Unofficial casual work isn't easy to find, but there's scope in the tourist resorts for barmaids, waiters, kitchen staff and so on. If you fancy working on a boat, tout around the offices of Zea Harbour in Piraeus. If you want to chance your last pennies, the national lottery is held on Mondays, winners announced in Tuesday's papers. Tickets from kiosks and street-sellers, price 500 dr, or 100 dr for a one-fifth ticket.

Taxes. Value Added Tax at varying rates is usually included in quoted prices. Most boat fares are subject to an additional tax of 5-8%, plus embarkation tax of 110 dr.

Getting Around

Details of all public transport services in and around Greece are given in the monthly *Key Travel Guide,* sold at bookstalls for around 250 dr.

CAR

Greek drivers are not exactly known for their courtesy — in fact they drive like mad-men: witness the little old ladies in the buses, crossing themselves at every bend in the road. The spine-chilling feat of three cars overtaking each other on a hairpin bend is not uncommon. Statistically, Greek roads are the most dangerous in Europe.

Rules and Requirements. A first aid kit is mandatory. It is illegal to carry petrol in a can. The minimum driving age for foreigners is that permitted in their own country. British drivers driving their own vehicles may use a standard British licence; otherwise an international permit is required, available at ELPA frontier offices for 3,000 dr (and 2 photos) on production of your own licence. The customs officer should enter in your passport the fact that you arrived with a vehicle.

Road Signs. All town signs are printed in Greek and Roman script.

Place Names. Corfu = Kerkyra; Salonica = Thessaloniki. Otherwise, English nomenclatures are similar to the original Greek.

Parking. A huge problem in central Athens and Thessaloniki, where in parts of the Green Zones, it is illegal to stop except at a meter. If you find a meter, the cost is 20-50 dr per hour. All towns have car parks and garages charging 300-500 dr a day.

Petrol. *Regular* (90 octane) costs 75 dr a litre; *super* (96 octane) costs 80 dr a litre (£1.35 per imperial gallon, $1.80 per US gallon). Unleaded petrol is widely available at 86 dr a litre. Petrol is generally more expensive outside Athens.

Tolls. Charges on the two main motorways: Athens-Katerini — 350 dr in three stages; Athens-Patras — 200 dr in two stages.

Touring Club. Automobile and Touring Club of Greece (ELPA), 2-4 Mesogion Street, Athens (Tel: 7791 615). They offer information and assistance, and their vans patrol the main routes. Dial 174 for information.

Breakdowns. ELPA runs a 24-hour rescue service in and around major towns: the number is normally 104. If this does not work telephone ELPA on the above number for advice. The service is free of charge to members of foreign affiliated clubs; others can receive assistance by joining ELPA on-the-spot for 5,000 dr.

Long Distance Taxis. (*Agoreia*). These operate between provincial towns on a very erratic timetable, and charge a fixed rate per person per route. They can be booked or contacted at garages and petrol stations.

TRAIN

Train and many long distance bus services are run by the Hellenic Railways Organisation (OSE). Information, tickets and reservations from the head office at 1 Karolou street, 104 37 Athens (Tel: 5222 491) or 6 Sina Street, 106 72 Athens (Tel: 3624 402). For OSE bus timetable — dial 5240 519.

Greek trains don't aim for speed, comfort or reliability. But they do offer a faithful picture of travel in the 20s — OK for Eric Ambler fans. There are two classes, first being 50% more expensive than second and offering less crowded compartments. You can change from second to first on the train by paying the necessary surcharge. Some trains (in the Peloponnese and Western Macedonia) have only one class. Second class single fares are around 3 dr per km (£0.18 pr $0.30 for 10 miles). The fastest train from Athens to Thessaloniki takes a shade over seven hours and costs 1,520 dr. One-way tickets are valid only for the day and train for which they are issued. Try to book in advance and reserve a seat.

Cheap Deals. Children under 4 travel free; children 4-10 at half price. Return tickets valid one month — 20% reduction.

Unlimited travel tourist cards are available for one to five persons, with validities of 5, 10, 15, 20 or 30 days (second class only).

BUS

The biggest operator on main routes is the OSE railway organisation, but KTEL

— a consortium of private companies — is more widespread. In most towns and cities there are a number of bus termini, so it is critical to ascertain the right one in advance. OSE international coach services to Sofia, Paris, Dortmund and Istanbul leave from Larissa Station (Tel: 8213 882); domestic services depart from 100 Kifissou Street or 260 Liossion Street. The tourist office at 2, Karageorgis Servias Street gives away leaflets with full details of services. Bus fares are more expensive than second class rail fares; Athens-Thessiloniki costs around 2,500 dr for the seven hour trip. Book in advance and board the bus early; overbooking is common.

MOTORCYCLE

Easy-riding on the Athenian asphalt practically amounts to suicide, but bikes and mopeds can be hired at garages and motor repair shops in the remoter suburbs. Although light motorcycles can be lethal in city traffic, these fiendish contraptions come into their own in villages, and especially on islands, where there are bike rental shops everywhere. Expect to pay around 3,000 dr per day for mopeds, scooters etc (any sort of licence will do). You may be asked to leave your passport as a deposit, but try to avoid this. Tolls for motorcycles on motorways are half the rate for cars.

AIR

Flying will save you a few hours, maybe even a whole day, but fares are more than twice as much as on land or sea. All internal flights are run by Olympic Airways whose terminal is at 96 Syngrou Ave (Tel: 9292 111).

Airport buses leave the terminal half-hourly and take 20 minutes to Hellinikon airport, fare 100 dr. At the airport, Olympic Airways use the West terminal (flight information: 9699 221); all others use the East (9811 201). To get from one to the other you must catch a transfer bus.

HITCH-HIKING

Little long-distance traffic, so brace yourself for long waits. The scenery, and the hospitality of the people who do pick you up, will easily make up for the time lost. Heading north from Athens to Thessaloniki, take the underground to its northern terminus; west to Corinth and Patras, get bus 818 out of town to Dafni. It's worth asking the truck drivers at the docks at Piraeus if you're after a long ride.

BOAT

Boats to the islands are run by variety a companies. Most ferries carry cars; and food is provided on board, but it's usually tasteless and expensive, so take your own. There are four classes: 1-3 and tourist, which usually comes above third; third class often means benches on the deck. Fares quoted in the brochures don't include taxes, which can add up to 10% of the fare. As an example of fares Piraeus-Heraklion costs 2,000-3,500 dr per passenger for a 12-hour trip. Children under 4 travel free; children 4-10, half-price. Be warned against the month of August: the first two weeks see rough seas as the annual *meltemi* wind blows; and around the 15th (Assumption Day) boats are crowded with pilgrims travelling to and from the island of Tinos. Ferries almost always leave punctually — or even a few minutes early -but do not necessarily arrive on time.

Hydrofoil services are spreading; the largest operator is *Ceres,* who serve nearby islands from Piraeus with their "Flying Dolphins". Journeys are roughly twice as fast (and expensive) as by ship.

Any tourist agency should be able to make reservations. For up to date information on sailings from Piraeus, call the Port Authority on 4175 657.

CITY TRANSPORT

Taxis. Taxis can be found at taxi ranks in larger cities, and in the main square or bus terminal in provincial towns. A ride in a Greek taxi is an absolute must for visitors — the driver, who is almost sure to speak some English, will give you a complete rundown on all Greek affairs, and lots of advice. There are two types of taxi: those with, and those without a meter. Meterless taxis should be avoided, as they overcharge. Charges in metered taxis in Athens are: flag-down rate — 25 dr, then 34 dr per km (£0.20 or $0.30, approx a mile) within the city perimeter zone, 51 dr per km outside the perimeter. The minimum total charge is 170 dr. Waiting time (likely to be long in central Athens) costs 300 dr per hour, and there are extra charges for luggage, nights and pick-ups at stations, ports and the airport.

Underground. Athens only — tickets bought at station entrances. One line — Piraeus-Kifissia, via Omonoia Square; runs 7 am-midnight. Not to be recommended on hot days or at rush hours; the service is free before 8 am, and can be impossibly crowded. Fare of 30 dr (Omonoia to Piraeus or Kifissia); 50 dr for the whole stretch.

Bus/Trolley Bus. City vehicles operate from 5 am-1 am, except the 24-hour buses between Athens and Piraeus. Smoking is not allowed in any buses. On one-man buses you pay the driver: otherwise you enter at the back and pay the conductor. Journeys are free (and crowded) before 8 am. Tickets cost 30 dr.

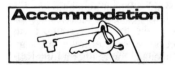
Accommodation

See the introduction for information on youth hostels, other hostels, and advance booking of accommodation.

Finding and Booking Accommodation. There's a 10% commission fee on rooms booked through a travel agent. For advance room reservations anywhere in Greece contact Greek Chamber of Hotels, 6 Aristidou Street, Athens (Tel: 3236 962). For last minute bookings in Athens, phone 3237 193, or go to the Tourist Office at 2 Karageorgi Servias Street, Outside Athens, contact the local Tourist Police.

Hotels/Pensions. There are six hotel classifications: de luxe and A-E, with minimum rates fixed for each category. E class double rooms cost from 1,570 dr (£6 or $9.50). In Patras and Thessaloniki, prices are raised by 20% during the carnival and international fair (respectively). All hotels offer discounts (up to 40%) out of season. Breakfast is not traditionally included, but A-D class hotels are allowed to charge for breakfast (around 500 dr) or demi-pension (lunch or dinner:

around 1,000 dr). You may face a surcharge of 10% if your stay is for less than three nights. Certain hotels in Athens offer accommodation on the roof for about 500 dr, which is highly recommended in summer. Ask other travellers — rather than tourist office — for current venues. Roofs apart, pensions are the cheapest solution in Athens; they are concentrated in the Plaka area, and charge around 800 dr per person per night. Out in the country they'll only cost 300 dr, with the possibility of haggling. The same applies to rooms in private homes — an ideal way of getting the feel of everyday life. Looks for *domatia* or "Rooms to Let" signs (in English, French, German or Italian). In Athens, there are some privately run hostels (about 600 dr a night) in the Syntagma Square area. Day rooms are available from noon-6 pm for half the nightly rate.

Be careful where you die; the *Guide des Hotels de Gréce* states that "in the case of the death of a visitor in a hotel, the heirs or executors are liable to pay to the hotel such expenses as may be incurred as a result of the visitor's death, including, if necessary, the redecoration or disinfection of the room and the replacement of the bedding".

Youth Hostels. Run by the Greek Youth Hostels Association, 4 Dragatsaniou St, Athens (Tel: 3237 590) A bed costs 450-650 dr. There are over 30 hotels around Greece and on the islands.

YMCA/YWCA. YMCA (known as *XAN*) at 28 Omirou Street, Athens (Tel: 36 26 970) and in Thessaloniki; YWCA (*XEN*) at 11 Amerikis Street, Athens (Tel: 36 26 180) and in Thessaloniki and Rethymnon (Crete). At the time of writing both YMCAs are closed for renovation: for the latest information contact the YMCA head office at 28, Homer and Academy Street, Athens (Tel: 3614 943).

Mountain Refuges. Maintained in most mountain areas by the Hellenic Alpine Club (HAC), 7 Karageorgi Servias Street, Athens (Tel: 3234 555), for the use of HAC members and members of many foreign alpine clubs at a normal rate (and for non-members at a higher rate). Contact the HAC for a list of refuges. For the unmanned refuges, keys must first be collected from the local HAC office.

Camping. About 90 sites. Prices 300-550 dr per person and per tent/caravan a night. No use haggling about the price at the 13 sites operated by the Tourist Organisation, but private ones are more flexible. In fact, you can pitch your tent just about anywhere, except close to archaeological sites. The main camp site for Athens is 12 km west in Dafni (bus 853 or 873). Some sites offer two, three or four-bedded huts from 1,200 dr per night.

Sleeping Out. Strictly speaking, foreign tourists are no longer allowed to sleep in the open, except in regimented enclosures termed "communal simple camping sites".

Communications

General information on telephones and English language newspapers and radio broadcasts is given in the introduction.

Post. Slow but sure seems the postal service's motto. Letter boxes are yellow and carry a table of postal rates in English. Main post offices keep normal shop hours, but branches may open mornings only. The central post office in Athens is at 100 Aeolou Street; the home of the Greek philatelic service is at 1 Apellou Street. There is a free poste restante service at all main post offices.

When writing to addresses in Greece, it is acceptable to use Latin characters. The street address should be followed by the town name and five-digit postcode; the code should be preceded by GR-when writing from abroad.

Telephones. Local calls requiring no code or prefix, can be made from the blue call boxes and from newspaper kiosks (which have no coin box, so pay the proprietor). International Direct Dialled calls can be made from ordinary telephones and special payphones with an orange ring around the top. They take only 5, 10 and 20 dr coins. The automatic dialling network is now quite extensive. The code for Athens and Piraeus is 01; Corfu City — 0661; Rhodes — 0241; Thessaloniki — 031. The international prefix is 00. The three central telephone bureaux in Athens are at 85 Patission Square (24 hours), Omonia Square Underground Station and 15 Stadiou Street (both open until midnight). Prices are cheaper between 9 pm and 5 am (6 am in winter).

The procedure for automatically dialled calls is: lift the receiver, wait for the dial tone (beeep-beeep, pause, beeep-beeep), insert at least one 10 dr coin, then dial. Unused money should be returned when you replace the receiver.

For IDD calls to UK inserts at least 20 dachma, dial 0044, dial UK area code, (minus initial 0) and local number, insert more coins on signal, check for refunds on hanging up. Dial 161 local international operator for collect and BT Chargecard calls. Any time you reach the international operator from a payphone you need a 5 drachma coin which is not returned at the end of the call.

If you can read Greek, you'll have no trouble with the directories, which come in two sections — alphabetical list of subscribers and yellow pages (hrysos odigos). Others can refer to the English language trade directory (green pages) arranged rather like the yellow pages.

Useful numbers in Athens: 1231 — information on all telecommunications services; 130 — directory enquiries (Athens); 131 — information on ex-directory numbers; 132 — directory enquiries (provinces); 151 — trunk calls; 161 — international calls; 141 — time; 148 — weather; 185 — news; 100 — police/emergency; 166 — first aid; 108 — coastguards; 171 — tourist police; 121 — out of order; 135 — complaints; 174 — motoring information; 161 — general information instructions (in English, German, French) for users of the International Telephone Services.

Telegrams. Telegrams can be sent from telephone exchanges (see above). By telephone, dial 155 but only from private telephones.

Newspapers. The Athenian English language daily *Athens News* contains job advertisements. *The Athenian* magazine is a poor imitation of the New Yorker and is useful only for its entertainment guide.

Broadcasting. Greek National Radio (ERT) broadcasts the news and weather in English on 412 m MW at 7.30am on weekdays, 15 minutes earlier on Sundays; also weather for shipping at 6.30am on Sundays, 6.35am for the rest of the week. In 1989 ERT also began broadcasting some north European satellite TV channels, to discourage Greeks from buying dish aerials.

The Greek Armed Forces Enlightenment Service (363 m MW) broadcasts the news in English each weekday at 3 and 11.05pm and at 6.35am on Sundays.

The American Forces Network runs two 24 hour radio stations on the mainland (188 m and 202 m). On Crete, AFN provides TV (channel A2) and radio (191 m).

Health and Hygiene

Vaccinations. A yellow fever vaccination certificate is required from all travellers arriving from an infected area.

Hygiene. The Greeks are clean people, at least compared with some of their neighbours. Nevertheless, it's not always advisable to drink tap water (check locally) and stomach upsets from one cause or another are not uncommon. In recent years, Greece has come pretty close to the areas infected by cholera, and typhoid.

Medical and Dental Treatment. EC citizens are entitled to treatment on the same terms as Greek nationals. In practice, this means long waits both to sort out the bureaucracy involved and to actually get treatment. Holders of E111 certificates can obtain free treatment and an 80% discount on prescribed drugs by taking the E111 to the IKA (Social Insurance Fund) office, or, in an emergency, by asking the hospital for free treatment under the IKA scheme. The IKA headquarters is at 8 Aghiou Constantinou St, 104 31 Athens. However, in remote areas and on small islands there are no IKA offices. If you have no option but to pay, you can claim a refund (whilst still in Greece) but it is likely to be less than half the total cost. Greek hospitals are not the cleanest institutions in Europe, and meals and laundry (where provided) have to be paid for.

Emergencies. Chemists are open during normal shop hours, but a number of them stay open day and night. Duty rotas are displayed in the local newspapers and in chemists' windows; or ring 107 for information. Other important numbers: 166 — for hospitals on duty; 105 — emergency Red Cross service; 7793 777 — poison clinic. 24-hour emergency service is maintained at the State Hospital, Mesogion Street (Tel: 7701 211); and the KAT Hospital in Kifissia (Tel: 8014 411).

Folklore. In the country, you're likely to find some unusual suggestions for medical treatment. Olive-oil is used as a cure for cuts, grazes and burns (including sunburn) as well as stomach upsets. Yoghurt is also suggested for sunburn (to run on, not to eat). Onions are reckoned to have medicinal qualities, and might be used in a poultice for sprains and bruises.

Entertainment

Nightlife. Greek nightlife is rather unorthodox by European standards, although in Athens you can go to cinemas (300-450 dr) (films are always shown in the original language), conventional theatres (750 dr or more with no reductions for students) and classical concerts. In the provinces, most cinemas are outdoor ones, and cost around 300 dr for a double bill. Bouzouki music is one of the most consistent elements of nightlife throughout the country, whether live, accompanied by impromptu dancing in a village square, or blaring from a juke-box loudspeaker. In the Athens area and other tourist resorts, tavernas with live (and usually drunk) bouzouki players, tend to be expensive rip-offs. Athens has a folk-dancing ensemble which performs in the open air theatre on Philopapou Hill, south of the Acropolis. Discos throughout the country close punctually at 2am.

Museums and Archaeological Sites. Greece's archaeological sites are a major attraction, and some of the most famous are within a stone's throw of the centre of Athens. Outside Athens (and the Acropolis), the most important archaeological sites are Delfi, Epidavros, Mycenae and Olympia. The most spectacular Byzantine sites are Mistra (near Sparta) and Meteora (Near Larissa). All sites have their own museums.

Sites and museums have varying hours, longer in summer than winter; many close for lunch from 12.30pm-4.00pm, or close for the day in mid-afternoon. Entrance fees are from 100-600 dr. Most museums and sites close on Mondays, and offer free admission on Sundays and holidays (when opening hours are much shorter). Fees are charged for photography.

Students get a 50% reduction at all times, but are granted free admission if travelling in a supervised group on a cultural tour. Free admission is also granted to single visitors who are professionally connected with the study of Greek antiquities (eg professors in classical studies), and members of foreign parliaments; applications for this privilege must be made to the General Directorate of Antiquities and Restoration, Museums Section, 14 Aristidou Street, Athens (Tel: 3243 056).

Eating out. Restaurants fall into four categories; 3rd, 2nd, 1st and luxury. Prices are controlled within each group — 3rd class restaurants, for instance, may charge 1000-1500 dr per meal (up to £5.50 or $9). Non-Greek restaurants (which are not common) are expensive. *Tavernas* offer a more modest decor and lower prices. There are two types — *psarotavernas* (specialising in sea-food), and *khasapotavernas* (meat and game). When taking a late lunch, beware of the effects of the siesta. The meal may well have been cooked at 11am and just reheated for you, sometimes with disastrous results. The big towns are witnessing a boom in pizza bars, steak houses and cafeterias. Not recommended; the native *moussaka* (minced lamb and aubergine), and ubiquitous *souvlaki* (kebab) are better bets. For starters try *taramosalata, houmous* or *melizanosalata,* respectively purées of cod roe, chick peas and aubergines. The correct name for the dessert popularly known as "shredded wheat with honey" is *kataifi.* The evening meal is eaten late: not before 7 or 8pm, often as late as 10 or 11pm, and even the smallest villages seem to be wide awake well after midnight.

Drinking. Non-alcoholic: tea is a rarity, always made with tea bags, and served either black or with lemon — ask for milk, and they'll think you're out of your mind. Coffee is more popular, but specify *nescafé* (around 150 dr) unless you want Greek coffee (80dr, with a free glass of water). (Turkish really). Milk fanatics must seek out the almost obsolete *galactopoleia,* which serve all kinds of milk products, including rice pudding and yoghurt.

Alcoholic: Wine is what everyone drinks. It comes in red (*kokkino*), white (*aspro*), and rosé (*kokkineli*); dry (*ksiros*), medium (*imigliko*) and sweet (*gliko*). *Demestica* and *St Helena* are the best white wines, and *Mavrodaphni* tops the reds. A special mention for *Retsina,* a white resin wine, cheapest of all, with a very idiosyncratic taste, though not at all unpleasant when you get used to it. In a food shop a half litre bottle or retsina should cost no more than a can of beer for a picnic. Beers, always served ice cold, cost about 150 dr.

The popular drinking-places are the *kafeneia,* which serve coffee, soft drinks, *ouzo* (aniseed — you know when it's been watered down because it goes cloudy), and beer, as well as light snacks. More trendy are the *zacharoplasteia* (like the Ilatian *paticcerias*), which are notoriously expensive. Along with night clubs and discos, they're the only place you can get whisky and gin. But the price — 300 dr for a glass — is unfavourable compared to 100 dr or less for a glass of ouzo in the kafeneion. If you want to buy ouzo to drink in your room it's cheapest to take your own bottle to the shop for a refill.

Licensing hours come into the same category as science fiction: the standard rule for most bars is to close when there are no more customers — often in the small hours of the morning.

Smoking. Tobacco is one of Greece's major export crops, so smoking's very cheap; it's dark tobacco, though, not Virginia. Plain cigarettes start at 110 dr a pack. Foreign brands cost a lot more, so acquire the taste of the local brands; Karelia and Papastratos filters aren't too bad. Cigars and pipe tobacco are of extremely low quality. Cigarette papers are unobtainable.

Police. The political changes of June, 1974, have taken most of the wind out of the sails of the previously powerful and omnipresent police, but their seven years of absolute power are still looked back on with nostalgia. People have been known to be held for up to a year awaiting trial. Never try to bribe them, especially the road police. The emergency number for the police is 100 or 109.

Laws. Tourists aren't likely to fall foul of the law, but drugs, nude bathing and antique smuggling are the most common pitfalls. Pocketing icons from little village churches can get you as much as five years. The Greeks are most concerned about the preservation of anything that could be described as an antiquity. Even underwater photography of antiques is an offence.

Care must be taken with hobbies such as aircraft, train and plane spotting, or even bird watching, particularly where cameras are involved. A healthy interest is sometimes misconstrued as spying.

Driving Offences. The road police (*trochaia*) are allowed to impose fines for motoring offences. Payment must be made at a central police station (or a "sub-magistrate's" court). You might run into trouble if you sell your car at random. To do it legally, you can only sell it to a non-Greek at a customs office. You must also notify the police. The alcohol limit is 0.5%. Penalties for drunken driving are loss of licence plus up to twelve months and a fine of up to 5,000 dr.

Drugs. There is no legal distinction between possession and supply; even for minute quantities of dope there is a minimum sentence of two years. The maximum is 20 years plus a fine, but can be even higher when conspiracy charges are added. Due to an unusual feature of the Greek legal system (whereby informing on someone who has committed a worse offence than you will earn a reprieve), informers are rife. Prison sentences can result from uncorroborated allegations or admissions of drug use at any time in the past. For supplying drugs to anyone under 18, the maximum penalty is life imprisonment and a 2,000,000 dr fine.

Legal Aid. There's no underground network in Greece, so no Release or similar organisations. In the past, even embassies have been pretty powerless.

For general information on useful contacts and complaints procedures, see the introduction.

Embassies and Consulates.
British Embassy, 1 Plutarchou Street, 106 75 Athens (7236 211).

British Vice-Consulates in Corfu, Crete, Patras, Rhodes, Samos and Thessaloniki.

American Embassy, 91 Vasilissis Sofias Avenue, Athens (7212 951).
American Consulate General, 59 Constantine Street, Thessaloniki (73941).

Canadian Embassy, 4 Ioannou Gennadiou Street, Athens (7239 511).

Lost Property. For things lost on any form of transport, try the head office or terminus of the company or line concerned. Athens has a lost property office at 16 Mesogion Street (Tel: 6436 460).

Baby-sitting. If your hotel can't arrange it, look up the baby-sitting agencies in the English part of the telephone directory. You could try these numbers (in Athens): 3237 190, 3222 265 and 6351 97.

Guides. Try the Union of Greek Lecturer Guides, 31 Voulis Street, Athens 118 (Tel: 3220 090).

Information. The National Tourist Office headquarters is at 2 Amerikis Street, Athens (Tel: 3223 111); 2 Karageorgi Servias Street, (Syntagna Square), Athens (Tel: 3222 545); 8 Aristotelous Square, Thessaloniki (Tel: 271 888). In most other towns, the information offices are manned by the Tourist Police, whose head office is at 7 Syngrou Avenue, Athens (Tel: 9214 392). For the multilingual 24-hour enquiry service dial 171.

The most complete compilation of facts on travel in Greece is the *Key Travel Guide for Greece and the Middle East,* which has bus, boat and train schedules, a list of hotels, telephone and telegraphic rates, and a whole supplement on travel around the Eastern Mediterranean. World wide distribution is by BAS Publications, 159 Mortlake Road, Surrey TW9 4AW.

Disabled Travellers. The National Foundation for the Rehabilitation of the Disabled (KAPAS) provide general help and information. Write to KAPAS, Neo Liosia (Kamatero), Attiki 5.

Youth and Student Travel. ISYTS, 11 Nikis Street, 2nd Floor, 105 57 Athens, plus many other agencies around Syntagma Square.

English Language Churches. St Paul's (Anglican), Fillelinon Street, Athens (Tel: 714 906); St Paul's (Catholic), Kifissia.

American Express. Constitution Square/2, Ermo Street, Athens (Tel: 3244 976-9); also in the Athens Hilton and Marriot hotels; and offices in Thesaloniki, Corfu, Heraklion, Santorini, Rhodes, Myconos and Patras.

Mount Athos

Europe's last remaining monastic state, on the easternmost of the three Halkidiki peninsulas, south-east of Thessaloniki, is open only to males. Boats with women aboard are not allowed within 500m of the coast. The peninsula contains 20 monasteries and a number of smaller religious communities. Men who want to visit the "Holy Mountain" should observe this procedure; first, obtain a letter of recommendation from your own Embassy or consul in Athens or Thessaloniki, who will give you his letter of recommendation. This is then taken to either the Directorate of Churches of the Ministry of Foreign Affairs, Directorate of Churches, 2, Zalokasto Street, Athens (Tel: 3626 894) or to the Ministry for Macedonia

-Thrace, 48 Eleftheriou Venizelon Street, Thessaloniki who will issue a permit. Young people aged under 18 may be allowed to visit Mount Athos provided they are accompanied by an adult. Only ten permits are issued per day. Clergymen are only admitted after special approval by his All Holiness the Ecumenicaal Patriarch in Constantinople, or by the Metropolitain of Thessaloniki.

Permits are handed in, with your passport, when you have entered the Peninsula. A token fee of 1,000 is levied. The permit allows the visitor(s) to stay up to four days in Mount Athos, with free food, wine and accommodation and free access to the monasteries. Take a supply of tinned food if you want to complement your daily meals. While the use of film cameras is permitted, the use of video and movie cameras and or tape recorders is strictly forbidden.

Calendar of Events

Public Holidays are shown in **bold.** Religious holidays marked * are Greek Orthodox dates which usually fall later than the Roman dates.

January 1	**New Year's Day**
January 6	**Epiphany;** celebrations at Kastoria, Pidni, Strymni
February	**Shrove Monday;** carnival festivities throughout the country
March 25	**Independence Day**
March/April	**Good Friday*, Easter Monday***
May 1	**Labour Day:** flower parades in several Athenian suburbs
May/June	**Whit Monday***
June-July	Drama Festival at Epidavros
July-September	Wine festivals at Alexandroupolis, Dafni, Rhodes
mid July-mid September	Athens Festival
July-September	Folklore festival at the theatre of Rhodes
late July-mid August	Filippi Drama Festival
August	Art and Literature Festival at Levkas
August 1-10	Festival of Cretan Dances at Aghios Nikolaos
August 15	**Assumption:** pilgrimages to the island of Tinos
mid August	Dodoni Drama Festival
September 1-20	International Trade Fair at Thessaloniki
September 14	Feast Day of the Holy Cross — religious celebrations
September-October	Grape festivals at Heraklion, Nea Aghialos, Tyrnavos
October	Demetria Festival of Theatre and Music at Thessaloniki
October 28	**National Day**
December 25, 26	**Christmas Day, St. Stephen's Day**

Cyprus

Area. 3,572 square miles   **Population:** 660,000

Capital. Nicosia (Lefkoŝa) — population 165,000.

Cyprus has had a long history of colonisation by the British, Greeks and Turks, and is now a divided island. The southern part is the Republic of Cyprus, a member of the British Commonwealth; the north, occupied by Turkey since the intervention of 1974, is called the Turkish Republic of Northern Cyprus (*Kibris*). It is not recognised by any country except Turkey. United Nations troops patrol the "green line" which divides the two sectors. This line, which earned its name from a line drawn on a map in green pencil, bisects the capital. Despite recent moves to improve relations, there is still considerable hostility.

Language. In the north, predominantly Turkish; in the south, Greek. English is spoken everywhere and British servicemen are still stationed in two Sovereign Bases in the south.

Entry. Since the closure of Nicosia airport, flights arrive at Larnaca or Paphos (for the south) and Ercan (in the north). Ferries sail to Famagusta and Kyrenia in the north, and Larnaca, Limassol and Paphos in the south. Visas are not required for either sector by travellers from the British Isles or North America. Customs allowances are fairly standard (200 cigarettes, one bottle of spirits etc).

Crossing the green line is difficult; it is sometimes possible, however, to obtain permission from the Public Information Office in Nicosia (near the Presidential Palace) for one-day visits from south to north. Travellers who arrive in the north of the island and cross to the south face deportation, since all northern gateways have been declared illegal ports of entry by the Government of the Republic of Cyprus. If your passport shows evidence of a visit to the north at any time since November 1983, you will be refused entry to the south.

Money. Cyprus pound (C£) = 100 cents; C£1 = £1.30 or $2.
Coins: 2c, 5c, 10c, 20c. Notes 50c, C£1, C£5, C£10.

In the north, the official currency is the Turkish lira at a rate of about TL 800 to £1, TL 550 to $1.

Up to C£50 in Cypriot currency may be imported or exported. Unlimited amounts of foreign currency and travellers cheques may be imported into the south, but these should be declared if you wish to re-export them.

Banks open 8.30 am-noon, Monday to Saturday. Centrally located Banks provide "afternoon tourist services" from Monday to Friday. Shops open on weekdays from 7.30 am-1.00 pm and 2.30-6.00, but are closed on Wednesday and Saturday afternoons. In tourist areas shops may keep longer hours.
Cyprus converted from the Imperial System of weights and measures to the Metric System in 1987.

Weather temperature reports are given in degrees Celsius, Petrol is sold by the litre, grocery items are in grammes and kilogrammes, fabric lengths are in metres and road speeds posted in kilometres per hour. Food is similar to that found in Greece, but is generally served at a hotter temperature.

Getting Around. By buses or by "service taxis" (usually huge Mercedes carrying six to seven passengers from town to town); or by private taxis (tariffs by taxi meter: prices are about 30c per mile). Car hire (for which any national driving licence will suffice) cost around £20 per day. Drive on the left: road distances are marked in miles. Hitch-hiking is quite feasible if you can stand the heat.

Communications. The Post Office at Eleftheria Square in Nicosia is open 7.30 am-2.00 pm and 3.30 pm-5.30 pm, Monday to Friday, 7.30 am-noon on Saturdays. Opening hours of other offices vary.

Telephone calls can be dialled direct throughout the island. Most of the western world can be reached from private telephones or green telephone booths. Payphones accept 2, 10 and 20c coins. Phonecards are available from banks and post offices. The international prefix is 00. For International Direct Dial calls to UK, insert 20c, dial 0044, UK area code (minus initial 0) and local number, insert more coins on signal. For telephone credit card or collect (reverse charge) calls dial 198 for the local international operator. These calls are not available from payphones.

Telegrams can be sent in Nicosia from the Central Telegraph Office, Egypt Avenue (Tel: 02-477111), which never closes.

Programmes in English are broadcast by CBC (TV and Radio) and BFBS (radio only).

The two English language newspapers are the daily Cyprus Mail and the Cyprus Weekly.

Accommodation. Reasonably plentiful in five-star down to one-star hotels. A double room in a one-star hotel can cost as little as C£10-12 per night. There are five youth hostels, which charge C£2-3 per night.

Health. Good insurance is recommended, since there are no reciprocal arrangements for free health care. Treatment though at the casualty department of Governmental Hospitals is provided free. All doctors speak foreign languages. Cyprus is free from the epidemic diseases and even the common infectious diseases are rare. Therefore no vaccination is required for international travellers.

Help and Information. Only Turkey has diplomatic relations with Northern Cyprus. In the south, the British High Commission is in Alexander Pallis Street, Nicosia (Tel: 473131). The American Embassy is on the corner of Dsitheon and Therissou Streets (Tel: 465151). The Canadian Consulate is at Themistocies Dervis Street (Tel: 451630). The Republic of Cyprus Tourism Organisation has its Head Office at 18, Theodotou Street, Nicosia (Tel: 443374) and offices at Larnaca Airport; and in Ayia Napa, Larnaca Town, Limassol and Paphos.

Public Holidays. In the south, as *Greece* but with the addition of Makarios' Day (January 19), EOKA Struggle Day (April 1) and Cypriot Independence Day (October 1). In the north, Muslim feasts depending on physical sighting of the moon and hence are variable from year to year.

The information above may change at any time, since inter-communal discussions between north and south are continuing. For latest developments contact the Cypriot High Commission in London.

Italy

VENICE   W.S

Area. 116,500 square miles   **Population.** 57,300,000

Capital. Rome (population: 2,827,000).

Weather. Don't assume that Italy is always hot; spring and autumn get a lot of rain and winters can be very cold in the whole country, although snow is rare as far south as Rome. The Alps have good ski conditions, and black ice and freezing fog are very real winter hazards throughout the north. However, you can rely on getting a respectable suntan in the summer.

THE PEOPLE

Italian society has an overwhelming Catholic influence, that controls family life (the woman's place is in the home) and produces a great resistance to change. Politically, however, Italy is fairly left-wing with an active women's movement and violent political strikes and demonstrations. Rural areas are still very conservative in their attitudes and the strength of the family remains intact.

Politics. Although the political system is often regarded by outsiders as corrupt, confused, and violent, the situation is now comparatively stable by Italian standards; however, feelings still run high. The Christian Democrats have dominated in the country since 1948, but in recent years the Communist party has effected a dramatic shift of power, and is now virtually the strongest party. As well as violent demonstrations from the left wing, the unemployed and the underpaid, governments have also suffered attacks from the strong feminist movement demanding much-needed legislative reform on the issues of rape, abortion and divorce. One factor common to all of the 50 or so governments since the war has been the attempt to shrink the vast economic gap between the rich north and the poor south. The Communist party enjoys a large amount of control of local government in the cities.

Religion. For all the political power the Communists hold, Italy is 95% Catholic. Most cities have Protestant churches, and there's a Protestant majority in some regions of the western Alps. Churches close from 12 or 1pm to 3 or 4pm, then reopen until 7 or 8pm. Be careful what you wear in churches — bare arms, legs and head are very much frowned on.

Language. Italian is the official language, but French is the native language in the Val d'Aosta, and German in the Alto Adige (around Bolzano). Both these regions have some degree of autonomy. Dialects are often difficult to understand, and in Sardinia and the Eastern Alps, they are recognised as separate languages. The Italians aren't good linguists, but French, German and English might get results, especially in tourist areas. If you speak Spanish or have studied Latin you should be able to read some Italian, and, speaking slowly, you might be able to converse.

Making Friends. Italians are always eager to open conversations, especially outside the large cities and tourist areas, where, after all, foreigners are commonplace. If you speak Italian, be prepared for lengthy interrogations on trains and buses. On the romance front, bear in mind the strongly chauvinistic bias of Italian society. Girls are virtually inaccessible to men (foreign or Italian); but men are free to chase whoever they please — the tales you've heard of bottom-pinching and general harassment are true, especially in the south. Italian men believe that foreign women are promiscuous and therefore egitimate prey. With such a social set-up, prostitution naturally thrives and is accepted.

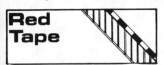

See the introduction for details of passports, customs regulations, duty free allowances, vaccinations and importing pets.

Passports and Visas. Holders of British, US and Canadian passports are allowed an initial stay of three months. This is renewable through the police. You're supposed to register with the police after three days (hotels and campsites do it automatically). Few people bother, but if the police want to get you, it could be for this. If you intend to request an extension to your three-month stay, you must also ask the police for a *permesso di soggiorno* within three days of your arrival.

Customs. Duty free allowances are as given in the introduction. Travellers under 17 are not entitled to the tobacco and alcohol allowances. All radios, including car radios, need a licence, available at the frontier for 1,000 l (valid three months). Export licences are required for antiques, works of modern art, and items worth over one million lire.

The unit of currency is the lira (l), plural lire.

£1 = 2,100 l   1,000 l = £0.47
$1 = 1,125 l   1,000 l = $0.88

For general information on handling, exchanging and raising money, see the introduction.

Coins. 5 l, 10 l, 20 l, 50 l, 100 l, 200 l, 500 l

Notes. 500 l (red/blue), 1,000 l (brown), 2,000 l (orange-green), 5,000 l (green-blue), 10,000 l (multi), 20,000 l (blue-grey), 50,000 l (brown), 100,000 l (brown).

As the volume of small change in circulation has increased, the use of sweets, stamps, bus tickets etc in lieu of change has decreased. However, don't be surprised to receive such things in place of coins — telephone *gettoni* (worth 200 l) are still quite acceptable and can be used as coins anywhere.

Import and Export. Regulations change frequently, so if you intend to import or export large amounts of foreign currency, or take more than 400,000 l of Italian notes in or out you should check before departure with the Italian State Tourist Office. Alternatively, ask the customs officer on your way into Italy whether you should complete form V2.

Banking Hours. Monday-Friday, 8.30am-1.20pm, plus an hour in the afternoon (often 3-4pm). The hours of exchange bureaux at airports, ports, main stations and frontier posts vary, but are usually open seven days a week, often late into the evening. The *bureau de change* at Rome's Fiumicino airport is open 24 hours. Most banks change a substantial service charge (typically 5,000 l) for exchanging money.

Shopping Hours. Vary from city to city, shop to shop, and season to season. By and large, expect shops to be open from 8.30 or 9am, closed between 1 and 4pm and then open until 7 or 8pm. The further north you go, the shorter the lunch breaks will be, and the earlier the shops will shut. Grocers' shops (*alimentari* or *supemercato*) are open until 7.30 or 8pm. A very few supermarkets may be open in the early afternoon, but if you assume that everyone takes a siesta, you won't be far wrong. Half day closing is also highly variable. On Sundays, very little will be open, except the occasional *alimentari,* bars, tobacconists, *tabacchi* and newspaper kiosks (*edicole*). In July and August, Saturday is nearly as bad.

Tipping. Hotels — 10-15%, not included in the bill. Restaurants — have a cover charge (*pane e coperto*) of around 3,000 l; service is often included in the bill (*servizio compresso*), otherwise, give 15%. Cafés, bars — the custom is to leave some small change (around 10%) in the saucer on the bar. Taxis — small change. Cinemas, theatres, toilets — 500 l for the usher(ette) or attendant. You may see the words *Nessun Mancia* displayed in public loos; it means no tipping, so ignore the attendant's saucer. Station porters — fixed charge of around 1,000 l per item.

Emergency Cash. Begging, busking and street-selling are illegal, though unlikely to be clamped down on. You can sell your blood at hospitals in the larger cities Citizens of EC countries are allowed to work without a work permit, but you should officially obtain a residence permit (*permesso di soggiorno*) from the local police. The best chances are in hotels and restaurants in summer. There is a national lottery, drawn weekly: bets are placed at the *Giuoco del Lotto* shops. The tickets sold in the streets are for major and less frequent lotteries, often connected with sporting events.

Details of employment opportunities during the skiing season can be found in Working in Ski Resorts-Europe (Vacation Work, £5.95).

Taxes. There's a sales tax (*Imposta sul Valore Aggiunto* — IVA) on everything. The standard rate is 18%, but rates vary from 2%-38% depending on the degree of luxury accorded to each item. Additional taxes are imposed on alcohol, bananas, coffee, margarine, petrol, sugar, tobacco and electrical goods: these are included in published prices.

 **Getting Around**

The information in this section is complementary to that given in the corresponding section in the introduction.

CAR

Roads are variable, but all well surfaced. *Autostrade* (motorways) are excellent and numerous, but cost a lot in toll money. South of Salerno, they're free. Italian drivers are dangerous but skilled, relying to a great extent on their brakes and horns. Keep the vehicle's registration document (log book) or rental agreement about your person at all times. If your car is stolen or towed away, the police won't co-operate until they're satisfied of your right to drive it.

Rules and Requirements. The UK pink driving licence is valid in Italy: other national licences must be accompanied by a translation into Italian (available for a small charge from motoring organisations abroad or ENIT offices at the main road frontiers into Italy). The minimum driving age is 18, but 21 for any car capable of over 180km/h (112mph). A red warning triangle is obligatory. The police are particularly strict about dipping headlights when approaching or following another car at night. Vehicles must have a left-hand rear view mirror (ie fitted to the passenger side on right-hand-drive cars). It is illegal to carry petrol in a can. It is compulsory to wear seat belts.

The maximum permissible level of alcohol is nil.

Traffic lights are often suspended above intersections; to discourage people from creeping over the line, the amber is sometimes cut out (this doesn't work).

Speed Limits. In towns speed limits are as signposted — usually 50km/h (31mph). Outside built up areas, speed limits are imposed according to the size of the vehicle's engine. The limits for cars under 600cc are 80km/h (50mph) on main roads and 90km/h (56mph) on motorways; for cars up to 900cc, the figures are 90km/h and 110km/h (69mph); up to 1,300cc, 100km/h (62mph) and 130km/h (81mph); and vehicles over 1,300cc, 110km/h and 140km/h (87mph).

Road signs. *Alt* — Stop; *Senso Vietato* or *Divieto di Accesso* — No Entry; *Entrara* — Entry; *Uscita* — Exit; *Lavori in Corso* — Road works; *Senso Unico* — One Way; *Rallentare* — Slow; *Vietato Ingresso Veicoli* — No Entry for Vehicles; *Casello* — Toll Booth; *Dare la precedenza* — Give Way; *Raccordo Anulare* — Ring Road; *Avanti* — on pedestrian signs, "go ahead"; on road signs, "drive at walking pace".

Place Names. English variations are usually close to the Italian originals — Roma, Milano, Napoli, etc. Florence is Firenze; Leghorn is Livorno; Turin is Turino; Venice is Venezia (Venedig in German, Venise in French).

Parking. *Sosta Vietata* = No parking; *Sosta Autorizzata* = Parking permitted — signs also gives the times parking is allowed. Members of the ACI (see below) enjoy special parking concessions. Parking fines have been raised to 200,000 l in a bid to cut down on illegal parking, and wheel clamps are being introduced in Rome and Milan.

Petrol. The octane grading is always marked on the pumps. A litre of *super* (94-98 octane) costs around 1,360 l, (£2.90 per imperial gallon or $4.50 per US gallon). Unleaded petrol costs 1,375 l per litre. Many petrol stations are closed from noon to 3pm.

There are four petrol voucher schemes which reduce petrol costs for motorists by 15; they are valid only for *super* petrol and for British registered vehicles. Coupons are available from CIT, 50 Conduit Street, London SW1 (Tel: 071-434 3844), Wasteel Travel, 121 Wilton Road, London SW1 (Tel: 071-834 7066), AA or RAC offices or ACI frontier offices. Drivers must buy the coupons in person and produce a passport and vehicle registration document. Participants in all these schemes receive a *carta carburante turistica* (tourist fuel card) which entitles the holder to the free ACI breakdown service (see below) and a number of motorway toll vouchers.

(1) *Northern Italy package* — £67.30. Comprises 12 petrol coupons worth 15,000 l each and 5 motorway vouchers worth 2,000 lire each.

(2) *Central Italy package* — £108.00. As (1) but with 3 extra motorway vouchers and an extra petrol voucher worth 120,000 lire which must be changed for six 2,000 l coupons at ENIT or ACI offices in Abruzzo, Basilicata, Calabria, Campania, Lazio, Molise, Puglia, Sardinia, Sicily.

(3) *Southern Italy package* — £148.70. As (1) but with 5 extra motorway vouchers and an extra petrol voucher worth 240,000 lire that must be changed for petrol coupons at ENIT or ACI offices in Basilicata, Calabria, Campania, Molise, Puglia, Sardinia, Sicily.

(4) *Southern Italy package* — £189.70. As (1) but with 5 additional motorway vouchers and an extra petrol voucher worth 360,000 l that must be exchanged for petrol coupons at ENIT or ACI offices in Basilicata, Calabria, Sardinia or Sicily: when changing this voucher motorists are given 8 additional motorway vouchers worth 2,000 l each.

Unused petrol coupons must be exchanged at the office that issued them.

Tolls. Although the *autostrade* (motorways) are excellent and numerous they are expensive in terms of tolls, which are assessed according to the power rating of the vehicle and the distance travelled. The toll for a journey from Milan to Rome is 36,500 L. Those who possess insufficient italian money may pay the toll in foreign currency. Foreign motorists buying petrol coupons receive a certain number of motorway toll vouchers, which can be used in full or part payment on most motorways. Anyone staying in Italy for a reasonable length of time who expects to be using the motorways a lot can obtain a credit card for the payment of tolls; details are obtainable from *Autostrade S.p.A.*, Direzione Generale Uffici, Casella, Postale 610, 50100 Firenze.

Touring Club. The *Automobile Club d'Italia* (ACI), via Marsala, 8, 00185 Rome (Tel: 4998) has offices at all main frontier posts, where foreign motorists can buy petrol coupons and take out temporary membership. The phone number of their assistance centre is 4212; it operates 24 hours a day with English speaking personnel who can advise on road conditions and give tourist information.

Accidents and Breakdowns. There are a number of different charges made for summoning the ACI *soccorso* (breakdown service), depending basically upon the amount of paperwork that you carry. Foreign motorists holding a membership card of a foreign motoring organisation only have to pay a call fee, (higher at night) and those bearing a FIA or AIT Assistance booklet can use the service free of charge. Others have to pay the full price, which is liable to be steep. To contact the ACI dial 116, or, on the motorways, use the press button emergency telephones located every 2 km. If you happen to break down on a stretch of motorway not equipped with these phones, you must wait by your car for a passing police car or breakdown vehicle. Complaints or other correspondence about the ACI service should be addressed to ACI Soccorso, Via Solferino 32, Rome. In cases of accident, dial 113 — this will get you in touch with the police and, if necessary, medical help.

TRAIN

The rail network is run by FS (Ferrovie dello Stato), Piazza della Croce Rossa 1, Rome. For information, dial 4775, or call in at the information office at Termini Station between 7 am-11.30 pm. This station has a morgue (for use of ticket holders only).

Trains have two classes, first costing 50-80% more than second. Second class fares are about 50 l per km (£3.80 or $6.10 per 100 miles). Trains come in five basic categories. *Diretto* and *locale* are slow trains, stopping everywhere. *Espresso* is faster; and *rapido* is an express which carries a 30% surcharge, may only have a first class, and may require seat reservation. *Super-Rapido* Inter-City are luxury first-class only trains running between the main Italian cities; a special supplement is charged, and seat reservation is compulsory. Booking in advance for any main route in summer is strongly recommended. If you are travelling by Expresso and your train arrives more than 30 minutes late FS will give you a credit equivalent to the cost of the Expresso supplement, which can be put towards the cost of you next rail ticket. Forms for claiming this credit should be available on the train or at station information desks.

First or second class couchettes cost 16,800 l, irrespective of the length of the journey. Sleeper berths cost between three and ten times as much, depending on the class and distance travelled.

Arrive early to be sure of a seat, as main routes are very crowded, and the multiplicity of special tariffs for groups such as soldiers and state workers can lead to large queues at ticket offices. Tickets bought on a train bear a surcharge of at least 6,000 l. Internal telegrams may be sent from all but *locale* trains; they cannot exceed 10 words, and cost around 6,000 l. Ask the guard for a special form. Telegrams can be received by rail passengers between 6 am-10 pm.

Cheap Deals. Children under 4 travel free; 4-12 years half fare. Men over 65 and women over 60 can buy a rail card for 18,000 l valid for 5 years and giving a 30% reduction: it is called the *Carta d'Argento.*

Unlimited travel tickets are available to non-residents only. Second class rates: £65 for 8 days; £79 for 15 days; £92 for 21 days; £112 for 30 days; first class rates are 35% higher. Extensions can be bought in Italy for all but the 8-day ticket.

Chilometrico tickets cost £60 (second class) for a combined total of 3,000 km between up to five people — it must be used for less than a maximum of 20 journeys.

For journeys up to 50 km, day return tickets earn a 15% discount; three-day return tickets on journeys 51-250 km yield the same saving.

People aged between 12 and 26 can buy the *Carta Verde* for 10,000 l; it gives a reduction of 20-30% on rail travel, depending on the date of travel, and is valid for one year.

CYCLE/MOTORCYCLE

Easy to hire in any city (from CIT offices and garages), but also quite dangerous in city traffic. The Italians go in for those tiny motorised cycles, for which you don't need a licence if you're over 14. In Rome, cycles can be rented from R. Collalti, Via del Pelligrino 81 (Tel: 654 1084).

AIR

Internal flights are operated by three companies: ATI (a subsidiary of Alitalia) — 4668 in Rome; Alisarda (serving Sardinia) — 475 1676; Itavia — 4988.

On internal flights there are reductions for families (one full fare, then 50% reductions), and 30% reductions for travel at night. Flight information for the airport in Rome is available on 724241 (Ciampino, the small airport for charter flights) or 60124 (Leonardo da Vinci/Fiumicino). Bus connections leave from the Alitalia Terminal at Via Giolitti 36, for both airports. An underground line from the centre of Rome to Fiumcino is under construction. Ciampiono can be reached by underground between 5.45 am and 10.30 pm: price 700 l. In Naples, take bus 12 from the station — the fare is 5000 l, and it runs from 7 am to midnight.

SEA

Times and prices of ferry services are given in the free booklet *Italy Travellers Hand-book*, published by the Italian tourist office. Book well in advance for services in summer.

HITCH-HIKING

Very fast on busy routes. The toll booths at motorway entrances are good places, as are motorway rest areas. For destination signs, you can use the two-letter codes for each town, as used on car number plates: MI = Milan, VE = Venice, NA = Naples, and so on. Rome is the exception (**ROMA**); RO = Rovigo.

However you try to get out of Rome, you'll be faced with awesome competition, so it's best to take a train as far out as possible. Going north, a train to Orte, then walking about 500 metres over the railway bridge to the A1 entrance, is one of many desperate ploys that have been known to work. Consult *Europe: a Manual for Hitch-hikers* for many more ideas on this subject. Avoid being dropped off the Milan Tangenziale, Bologna Periferico, Rome Raccordo Annulare or Naples Circolare (although the northern part of the Circolare is not bad for hitching north out of Naples). Better to get off at a busy service area before you reach these towns, and wait for a lift going right past them. In the north, many passes are closed from November through to March, but strategic tunnels and the Brenner Pass usually remain open.

CITY TRANSPORT

Taxis. Mostly yellow. They don't cruise, but there are many stands, and you can telephone for them; in Rome, 3570. Prices vary, but reckon on (at least) 2,300 l fixed charge plus 1,000 l per km (around £1.50 or $2 for a two mile journey).

There are supplements for night journeys, Sundays, luggage, telephone bookings and leaving the city limits. In Naples, haggle.

Boats in Venice. The car park is in the Piazzale Roma and then you either walk or go by boat. *Vaporetti* are the bus equivalent (flat fare of 1,500 l, or 8,000 l for a 24 hour ticket) *motoscafi* are taxis. *Gondole* are prohibitively expensive — about 140 l per hour for up to five people, more after 4 pm.

Bus/Tram/Underground. There are bus stations, or at least information offices, close to railway stations. All towns have a flat rate for journeys within the urban network; the usual rate is 600 l-700 l, often with a time limit of one or two hours. The discount for buying a book of 10 is usually 100 l per ticket. Cancel your pre-purchased ticket in an automatic machine. Tickets can be bought from any *tabachi* or from machines which accept a variety of coins.

There are undergrounds in Rome and Milan with a fixed fare of 700 l. Tickets are bought from automatic dispensers. Naples is building.

Cheap Deals. In Rome weekly *Tessera* tickets are available for 10,000 l.

See the introduction for information on youth hostels, other hostels, and advance booking of accommodation.

Hotels/Pensions. Hotels are graded from one to five stars. Prices are strictly controlled and should be posted inside every room. A double room in a modest, centrally located pension in Rome costs about 46,000 l; elsewhere it would be 30-35,000 l. Meals, including breakfast, are optional for short stays, but pensions are entitled to impose half board if you stay for a considerable length of time. Outside the tourist seasons, you usually get reductions: haggle if the place looks empty.

Day hotels (*Alberghi diurni*) can be found in many towns and cities, usually near railway stations. They are open from 06.00 to midnight and provide baths, laundry, hairdressers and reading rooms, but no sleeping accommodation.

Guests in all types of hotels and pensions are required by law to obtain a *recevuta fiscalo* (an official receipt, showing the tax paid) upon settling the bill but don't be too surprised if you are not given one. Tax rates are higher for luxury hotels (18%) than for lesser hotels and pensions (10%).

Youth Hostels. *Associazione Italiana Alberghi per la Gioventu,* Palazzo della Civilitá del Lavoro, EUR 00144 Rome (Tel: 06 4623 42) for free map and list of 52 hostels. The basic cost is 10,000 l per night, with higher charge for superior hostels.

Student Hostels. Out of term-time, apply to the *Casa dello Studente* in University towns for rooms. The *Guide for Foreign Students* is available from the Ministry of Education, Viale Trastevere, Rome.

Cottages and Farmhouses. To rent the Italian equivalent of a French *gîte,* contact *Agriturist,* Corso V Emanuele 101, Rome (Tel: 06 6512 342). Prices range from 3,500 to 8,000 per person per night.

Mountain Huts (*Rifugi Alpini*). There are about 465 of these in the Alps, overnight prices starting around 6,000 l with a 20% surcharge in winter. Details from the *Club Alpino italiano,* Via Ugo Foscolo 3, Milano (Tel: 720 22 555).

Camping. The police might hassle you if you camp in any old field without the owner's permission. In theory, you're allowed to camp only at Italy's 2,100 registered campsites. Prices are around 6,500 l per person, 3,500 l per tent, plus 6,000 l for a car. *Federcampeggio,* Casella Postale 23, 50041 Calenzano (Florence) or Italian State Tourist Offices abroad can provide you with a map and list of campsites. Try and get youth hostel and/or student reductions if you've got cards. The site in Rome is on Via Aurelia, southwest of the Vatican.

Sleeping out. The police aren't too happy about it, and stations tend to throw you out if you don't have a ticket. Some otherwise attractive locations in towns (notably the Borghese Gardens in Rome) have a bad safety record when it comes to muggings and thefts. Never sleep out in Naples. Advice for cities is to buy a ticket to the nearest suburban station and sleep in the station (most suburban stations tolerate this, central stations don't).

Finding and Booking Accommodation. Provincial Tourist Offices (EPT) carry lists of hotels and can make bookings for you. If you reach a town outside office hours, head for the station. The cheapest hotels are usually alongside the stations, expensive ones in front. Stations in large cities usually have a hotel booking agency on the premises.

Communications

General information on telephones and English language newspapers and radio broadcasts is given in the introduction.

Post. Letterboxes are usually red, sometimes with two slits, one for the city (*la citta*) and one for elsewhere (*Tutte le Altre Destinazioni*), or one for Italy (*interno*) and one for abroad (*estero*). Stamps can be bought from post offices, tobacconists (*tabacchi*, marked by a large blue "T") and some bars which double as tobacconists. Post offices are open 8.30 am-2 pm Monday-Friday, until noon on Saturday; central offices in cities up to 9 pm. Poste restante letters should be addressed *Fermo Posta*; a small fee is payable upon collection. Main post offices have a philatelic counter, marked *Sportello Filatelico.*

The correct way to address mail is name; town (in capitals, preceded by the five-figure code); street (name then number). The town code should be preceded by the country code I- when writing from abroad.

Telephone. Most new payphones take 100 l, 200 l and 500 l coins as well as gettoni (tokens), but some older payphones accept only gettoni. These cost 200 l at the nearest bar kiosk, or (occasionally) slot machine. On one side they have one groove, on the other two: there is only one way to put them in. There are two kinds of pay-telephone. The black ones have a knob beside the slot which holds the gettone in place until you get a reply; then press it. The yellow, gold and red ones have no knob and can be used for long distance calls (and, in larger towns and cities for international calls), then dial when you hear the tone. Unused coins or tokens will cascade around your feet when you hang up — some phones have a button you must press to return your investment. Every cafe has a telephone as well — some work on gettoni, others are metered and you pay at the bar when you've finished. There are a growing number of cardphones, which obviate the need for long amounts of change — ask for a scheda magnetica at offices of SIP, the Italian telecommunications organisation.

Local calls cost 200 l, then rates rise fast. Long-distance and international calls are most easily made at telephone offices where calls are metered, but can, in theory, be dialled direct to most exchanges from call boxes. Area codes include; Rome — 06, Milan — 02, Napels — 082, Venice — 041, Florence — 055. The international prefix is 00, except when calling an adjacent country from some frontier regions.

The dial direct to the UK insert *gettoni* or coins (200 l). Dial 00 44 followed by UK area code (minus initial 0) and local number; for BT Chargecard and Collect (reverse charge) calls dial 15 for the local operator from call offices, or from designated phones in post officc and airports dail 15. UK direct is available from telephone bureau located in major cities and airports. Dial 10 44 from these designated telephones.

Local calls are half price on Sundays and holidays; and from 10pm Monday — Saturday until 8am next day. There are surcharges on calls made 9.30am — 12.30pm, Monday-Friday.

There should be a directory in every public phone booth but in practice there often isn't. Café/bars which have a telephone booth at the back may have directories for the whole country. There are two standard sections — personal and commercial. The personal directory is first divided alphabetically into towns or villages, subscribers then listed alphabetically within these divisions. Information (in Italian only) and code numbers are given at the beginning of the personal directory.

Useful numbers (in Rome, elsewhere check): emergency — (fire, ambulance, police) — 113; breakdowns — 116; intercontinental calls — 170; European calls — 15 (operator), 184 (information); directory enquiries — 12 (local), 181 (long distance); time — 161; news — 190; postal information — 160; horoscope — 195; alarm calls — 114; recipe of the day — 1991.

Telegrams. Operated by *Italcable*, who have offices attached to all major post offices; the central office in large cities is open 24 hours. Or dial 186.

Newspapers. *La Stampa* (published in Turin) and *La Republica Corriere della Sera* (Milan) are the only Italian newspapers with claims to a national circulation. Rome's most prominent English language publication is *This Week in Rome*, 4,000 l from kiosks.

Broadcasting. American Forces Network has FM stations at San Vito (107 MHz). Vicenza (108 MHz), and several stations on 106 MHz. An interesting feature of Italian broadcasting is that, due to a legal loophole, unlicensed stations are not banned from transmitting. There are estimated to be about 1,000 radio and 650 television stations, with a sprinkling of the latter providing soft porn.

Health and Hygiene

For information on hygiene, first aid, insurance and medical treatment, see the introduction.

Hygiene. Of all the Mediterranean countries, Italy has one of the worst records for sea pollution. It is not unknown for gently shelving beaches to become putrid and unsafe for use. Do not ignore warning notices. The coastal areas, particularly in the south, have had cases of cholera and typhoid in the past.

Drinking water is generally safe; *acqua non potabile* means don't drink it. Petrol stations, particularly AGIP, are very good places for a shower or bath and generally spotless. Other Italian toilets *(gabinetti)* are sometimes of the hole-in-the-floor variety. You're allowed to use café toilets without buying a drink.

Reciprocal Agreements. Only for British travellers with Form E111 (see the introduction). Take form E111 to the local insurance authority, either *Unita Sanitario Locale* (USL) or *Struttura Amministrava Unificata de Base* (SAUB). They will provide a treatment certificate and list of participating doctors and dentists, who will treat you free of charge. Without the certificate, you will have to pay the full fee and will probably not get a refund. Take any prescriptions, along with the certificate to a chemist *(farmacia)*; you must pay a percentage of the cost of each medicine. If the doctor thinks you should be in hospital, he will give you a certificate *(proposta di ricovero)* entitling you to free treatment in participating hospitals (list from USL or SAUB). In emergencies, take Form E111 to a participating (public) hospital and ask them to contact USL or SAUB on your behalf.

Emergencies. If you fall seriously ill, the best thing to do is get on a plane, or just head for Switzerland — Italian hospitals are often terrible. The emergency number to call an ambulance is 113. There are emergency 24-hour clinics at all hospitals, airports, ports and stations (ask for *pronto soccorso).* In small towns, chemists have a rota — look in any chemist's window or dial 110. Larger towns have 24-hour pharmacies, listed in the directory under *Farmacie con Servizio di Pronto Soccorso e Notturno.* Rome has four — Via Europa, 28; Piazza Barberini 49; Via Portense; and Piazza Ragusa 14. For the doctors' rota, look up *Guardia Medica* or dial 1921 for information.

Sport. By far the most popular spectator sport is soccer, about which the Italians are hysterically enthusiastic as befits the hosts of the 1990 World Cup. The best teams are Juventus of Turin and the two Milan clubs, AC and Internazionale. Don't show this page to the supporters of any other team. Other popular spectator sports include cycling, motor racing, motor cycle racing, horse racing and basketball.

Beaches. Many are private, with fees charged for the (compulsory) hire of sun beds. However, there is usually a strip of free beach between the boundary of the private sector and the high water mark. In addition, stretches of free beach — provided by local councils — can usually be found every few hundred yards in between the private beaches.

Nightlife. Local newspapers will give all the essential information, plus telephone numbers for booking. Theatre and opera performances are usually scheduled for 9pm, but many start later; they have numerous intervals and end very late. The shows are quite different from London and New York, with plenty of audience participation. Expect to pay from 2,000l for a seat. *La Scala* in Milian is the best known opera house but in summer you can also see performances in some archaeological sites — notably, the arena at Verona and the Terme di Caracalla in Rome.

Cinemas usually show films dubbed in Italian. *Prima visione* cinemas (5,000 l and up) show new releases. *Seconda visione* (second time around) are much cheaper but you may have to sit on hard wooden seats. There's also the usual range of nightclubs both in and outdoors, but many Italians' idea of a night out is either a long slow meal in a restaurant or going to the movies.

Casinos. Only four Italian towns, all in the north of the country, have casinos. They are at Venice, San Remo, St. Vincent (in the Aosta Valley) and Campione (on Lake Lugano). From April-September, the Venice casino can be found at the Lido; during the rest of the year, in the Palazzo Vendramin. Only visitors over the age of 18 are admitted to Italian casinos: locals are prohibited from using them.

Museums and Galleries. There are two types — city and state. City museums vary in prices, opening hours and reactions to student cards. Many are shut on Sunday afternoons and all day Monday. State museums and galleries (including most archaeological sites) also close on Mondays; on Sundays and public holidays they open from 9am to 1pm, on other days 9am-2pm. Charges are normally around 2,000-5,000 l, with reductions for students and other worthy causes. Admission is free for tourists aged under 18 and over 60 if their country has a reciprocal agreement with the Italian Government: check at the entrance.

The Naples Tourist Board offer five-hour minibus tours taking in Pompeii and Vesuvius for which represent good value if you're into volcanoes. The Leaning Tower of Pisa was recently closed for structural work to stop it toppling: check with a tourist office before making a special trip to see it.

Eating out. Restaurant meals start at around 8,000 l (£3.50 or $6). The cheapest restaurants are *trattorie* (but not all *trattorie* are cheap). The authentic ones catering for Italians may have no menus — trust them, but don't be afraid to ask prices and perhaps walk out. Many restaurants have a *menu turistico* which will give you a whole specified meal for around 10-15,000 including wine or mineral water and tip. Average meal times are 1-2pm for lunch; 8-10pm for dinner. To choose a restaurant check the cover charge on the menu: 1,000 l indicates a modest restaurant, 3,000 l an upmarket one.

A *tavola calda* or *rosticcerial* is a more casual, sometimes self-service place. A *pizzeria* serves *pizza*. Two types: the very cheap, on-the-spot *pizzeria* that sells by weight and often does a take-away service *(al taglio)* at ridiculously cheap prices; and a flashier type — primarily a medium-price restaurant. For a snack, try *panini* (sandwiches) or *toast* (a toasted sandwich).

Every restaurant closes one day a week *(chiusura settimanale)*. It says which day on the door. It's worth checking beforehand, if you have your eye on a specific place.

You are required by law to obtain an official receipt *(recevuta fiscale)* whenever you eat a meal out in Italy. It must show the cost of each part of the meal, and include IVA tax, the avoidance of which this law is intended to stop. In theory fines can be heavy if you're caught leaving a restaurant without the receipt: in practice you may never be given one during your time in Italy.

Vegetarians can seek advice on where to eat from the *Associazione Vegetariana Italiana*, Viale Gran Sasso 38, Milan. The *Unione Communita Israelitiche Italiana*, Lungotevere Cenci 9, Rome, can provide the addresses of Kosher restaurants. If you have a craving for real tea, scones and muffins while in Rome, visit the Babington Tea Rooms by the Piazza di Spagna.

Drinking. Café/bars are open throughout the day, and some are always open late. Some have TV and many have pinball. No age restrictions. The Italians drink a lot but rarely get drunk. Wine is the most common drink, red or white *(rosso or bianco)*. The expression for local wine is *vino locale* or *vino regionale*. The beer is sweet and fizzy; for a stronger, pricier brew ask for *birra estera* (foreign). *Birra dalla spina* means "from the tap", but don't expect real ale. Wine is cheaper and better; very cheap in supermarkets. The most common and cheapest spirit is *grappa* — made from distilled grape juice. Aperatifs are popular: try *Cinar* (made from artichokes) or any other *amaro* (bitter drink).

Most bars charge more if you sit at a table than if you drink at the bar, while many bars don't have chairs at all. The normal way to pay, if the waiter won't take your money, is to take your bill to the cashier. Some bars work the other way round — you pay for your drink at the cash desk, then take the receipt to the bar to place your order. If you are on a strict budget, stay clear of costly tourist traps, where you may find yourself paying well over the odds for your drink. Even railway stations can be bad value, as you find yourself paying over 1,500 l for a *cappucino* normally costing around 1,000 l or 4,000 l for an aperatif which normally costs 1,000 l.

Smoking. Tobacco, like salt, is nationalised. American brands are available, but more expensive. The standard cigarettes, *Nazionali* (about 1,300 l a pack) are supposedly like Orwell's *Victory* cigarettes, though you get used to them. Unless you ask for tipped *(con filtro)*, you'll get plain. "Duty-free" *Marlboro* cigarettes are sold throughout the south by street vendors. Usually these are the genuine article, smuggled in by sea, but some imitations contain cabbage.

Police. Italian police can be rough and are known to be trigger-happy; never run away, they'll most likely shoot. they have little respect for suspects, but can be quite friendly if you stay on the right side of them (rather like bears). Your most likely contact with them is likely to be to report stolen possessions; they will probably show a hearty lack of interest. There are different types of police, recognisable by their uniforms. The green ones can be dangerous, but the flashy blue ones with red and white braid (*carabinieri*) are quite well-mannered. The emergency number for calling the *carabinieri* is 112. The police headquarters in Rome is at via San Vitale 15, where there is a special information office for tourists: dial 4686, extension 2858.

Crimes. Mugging is not as common as you might think, but watch out for bag-snatchers — they often ride motorbikes with covered number plates, or mopeds, which do not need number plates. Also, when you are stationary in a car in a traffic jam, a hand may suddenly reach in and snatch an unguarded or loosely held handbag. You should also exercise great caution in railway stations: pairs or small groups of children may jostle you or distract your attention with an opened newspaper while one of their number goes for your wallet.

Laws. Italian law is based on the Civil Code, unreconstructed since Mussolini drew it up, therefore very Fascist in outlook.

Possession of even a small quantity of drugs is an offences.

For less serious offences (speeding, parking, indiscreet nude bathing, camping in the middle of a motorway, etc) you'll get away with an on-the-spot fine. The maximum instant fine is 300,000 lira. Unless you know the Civil Code backwards, pay up. You could try pleading ignorance, but start co-operating at the first signs of anger.

As for politics, no one should bother you if you're merely a peaceful dabbler. But stay clear of demonstrations, especially when you see the green-uniformed police with visors. They can get violent.

If you do happen to end up in jail, you have to put up with Italian law which has no *habeas corpus*. If it takes them a few years to arrange your trial, you have to sit it out in jail. There is no bail, but you won't be kept languishing in jail if you only have a parking ticket.

Legal Aid. Get in touch with your embassy or consulate. They will be unenthusiastic but they will get you the legal necessities. According to the Civil Code, you can demand as lawyer before you say anything. If you are poor and can prove it, a judge will choose a free lawyer for you.

Nude Bathing. The legal position is highly confused. Recent appeals to the Supreme Court by those convicted of total nudity have failed, but the Court is equivocal on the subject of toplessness. Since police attitudes vary from one resort to another, the best advice is to watch what others are doing.

Help and Information

For general information on useful contacts and complaints procedures, see the introduction.

Embassies and Consulates.
British Embassy, Via XX Settembre 80a, 00187 Rome (475 5441).
British Consulate General, Via XII Ottobre 2/132, 16121 Genoa (564 883).
British Consulate General, Via San Paolo 7, 20121 Milan (869 3442).
British Consulate General, Via Francesco Crispi 122, 80122 Naples (66 3511).
There are also British Consulates in Florence, Trieste and Venice.

American Embassy, Via Vittorio Veneto 119, Rome (46741).
American Consulate General, Piazza della Repubblica 32, Milan (652 841).
There are also American Consulates in Genoa, Naples and Palermo; and consulates in Florence, Trieste and Turin.

Canadian Embassy, Via G.B. de Rossi 17, Rome (855 341).
Canadian Consulate General, Via Vittori Pisani 19, Milan (669 7451).

Lost Property. For things lost in any form of public transport, apply to the appropriate authorities. Otherwise, the nearest police station.

Baby-sitting. Virtually impossible, since Italian *bambini* are never let out of their mother's sight. You'll have trouble finding an agency, but see what your hotel can suggest.

Information. There is a comprehensive network of tourist information offices, ranging from the Provincial Tourist Boards (EPT) in 94 major towns, to the more limited local tourist offices (*Azienda Autonoma di Soggiorno* — AS) in over 400 smaller towns. The Rome office is at Via Parigi 11 (Tel: 461 851) with branches at Fiumicino airport and Termini station. Outside Italy, consult the Italian State Tourist Office (ENIT), which also has frontier offices at Imperia, Como and Brenner. For travel information, the CIT (pronounced *cheet*) offices in major towns are quite useful.

Free Maps. The best are issued by AGIP petrol stations.

Disabled Travellers. The *Associazione Italiana per l'Assistenza agli Spastici*, via Cipro 4H, Rome will provide general help and information.

Student Travel. CTS, Via Nazionale 66, 00184 Rome (Tel: 479 931). CTS, Pia Sant'Antonio 2, 20122 Milan (Tel: 5830 4121); there are CTS offices in many other cities. ESTC, Largo Brancaccio 55, 00184 Rome.

English Language Churches in Rome. All Saints (Anglican), Via Bubuino 153 (Tel: 679 4537); St. Paul's (American Episcopal), Via Napoli 88 (Tel: 474 3569); St. Andrew's (Church of Scotland), Via XX Settembre 7 (Tel: 475 1627), San Silvestro (English-speaking Catholic), Piazza San Silvestro. (Tel: 6785 609).

American Express. Piazza di Spagna 38, Rome (Tel: 67641). Plus offices in 14 other cities.

Calendar of Events

Public Holidays are shown in **bold.** If a holiday falls on a Thursday or Tuesday it is common practice to turn it into a long weekend. Many other religious days are celebrated locally.

January 1	**New Year's Day**
January 6	**Epithany**
February	Carnival at Viareggio
	Orange Blossom Festival at Agrigento
March/April	**Easter Monday** — festivals everywhere
April (last 2 weeks)	International Trade Fair at Milan
April 25	**Liberation Day**
May 1	**Labour Day**
May 1-4	Feast of St Efisio at Cagliari
May (first Thursday)	Festival of St Domenico (snake festival) at Cocullo
May	Vallelunga Grand Prix, Rome
	Music Festival at Florence
June 5	Tournament of the bridge, Pisa
June 24 and 28	Mediaeval pageantry and football, Florence
June/July	*Due Mondi* Festival at Spoleto
July 2	First *Palio* (mediaeval pageantry and bareback horse racing around the city square) at Siena
	Beginning of opera season in Verona amphitheatre
August (first Sunday)	Tournament of Quintana at Ascoli Piceno
August 15	**Assumption**
August 16	Second *Palio* at Siena
	Beginning of opera season in Verona amphitheatre
August	International Film Festival at Venice
September	Car and Motorcycle Grand Prix at Monza
October	Truffle Fair at Alba
November 1	**All Saints' Day**
November	International Car Show, Turin
December	**Conception Day**
December 25, 26	**Christmas**

Vatican City

The Vatican enclave is a tiny independent state on the west side of the Tiber in Rome. Although entry to the Vatican Palace itself is not permitted visitors are allowed into St Peter's Square and St Peter's Basilica between 7am to 7pm without charge. The Vatican Museums and the Sistine Chapel are open from 9am to 2pm Mondays-Saturdays around the year: they are also open from 2 to 5pm on weekdays from July to September. Entrance costs 8,000 l, or 4,000 l to students. You can save yourself the 15 minute walk from St Peter's Square to the Museums by catching the shuttle bus (1,000 l) from the Information Office. (Tel: 6981 4468) there. From the same Office you can take one of the offered minibus trips that are run between March and October, leaving at 10am. These go to the Gardens and Sistine Chapel (Mondays and Thursdays, 19,000 l), or the Gardens and St Peter's (Tuesdays and Saturdays, 8,000 l).

The Vatican mints a few of its own coins, which are valid throughout Italy, just as Italian currency is valid in the Vatican. It also issues its own stamps, available from post offices around St. Peter's.

Papal audiences are usually held every Wednesday either in St Peter's Square or the Audience Room, at 11am in Castel Gandolfo. To participate at either, apply to the *Prefettura della Cassa Pontificia,* 00120 Citta del Vaticano indicating the desired date and the nationality and number of desired participants giving between two and 30 days' notice. Catholics should take a letter of introduction from their parish priest.

Vatican Radio broadcasts in English daily at 1.45pm and 8.30pm.

Canadian Embassy to the Holy See, Via della Conciliazone 4 (Tel: 654 7316). Otherwise refer to consular offices in Rome.

San Marino

The Most Serene Republic of San Marino is a 25 square mile chunk of the Apennines, entirely surrounded by Italy, and only 12 miles from the Adriatic coast at Rimini. It claims to be the world's oldest republic, founded, according to legend, in 301 AD. The 22,500 inhabitants are ruled by a 60-man Grand General Council, elected every five years. It is headed by two Regent Captains who are elected every six months and instated with much ceremony on April 1st and October 1st each year. The government is governed by a Communist Christian Democrat coalition.

Italian currency is used, but San Marino coins have also been minted since 1971 (including some gold ones); these are legal tender, as well as being collectors' items, but are hard to use outside the republic. Only San Marino stamps may be used, and Italian postal and telephone rates are in force. Useful numbers: emergency — 113; taxis — 991 441.

Information. *Ufficio di State per il Turismo,* Palazzo del Turismo, 47031 San Marino (Tel: 992 101).

Malta

Malta GC (population 360,000) is a group of islands between Sicily and North Africa, covering an area of 122 square miles. A former British colony, the islands are now independent; the George Cross was awarded to the islanders for their bravery in resisting the German bombing and Italian blockade in 1942. Only the three largest islands are inhabited — Malta, Gozo and Comino — all connected by cheap ferries. The islands' popularity among the British is due to the combination of sun, sea and sand, plus the fact that English is spoken everywhere (although there is a native Maltese language, of Semitic origin, and Italian is also widely spoken).

Entry. If you wish to stay more than three months, contact the Principal Immigration Officer, General Police Headquarters, Floriana (Tel: 224001). Duty free customs allowances are granted on tobacco and alcohol — the usual litre of spirits plus 200 cigarettes and one bottle of wine — and articles intended for personal use. — You may only bring in up to £M50 in local currency.

Money. The currency is the Maltese Lira (£M): £M 1 = 100 cents = 1,000 mils.

£1 = £M 0.55 $1 = £M 0.35   £M 1 = £1.80   £M 1 = $2.90

Coins. 2 m, 3 m, 5 m, 1 c, 2 c, 5 c, 10 c, 25 c, 50 c, £M1. Silver and gold coins of higher values are issued (at a premium) by the Central Bank, who also issue permits for their export.

Notes. £M 1, £M 2, £M 5, £M 10, £M 20, £M 25, £M 50
Imports of Maltese currency are limited to £M 50, exports to £M 25, plus foreign currency and travellers cheques to the value imported and declared. Banks are open Monday-Friday, 8.30am-12.30pm; some open 5-7pm and closing times may be 30 minutes earlier in winter. Arriving or departing passengers can use the 24-hour exchange facilities at Luqa airport. Shops open 9am-7pm (8pm on Saturdays), but most close from 1 to 3.30pm for the siesta.

Getting Around. Most travellers arrive by air; for flight information at Luqa airport, dial 622901. Malta can also be reached by car ferry from Syracuse and Catania on Sicily. For car bookings on the Marfa-Mgarr ferry between Malta and Gozo, phone 603 964. Car hire on the islands is amongst the cheapest in Europe, costing as little as £M 6 per day or £M 35 per week. There are no cars on Comino. The maximum speed limit is 40 mph (25 mph in built-up areas). As in Britain, traffic drives on the left.

The island of Malta is served by a cheap and comprehensive bus network. The Valletta bus terminal is at City Gate (Tel: 624001). Taxis, which are all metered at the same rates (about 30 cents per mile), have red number plates with the word *Taxi* printed in white. The Gozo Taxi Association has a booking and information office at Mgarr (Tel: 76543). For more expensive travel there are the *karrozin* (horse drawn cabs) and *dghajjes* (taxi-boats). Cycles can be hired from the Cycle Store, 78 d'Agrens Road, Msida (Tel: 31967); and the Fun Rental Centre, 181 Strand, Gzira (Tel: 30758) for about £M 2 per day. Hitch-hiking is excellent.

Accommodation. There are no organised camping or caravan sites, but the Floriana police anticipate little trouble if you pitch your tent sensibly, and not close to the edge of the water along sandy beaches.

Communications. The main post office is in Merchant's Street, Valletta (Tel: 624421). Telegrams can be sent from any post office during office hours; or round the clock from the main telegraph office in St. George's Road, St. Julians (or dial 34042). The Valletta telegraph office in St. John's Square is open 8am-6.30pm on weekdays; the Luga airport office 7am — 6.45pm daily. International telephone calls can be made from these, and also the Bisarra St office in Sliema (open 8.30am — 9.30pm except Sundays) and the Republic St office in Victoria on Gozo (open daily). When dialling direct, the international prefix is 0; for IDD calls to UK dial 0 44, followed by area code (minus initial 0) and local number. Via the international operator, dial 994; collect calls only are available. Telephone information — 91; complaints — 93; police — 99; ambulance — 96; road accidents — 88; time — 95 (these numbers are for Malta — in Gozo and Comino a preceding 0 is necessary). The telephone directory gives all information in both Maltese and English.

Radio Malta broadcasts mostly in Italian and Maltese, as does Maltese TV. However, there is an English service on 98.7 MHz FM daily from 8am to 8pm.

Health and Hygiene. The main health risk is from the sand flies that occasionally blow in from North Africa and can cause a nasty fever — nothing dangerous.

An appropriate vaccination certificate is required by travellers arriving from areas affected by yellow fever or cholera.

Under a reciprocal agreement, British visitors who are staying for less than 30 days can obtain, on production of their passport, free out-patient treatment at St. Luke's Hospital, Gwardamangia (Tel: 621251); and in-patient treatment for a nominal fee; extra charges are made for surgery and X-rays. Otherwise, charges for medical and dental treatment and drugs are payable in full. Dentures can be repaired within two hours at 71 Norfolk St. Siliema.

Disabled Travellers. Disabled visitors can seek advice and help from Mr John A. Micallet, Centre for the Physically Handicapped, Corradino. Help for blind visitors, including the loan of a braille map of the islands, is offered by Mr Joseph Burlo, Malta Society for the Blind, 1 Tigne Terrace, Sliema (Tel: 332104).

Babysitting. Promotion Services (Tel: 30120) will arrange a babysitter at 24 hours notice if you call them between 8.30am — 1pm Monday to Friday.

Addresses. The Malta National Tourist Office, 11 City Gate Arcade, Valletta (Tel: 224444) published the booklet *Coming Events*. Postal enquirers to NTOM, 280 Republic Street, Walletta.

British High Commission, 7 St. Anne St, Floriana (Tel: 233134).
American Embassy, Development House, St. Anne St, Floriana (Tel: 623653).
Student Travel: NSTS, 220 St. Paul St. Valletta (Tel: 624983).
American Express, 14 Zachary St, Valletta (Tel: 624312).

Public Holidays. January 1; February 10 (St. Paul's Day); Good Friday; March 31 (Freedom Day); May 1 (Worker's Day); June 7 (Sette Guigno Anniversary); June 29 (Muarja); August 15 (Assumption); September 8 (Our Lady of Victories); September 21 (Independence Day); December 8 (Immaculate Conception); December 13 (Republic Day); December 25 (Christmas).

Netherlands

KINDERDIJK

W.S.

Area. 16,000 square miles

Population. 14,700,000

Capital. Amsterdam (population: 679,000).

Seat of Government. The Hague (population: 500,000).

Weather. Changeable: temperatures don't reach any extremes, and August has the distinction of being the wettest month. Even in summer you'll need a raincoat with you and something warm for the evenings. Winters are dark and wet, with a fair sprinkling of snow, and the North Sea sometimes freezes round the edges.

THE PEOPLE

The real Netherlands is far removed from the tourist brochure image of a country populated by nubile blondes in lace bonnets, and wizened old pipe-smoking sailors in clogs. In reality, it is a mixture of traditional puritanism and advanced liberalism. The narrow-mindedly conservative are found side by side with a progressive, even amoral, younger generation.

Politics. The Netherlands is a constitutional monarchy, with the monarch (Queen Beatrix) as nominal head of state, but the real power lies with the Prime Minister, his ministers and the two-chamber Parliament, known as the States General. The country is governed by a coalition of Christian Democrats and liberals.

Religion. 40% Catholic. 25% Dutch Reformed (Protestant); Catholics in the south,

168

Protestants in the north. Most Dutch Catholics are liberal and opposed to Vatican doctrine on many social issues.

Language. Dutch (as opposed to double Dutch) is closely related to German, which it resembles in accent and intonation. Friesland has a language of its own; the other regional dialects don't differ much from standard Dutch. If you don't speak Dutch, don't worry — almost everyone speaks English . . . and French and German.

Making Friends. Although they may at first seem aloof and reserved, the Dutch can be very friendly and hospitable. The older generation tend to be fairly formal: handshaking is widespread at all age levels, but you can't really hold a long conversation with the older people until you know them well. If you want to experience Dutch family life at first hand, the Amsterdam VVV runs a scheme called "Get in Touch with Dutch". Alternatively, since no-one uses curtains in their front room, you can simply look through any window.

The young generation have a very open attitude towards sex. Look in the personal columns of newspapers for an idea of the acceptance of paid companionship, blind dates, and computer dating. Walk round the Zeedijk in Amsterdam for an idea of attitudes towards commercialised sex.

See the introduction for details of passports customs regulations, duty free allowances, vaccinations and importing pets.

Passport and Visas. Holders of British, US and Canadian passports are allowed to stay three months. For extensions, apply to the police.

Customs. Travellers, especially long-haired hitch-hikers, have been known to be turned back because they have "insufficient funds", although an exact sum isn't specified. If you are able to show a return ticket, your chances are greatly enhanced. Duty free allowances are basically the same as in the introduction, with additional restrictions on tea and coffee (amounts given under *Belgium*). Travellers under 15 are not entitled to the alcohol, coffee or tobacco allowances. If you wish to take bulbs home, it's simplest to have them forwarded direct by a bulb dealer — export laws are complex.

100 cents (c) = 1 guilder or florin (fl)
£1 = fl3.30   fl1 = £0.30
$1 = fl2.00   fl1 = $0.50

For general information on handling, exchanging and raising money, see the introduction.

Coins. 5c (*stuiver*), 10c (*dubbeltje*), 25c (*kwartje*), fl 1 (*gulden* or *florijn*), fl 2.5 (*rijksdaalder*), fl 5 (*five guilder*).

Don't confuse the fl 1 and fl 2.50 coins: there's only a slight difference in size. All bank notes are marked in braille for the benefit of the blind.

Notes. fl 5 (green), fl 10 (blue), fl 25 (red), fl 100 (brown), fl 1,000 (green).

Banking Hours. Monday-Friday, 9 am-4 or 5 pm. Exchange bureaux at airports, ports, frontier posts and rail stations, are open from 6 am to 11 pm or midnight, including Sundays. Money can be changed, and cheques cashed, on many international trains.

Shopping Hours. Weekdays 8.30 or 9 am-5.30 or 6 pm (tobacconists 7 pm), Saturdays 9 am-5 pm. Late-opening — Amsterdam and The Hague: 9 pm Thursdays. Rotterdam: 9 pm Fridays. Half-day closing varies from place to place; Wednesday afternoon is the commonest, but food shops and department stores close on Monday morning instead.

Import and Export. No restrictions for non-residents.

Tipping. Hotels, restaurants, cafés — 12%, usually included in the bill (*bediening inbegrepen*). Taxis — in Amsterdam, included in the fare; elsewhere, 15%. Porters — available at Amsterdam, Rotterdam and Utrecht (Central Stations) and at Hook of Holland for trains connecting to the Harwich ferry; fl 2 per item; a tip is expected in addition. Lavatory attendants: 25 or 50 cents.

Emergency Cash. Begging, street-selling and busking are illegal, and the police can be quite severe. The work situation isn't too good, because of high unemployment, but wages are high. The most efficient way to find work is to look under *Uitzenburos* (employment agencies) in the yellow pages and register with as many as possible.

Taxes. Value added tax (BTW) of 18% on meal prices and hotel bills is normally included in menus and price lists. BTW of 18% on luxury items in the shops; 4% on basic necessities. Business travellers can reclaim tax paid on certain expenses from Invoerrechten en Accijnsen, Waldorpstraat 440, The Hague.

Getting Around

The information in this section is complementary to that given in the corresponding section in the introduction.

CAR

Holland has one of Europe's best road networks. Cyclists are the main hazard, choking the roads in and near the large cities at rush hours. Motorways are toll-free and fast-flowing, except when interrupted by traffic lights controlling swing bridges. Dial (06-910 910 90) for information on road conditions, including hold-ups and weather reports.

Rules and requirements. A red warning triangle is obligatory. Seat belts must be worn at all times by drivers and front seat passengers; children under 12 are banned from the front seat. Trams, funeral processions and military convoys have absolute priority and will assert it. When turning right, watch out for cyclists alongside you, to whom you should give way. Minimum driving age — 18.

Road signs. Through routes are indicated by the sign *Doorgaand Verker,* or by rectangular blue signs with a slender white arrow. Slow — *Langzaam rijden;* Single line — *Een file;* Danger — *Gevaar;* Bicycles — *Fietsen.* In built up areas with a blue sign bearing a white house, traffic should proceed at walking pace.

Place Names. The Hague = 's Gravenhage or Den Haag; Flushing = Vlissingen.

Parking. The most common methods of control are meters (25c, fl 1 or fl 2 coins — at a rate of fl 5 an hour in city centres); and blue zones — discs available (for fl 1) from police stations, ANWB offices and VVV's. Take care when parking by canals: engage low gear and check that the handbrake is full on.

Petrol. Two grades of unleaded petrol — 91 octane (*normal*) costs about fl 1.69 a litre; *super* (99 octane) is fl 1.89. Super leaded petrol cost about fl 1.75 a litre (£2.40 per UK gallon, $3.30 per US gallon).

Touring Clubs. KNAC, Westulietweg 118, Leidschendam (Tel: 070 997 451); ANWB, Wassenaarseweg 220, The Hague (Tel: 070 147 147).

Breakdowns. Motorways and main roads are patrolled by the ANWB *Wegenwacht* vans; or, for 24-hour breakdown service, they can be summoned by dialling 06-0888. Subscribers to foreign touring plans receive these services free; others must pay around fl 75 for temporary ANWB membership.

Accidents. To call the police, dial 22 22 22 in the Hague. Elsewhere the number for emergency services is generally 001 (0011 in Friesland).

TRAIN

The rail network is run by *Nederlandse Spoorwegen* (NS), Moreelsepark 1, 3511 EP Utrecht (Tel: 35 91 11). For information about international rail traffic in Amsterdam dial 20 22 66: for information about trains and other public transport inside the Netherlands dial 06-899 1121.

There are two classes, first costing 50% more than second. Second class single fares cost about fl 3 for 10 km (about £1.50 or $2 for 10 miles). Timetables (*Spoorboekje*) are published annually in May and are on sale at stations, bookshops and some post offices. It is neither possible nor necessary to make advance seat reservations. You can board a train without a ticket, or switch from second to first class on the train, but you'll be surcharged fl 3.50 by the conductor. Breaks of journey are allowed, but hang on to your ticket.

Cheap Deals. Children under 4 travel free: children aged 4-11 get a 40% discount. A fare paying adult can take up to three children for 1 fl each: ask for a *Roadrunner* ticket.

Unlimited travel cards: as well as the Benelux Tourrail system (see Belgium for details) travellers can buy a seven day or monthly *Rail Rover* for fl 108 or fl 419 respectively for second class rail travel within the Netherlands. Add on supplements of fl 20.15 or fl 65.75 allow unlimited city transport. There is also a one day *Rail Rover* costing fl 52.50, with a supplement of fl 5.25 for city transport.

Dutch Railways run cheap day excursions to over 40 places of interest: details can be found in the booklet *Er-op-Uit!* (fl 3.95 from stations).

BICYCLE

There are around 1,500,000 bicycles in Holland, and each year half a million are stolen.

Cycles can be hired at an hourly or daily rate from main railway stations and bike dealers for around fl 7.50 per day (with a discount at railway stations for those who can show a railway ticket). You may be required to leave a deposit of fl 200, which you will lose if the bike is stolen. Motorways are forbidden territory, but there is invariably a cycle track nearby, marked by a round blue sign with a white bicycle superimposed.

HITCH-HIKING

Prospects are good once out of towns. Displaying a flag is recommended. To get out of Amsterdam, take tram 6, 16 or 24 to the Olympic Stadium for Rotterdam; line 25 to the terminus at Europabrug for Utrecht and points south and east.

AIR

Schiphol airport is accessible from all over Holland — buses from the Hague, Utrecht, Delft, Leiden and Eindhoven operate regularly, as well as services from Central Station and major hotels. Trains to and from Leiden (with alternate services for the Hague and Rotterdam) operate every 15 minutes from 5 am to midnight. A train to the Central station costs fl 14.40. The 20 minute taxi ride from cental Amsterdam to the airport costs fl 60. For flight information, dial 601 0966.

CITY TRANSPORT

Taxis. There are taxi stands at stations, airports and other random points; if the light on the roof is on, they can also be hailed, but don't always respond if it involves a tricky manoeuvre. Otherwise, telephone (*Taxis* in the directory; in Amsterdam dial 77 77 77 for the Central Taxi Office at Prins Hendrikskade 43). In Amsterdam, meters start at fl 3, then fl 3.50 per km (£1.00 or $1.60 a mile), inclusive of the 15% tip.

Bus/Tram/Underground. All urban transport in Holland has a uniform ticket system. You buy a *Nationale Strippenkaart* valid for 15 or 45 zones, for fl 8.85 or fl 25.85 respectively, from tobacconists, post offices and some local tourist offices and public transport kiosks. You can buy cards from the drivers of buses or trams but it will cost slightly more. Once you have a ticket, you may use it for any journey according to local zone and time regulations, and transfers are allowed. You punch the ticket in the machines provided, or get the driver to stamp if for you.

A "surcharge" of fl 26 is payable for travelling without a ticket (or an insufficiently stamped ticket).

For transport information in Amsterdam, dial 16 00 22: in Rotterdam, 13 75 38.

Cheap deals. Details of day tickets are given in English on the back of each card. For unlimited travel on urban transport throughout Holland, simply buy two ten-strip tickets and get the driver to stamp the two cards simultaneously. For the Hague-Amsterdam-Rotterdam area, you need only get one ten-strip card validated. In Amsterdam, an alternative to strip-tickets is the one-day tourist ticket for fl 8.85, which allows unlimited travel within the city. It can be bought from the information office opposite Central Station.

See the introduction for information on youth hostels, other hostels, and advance booking of accommodation.

Hotels/Motels. You are assured of absolute cleanliness in all Dutch hotels, which are graded from one to five stars, one being the highest standard. They are obliged by law to have a price list available for inspection at the reception desk. Prices start at about fl 75 (£22 or $37) for a double room with breakfast, and usually include 15% service and 18% tax. Prices for single rooms are around two-thirds of the price of doubles. The *Amsterdam Way* Scheme offers discount rates in 26 hotels of different grades between November 1st and March 31st.

Youth Hostels. The head office is: *Nederlandse Jeugdherberg Centrale* (NJHC), Prof Tulppein 4, 1018GX, Amsterdam (Tel: 55 13 155). All hostels offer full board as well as bed and breakfast, which costs fl 18.50 for members of the IYHF and fl 23.50 for non-members regardless of category.

Dormitories. Following in footsteps of the famous Amsterdam Sleep-ins, dormitory hostels can be found in many towns, some only opening in the summer; prices start at around fl 8 per person per night (bed and breakfast). Details from MAIC, Hartenstroaat 16-18, Amsterdam (Tel: 020 24 09 77). Beware of people who approach you and offer to find you somewhere to stay for the night; they will probably be receiving commission, which thus raises the cost of the places they represent.

Camping. In general, camping is only allowed on special camp-sites, which are usually very well equipped. Prices are in the region of fl 5 per person, caravan or trailer, with sometimes an extra nominal charge for cars and tents.

Sleeping out. Legal, but the police might bother you if you're in a very public place. You can only be arrested for vagrancy if you have no money. Stations are inadvisable unless you have a ticket.

Finding and Booking Accommodation. If you go at bulb-time (April-May), at Easter, Whitsun or Christmas, or in June, July, or August, you should book early. When booking in advance, you may be required to pay a deposit of 25%, retainable if you cancel at short notice. You can book rooms anywhere in Holland through the National Reservations Centre, PO Box 404, 2260 AK Leidschendam (Tel: 070-20 25 00). The NRC also takes bookings for camping huts (fl 44 per night), theatre tickets, bungalows and self catering accommodation. Alternatively, you can do it yourself with the help of the hotel guide issued free by Netherlands National Tourist Offices. They will also provide lists of camp sites, camping houses and farms.

For a small fee, you can also use the *VVV Logies* service, either for bookings in the same town or elsewhere in Holland. You must go to the VVV in person. Rooms anywhere in Holland can also be booked at VVV frontier offices on the E10 and E36 motorways and at the port of Hook of Holland. VVVs are always the best bet for last minute bookings.

Communications

General information on telephones and English language newspapers and radio broadcasts is given in the introduction.

Post. Post offices are open 9am-5pm Monday-Friday; some also open 9am-4pm on Saturdays. The main post office in Amsterdam (where letters addressed to Poste Restante, Amsterdam should arrive) is at Nieuwe Zjjds Voorburgwal 182 (open until 6pm on weekdays, and 8.30pm on Thursdays); the post office at Oosterdokskade is open till 9pm. Stamps can also be bought at card shops and tobacconists. Mail boxes are red, and are no longer found on the back of Amsterdam's trams. There is a free restante service *(Postliggen)* at all main post offices.

Large post offices have their own philatelic counters. There is a central philatelic service at Beatrixslaan 11, The Hague (Tel: 75 77 44), for all current issues of the Netherlands, Surinam and Dutch Antilles. Most post offices sell tape cassettes which allow voiced messages of up to ten minutes to be sent through the post.

The correct way to address mail is: name; street (name, then number); town, preceded by a post code consisting of four digits and two letters (and the letters NL if writing from abroad).

Telephone. Within Holland all calls are automatic. Public telephones take 25c fl 1 and fl 2.50 coins; 50c gives you unlimited time for local calls. Lift the receiver, insert 50c, dial — if there's no reply, your money will be returned. For long distance calls, the same procedure applies, but pause after dialling the area code (or after dialling the international prefix — 09), until you hear a new dialling tone. Long distance and international calls can be made from all public telephones. Operating instructions are often displayed in English. The codes for the main cities are Amsterdam — 02; Rotterdam — 010; The Hague — 070; Utrecht — 030. Delete the initial zero on a number if calling from the UK. Calls within Europe are 50% cheaper at weekends, and at night from 6pm-8pm. There is an audible (buzzing) warning when your money is running out.

Long distance and international calls can also be made at telegraph offices, attached to main post offices. In Amsterdam, the office at NZ Voorburgwal is open round the clock. For IDD calls to UK, insert at least 2 25c coins, dial 09, wait for 2nd tone, dial 44 dial UK area code (Minus initial 0), dial local number insert more coins on signal. For the operator, dial 008 (domestic). International operator for collect & BT chargecard calls is 06 (dial tone) 0410. For access from cardphones insert *Telefoonkaart*: the card will not be credited for UK direct calls dial 06 (await 2nd dial tone) 022 99 44. Payphones require a 25c piece which will be returned. Other useful numbers: 22 22 22 — police (emergency); 131313 — ambulance; 212121 — fire; 0017 — postal information; 088 — directory enquiries.

Each town or area has its own commercial directory *(Gouden Gids)*, but the whole country is covered by nine fat personal directories *(Woonplaatsen):* Volume I is Amsterdam; Volume II The Hague; Volume III Rotterdam; Volumes IV-IX include the other towns and villages in alphabetical order. Note that the diphthong IJ is treated as one letter between Y and Z in the alphabet.

Yellow pages have an index in English; and a few emergency numbers on the front pages, along with descriptions of the warnings you'll hear in case of an invasion: air raid warning — 1 minute of undulating siren; fall out warning — three $\frac{1}{2}$ minute undulating sirens with $\frac{1}{2}$ minute pauses; all clear — one minute's steady tone.

Telegrams. Can be sent from any post office or telegraph office, or by telephone — 009 for domestic, 0019 for international.

Newspapers. For what's on in Amsterdam, try the weekly *Amsterdam This Week,* fl 1, published by the VVV, or the magazines *Agenda* and *Uitkramt.*

Broadcasting. American Forces Network operate the following FM stations: Brunssum — 89.15 MHz; Camp New Amsterdam (Soesterberg) — 93.1 MHz; Maastricht — 93.4 MHz; Volkel Air Base — 93.6 MHz. Most British radio and television programmes can be received in southern coastal areas.

Emergency messages (contact ANWB — 070-26 44 26 — if you want to place one) are transmitted at 5.55pm on Hilversum 2 (746 kHz AM) and at 10.55pm on Hilversum 3 (674 kHz AM).

Health and Hygiene

For information on hygiene, first aid, medical treatment and insurance, see the introduction.

Hygiene. Holland is a very clean country and the chances of illness or disease are low. Tap water is drinkable everywhere.

Treatment. Medical and dental treatment is expensive, but emergencies will always be dealt with free, even if you're broke and uninsured.

Reciprocal Agreement. Only for British visitors with Form E111 (see the introduction). Take both the original and photocopy of your E111 to a doctor (for free treatment) or dentist (part payment), or to a pharmacy for free prescriptions. Not all doctors and dentists belong to the scheme — information from the *Algemeen Nederlands Onderling Ziekenfonds* (ANOZ), Kaap Hoorndreef 24-28, Utrecht (Tel: 61 88 81). Free hospital treatment is subject to ANOZ approval — this is normally arranged by a doctor, but if you enter hospital without ANOZ approval, show the E111 to the hospital authorities and ask them to contact ANOZ immediately. If you have to pay, contact ANOZ before leaving the Netherlands to obtain a refund.

Pharmacies. Open Monday-Friday, 9am-5.30pm. At least one in every town is either open or on call all night and at weekends; look in the local rag, or in chemists' windows; or, in Amsterdam, dial 44 77 39.

Emergencies. Ambulance — 13 13 13. For emergency treatment in Amsterdam, dial 555 59 11; in Rotterdam 13 50 00; in the Hague, 22 21 11. There are 24-hour first aid stations in all hospitals; the most central are at Grimburgwal 10 and Helmersstraat 104. 24-hour medical or psychological help from Projekt C-Gebouw, Lauriergracht 116 (Tel: 25 36 52). VD clinics at Groenburgwal 44 and Van Oldenbarneveldtstraat 42.

Entertainment

Sport. Soccer is the most enthusiastically-supported game, reflecting the consistently good performance by the national team. Ajax (pronounced *eye-ack*) of Amsterdam and Feyernoord are the best clubs. Skating is very popular, with the Eleven Cities Tour being the premier event. This 124-mile marathon around the canals and lakes of Friesland takes place only in the coldest of winters: only 13 times since its inception in 1090, most recently in 1985. Contrary to some expectations, skiing is popular on the hills around Maastricht in the extreme south of the country.

Museums. Amsterdam has some outstanding museums: the *Rijksmuseum* (Stadhouderskade 42), which includes Rembrandt's "Night Watch"; the National Museum (Paulus Potterstraat 7), devoted to Van Gogh; and the Stedelijk Museum (Paulus Potterstraat 13), for modern art. Most charge around fl 5 for admission, but you can buy a museum card for allowing unlimited visits to all of the Netherlands' 350 museums. It costs fl 15 for those under 26 or fl 30 for those over 26.

Nightlife. Amsterdam has absolutely everything from the classiest opera to the seediest strip joints. Cinemas invariably show films in the original language; tickets cost around fl 12. For theatre in English, look out for the shows by Paul van Vliet. Discotheques are very popular — the most famous (or infamous) are the *Paradiso* and the *Cosmos*.

Eating out. Restaurant meals start at about fl 16 (£5 or $8). Look for places displaying a "tourist menu" (sign — fork wearing a hat and a camera), which will give you a three-course meal for fl 19.90. Indonesian restaurants are generally cheaper than their domestic equivalents. Whether you go, the service is likely to be courteous; but sometimes painfully slow. For cheap lunches, try university canteens — known as *Mensa* — where no ID is required; Amsterdam Mensa is at Damstraat 3. Or try a sandwich shop *(Broodjeswinkel) or eetcafe* (eating house). At any time of day or night, hot or cold snacks can be obtained from coin-operated *Automaaten* in all towns, and at all large railway stations. The national dish — *ertwensoep*, a thick pea soup — is traditionally served only from October to March, but is usually cheap and filling.

Drinking. Licensing laws don't really seem to have occurred to the Dutch. Bars usually stay open till well after midnight, often till 3am, and re-open at 10am. The age limit is 16 (for beer only) or 18 (for everything).

Beer is the most popular drink, and the one most frequently drunk at mealtimes. In a bar, a half-litre of beer (about a pint) costs fl 2.50 or so. The light beer is called *Pils*, the heavier dark beer, *Bockbier* or stout. The Amstel and Heineken breweries offer free beer to those who survive the mandatory tour. Gin *(Jenever)* does not mix well, except with coke. A reasonable tot costs about fl 2.50. Other typical Dutch drinks include lemon and redcurrant gins, and *advocaat*. Treat Dutch brandy with great caution.

Smoking. Cigarettes cost around fl 4.25 per packet of Dutch, German or American brands. For the same price you can buy 50g of cigarette tobacco plus papers *(Samson* or *Drum* being the most popular rolling tobacco) which will yield at least twice as many cigarettes. Dutch cigars and pipe tobacco are both of an outstandingly high quality. The best brand names are *Clan* and *Holland House* for pipe tobacco; *Ritmeester, Wintermans* and *Schimmelpenninck* for cigars.

Crime. Holland has the second-highest theft rate in Europe, just behind Britain, much of it drug-related. Although assault is rare, intoxicated foreigners are popular targets among robbers.

Police. The head police station in Amsterdam is at Elandsgracht 117 (Tel: 559 91 11); the emergency number is 22 22 22 in most areas, 14 14 14 in some.

Nude Bathing. Generally illegal, but permitted on five beaches — Scheveningen, Zandvoort, Hook of Holland, Texel and Callantsoog.

Drunken Driving. Fines and loss of licence are the standard penalties with imprisonment possible for those greatly over the limit.

Drugs. Possession of small quantities of soft drugs is an offence, but will normally be tolerated. Possession of over 30g is a crime, and will be treated more seriously. Holland has a serious problem with hard drug addiction, and possession will be dealt with severely.

Legal Aid. There are special legal aid offices in more large towns known as *Bureau voor Rechtshulp.* The address in Amsterdam is Droogbak 1a (Tel: 24 27 57); The Hague — Javastraat 27a (Tel: 63 49 58). Otherwise, try your embassy.

For general information on useful contacts and complaints procedures, see the introduction.

Embassies and Consulates.

British Embassy, Lange Voorhout 10, 2514 ED The Hague (64 58 00).
British Consulate General, Koningslaan 44, 1075 AE Amsterdam (76 43 43).

American Embassy, Lange Voorhout 102, 2514 EJ The Hague (62 49 11).
American Consulate General, Museumplein 19, Amsterdam (64 56 61).
American Consulate General, Vlarmarkt 1, Rotterdam (1 11 75 86).

Canadian Embassy, Sophialaan 5-7, The Hague (61 41 11).

Lost Property. For general lost property, contact the police. In Amsterdam, the Police Lost Property Department is open from 10.30am-4pm (Tel: 75 25 50). For property lost on a bus or tram, telephone the municipal tramway office (Tel: 16 01 28 in Amsterdam). For things left in taxis, call 77 77 77 in Amsterdam, or the office of the particular taxi company.

Baby-sitting. Local VVVs can help find baby-sitters. Charges are about fl 5 an hour (more after midnight).

Gay information. Contact *COC,* Rozenstraat 14, Amsterdam (Tel: 26 30 87).

Guides. The Dutch Amateur Guides Association, consisting mainly of students and school children, offer their services free to visitors. They can be contacted through the local VVV. Or contact the *GUIDOR* Guide Service (12 34 56) if you feel like paying for your tour.

Information. There are some 450 VVVs (tourist offices) spread around the country. Always centrally situated, usually next to the main station, they are indicated by blue and white triangular signs. They offer free advice and information on virtually any subject. In Amsterdam, the central VVV is at Rokin 5 (Tel: 26 64 44). There are branch offices at Stationsplein and Utrechtseweg. Rotterdam VVV is at Stadhuisplein 19 (Tel: 13 60 00).

Help. MAIC (Social Advice and Information Centres) has an office at Hartenstraat 16-18, Amsterdam (Tel: 020 24 09 77), and in Amersfoort, Arnhem, Breda, Enschede, Gorkum, Haarlem, The Hague, Utrecht, Wageningen and Woudrichem.

Disabled Travellers. *Holidays for People with Physical or Sensory Disabilities* is a free booklet (send six international reply coupons for postal delivery abroad) issued by the Nederlandse Vereniging voor Revaliditie ((NVR), Postbus 323, Utrecht, giving information on hotels and other establishments, and their practicability regarding wheelchairs. It covers all of Europe. The Red Cross provide wheelchairs for the use of the disabled at major railway stations.

Student Travel. NBBS, Dam 17, Amsterdam (Tel: 20 50 71); in Rotterdam at Meent 126 (Tel: 414 98 22); in Leiden, Breestraat 52 (Tel: 14 19 97).

Student Organisations. For general information on studying in the Netherlands, contact the Foreign Student Service (FSS), Oranje Nassaulaan 5, 1075 AH Amsterdam (Tel: 71 59 15) for their publications *Vademecum: a concise guide to studying in the Netherlands for foreigners.*

Youth Information Centres. JAC is a youth organisation for any kind of help or information. The Amsterdam office is at Amstel 30 (Tel: 24 29 49). Here, and at many other places in Amsterdam, you can pick up the free leaflet *Use It* — a guide to the city for young people. Other JAC addresses: Eendrachtsweg 69, Rotterdam (Tel: 13 64 28); Oude Gracht 371, Utrecht (Tel: 31 02 67); Social Unit, The Hague (Tel: 39 99 43).

English Language Churches. Christ Church (Anglican), Groenburgwal 42 (Tel: 24 88 77); English Reformed Church, Begijnhof (Tel: 72 22 21).

American Express. Damrak 66, Amsterdam (Tel: 26 20 42); and offices in Enschede, The Hague and Rotterdam.

Calendar of Events

	Public Holidays are shown in **bold**
January 1	**New Year's Day**
February	Shrovetide Carnivals, especially in the provinces of Limburg and North Brabant.
March/April	**Good Friday, Easter Monday**
March-May	Open air bulb show at Keukenhof, Lisse; bulb field in bloom throughout Holland
April	Arts and Antiques Fair at Breda
April 10	**Queen's Birthday**
May/June	**Ascension Day, Whit Monday**
May-September	Cheese markets at Alkmaar (Friday mornings) and Gouda (Thursday mornings)
June	Holland Festival (theatre and music) in Amsterdam, the Hague and Rotterdam
	Dutch Grand Prix at Zandvoort
July	Liliade flower show at Akersloot
early August	Gladioli show at Middelharnis
	Floral parade from Rijnsburg-Leiden

mid August	Floral parade at Katwijk aan Zee and Leersum
late August	Floral parades at Winterswijk and Eelds-Paterswolde
early September	Dahlia Show at Almelo
	Floral parades at Aalsmeer and Zundert
	Arts and Antiques Fair at Delft
mid September	Floral parades at Frederiksoord and Valkenswaard
	Fruit and flower parade at Tiel
early October	Festival at Leiden
	Flower shows at Laren and Enschede
November-December	St Nicholas celebrations in many towns, culminating in the saint's birthday on December 5
December 25, 26	**Christmas Day, Boxing Day**

Liberation Day (May 5) is celebrated only when the year ends in 5 or 0 — so 1995 will be the next such year. The Dutch celebrate St. Nicholas' Day on December 5 and many businesses close at noon for this purpose.

TOWER OF BELÉM, LISBON   W.S.

Portugal

Area. 36,390 square miles   **Population.** 10,100,000

Capital. Lisbon (population: 850,000).

Weather. Temperatures are high, but cooler near the coast and in Madeira and the Azores — Lisbon rarely gets hotter than 85°F. Inland, the temperature often rises above 100°F in the summer; but winters are mild — about 60°F average in the Algarve for January. The rain is concentrated into the period from November to February.

THE PEOPLE

The Portuguese are very friendly people, less temperamental than the Spanish, and always neat and courteous. The overall atmosphere is one of tranquillity, boarding on lethargy. The characteristic Portuguese sense of melancholy possibly stems from the county's chequered history. After a series of invasions (Romans, Barbarians, Goths, Visigoths and Moors), a wealthy kingdom emerged which led the world in exploration and colonialism throughout the Middle Ages. This kingdom was devastated by two major events — the earthquake of 1775 and Napoleon's Peninsular Campaign 50 years later — from which Portugal has never fully recovered.

Politics. Until the coup d'état of April 25, 1974, Portugal was a dictatorship under Premiers Salazar, then Caetano. After the first elections for nearly fifty years, the country settled into a democratic regime, which survived several major counter-revolutionary attempts. In 1987 the Social Democratic Party became the first government to have a majority since the restoration of democracy.

Religion. Over 97% Catholic, although complete religious freedom is guaranteed under the constitution. As in all Catholic countries, be careful what you wear in churches (no bare arms or legs).

Language. The official language is Portuguese, a romance language closely related to Spanish, but pronounced very differently. A knowledge of Spanish will help you to read Portuguese, but not necessarily to speak it. Many Portuguese understand Spanish, but their national pride is easily offended by its use. Otherwise, French is the most commonly spoken foreign language, followed by English. *Portugal Welcomes You*, a free booklet available from tourist offices, includes a brief list of useful Portuguese phrases such as "I don't understand", "I don't know", "Please help me", etc.

Making Friends. The Portuguese are extremely polite, and more formal than the people in most other Mediterranean countries. They also take a great pride in their personal appearance, young and old alike, and expect others to conform to their standards. Formality, along with Catholic morality, also governs boy-girl relationships. Marriage is still a sacrosanct status (although divorce was recently legalised), and inviting a girl out might be misconstrued as a declaration of undying love. There are more liberal attitudes in the major tourist areas.

Red Tape

See the introduction for details of passports, customs regulations, duty free allowances, vaccinations and importing pets.

Passports and Visas. British subjects can stay up to three months without formality. Canadian and US passport holders require a visa to visit the Azores; elsewhere, they are allowed to stay up to 60 days without additional paperwork. For longer stays, apply to the police; in Lisbon to the Foreigner's Registration Service, Rua Cons. José Silvestre Ribeiro, Lote 22 (Tel: 714 1027). Some travellers have been turned away through lack of funds; the minimum seems to be 2,000 $00 per day with at least 10,000 $00.

Customs. Inspections are relatively common, and drugs are very much taboo. There are strict rules regarding the import of fire-arms, including 30,000 $00 deposit, refundable only when leaving the country from the same point of entry. Duty-free allowances are as shown in the introduction.

Frontier Posts. None of the 12 road frontiers with Spain remains open at night, most closing around midnight in summer, 9 pm in winter; and reopening at 7 am. The La Guardia-Caminha crossing is open only 9.30 am-6 pm all year. The car ferry from Ayamonte (Spain) to Vila Real in the south of Portugal operates from around 7 am-9 pm (winter) or 11 pm (summer).

100 centavos = 1 escudo (1 \$00)
£1 = 250 \$00   10 \$00 = £0.04
\$1 = 155 \$00   10 \$00 = \$0.06

For general information on handling exchanging and raising money, see the introduction. The inflation rate of around 10% means that the exchange rates quoted above are likely to change; sterling and dollar equivalents of prices quoted in this chapter, however, should remain fairly constant.

Coins. 0 \$50, 1 \$00, 2 \$50, 5 \$00, 20 \$00, 25 \$00.

Notes. 50 \$00, 100 \$00, 500 \$00, 1,000 \$00, 5,000 \$00 (all multicolored).

Older people might still quote prices in the traditional units of *mil reis* (1 \$00) and *conto* (1,000 \$00).

Banking Hours. Monday-Friday, 8.30 am-11.45 pm and 1-2.45 pm. In central Lisbon some banks also open 6-9 pm on weekdays. The *bureau de change* at Lisbon airport stays open 24 hours. Elsewhere, hotels are always willing to change money at poor rates of exchange. Even among banks charges vary widely, with some charging no commission and other taking up to 10%.

Shopping Hours. 9 am-1 pm, Monday-Saturday; and 3-7 pm, Monday-Friday. The lunch break may be longer in summer.

Import and Export. There are no restrictions on the amount of excudos or foreign currency that may be brought into Portugal, but if you want to take out more than 50,000 \$00 in escudos or 100,000 \$00 in foreign currency you must be able to prove that you brought in at least that amount.

Emergency Cash. Despite Portugal's membership of the Common Market, full employment rights for EC citizens will not come into effect until 1993. Work prospects are poor, but if you find a job you can work legally for 30 days without a permit.

Work in the catering trade is very hard to find. All employees are required to undergo medical tests (including X-rays), and anyone working without the official pass is subject to a heavy fine. More encouraging for English-speaking travellers is canvassing on the Algarve: accosting tourists with tempting invitations to view time-sharing apartments. This also works the other way; for free champagne, food money (typically 1,000 \$00), take up any opportunities offered — but be prepared to endure the hardest of hard sells.

Tipping. Hotels, restaurants and cafés — 10%, usually included in the bill (*serviĉo incluido*) if not, tip 10-15%, but not less than 25 \$00. Station porters — 100 \$00 per item.

Taxes. Value Added Tax is gradually replacing the variety of retail and tourist taxes. Expect to pay 8% on most things, 17% on luxury items.

The information in this section is complementary to that given in the corresponding section in the introduction.

CAR

Roads surfaces range from abysmal to surprisingly good; country roads tend to be narrow and winding. The natives drive fast and recklessly, relying to a large degree on their horns. Each summer has an alarming number of accidents. The only toll roads are short stretches of motorway around Oporto and Lisbon, including the 25th April Bridge (originally called the Salazar Bridge), leading south over the Tagus out of Lisbon; the toll gate (*portagem*) is on the south side.

Rules and Requirements. Horns may not be used in urban areas during the hours of darkness. If you are driving a vehicle not registered in your name, the owner's written permission must be given on a special authorization form issued by motoring organisations. Trams (in Lisbon and Oporto) must be overtaken on the left; you are not allowed to pass stationary trams until all passengers have finished entering or leaving. The minimum driving age is 18. Drivers who have held a full licence for less than a year must display a yellow disk bearing the figure '90' and are restricted to 90 km/h. Discs are obtainable from ACP shops.

Cars which use liquid petroleum gas either instead or as well as petrol are banned. It is illegal to carry petrol in a car.

Parking. Except in one-way streets, you may park only on the right-hand side of the road. Parking is not allowed within 3 metres of a tram stop, 15 m of a bus stop, 20 m of a road junction, nor in front of entrances to schools, parks, theatres or churches. Oporto has some parking meters. No Parking = *Estacionamento Probido.*

Petrol. 119 $00 for a litre of *super* (96 octane), ie £2.15 per imperial gallon, $2.90 per US gallon. Or 115 $00 for 85 octane (*regular*). Unleaded petrol costs 119 $00 per litre. Some foreign brands are available, as well as the Portuguese-owned *GALP.* Filling stations are few and far between in the remoter areas.

Touring Clubs. *Automòvel Club de Portugal* (ACP), Rua Rosa Araùjo 24 (Tel: 56 39 31).

Accidents and Breakdowns. Should anything go wrong, Portuguese mechanics are very skilled and cheap. Most service stations shut at 1 pm on Saturday. ACP runs a 24-hour towing and breakdown service from offices in Lisbon and Porto for members of affiliated motoring organisations including the AA and RAC. In Lisbon, the office is at Avenida Bardosa de Bocage 24 (Tel: 73 61 21), and in Oporto at Rua Goncalo Cristovao 2 (Tel: 31 67 32). These two central offices will call the nearest office for you. In cases of accident, the police must be called. The emergency number is 115. Details of accident damage should be reported to the Insitiuto Nacional de Seguros, AV 5 de Outubro, 1094 Lisbon.

TRAIN

The state-run system is run by Caminhos de Ferro Portugueses (CP). Second class costs 900 $00 per 100 km (£3.60 or $5.80 per 100 miles), first class is 60% more expensive. Smoking is prohibited on all journeys of less than one hour. The international station in Lisbon is the Santa Apolonia. Stations to Sintra are served from Rossio and Campolide, and to Estoril from Cais do Sodrè. Southbound trains start from Barreiro, south of the Tagus. Boat connections run from Terreiro do

Paco pier at the Praça do Comércio. For rail information, dial 32 62 26 in Lisbon, 2 27 22 in Oporto.

Cheap Deals. Children under 4 free; 4-12 half fare. Over 65s: half fare on proof of age.

There are 20% reductions on return tickets used on blue days. The Kilometric Ticket allows up to 5,000 km of travel for 25,000 $00 (2nd class). Touristic Tickets are also available, allowing unlimited travel over a set period of time. They cost 1,145 $00 for seven days, 18,300 $00 for 14 days and 26,140 $00 for 21 days.

BUS

Most services, both local and long-distance, are operated by *Rodoviaria Nacional* (RN). Fares are slightly higher than second class rail fares. Tickets for local services can be bought on the bus. For long-distance runs, buy tickets from bus stations or RN travel agencies. Smoking is permitted only on journeys of one hour or more, and then only in the last three rows of seats. Some services are operated by luxury *expresso qualidade* buses at higher fares. The cental coach station in Lisbon is on Avenida Casal Ribeiro (metro to Saldanha). On Madeira and Azores, buses are the only form of public transport.

AIR

Internal flights are operated by TAP (89 91 21 for flight information in Lisbon) and in the Azores, by SATA. For flight information at Savacem, dial 802060. A departure tax of around 500 $00 is levied on domestic flights. 1,000 $00 on international departures. Tax is normally included in the fare for charter flights.

Air links to and between the Azores are limited, and seats should be booked well in advance.

HITCH-HIKING

Good on the whole, but there's no long-distance traffic on the minor roads. You'll always have better luck if you're neatly dressed. To clear Lisbon when hitching north, take bus 1, 8, 10, 19 or 22 to the airport roundabout. Going south, try one of the approach roads to the Tagus Bridge, eg Alcantara (tram 19 from Praça de Comércio). The Algarve coast road is crawling with hitchers in summer.

CITY TRANSPORT

Taxis. Easily recognised: black with green roofs, usually rambling old Mercedes. Fares are 34 $00 for the first 360 metres, then 50 $00 per kilometre. You must get out on the pavement side. No more than four passengers are allowed in one taxi. A surcharge of 50% may be imposed if luggage weighs more than 30 kg. Fares are 20% higher between 10 pm and 6 am.

Bus/Tram/Underground. Lisbon city transport is run by the Companhia Carris de Ferro de Lisboa, Rua 1° de Maio 101-103, Lisbon 3 (Tel: 63 20 21).

The metro is a roughly U-shaped line, with the city centre at the base of the

U and two branches on the western side. It operates from 6 am-1 am. Trains have either two or four carriages, but two station platforms are too short for four carriages, so play safe and use the front two. The problem stations (Parque and Socorro) do not have a green circle on the route maps. The flat fare is 40 $00, or you can buy a book of 10 tickets for 320 $00.

The old Lisbon fleet of British double-decker buses is gradually being superseded by new single-deck Volvos. The word for bus stop and tram stop is *Paragem*. Bus stops are always at the side of the road; tram stops have the *Paragem* sign suspended over the middle of the road. Services run from 5 am-1 am. Fares are graded by zones: 30 $00-60 $00 on trams; 30 $00-90 $00 on buses.

Four and seven day tourist tickets (*semanal turisticos*) are available. Tram routes 10, 11, 12 and 28 offer some spectacular sights.

Lifts. To tackle the steep hills in Lisbon, there are a number of funicular railways called *lifts* or *elevadores*, which charge 22 $50.

Boat. The passenger ferries crossing the Tagus from Lisbon cost 46-60 $00, but if you buy a train ticket from Lisbon to the south, the boat ride is included in the fare.

See the introduction for information on youth hostels, other hostels, and advance booking of accommodation.

Hotels/Boarding Houses. All hotel accommodation is strictly controlled by the State Tourist Board. Hotels are graded from five stars to one; inns and boarding houses, known as *estalagen, albergaria* or *pensão,* follow the same system.

A 4-star *pensão* is roughly on a par with a 3-star hotel. Rates must be displayed in the hotel entrance and in each room; there is an official complaints book (*livro de reclamações*), which the management must produce on request. Complaints can also be made to the local Tourist Board.

A double room in a 3-star hotel costs at least 3,500 $00 (£14 or $22); in a 2-star *pensão*, a double room can cost 2,000 $00 (£8 or $13) or less. Prices in hotels outside Lisbon and the Algarve will be about 10-15% less. In the Algarve, there is also a 15% discount during the off-season (November-February). Single rooms are less numerous than doubles, and are about 30% cheaper. Children under 8 who share a parent's room are entitled to a 50% reduction.

Establishments that offer only bed and breakfast are distinguished by the word *residencial* in brackets after the hotel's name. In other hotels, full board is available for stays of more than two days, but make sure you come to an agreement with the proprietor — he can make an extra charge for meals not taken; but you are not forced to accept full board in the first place.

Manor Houses. Rooms are available for a minimum of three nights per stay in a number of privately owned old manor houses, particularly in the north of the country. Prices per night for a double room, including a private bathroom and breakfast, range from around 5,500 $00 to over 10,000 $00. For further information or to make a booking contact TURIHAB, Delegação de Turismo de Ponte da Lima, Praĉu da Repùblica, 4990 Ponte de Lima (Tel: 058-94 23 35).

Motels. Long-distance routes have a sprinkling of rather characterless motels, graded as two or three-star.

Pousadas. These are state-run inns, 32 in number, situated in the remoter parts of the country, and designed to provide tourists with typically Portuguese cuisine and atmosphere. Some are housed in castles, palaces and monasteries. You can stop for a meal, even if you don't stay the night. During the summer, you aren't allowed to stay in any one *pousada* for more than three nights. Prices range from 8,100 $00 to 14,400 $00 for a double room plus breakfast between July 1st and September 30th (rates are lower at other times of year). Pousadas are graded B (the lowest), C or CH. Bookings can be made through ENATUR, Av Santa Joana Princesa 10A, 1700 Lisbon (Tel: 88 12 21).

Hostels. Youth hostels are run by the *Associação Portuguesa de pousadas de Juventude,* Rua Andrade Corvo 46, 1000 Lisbon (Tel: 57 10 54). Charges begin at around 550 $00 per night, rising to 700 $00 per night in Lisbon and Porto from July to September.

Camping. By and large, camping is not too popular in Portugal, as there is an abundance of cheap accommodation. Charges begin at around 250 $00 per person. The Portuguese camping association has its headquarters at Rua da Voz G. Perfia, 1100 Lisbon (Tel: 86 23 50). Sites are graded from four down to one star, or *privativo.* Many of the 87 sites require a camping carnet. Away from official sites, camping is allowed with the landowner's permission except in towns, near reservoirs or within 1 km of a beach or official camp site. Details of sites can be found in the *Portugal Camping* brochure, free from tourist offices.

Sleeping out. Not strictly legal, but no problem with weather.

Finding and Booking Accommodation. The Portuguese National Tourist Offices can supply lists of hotels, *pensões* and *pousadas.* The Lisbon Tourist Office can help you find a room either in Lisbon or in the provinces. Book well in advance for any sort of accommodation in the Algarve.

General information on telephones and English language newspapers and radio broadcasts is given in the introduction.

Post. Mail boxes are painted red with a white hoop and marked *Correio.* Stamps (*selos*) are sold at post offices (also marked *Correio*) and hotels. There are all-night post office in the Praça dos Restauradores in Lisbon, and at Lisbon airport. Main post offices have philatelic counters and a free poste restante service: address mail to *Posta Restante, Correio,* and the name of the town.

The correct way to address mail is: name; street (name then number); postcode; town, followed by district number (if applicable) and, if writing from abroad preceded by the code letter P.

Telephone. Public call boxes take 25 and 50 $00 coins. Dial first, insert 25 $00 when you hear a reply. It'll buzz when it wants more money. The time expiry warning is a visible signal. Card phones — for which you buy a prepaid card from post offices worth 50 or 120 units — are becoming widespread. For the local operator, dial 9. Long distance calls can usually be dialled direct; the international prefix is 00. For International Direct Dial calls to the UK, dial 00 44 followed by the UK area code (minus initial 0) and local number. To make long distance calls through the operator dial 19. BT Chargecard and collect calls are available by dialling 099 for the international operator. Alternatively, these calls can be placed at a telegraph office, attached to central post offices (24-hour service at Lisbon Airport and Praca dos Restauradores). The cheap period for all calls is 8 pm-8 am.

Directories are divided into the usual two sections — alphabetical and commercial (yellow pages); outside Lisbon and Oporto, the alphabetical directory is first sub-divided into areas (see the map at the front). The yellow pages have an English index.

Useful numbers in Lisbon (elsewhere check the directory): Information — 16; Time — 15; Fire — 115; Early morning alarm -180; Police (emergency) — 115; Ambulance — 115; Tourist information — 57 50 86.

Telegrams. For the Iberian peninsula, dial 10 for the Post Office service. For countries other than Spain and Portugal dial 32 98 11 for Radio Marconi. Or go to any telegraph office or main post office.

Newspapers. Look out for *Anglo-Portuguese News* and, in the Algarve, the *Algarve Magazine* and *Algarve News*.

Broadcasting. News, weather and general information are broadcast in English daily by *Radiodifusão Portuguesa E.P.* from 8.30 pm-9 pm. *Holidays in Portugal* is broadcast daily from 8.15-8.30 am on 765 kHz AM and 94.3 MHz FM. The television channel RTP1 shows some material in English, including *Top of the Pops* (broadcast on the Sunday following Thursday's transmission in Britain).

Health and Hygiene

Vaccinations. A yellow fever certificate is required by travellers arriving in Madeira or the Azores from infected areas.

Hygiene. Tap water is reckoned to be drinkable, at least in the towns; if you want to play safe, buy mineral water. Portugal is not as liable to disease as Spain, but, as a point of interest, Oporto had an outbreak of cholera in 1975.

Treatment. British passport holders are entitled to free inpatient treatment in a general ward of a public hospital on production of their passport, reduced rates for out-patient visits to public hospitals and health clinics; and cut-price prescribed medicines. There are British hospitals at Rua Saraiva de Carvalho 49, Lisbon 3 (Tel: 60 20 20); and Rua da Bandeirinha, Oporto (Tel: 2 12 02).

Emergencies. Chemists (*farmacias*) keep a duty rota in the main cities. The list is posted in pharmacy windows, or dial 16 for information. In Lisbon, the emergency number for first aid is 115; and for poisons — 76 11 76. The main dental clinic (round the clock) is at Calçada Bento da Rocha Cabral 1, Lisbon (Tel: 68 41 91).

Entertainment

Bull Fights. There are two methods of bull-fighting — the *matador* fights, in which the bull-fighter is on foot; and the *toirada à antiga,* in which the bull-fighter dresses up in an 18th-century costume and rides a horse.

In both types of fight, it is forbidden to kill the bull (and has been since 1799). The bull-ring in Lisbon, an ornate building in 19th-century Muscovite style, is known as the *Campo Pequeno*. Tickets cost as little as 1,000 $00 in the sun, 5,000 $00 in the shade, from the bull-ring or hotel desks. For all but the most important fights, you should be able to buy tickets at the ring at the time of the flight. In summer, there's a televised bull-fight every Thursday.

Nightlife. The folklore thing in Portugal is *fado*. The word means fate, and describes quite well the sad, resigned nostalgia of this music. Like flamenco, fado is spontaneous and natural, but there the similarity ends. The best fado restaurants are in the Alfama and Bairro Alto districts of Lisbon. The finest quality singing is said by many to be in Parrerinha d'Alfama, Largo do Chafariz de Dentro, in the Alfama. Try to avoid the fado restaurants that figure in the guided tours, as they will be expensive. The Lisbon fun fair is popular throughout the year; metro to Entre Campos.

Museums and Galleries. Opening hours are 10 am-5 pm. Most museums close on Mondays. Charges range from 100 $00-400 $00: entrance is usually free on Sundays. The Coach Museum (in Belém) is free on Thursdays and Sundays, and the Museu da Arte Antiga is free on Monday mornings.

Eating out. Cheap restaurants are recognised by the lack of chrome and menu translations, and the presence of natives rather than tourists. Expect to pay about 2,500 $00 (£10 or $16) for a good three-course meal including wine in an ordinary, unpretentious restaurant. Menus will usually be displayed outside. In Lisbon, the best areas to find good, cheap restaurants are: Rua dos Corrieiros, in the Baixa district; the rua Primavera, in the Bairro Alta; the Calçada do Garcia, below the Castle of St. George; and the rua das Portas de Santo Antão, behind Rossio Square. Fish is good in coastal cities and towns; *sardinhas* (sardines) and *bacalhau* (cod) are common and cheap. On and near beaches, you can get a cheap steak sandwich *(prego)* for a lunchtime snack, from one of the mobile shops.

Drinking. No licensing hours or age restrictions. The Portuguese drink in a variety of establishments, ranging from dark, grimy, fly-infected taverns, through ordinary bars and cafés to the appetizing *pastelarias* that serve cakes and pastries. The main drinks are beer and wine, as well as a cheap brandy distilled from either grapes or sugar cane. Beer at around 90$00 a glass is mainly of the lager variety, but Lisbon also has a stout *(cerveja preta)*. Wine costs 50 $00 for a large glass. With a meal ask for a cheap local wine, called *vinho da casa* or *vinho da região*. The best wines are the reds of Dão and Colares; and the dry whites of Borba and Dão. For free tastings go to the left bank in Oporto. However, in Lisbon the port producers run a cellar called the *Solar de Vinho do Porto* where you can choose from hundreds of varieties at reasonably low prices in opulent surroundings. It is opposite the top station of the *elevadore* from the Praça dos Restauradores, on Rua de São Pedro de Alcantara. Grape brandy is called *aguardente;* the more fiery molasses brandy is known as *bagaço*. *Brandymel* is a popular honey liqueur.

Smoking. Cigarettes are cheap and strong, local brands costing about 127 $00 for 20. American, French and some British cigarettes are available at tobacconists, but at 150 $00 are more expensive.

The Law

Police. The police force is divided into three major sections — Frontier Police (*Guarda Fiscal*) who wear bule peaked caps; in urban areas, Security Police (*Policia de Segurança Publica*), in grey uniforms; and in rural areas, Traffic Police (*Guarda Nacional Republicana*), in green berets. In Lisbon, the central police station is the *Governo Civil* on Rua do Capelo (Tel: 36 61 41 or 3 55 63). In emergencies dial 115. For the crime department, dial 53 53 80.

Laws. You aren't likely to fall foul of the police, but you'd be wise not to dabble in Portuguese politics, even though things now seem to have settled down. Some visitors have been tempted to pick oranges growing in public squares. These are saved for the needy of the area, and less needy tourists have suffered heavy penalties.

Nude Bathing. Nude bathing is against the law, but still practised at some resorts in the Algarve. Although even bikinis were illegal until a few years ago toplessness is the norm on many beaches in the Algarve. Even so, keep scanty beachwear for the beach.

Driving Offences. On-the-spot fines for speeding, etc, but you could be locked away for drunken driving.

Drugs. There is no real scene in Portugal, and the authorities aim to keep it that way. Fine and up to two years for possession; 2-8 years for selling.

Legal Aid. There's no state scheme, so your only chance of help is the nearest consulate. If you're arrested, you're entitled to contact your consulate before you say anything.

Help and Information

For general information on useful contacts and complaints procedures, see the introduction.

Embassies and Consulates.
British Embassy, Rua de Santo Domingos à Lapa 35-39, 1296 Lisbon (66 11 91).
British Consulate, Av de Boavista 3072, 4100 Oporto (68 47 89).
There are also British Consulates in Portimão and the Azores, and an Honorary Consulate in Madeira.

American Embassy, Av Forcas Armadas, Lisbon (726 66 00).
American Consulate, Rua Julio Dinis 826, Aptdo. 88, Oporto (6 30 94).
There is an American Consulate in the Azores; and a Consular agency in Madeira.
Canadian Embassy, Rua Rosa Araújo 2, Lisbon 2 (56 38 21).

Lost Property. For things lost in Lisbon taxis, go to the *Sindicato dos Motoristas*, Av Visconde de Valbom 31. For things lost in Lisbon trams, buses, trains or lifts, go to Largo do Carmo, near the Santa Justa lift (Tel: 37 08 77). Otherwise, go to the police; in Lisbon to the *Governo Civil* on Rua do Capelo.

Baby-sitting. Try *Hospederias de Portugal*, 45a Prazeres, Lisbon 2 (Tel: 60 43 53).

Guides/Interpreters. The official organisation in Lisbon is the Syndicate of Interpreters and Guides, Rua do Telhal 43 (Tel: 36 71 70).

Information. The main tourist office not far from Rossio station at Av António Augusto de Aguiar 86, Lisbon (Tel: 57 50 15 or 57 50 86); other offices at the airport and Santa Apolonia station. In Oporto, at Praça D João I, 25 4Dt (Tel: 31 39 57). The word for tourist office is *Turismo* — there's one in every large town. (*Viagens Turismo* means sightseeing tours, usually in luxury coaches at luxury prices.)

For information in English, dial 36 94 50 in Lisbon.

Disabled Travellers. Help and advice from the Secretariado National de Rehabilitação, Av Conde Valbom 63, 1000 Lisbon.

Free Maps. National and local tourist offices. Lisbon city transport maps and timetables are sold at the bottom of the Santa Justa Lift.

Student Travel. Tagus, Praĉa de Londres 9B, 1000 Lisbon.

English Language Churches. St. George's (Anglican), Rua da Estrela 4, Lisbon (Tel: 66 30 10); St. Andrew's (Scottish Presbyterian), Rua da Arriaga 13, Lisbon (Tel: 66 26 40).

American Express. Star Travel Service, Av Sidonio Pais 4a, Lisbon (Tel: 53 98 71); and Praça dos Restauradores 14, Lisbon (Tel: 346 25 01). Offices in Estoril, Faro, Funchal (Madeira), Guimaraes, Oporto, Porto Santo, Portimâo and Praia da Vitoria (Azores).

Calendar of Events

Public Holidays are shown in **bold**. Those marked* are not observed in all areas.

January 1	**New Year's Day**
February	Carnival celebrations at Loulé
February/March	**Shrove Monday**
March/April	**Good Friday:** Holy week processions in Braga
April 25	**National Day**
May 12-13	Pilgrimages to Fatima
late May	Burning the Ribbons — student celebrations at Coimbra
May/June	**Corpus Christi**
June	International Festival in Lisbon
June 10	**Day of Camões**
June 13	**St. Anthony's Day*** (Lisbon)
June 24	**St. John's Day*** (Oporto)
early July	Festival of the Red Waistcoat at Vila Franca de Xira — bull-running, processions and dancing
August	Pilgrimage and Fair at Viana do Castelo
August 15	**Assumption**
mid September	Fair at Nazare — processions and bull fights
late September	Grape festivals in Curia and the Douro Vally
October 5	**Proclamation of the Republic (1910)***
October 12-13	Pilgrimages to Fatima
late October	Festivals in Faro and Monchique
November 1	**All Saint's Day**
December 1	**Independence Day**
December 8	**Conception**
December 24, 25	**Christmas**

Celebrations for most religious festivals usually begin the previous evening.

Spain

Area. 194,885 square miles   **Population.** 39,000,000

Capital. Madrid (population: 3,158,000).

Weather. The weather is one of the main factors in Spain's popularity with tourists. If anything, it's too hot in summer, and even in the middle of winter, the sun can be relied upon on the Costa del Sol and in the Canary Islands. Such rain as there is, falls mainly on the plains of the north and along the Atlantic coast; but very little falls on the southern plains, which, in some places, are little more than desert, popular with the makers of cowboy movies. In winter, snow is also common on the plains, and there are good ski conditions in the Pyrenees and the Guadarrama and Sierra Nevada ranges.

THE PEOPLE

The traditional image of the Spaniards is conjured up by the word *mañana*, which literally means "tomorrow", but in fact means "sometime" or "never". The word typifies easy-going procrastination, a way of life that is nowadays being replaced by a growing political concern and activity.

Politics. With Franco's regime coming to an end in 1975, the last dictatorship in western Europe bit the dust, and Franco's appointed successor, Prince Juan Carlos de Borbon, took over as the legitimate heir to the Spanish throne. He survived the attempted *coup* of 1981, and his influence led to the acceptance of Spain into

191

the Common Market. The change to democratic rule has been gradual — of necessity, due to the strong right wing elements at the forefront of national politics. United national politics are also held back by regional dissension. Although both Catalonia and the Basque region have a fair amount of autonomy, the Basque separatist group ETA have continued their campaign by attacking police, and more recently Mediterranean beaches. As a result, the police are extremely nervous and trigger-happy.

Religion. Spain is officially Roman Catholic (and it shows), but tolerance to other religions is much greater than it used to be. Take care what you wear in churches — beachwear is out, as are shorts on men and jeans on women.

Language. The official language in Spain is Spanish, or Castilian, the language originally spoken in Castile. Three other regional languages are used — Catalan in the north-east and the Balearics, Galician in the extreme north-west, and Basque along the French border in the Western Pyrenees. Of these, only Basque is unrelated to Spanish. The worst dialect from the point of view of the Spanish-speaking tourist is in the South. If you don't speak Spanish, you might be able to read it if you speak other Romance languages such as Portuguese, French or Italian. In all tourist resorts, you'll find people who speak English, in varying degrees of fluency. In the north you should find plenty who speak French.

Making Friends. Attitudes vary from region to region — northern Spaniards tend to be more businesslike and less friendly than their southern compatriots. In the less tourist-exploited areas, particularly inland, the natives' natural curiosity should be a good enough ice-breaker.

Socially, the impact of tourists, particularly women, from more permissive societies, has created an artificial flesh market in many resorts. Spanish men have turned their backs on the over-protected Spanish girls, and now consider any foreign women as fair game. This is all very well for the girls who have set their sights on those beady-eyed Spanish waiters, but if you have a harmless friendship in mind, remember that the Spaniards have come to expect more. Men will have little luck with the Spanish señoritas.

Red Tape

See the introduction for details of passports, customs regulations, duty free allowances, vaccinations and importing pets.

Passports and Visas. A valid passport is all British, American, Canadian and Australian people need to enter Spain (including the Balearic and Canary Islands, Ceuta and Melilla), but unaccompanied people under 18 are not allowed into Spain unless they carry a letter of consent from their parent or guardian. Subject to this condition, you are allowed to stay up to 90 days; if you wish to stay longer, apply for a 90-day extension (*permanencia*) at the local police station, or, in Madrid at the *Sección de Extranjeros, Dirección General de Seguridad* (Alien's Section of the Police Department — Tel: 222 04 35).

Customs. Spanish customs are generally lenient about anything which can fairly be classed as "personal belongings". There are three things you'd be wise not to carry: drugs, political propaganda, and pornographic (or even semi-pornographic) literature.

Duty-free allowances are standard EC amounts, but unless you have a penchant or Scotch or a particular brand of cigarettes, you'll find alcohol and tobacco much heaper in Spain.

100 centimos (c) = 1 peseta (pta).
£1 = 185 ptas   100 ptas = £0.54
$1 = 115 ptas   100 ptas = $0.86

For general information on handling, xchanging and raising money, see the introduction.

oins. 1 pta, 2 ptas, 5 ptas, 10 ptas, 25 ptas, 100 ptas, ptas 500.

Jotes. 100 ptas (brown), 500 ptas (blue), 1,000 ptas (green), 5,000 ptas (purple), 0,000 ptas (purple).
The 5 ptas coin is known colloquially as a *duro*.

anking Hours. 8.30 am-2.00 pm, Monday-Friday. On Saturdays banks open from 30 am to 1 pm (12.30 in summer). The exchange offices at Atocha and Chamartin ations in Madrid, and Sants station in Barcelona, are open daily. Many hotels nd travel agencies also change money, but at a lower rate.

hopping Hours. 9 or 10 am-1 or 1.30 pm and 3.30 or 4.30 pm-7 or 8 pm Monday-riday, morning only on Saturday. The afternoon siesta period is shorter in winter an in summer. In some cities, some of the larger shops and stores stay open lunch-time.

nport and Export. No restrictions on foreign currency and travellers' cheques, or on the import of Spanish notes, but declare them if you are bringing in more an the equivalent of 500,000 ptas, or 100,000 in ptas; no more than 100,000 ptas ay be exported. You can take out foreign currency up to the amount declared 1 arrival.

ipping. Restaurants and bars — the service charge (15%) is nearly always included *ervicio incluido*), but a tip is also expected — 10% will do; if you have your inks at the bar, a tip isn't obligatory, but a few pesetas are expected. Taxis — dd another 10% if driver carries luggage. Hotels — service charges included. ation porters — operate at fixed rates; tip them, in addition, 20 ptas per bag.

axes. Value added tax of 6% is charged on hotel and restaurant bills, 12% on ost other non-food items.

mergency Cash. Begging and street-selling are illegal, but if you paint or make wellery you should do well in tourist resorts. Try buying some postcards and •ing blown-up pen and ink sketches of the scenes.
Large supermarkets in city suburbs often have enough free *degustaciones* for full meal.
Selling blood is a viable proposition — the money will feed you for a few days. y any hospital; blood is *sangre*.
Work prospects are least bad for pretty girls, who may be able to work as rmaids in tourist areas (although they and the bar owner risk heavy fines). Skilled desmen (carpenters, electricians, plumbers and even hairdressers) may find there ills in demand, especially if they carry the tools of their trade with them. Teaching iglish is also a possibility.

Betting is technically illegal, but there are a number of local and national lotteries, with funds going to charity. One of the national lotteries is for the blind — tickets can be bought either from blind street-sellers or at the kiosks marked *Cupon pro Ciegos,* which is also where results are published. The largest lottery is *El Gordo* ("the big one"), which dates back over 200 years. The prize fund is around 300,000,000 ptas, with a first prize of 60 million ptas. It is drawn around Christmas.

Getting Around

The information in this section is complementary to that given in the corresponding section in the introduction.

CAR

Although you might get stuck behind a horse and cart (or, more likely, a mule and cart), even on apparently major roads, the main through routes are now wide enough to take tourist traffic. If you take to minor roads expect bad surfaces and large potholes. Motorways are springing up around large towns, the longest single stretch being the A7 along the Mediterranean coast. In Madrid, dial 441 72 22 or 459 50 00 for information on road conditions.

Rules and Requirements. The new pink British driving licence is acceptable otherwise, an international driving licence — or Spanish translation of a national licence, endorsed by a Spanish Consulate — is necessary. Drivers and front seat passengers must wear seat belts outside built up areas; it is recommended that children under 14 do not travel in the front seat. At night, sidelights alone must be used in built up areas (unlike the rest of Europe, where this is banned), and in daylight dipped headlights must be used on motorways and fast dual carriageways. A spare set of bulbs must be carried. A disconcerting local custom is that drivers flash their indicators when they are being overtaken, to show that they are aware of the other vehicle. Three-point turns and reversing into side streets are forbidden in towns. The minimum driving age is 18.

Tolls. Only urban stretches of motorway are toll free. The length of the A7 from La Junquera to Alicante costs 4,235 ptas. A useful map of all Spanish *autopistas* is available free from ASETA, calle Estébanez Calderón 3, Madrid 20.

Road Signs. *Peligro* — Danger; *Cuidado (Precaución)* — Caution; *Ceda el paso* — Give Way; *Obras* — Road works.

Parking. Keep moving when you're confronted with a sign saying *Estacionamiento Prohibido* (No Parking). In towns, car parks are indicated by signs marked 'P' Never park facing on-coming traffic. On one way streets the alternate day system may operate — see the introduction — but the system is being phased out. In blue zones the maximum waiting period is 1½ hours. Parking tickets for 30, 60 or 90 minutes are available from tobacconists.

Petrol. All petrol is supplied through the official agency CAMPSA, which has standardised prices. There are two grades of leaded petrol *normal* (92 octane) and *super* (97 octane). Super sells at 74 ptas a litre (£1.80 per UK gallon or $2.4 per US gallon). Unleaded petrol (95 octane) sells for 69 ptas a litre.

Touring Clubs. Real Automóvil Club de Españā (RACE), José Abascal, 10, 28003 Madrid (Tel: 447 3200).

Accidents and Breakdowns. Despite the fact that agencies for foreign cars will only be found in the larger towns, you will find that mechanics in the provinces will give efficient service. On the occasions when you have to wait for a spare part, be prepared to wait for a matter of several days.

The *Guardia Civil* has set up a system as *Ayudda en Carretera,* which operates on major roads throughout the country. The roadside SOS telephones are connected to the nearest police station, which sends out a breakdown van with first aid equipment. The van driver can also radio for an ambulance if needed. There is a small charge for work done and spare parts used. Alternatively, in cases of accident, contact the nearest *Guardia Civil* station. See *The Law* for the advisability of taking out bail bonds, and the question of liability in accidents.

TRAIN

Most railways are run by the national network, RENFE (*Red Nacional de los Ferrocarriles Españoles*). The monthly *Guia Horarios* contains details of all rail, bus, air and sea services in Spain. It is sold at station bookstalls. The RENFE head office in Madrid is at Alcala 44. For train information call 733 30 00 or 733 22 00 in Madrid, or 322 41 42 in Barcelona.

Trains are graded by their speed, and priced accordingly. *Talgo,* Inter-City, ELT *(Electrotren)* and TER (*Tren Español Rapido*) require the largest supplements. A smaller supplement is payable for the next grade, *rapido,* which is not at all what its name implies, and the *correo* (slowest of all) is to be avoided at all costs for long journeys. All trains have a first and a second class first costing 50% more than second. The basic rate for second class travel is around 45 ptas per 10 km (£0.41 or $0.65 for 10 miles), but supplements can almost double this. Many lines are single track and thus highly susceptible to delays.

If you enter Spain by rail from France, be prepared in most cases to change trains at the border, because of the difference in track size.

If you board a train without a ticket, you can pay the conductor on the train, but he has the right to charge you double. In fact, it's always advisable to reserve seats in advance because you might not be allowed on a train if there are no seats free. Reservations should not be made at stations, since ticket offices there have very erratic opening hours. Instead, go to the RENFE office in town (usually open 9am-2 pm) or any travel agent.

The Spanish version of the Orient Express is known as *Al Andalus;* this luxurious train takes around 70 passengers on week-long tours of the historical cities of Andalucia. Contact the National Tourist Office for details of this and other special trains.

Cheap Deals. Children under 4 travel free; 4-12, half fare. Discounts of 20% are granted on return journeys of over 200 km on off-peak "blue" days (*dias azules*); the *Cheque-tren* system allows you to buy vouchers that can be used in payment for rail travel, giving a discount of 15%.

The *Tarjeta Turistica* (Tourist Card) is available only to people not resident in Spain and gives unlimited rail travel for 8, 15 or 22 days. Card holders do not need to pay any supplements apart from those for sleeping facilities and making seat reservations. The card can be bought from RENFE stations in Spain, or in

Britain from Wasteels Travel, 121 Wilton Road, London SW1V 1JZ (Tel: 071-834 7066). In Britain the 8 day card costs £50 in second class (£70 in first class); the 15 day card costs £80 (£115); and the 22 day card costs £105 (£130).

BUS

RENFE and numerous private operators run long distance bus services at similar fares to trains. Most cities have two or more bus stations, so check before you set off for a bus.

AIR

There are frequent flights between the main cities, and an hourly service between Madrid and Barcelona. The national airline Iberia, its domestic subsidiary Aviaco or any travel agency will supply information and tickets.

In Madrid, buses leave for Barajas Airport from the Iberia Terminal in Plaza de Colon: the fare is 200 ptas. Flight information at Barajas — dial 8343-46. In Barcelona, take the train from Sants Station (every 15 minutes, journey time 30 minutes, price 200 ptas) to Prat airport. Flight information -dial 370 1011.

HITCH-HIKING

Hitching is not illegal, but it is discouraged. The Spanish don't really understand the phenomenon of hitch-hikers, especially long-haired ones, and the general scarcity of cars makes it altogether slow going. To avoid disappointment, don't reckon on more than 300 km per day, on average. This may come as a 9-hour wait one day, and a 600km lift first thing next morning. If a horse and cart stops, take it.

From Madrid, take the *metro* line 1 to Plaza de Castilla for the NI north; line 4 or 7 to America for the NII east to Barcelona; for the NIV south line 3 or 6 to Legazpi, then cross the Peunte de Andalucia for the Autovia Cuidad de Los Angeles.

CITY TRANSPORT

Taxis. In Madrid, taxis are mostly white, but a few are black with a thin red band; in Barcelona, black with yellow doors. Prices vary from town to town: in Madrid there is a 100 ptas flag-down charge, then around 40 ptas per km (£0.36 or $0.58 a mile). There may also be supplements to and from railway stations, airports, football stadiums and bullrings. Never trust a taxi that doesn't have a meter — they often operate as chauffeur-driven cars, and charge accordingly. When travelling outside the town boundary (eg to the airport), ask about the fare beforehand. When a taxi-driver takes you over the boundary, he is any case obliged to stop there are inform you of the rate if you wish to travel further.

Bus/Underground. Barcelona, Madrid and Valencia each have an underground railway network *(metro)*. There is a set fare of 65 ptas or you can buy a ticket valid for ten trips for 410 ptas. Before 8am, you can buy a cheap day return for 75 ptas. Most metro stations have ticket-vending machines, but you can also buy tickets at the counter. You may encounter people selling cut-price tickets at station entrances. There are usually tickets bought at a reduced rate (eg for children) and are not recommended for adults. The metro runs until 1.30 daily.

Buses also have fixed fares, in Madrid 65 patas, or you can buy a *bono bus* ticket for 370 ptas that is valid for 10 journeys. The door to get in is marked *Entrada*, if this is at the front, pay the driver, of it's at the back, pay the conductor, who usually sits by the door, or use the ticket machine. Buses run until 11.30pm.

Accommodation

See the introduction for information on youth hostels, other hostels and advance booking of accommodation.

Hotels. Hotels, and all other types of accommodation, are officially inspected and classified by the *Secretaria de Estedo de Turismo.* Hotel classifications range from one to five starts. The star classifications are worked out bureaucratically, so it may happen that you'll find really comfortable hotels that would merit an extra star (and therefore a price rise) if, for instance, they had a lift, or another bathroom. All Spanish hotels have a laundry and ironing service.

Room prices start around 2,000 ptas (£11 or $17) for a double room: singles are 40% cheaper. All prices must be visibly displayed in every room; there is a minimum and maximum limit, and needless to say, you must be ready to pay the maximum. Prices are usually quoted for the room only; breakfast is generally an optional extra, charged separately; but in some lower category hotels, you may be charged for demi-pension, whether you actually eat there or not.

Hotels usually increase prices by 15% for two months of the year, during their high season. This is generally July and August, but in skiing areas it may be taken in winter.

If you think you're being overcharged, ask the hotel for (and fill in) one of their official complaint forms *(hojas de reclamaciones),* of which all hotels should have a stock. Threaten to contact the Provincial Tourist Board if the hotel has no forms, or if you're otherwise unsatisfied.

Pensiones and Hostales. These categories are the rock-bottom in cheap accommodation, starting at about 900 ptas (around £5 or $8). They don't go above three stars, and prices are usually computed per person, taking into consideration the number of other people you're sharing a room with. Don't expect any luxuries - for 900 ptas, you might be sharing a room with cochroaches as well as human occupants. At that price, expect holes in the floor for lavatories and no hot water.

Paradores, Albergues and Refugios. These names apply to three types of State-run accommodation for tourists which are quite expensive but very good value. *Paradores* range from 2-4 stars, and usually take the form of old castles or stately homes, decorated in the style of the region, and serving local specialities as well as standard cuisine. There are, however, some modern *paradores* along the Mediterranean coast. Prices for a double room in high season are in the range of 4,000-7,000 ptas. Most *Paradores* are only small, so it's advisable to book in advance. For further information or to make a booking contact *Paradores de Turismo,* Velazquez St. 18, 28001 Madrid (Tel: 435 9700 or 435 97 44). NTOs can also supply addresses of paradores. These may be booked through Keytel International, 402 Edgeware Road, London W2 1ED (Tel: 402 8182). Brittany Ferries offer cut-price vouchers for paradores in connection with their Plymouth-Santander ferries; details from travel agents.

The *albergues* and *refugios* are run on the same lines as the *paradores,* although they are not always so grand (therefore a little cheaper). The main purpose is to provide accommodation in the more isolated parts. *Albergues* will be found along main roads, and are only intended for overnight stops. *Refugios* will only be found way off the beaten track, and are intended primarily for hikers and mountaineers.

Youth Hostels. For information, apply to the *Red Espanola de Albergues Jeveniles,* José Ortega de Gasset 71, 28006 Madrid (Tel: 401 1300).

Camping. There are almost 800 camping sites in Spain. Sites are variable in terms of cleanliness and facilities, but on the whole the standard is high. Prices also vary, but allow at least 200 ptas a night per person, per tent and per car. Information can be obtained from the *Federacion Espanola de Empresarios de Campings,* Gran Via 88, 28013 Madrid (Tel: 242 3168). Camping outside official sites is not permitted in dry river beds liable to flood, urban areas, or close to roads, military bases, sources of drinking water within 1km of an official camp site and some minicipalities do not allow camping on public land.. Elsewhere it is allowed with the landowner's permission.

Sleeping out. Climatically, it's no problem for most of the year; beaches on the south coast are often frequented by the locals, who have an uncanny knack of knowing when it's going to rain, so a deserted beach is probably a bad omen. Well-known areas for sleeping out are patrolled by the *Guardia Civil;* they should only take you in for vagrancy if you have hardly any money on you. They'll probably wake you up to find out. Expect trouble in towns.

Finding and Booking Accommodation. List of hotels and their facilities are issued free by local tourist offices. A national list is available from National Tourist Offices. The complete hotel list, *Guiá Oficial de Hoteles,* is published around Easter.

In general, it's advisable to book in advance, especially at popular resorts during summer or at festival times. If you reach town late in the day without room, the tourist office can give you a list, but is not allowed to make reservations for you. Larger towns have *Brujula* offices — the offical room-finding service — which will charge a small fee for their services. They have offices at stations, airports, and on main roads entering cities.

If you arrive late in the evening, and the normal channels are closed, don't hesitate to ask a nightwatchman, waiter, barman or taxi-driver. The other late-night problem is getting locked out of your hotel or pension, most of which, especially in the lower categories, close faithfully at 11pm. Just stand at the gate and clap your hands. The night porter will come jangling his keys, expecting a small tip for letting you in. Don't disappoint his (100 ptas will do), in case you need him again.

Communications

General information on telephones and English language newspapers and radio broadcasts is given in the introduction.

Post. Post offices are open between 9am and 2pm, Monday-Saturday. Postboxes are coloured red, with a yellow band (like the Spanish flag), and often have two parts; one marked *ciudad* (for local mail), the other — *provincias y extranjero* (for the rest of the country and abroad). Stamps are sold at post offices and at the *estancos,* or tobacconists' shops, easily spotted by the Spanish flag painted outside. In Madrid the main post office *(Palacio de Communicaciones)* is the Plaza de Cibeles (Tel: 221 40 04). Main post offices usually have a special counter for philatelists. Madrid has a market (open Sundays 10am-2pm) in the Plaza Mayor. A similar one takes place in Barcelona's Plaza Real.

There is a poste restante service at all main post offices, with a charge of 10 ptas for collection. Letters should be addressed *Lista de Correos,* the name of the town, and the province.

The correct way to address mail is: name, street (name, then number); town, preceded by a code number, which, in turn, is preceded by the country code E-f writing from abroad. Large cities are also followed by a zone number.

Telephones. Telephone booths are now not an uncommon sight, but they don't have a directory. If you need one, go to the nearest bar or cafeteria. Public phones take 5, 25, 50 and 100 ptas coins; those marked *Telefono Internactional* are good for international calls (for which the minimum charge is 50 ptas). Some bars have metered phones — pay at the bar when you've finished your call. Calls are cheaper at weekends and at night (10pm — 8am).

The easiest way to make long-distance or international calls is at the *locutorio publico* (telephone office), usually known simply as *telefonos*. In Madrid, there's a 24-hour service at Plaza de la Cibeles. Go to the counter and give the number you want to call, stating country, province and town (even if you know the codes); when the call is ready, you'll be transferred to one of the numbered booths; pay on the way out. For calls that you can dial direct, Madrid is 1, Barcelona 3. Insert the money first, then lift the receiver, and dial when you hear the dialling tone. For international calls, pause after dialling the international prefix (07), then continue when you hear a new dialling tone. For international direct dial calls to the UK place at least 150 ptas in sloping groove at the top of the coin box. Do not press button to left or dial as you may lose your money. Lift receiver dial 07 (wait for 2nd tone) dial 44 then UK area code (minus initial 0) and local number. Coins will drop in as needed. Insert more coins when warning sounds. Unused coins refunded. Commercial credit cards are accepted by some phones in main cities. To make collect or BT chargecard calls dial 008 in Madrid or Barcelona; else-where on mainland Spain dial 9398 or 9198. Collect and BT Chargecard calls can not be made from payphones on the Balearic or Canary Islands.

Telephone directories come in two sections: alphabetical subscriber list, and yellow (commercial) pages. In the alphabetical list, names beginning with *Ch* appear after *C*; those beginning *Ll* after *L*; and *Ñ* after *N*. All the essential numbers are listed at the front, but they vary from place to place. Numbers in Madrid include: information — 003; sports information — 097; time — 093; police — 091; weather — 094; ambulance — 092; fire *(bomberos)* — 232 32 32; international enquiries — 008; news — 095.

Telegrams. Can be sent in person at post offices, which in main cities, keep up 24-hour telegraph service (at Plaza de la Cibeles in Madrid). By telephone, look up TELEBEN in the directory; in Madrid dial 222 47 94 to send telegrams, 221 0 04 for information.

Newspapers. English language papers of varying vintage appear spasmodically in street kiosks.

Health and Hygiene

For general information on health, hygiene, first aid, medical treatment and insurance, see the introduction.

Hygiene. Standards of hygiene in Spain are not high, and tourists have been known to contract dysentery and hepatitis, as well as the regular stomach upsets that can be easily cured by a plain diet and light medicines. Most tap water (and ice cubes) should be safe, but if you're dubious stick to bottled drinks. More serious illnesses, like typhoid, poliomyelitis and cholera, occasionally find their way over from North Africa; there have also been several cases of rabies.

Treatment. EC Citizens are entitled to treatment on the same terms as Spanish nationals. For holders of the E111 hospital and medical treatment are free, but you have to pay for dental treatment and up to 40% of the cost of prescriptions. For free treatment you must use doctors or hospitals participating in the national social security scheme; get their addresses from Provincial Offices (*Direction Provincial*) or local offices (*Agencies*) of the *Instituto Nacional de la Segundad Social* (INSS). It can be time-consuming to track down an INSS doctor, so you are recommended to take out private medical insurance which gives you the option of using a private doctor.

Emergencies. Chemists are easily recognised by the cross — red or green — that they use as a shop sign. You will always find one open at any time, day and night, holidays and weekends. If the nearest pharmacy is shut, look for the list of *farmacias de turno* (duty chemists) in the window. The list is also published in local papers. If you need emergency medical treatment, turn to the telephone directory and look up either *médico de urgencia* or *servicio médico de urgencia* — it'll be at the beginning of the book, as well as on the yellow pages. For ambulances, dial 092. Madrid has a 24-hour first aid station at Don Ramòn de la Cruz 93 (Tel: 734 55 00). In smaller towns, a limited first aid service may be run by the *dispensario* in the Town Hall (*ayuntamiento*).

Entertainment

Sport. Bull-fighting is the most Spanish of spectator sports, although connoisseurs see red when the *fiesta nacional* is called a sport — it is held to be an art. The season runs from March-October, and there are fights every Sunday afternoon (5 or 5.30 pm) in most cities. The further from the arena, the cheaper the seat; seats are also divided into *sol* and *sombra* (sun and shade), the ones in the sun being cheapest. Tickets can be bought at the bull-ring itself, hotel desks or at special booking offices (*oficinas de reservationes de la empresa de la plaza de torros*). To see the best bull-fighters, you have to book well in advance. Children under 14 are not admitted.

Pelota or *fronton* is originally a Basque game, now played in all parts of Spain, and well worth watching, or even betting on. It's played on a court like an enormous squash court, and the game resembles a faster version of fives, except that the glove has a basket-shaped extension, for catching the ball and flinging it back at the wall. The cental court in Madrid is on the Calle Villaneuva, where games are played daily at 6 pm and/or 11 pm. Soccer is fanatically supported; the best team at present is Barcelona.

Eating out. If you only see the Mediterranean coast of spain, and only eat in the tourist cafés, you might think that Spanish eating habits are exactly the same as in England — bacon and eggs, toast and marmalade for breakfast, take-away fish and chips, and oodles of "tea like auntie makes it". The local elevenses — *chocolate y churros* — is cheap and delicious.

Olive oil and garlic are two of the ingredients foreigners will just have to get used to if they intent to try Spanish cooking. Contrary to popular belief, it's not these ingredients that cause "Spanish gut" — this is usually attributable to excesses of one sort or another, like cheap wine. The standard dessert is *flan* — creme caramel.

Instead of stars, Spanish restaurants are classified by means of forks, one to five. Like hotels, they are very strictly controlled as far as standards and prices are concerned. One official rule is that all restaurants should provide a *menu del dia,* inclusive of everything, even wine. This is much cheaper than eating á la carte. If the *menu del dia* is not displayed at the door, ask the waiter for it. If they don't offer you one, ask for the complaints book and you might get results. If you shop around you should be able to find a set meal for around 800 ptas: expect to pay from 2,000 ptas if you choose from the menu. Just a main course in a modest establishment should be around 400 ptas.

The so-called cafeterias are not self-service, and usually they're not as cheap as restaurants or a similar standard. They are considered as rather trendy places, often with plastic decor, and a pseudo-American atmosphere.

Hamburger vans and fish and chip shops will be found in all Spanish tourist resorts, but they are an imported phenomenon, which should be avoided on principle. *Calamares* (squids) and other types of fish and shellfish (*mariscos*) are often sold, fried in batter, on a take-away basis, usually with bread or genuine Spanish chips as an optional extra.

Drinking. Wine is the national drink in Spain. The best wines, ranking with French vintages, come from la Rioja, just south of the Basque provinces. *Valdepeñas,* from la Mancha, south-east of Madrid, is not of the same quality, but still an excellent table wine. Other good wines are produced in Tarragona, Carinena, Jumilla and Zamora. The Penades, just south of Barcelona, is an important sparkling-wine area. Sherry is produced only in Jerez de la Frontera. Free tours of the *bodegas* (including a tasting of several varieties) should be booked in advance. They take place only in the morning; don't plan any coherent activity for the afternoon.

A one-litre bottle of ordinary wine costs about 70 ptas., of which some 5 ptas are the returnable deposit on the bottle (or go back and have the bottle filled up again). Superior brands of wine cost 400 ptas or more.

Spanish beer does not aim for superlative quality, but is drunk merely as a thirst-quencher and always served chilled. *San Miguel* is reliable brand. It is often drunk with *tapas,* small snacks, which serve as an hors d'oeuvre before a main meal. There is a tradition in Madrid of going from tapas bar to tapas bar. A bottle of reasonable Spanish gin or brandy costs less than 500 ptas. The best brandies, such as *Carlos I,* costs 2,000 ptas or more. Imported alcohol is even dearer.

Bars are open from 7 am or earlier until well after midnight, and they all serve coffee, alcoholic and soft drinks at any time. Average prices are 80 ptas for a glass of beer, about the same of a cup of coffee, and about 100 ptas for a brandy, gin or liqueur. For really cheap wines, and an almost medieval atmosphere, go to one of the lower-class *tavernas* or *bodegas,* where wine comes straight from the wood.

Smoking. Spain is a tobacco-producing nation, although the native light tobacco doesn't compare with the American, prices starting at about 100 ptas a pack. However, proper Virginia cigarettes — American brands being much more common than English — sell at over 200 ptas a pack. The cheapest cigarettes are *Ducados* (black tobacco); they are very strong and not to everyone's taste. On street corners, you may find beggars selling cigarettes singly: this is the most expensive way to buy your smokes.

The Law

Police. Spanish police fall into three basic categories: *policia armada,* in a brown uniform — they stand guard outside banks and public buildings; *guardia civil,* in green uniforms, with shiny black three-cornered hats — they patrol rural areas; and *guardia urbana* — urban police. The emergency number to contact the police is 091.

Crime. Despite widely-publicised attacks on British holidaymakers at Mediterranean resorts, mugging is not commonplace. More prevalent are the *semáforazos* who rob cars which stop at lights (*semáforos* = traffic lights). Initially they attacked only cars with wound-down windows, but now have taken to smashing any windows that take their fancy. Handbag snatching is also widespread.

Laws. If you fall foul of the Spanish police, it's wise not to argue. Just be apologetic and hope they let you off. Identification must be carried at all times, and only a document with a photo will do. As tourist, you shouldn't expect too much trouble from the police. Cross the road against a red light and you might get whistled at and sent back. Vagrancy and drunkenness are reasons to be imprisoned for a night or two. Photographing military installations may qualify you for a longer stay. Spanish prison is no joke — no three-course meals, and little chance of getting through to your Consulate immediately.

The Spanish legislative system is years behind the rest of Western Europe. You can be held for 60 days with no charge against you, and no contact with the outside world. Once charged, you can wait up to a year for trial, and trials show little sense of justice. Acquittal is rare, and it seems that the longer they hold you before trial, the less they feel justified in acquitting you. Start despairing when you're arrested.

Nude Bathing. Nudity is theoretically legal as long as no-one is offended, but in some areas there are strong local objections, in many cases led by the Church.

Driving Offences. Fines for speeding, etc, get a 20% reduction if paid on the spot. Spaniards have the alternative of paying within ten days, but visiting motorists must pay at once or have their car confiscated, unless they can name someone in Spain who will guarantee that the fine will be paid. As stated on the back of the receipt, you may appeal against a fine. Do this in writing to the Town Hall, if the alleged offence was committed within a town, or, in country areas, to the *Jefatura de Tráfico* (Traffic Headquarters) in the provincial capital within ten days. If you hear no reply, it means the appeal has been dismissed.

Bail Bonds. Under Spanish law, if you're involved in an accident, you may be held in prison and/or your car confiscated. The alternative is bail, for which you can cover yourself as an extension of your travel insurance policy. Bail bonds are not required by law, but are obviously advisable, since investigations of this kind can take a long time, and you won't be let out unless you can raise the cash. When liability is established you are in trouble if the verdict is against you. As well as losing the bail (or bonds), you risk a fine, plus imprisonment if gross neglect is proved — as it almost certainly will be if alcohol is involved.

Drugs. No legal distinction between possession and supply. The maximum sentence is 11 years and is frequently administered. It is not a good idea to try importing from North Africa.

Legal Aid. Since the youth movement carries little weight in Spain, there are no alternative organisations like Release. When in a jam, the Consulate's your only hope, and they have very little influence.

For information on useful contacts and complaints procedures, see the introduction.

Embassies and Consulates.
British Embassy, Calle de Fernando el Santo 16, Madrid 14 (Tel: 419 02 00).
British Consulate General, Avda. Diagonal 477/13, Barcelona 36 (Tel: 322 21 51).
British Consulate General, Almeda Urguijo 2-8, Bilbao 8 (Tel: 415 76 00).

There are British consulates in Algeciras, Alicante, Las Palmas, Malaga, Palma de Mallorca, Santa Cruz de Tenerife, Santander, Seville, Tarragona and Vigo; and vice-consulates in Ibiza and Menorca.

American Embassy, Serrano 75, Madrid (Tel: 276 34 00).
American Consulate General, Via Layetana 33, Barcelona (Tel: 319 95 50).

There is an American consulate in Bilbao, and consular agencies in Ibiza, Las Palmas, Malaga, Palma de Mallorca and Valencia.

Canadian Embassy, Calle Nuñez de Bilboa de Bilboa 35, Madrid (Tel: 431 43 00).

Lost Property. In Madrid, the central lost property office is the Oficina de objetos perdidos, Plaza de Chamberi 4 (Tel: 448 79 26). Elsewhere, try the police.

Baby-sitting. There are no formal agencies that deal with baby-sitting, and the answer is either to ask at your hotel, or look for offers in the classified section of the local paper. In university towns, you could also look on the notice-boards at the university.

Information. The General State Information Office is at Callé Maria de Molina, 50 Madrid (Tel: 411 61 62), with branches in over 50 cities. This network is supplemented by local or city tourist offices: the Madrid city tourist office is at Plaza Mayor 3 (Tel: 266 5477). There are also offices at Madrid Airport and Chamartin Station.

Complaints. Complaints books (*libros de reclamaciones*) are kept in hotels, camp sites, restaurants, railway stations, and petrol stations. Ask for it, if you have any reason to complain; it should be made available to you on request. If you are refused access to it, make your complaint in writing, before you leave Spain, to the *Responsable de Turismo* of the local Community Autonomy.

Free Maps. Free road maps from Spanish National Tourist Offices. City street plans from the local tourist offices. If the free road map isn't detailed enough, try the maps published in Spain by Firestone — from bookshops and some garages.

Disabled Travellers. General help and information from INSERSO, C/Maria de Guzmén, 52, Madrid (Tel: 256 26 05).

Student and Youth Travel. TIVE, José Ortega Gassett, 71, 28006 Madrid (Tel: 401 13 00).

English Language Church. St. George's (Anglican), Calle de Hermosilla 43, Madrid (Tel: 274 51 55).

American Express. Plaza de las Cortes 2, Madrid (Tel: 429 57 75); Paseo de Gracia 101, Barcelona (Tel: 217 00 70); and representatives in Granada, Ibiza, La Coruña, Lanzarote, Mahon, Malaga, Palma, Santiago, Seville, Tenerife and Vigo.

Calendar of Events

Public Holidays are shown in **bold.** Various other saints' days are observed locally.

January 1	**New Year's Day**
January 6	**Epiphany**
March 12-19	*Fallas* in Valencia
March 19	**St. Joseph's Day**
March	Holy week: celebrations throughout Spain, with spectacular processions at Granada, Lorca, Malaga, Murcia, Seville, Valladolid
March/April	**Good Friday**
mid April	*Feria* in Seville
May 1	**Labour Day**
May 1-5	Festival and Fair at Jerez
May/June	**Ascension Day**
May 25-31	Folk dancing festivals at Cordoba and Alhaurin el Grande (Malaga)
May/June	**Corpus Christi:** *Romeria* (pilgrimage) in Almente
June 29	**St Peter's Day:** festivities in Burgos
early July	Bull-running and San Fermin festival in Pamplona
July 18	Battle of flowers at Valencia
July 25	**St. James' Day**
August 15	**Assumption:** ancient religious plays and celebrations at Elche and La Alberca-Sequeros
August 27	Festival and battle of flowers at Laredo (Santander)
September 1-15	Wine festival at Jerez de la Frontera
September	Festivals at Tarragona and Salamanca
September 29	Pilgrimage through the gypsy quarters of Granada
October 7-15	Festivals at Avila and Zaragoza
October 12	**Columbus Day**
November 1	**All Saints' Day**
December 8	**Conception**
December 12	Fiesta in the Monastery of the Lady of Guadalupe (Caceres)
December 24	Festival of the Black Virgin at Montserrat (Barcelona)
December 25	**Christmas Day**

Andorra

Area. 175 square miles   **Population.** 48,000
Capital. Andorra la Vella (population: 15,600)

Andorra lies in the heart of the Pyrenees between Spain and France, and can be seen as an extension of both countries. The small state is officially ruled jointly by the co-princes — the President of France and the Bishop of Urgell — but Andorra also has its own democratically-elected government. The vote was given to women in 1970. The official language is Catalan, although both French and Spanish are widely spoken. French and Spanish money are both legal tender; and Andorran stamps are printed in both currencies — those in pesetas going by the Spanish postal service, those in francs going by the faster but more expensive French service. Within Andorra itself, the postal service is free. Telephones are linked to the French system — the area code being 078.

Frontier formalities on entering Andorra are non-existent — if you want an Andorran stamp in your passport you must go to the Sindicat d'Iniciativa. Because of the absence of taxes, however, goods taken out of Andorra are likely to be closely inspected by the French or Spanish custom authorities.

Apart from the fresh air, and the tranquillity of a still almost unspoilt country, Andorra is also popular for ski-ing — most centres are open from November to May. For ski-ing information, contact the *Esqui Club d'Andorra,* Urbanització Babot, Andorra la Vella (Tel: 20-010). For general tourist information, contact the *Sindicat d'Iniciativa,* Carrer Dr Vilanova, Andorra la Vella (Tel: 20-2-14). In emergencies, the two important numbers are 21-2-22 for the police; and 20-0-20 for the fire or ambulance services.

Gibraltar

Area. 2½ square miles   **Population.** 30,000

The land frontier at La Linea re-opened in February 1985 after 16 years of the Spanish blockade.

Despite Spanish claims to the Rock, Gibraltar remains British to the core. The language is English, the policemen wear bobbies' helmets, Imperial weights and measures and metric weights are also used, and the currency is sterling. Among the un-British aspects of the territory, the most notable are the Mediterranean climate and the fact that traffic drives on the right.

Money. British notes and coins are in use; Gibraltar notes are printed in denominations of £1, £5, £10 and £ 20, and £50 which get a lower exchange rate abroad. There are no restrictions on currency imports, but you can only take out currency notes which you have declared on arrival. Banks are open from 9am to 3.30pm, Monday-Friday reopening from 4.30 to 6pm on Fridays. There is no

VAT in Gibraltar — cigarettes are from 38p to 58p for 20, whisky is £4 a bottle and a litre of petrol costs about 38p (£1.71 per UK gallon, $2.28 per US gallon). Most shops remain open until 7pm at least. Service charges of 12% are added to hotel and restaurant bills; otherwise, give 10% tips to waiters, taxi drivers, etc.

Getting Around. With only small distances to worry about, transport is not expensive. Buses have a set fare of 30p for adults and 15p for children under 12; Taxis charge around £1 ($1.60) per mile with extra charges at night and Bank Holidays — tariff card available on request. Prices for a horse-drawn taxi (gharry)) should be negotiated in advance. Car hire rates are two levels, depending on whether you remain in Gibraltar (much cheaper) or venture into Spain. The minimum driving age is 18. Within the urban area, the maximum speed is 20mph; outside 30mph.

Accommodation. Options are limited; the cheapest rooms can be found at the Queens Hotel around £18 ($29) per single room and £26 ($42) per twin room. It is cheaper to find a "pension" in La Linea, just across the border.

Communications. The main post office is at 104 Main Street; telegrams can be sent from Gibraltar Telecommunications International Ltd, 60 Main Street or 18 South Barrack Road (open from 9.00am-1.00pm, 2.00pm-5.00pm — tel 78973). Local telephone calls cost 10p; all international calls must be made from private phones, car phones, public telephone, post offices or via the operator. The Gibraltar Broadcasting Corporation runs one TV channel 7pm — midnight daily, plus Saturday and Sunday afternoons; and one radio channel (in Spanish and English) on VHF 91.3, 100.5 MHZ & MW 206M 14.58 KHZ from 8am to midnight daily. BFBS Gibraltar broadcasts on 89.4, 93.5 and 97.8 MHz FM. There are three turf accountants on the Rock, on whose premises commentaries on British horse and greyhound races can be heard.

Health. British visitors can benefit from reciprocal agreement whereby a nominal change is made for prescription drugs; out-patient treatment and dental extractions at St Bernard's Hospital. Other medical and dental charges must be paid in full. The number for accidents and emergencies is 199.

Information. Gibraltar Tourism Agency, Cathedral Square (Tel: 76400)

American Express. Bland Ltd, Cloister Building, Irish Town (Tel: 78061).

Public Holidays. January 1; Commonwealth Day (March 10); Good Friday; Easter Monday; May 1; Spring Bank Holiday (3rd Friday in May); Queen's Birthday (June 14); Summer Bank Holiday (last Monday in August); Christmas Day; December 26.

Switzerland

Area. 15,941 square miles

Population. 6,600,000

Capital. Bern (population 145,000)

Commercial Capital. Zurich (population: 349,000)

Weather. Because of the Alps, the weather is very changeable, and light rainwear is recommended even in summer; heavy woollens and coats in winter. The areas south of the Alps have an almost Mediterranean climate, with mild winters, sheltered by the Alps from the cold north wind known as *la bise*. The alpine area itself is very fickle — usually warm summers, but with sudden downpours of rain; and cold winters (especially at night), but not without the chance of high daytime temperatures at the main ski resorts. Many of the mountain passes are blocked in winter, and enough snow lingers on the slopes to keep high-altitude ski resorts open during the summer. Daily weather reports covering the major resorts are displayed in all large railway stations and post offices.

THE PEOPLE

It's difficult to generalise about the Swiss, since the nation is made up of three major racial groups — French, German and Italian, not to mention a vast number of immigrants. As a generalisation, the Swiss are hard-working and go to bed early so they can get up early — through you might not believe this if you wander through Geneva at 2 am. The reputation of the Swiss bankers (the gnomes of Zurich) is based on this hard-working attitude, rather than the ability to make a bit of quick money.

Politics. The Swiss confederation (*Confederatio Helvetica*) began in 1291 with the alliance of the three original cantons — Uri, Schwyz and Unterwalden. There are 25 cantons, which are to some degree autonomous, though national politics are run by the bi-cameral Federal Assembly. Switzerland has been neutral since 1515, a fact that has made it a seat of several international organisations, including the League of Nations, then the United Nations and many of its agencies. Swiss politics may be advanced in many ways, but in one way it's behind other European countries — Swiss women were only given the vote in 1976.

Religion. Switzerland is split almost equally between Catholics and Protestants, but there is complete freedom of religion.

Language. There are four official languages — German (70%), French (20%), Italian (9%) and Romansch (1%). German is spoken in the northern areas, and in one solitary village (Bosco Gurin) in the Italian-speaking area. Although proper German (*Hochdeutsch*) is used in education and official matters, the spoken language (*Schweizerdeutsch*) is a very difficult dialect. There are no such dialect problems in the French-speaking area (along the French frontier in the west) or the Italian-speaking area (in the cantons of Ticino and part of Graubünden). Romansch is spoken only in a small part of the canton Graüünden in the south east. It is a Latin-derived dialect, which is both difficult and unnecessary to understand. If you can't get by in any of these languages, English is widely spoken, especially in the cities.

Making Friends. As in most of Europe, handshaking is widespread, and formalities among the Swiss are still quite strictly observed: you won't be on Christian name terms until you know someone quite well. This is more true among the German sector of the population than among the more outgoing French and Italian populations. An over-long conversation at an early stage of acquaintanceship may easily be misconstrued as prying. You'll rarely be invited to a Swiss home, since most of their entertaining is done in restaurants — but this custom is breaking down because of the high cost of eating out. If you are invited into a Swiss home for a meal, it's customary to take flowers for the hostess. When sitting down, it is acceptable to cross your legs but not to stretch them out. Men should not have their hands in their pockets during conversation.

The younger generation is, of course, less formal than the older generation, and are very straightforward in their attitudes. The après-ski scene is traditionally thought out as an ideal breeding-grounding for romance and rightly so. But the really keen skier will have little energy left for nightlife. Ski-lifts are a good meeting place, and in the two-person lifts, it's very impolite not to speak to your fellow-traveller. In towns, the best meeting places are the cafés, where total strangers can easily start up a conversation, without offence. An interesting comment on the orderliness of Swiss life and society is the fact that all prostitutes have to be officially registered, and strict health checks are periodically carried out. All very ' neat and tidy.

See the introduction for details of passports, customs regulations, duty free allowances, vaccinations and importing pets.

Passports and Visas. Holders of British, and US and Canadian passports are allowed to stay in Switzerland for three months; for extensions, apply to the police or, in large towns, to the *police des étrangers* or *Fremdenpolizei*.

Customs. The duty free allowances are: 2 litres alcohol up to 25° and 1 litre over 25°; 200 cigarettes or 50 cigars or 250 grams tobacco; 125 ml perfume; 10 unexposed films; and 125 g of butter. Non-European residents are entitled to double the amounts of tobacco goods and perfume. In addition, all visitors may import items intended for personal use and other non-commercial items to the value of SFr 100 (SFr 50 if under 17). Travellers under 17 are not entitled to the tobacco and alcohol allowances. The import or firearms, drugs, meat and other animal products is restricted. The import of absinthe and anaesthetics is forbidden.

100 centimes (c) = 1 franc (SFr)
£1 = SFr 2.55   SFr 1 = £0.40
$1 = SFr 1.60   SFr 1 = $0.60

For general information on handling, exchanging and raising money, see the introduction.

Coins. 5 c, 10 c, 20 c, 50 c, SFr 1, SFr 2, SFr 5.
Centimes are *Rappen* in German, *centesimi* in Italian.
A franc is *Frank* in German, *franco* in Italian.

Notes. SFr 10 (violet), SFr 20 (mauve), SFr50 (green), SFr 100 (blue), SFr 500 (brown), SFr 1,000 (violet).

Banking Hours. Monday-Friday 8.30 am-noon and 2-4.30 pm approximately. Resorts and large cities may have longer opening hours. All main stations and airports have exchange facilities, with more generous opening hours than banks, and usually a seven-day service. Those at Zurich and Geneva airports are open 6.30 am-11 pm daily. The bigger hotels will change money, but at a lower rate. Beware also of private, unofficial exchange bureaux, particularly in frontier towns, where you can lose up to 5%.

Shopping Hours. 8 or 8.30 am-6.30 pm, Tuesday-Friday, with an optional lunch break. 12-2 pm. Most shops close at 4 pm on Saturdays and stay closed on Monday mornings. Small shops close one afternoon a week, but this varies not only from town to town but from one area of a town to another. Some discount stores and supermarkets have special late opening hours, usually on Thursdays.

Import and Export. No restrictions.

Tipping. Hotels, restaurants — 15%, always included. Service included is *service compris* in French, *einschliesslich Bedienung* in German, *servizio compresso* in Italian. Taxis — 15% (usually included on the meter). Station porters — SFr 2 per item for up to 15 minutes, then SFr 1 for each extra 15 minutes. The British Overseas Trade Board recommends: "when accepting hospitality in a private house, it is usual when leaving to give SFr 2 to the servant who hands you your coat and hat and SFr 5-10 to the cook or maid."

Emergency Cash. Although about 20% of the population are foreigners, prospects are not very good, with very tight restrictions on work permits, and very little work in the first place. Seasonal work, like grape picking (October) and hotels and restaurants (winter and summer in the Alps) are possible, but illegal on a casual basis. See *Working in Ski Resorts: Europe* and *Work Your Way Around the World* (Vacation Work, £5.95 and £7.95 respectively) for the possibilities. If you wish to take up work legally, you must obtain a work permit before entering Switzerland, have your chest X-rayed at a Swiss clinic, and then register at the Aliens Police. If you apply for a work permit after you arrive it will be refused and not reconsidered until at least a month after you have left the country.

Getting Around

The information in this section is complementary to that given in the corresponding section in the introduction.

CAR

Swiss roads are on the whole, crowded, most of them being narrow and winding but the surfaces are excellent. There are over 600 miles of motorways but these are expensive for temporary visitors. Motorists using the network pay an annual tax of SFr 30, at frontier posts or through motoring organisations abroad. Evidence of payment is a tax disc displayed inside the windscreen. Caravans and trailers require an additional payment of SFr 30. For road conditions anywhere in the country, including the winter accessibility of mountain passes, dial 163. Many passes close from November to May or June.

Rules and Requirements. On mountain roads, the yellow postal coaches have absolute priority, and any instructions issued by their drivers have the authority of law; otherwise, uphill traffic has priority; in towns, trams have priority.

On some mountain roads, snow chains are obligatory — watch the signs at the bottom of the passes. Chains can be hired from most garages.

You may not wear ski boots while driving. Drivers and front seat passengers must wear seat belts at all times; children under 12 may not travel in the front seat.

Motorcyclists must ride with dipped headlights at all times; others must use dipped headlights in tunnels (however short) and in poor daytime visibility, including heavy rain.

Drivers who wear spectacles must carry a spare pair at all times.

Roof racks cannot carry a load of more than 50 kg if the car was registered after 1980, or 10% of the cars unladen weight if it was registered before then.

The minimum age for driving is 18.

Insurance. Claims should, in the first instance, be addressed to the *Zürich Versicher ungsgesellschaft,* Mythenquay 2, 8002 Zurich (Tel: 205 21 21).

Road Signs. Mostly follow the international pattern, but motorways and semi-motorways have green, not blue, signs.

Place Names. Many towns have an official name in one language, and an unofficial name (or orthographical variation) in another. Thus Neuchâtel is known locally as Neuenburg among German speakers. Geneva is Genève in French (the official version), but Genf in German. Very few towns have two official names, for instance Bern (German)/Berne (French); Biel (German)/Bienne (French). Cantons too have unofficial names; Ticino (Italian) is Tessin in French; Graubünden (German) is Grisons in French.

Parking. Basel, Bern, Geneva and a few other towns have disc parking (blue zones). Discs are available free from police stations, restaurants, garages, kiosks and ACS or TCS offices. Meters are also in use in many towns. When parking on hills, put the car in the lowest uphill gear, handbrake full on, and, to be safe, use chocks. No Parking is *Stationierungsverbot* (German), *Sosta Vietata* (Italian) or *Interdiction de Stationner* (French).

The standard advice given by Zurich police is to park in one of the no time limit car parks at the edge of town and continue into town by tram or bus. Maps of parking facilities are available from Zurich City Police, Bahnhofquai 3 (Tel: 29 40 11).

Petrol. There is only one grade of leaded petrol: *super* (96-98 octane), costs around SFr 1 per litre (£1.77 per UK gallon, $2.34 per US gallon). Unleaded costs around SFr 0.90 a litre. Prices are slightly higher in mountain areas.

Car Transport by Rail. Whether to by-pass the closed roads in winter, or just to save time and effort in summer, you can put you car on a train to avoid the Lötschberg Pass; Kandersteg to Goppenstein (SFr 15), Brig (SFr 30) or Iselle (SFr 42). These fares include all passengers.

Touring Clubs. *Automobil Club der Schweiz* (ACS), Wasserwerkgasse 39, 3000 Bern 13 (Tel: 22 47 22); *Touring Club Suisse* (TCS), 9 rue Pierre-Fatio, 1211 Geneva 3 (Tel: 737 12 12); *Verkehrs-Club der Schweiz,* Bahnhofstr 8, 3360 Herzogenbuchsee — (Tel: 61 51 51).

Accidents and Breakdowns. The TCS operates a 24-hour breakdown service; phone 140. In accidents involving personal injury the police must be informed (dial: 117). There are emergency telephones every 1.6 km on motorways and divided roads, and at irregular intervals on mountain passes.

TRAIN

There are two classes; first costs about 50% more than second. Second-class single fares work out at SFr 3 for 10 km, SFr 25 for 100 km (£16 or $26 for 100 miles), SFr 75 for 500 km. Seat reservations can be made only for international journeys.

The head office of Swiss Federal Railways (SSB) is Hochschulstrasse 6, 3030 Bern (Tel: 60 11 11).

Cheap Deals. Children under 16 travel free, and unmarried children aged 25 at half price, if accompanied by a parent with a valid ticket on the free Swiss Family Card scheme.

POSTAL COACHES

These belong to the Postal Organisation (PTT) and carry mail as well as passengers. They travel where railways don't go (ie up the mountains) and are, in fact, an extension of the railway system with timetables that dovetail with train times. Prices are similar, and coach stations in the towns are usually next to rail stations.

A seven day pass is available for SFr 25-58 depending on the region covered giving unlimited travel on postal coaches in that region. See also *Joint Transport Tickets* below.

BOAT

The lakes offer ample opportunity for sailing, rowing or participating in a boat trip (see *Joint Transport Tickets)*. There are car ferries on Lake Constance (Romanshorn to Friedrichshafen: 40 minutes; Meersburg to Konstanz: 20 minutes), Lake Lucerne (Gersau to Beckenried: 25 minutes) and Lake Zurich (Meilen to Horgen: 10 minutes).

MOUNTAIN RAILWAYS

Local Winter Sports Season Tickets are issued from November to June for reduced rate travel by mountain railways, funiculars, cableways and ski-lifts; details from local tourist offices.

JOINT TRANSPORT TICKETS

Timetables for all services can be bought from National Trust Offices or major Swiss stations. They appear in May.

The following tickets are valid for travel by train, postal coach, and boat, and in some cases cableways and funiculars. Most can be bought (on production of your passport) at the railway information offices in Basel, Bern, Geneva, Interlaken, Lausanne, Lucerne, Lugano, Montreux and Zurich; at Geneva and Zurich airports; or at Swiss National Tourist Offices abroad.

Swiss Pass — unlimited rail, boat or postal coach travel, plus free use of trams and buses in 24 Swiss towns, and 25% reductions on many cable cars and funiculars. The pass costs SFr 195 (SF2 280 1st class) for 8 days; SFr 235 (SFr 335) for 15 days; and SFr 325 (SFr 465) for a month. A new Swiss Card Flexipass is also available for use on any three days within a 15 day period for SFr 160 (SFr 235 1st class).

Half-fare Travel Card; offers 50% reduction on fares. The cost is SFr 65 for a month or SFr110 for a year. Holders of these tickets may buy Day Cards offering unlimited travel on the above systems for one day each in blocks of six for SFr 170 (SFr 270 1st class).

Regional Passes — holders of any of the above cards receive 20% discount on these regional unlimited travel tickets which are issued for seven or 15 days in 1st or 2nd class in nine areas of Switzerland. Prices range from SFr 50 in 2nd class in the Locarno/Ascona region to SFr 147 1st class in the Graubunden region. The tickets allow unlimited travel on two out the seven days or seven of the fifteen days; on the other days it allows reductions of 25%-50%.

Swiss Card — permits a one day journey from any border point to any destination in Switzerland, and a return journey, and allows any additional journey to be made at half price. The card is valid for one month and costs SFr 100 (SFr 125 1st class).

Transfer Ticket. Permits a one day journey from any border point to any Swiss destination and a return journey, to be made inside a month. The cost is SFr 70 (SFr 100 1st class). This is only available outside Switzerland.

Family Cards. Obtainable free from any Swiss National Tourist Office or railway station, these permit an adult holding one of the above tickets or a full fare ticket to take their children aged 6-16 free and children 16-25 at half fare. The ticket is only available outside Switzerland.

CYCLE/MOTORCYCLE

Swiss bicycles carry number plates, but these are not necessary for imported vehicles. Bicycles can be hired from main railway stations for SFr 14 a day. For route suggestions, contact the Swiss Cyclists' and Motor-Cyclists' Federation, Schaffhauserstr. 272, 8023 Zurich (Tel: 311 9220).

AIR

The Zurich Airport Authority (Tel: 816 22 11; flight information — 812 71 11) issues a general guide, parking plans, and a guide for the handicapped (all in English). Airport trains take ten minutes from the Hauptbahnhof. The fare is SFr 4.20. There are also direct trains from Zurich Airport to Bern. From Geneva Airport you can take a train (SFr 3.40) or bus no. 10 (SFr 1.50) Basel airport is actually in France (near Mulhouse) and is connected to the city by a land corridor.

The *Fly-Gepack* scheme allows luggage to be checked-in at most city and resort railway stations for flights via Geneva or Zurich. The fee is SFr9.

HITCH-HIKING

Legal, except on motorways. Pretty slow. Best results if you're neatly dressed. If you secure a lift, and they like you, the Swiss can be extraordinarily hospitable.

CITY TRANSPORT

Taxis. No particular make of car is used, so look for the signs on the roof. Taxis can be hailed, or you may prefer to telephone or hunt one out at a taxi-rank. The rate is about SFr2 per km (£1.30 or $2.10 per mile) with a minimum charge of 5SFr. These rates increase by 50% outside city limits, so, for long journeys, try to agree on a price beforehand.

Underground. The only metro is in Lausanne, which is actually a kind of funicular railway. It travels from the city centre, via the railway station, to Ouchy along the lakeside. Fares are based on length of journey.

Bus/Tram. In Zurich city transport is very much do-it-yourself — you buy your ticket from automatic machines at bus or tram stops (flat fares of SFr 1.50 up to 5 stops; SFr 2 for 6 stops of more); then you must press the button before you reach your stop) — do not get in at the door by the driver. The coins you need for the vending machines are 10c., 20c., 50c. and SFr1. The fine for travelling without a ticket (delicately called a "supplementary charge") is SFr50 plus the cost of the journey.

The Zurich City Transport Office (VBZ) is at Bahnhofquai 5, 8001 Zurich (Tel: 221 03 55); there is an information and sales office in the underground shopping centre *(Shopville)* under the Central Station. As well as single ride tickets you can buy an unlimited travel day ticket — at the VBZ offices or at most newsagents — for SFr5.

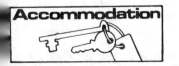

See the introduction for information on youth hostels, other hostels and advance booking of accommodation.

Hotels/Motels. The star rating system for hotels runs from five down to one-star. Prices are highest in Zurich, where the cheapest double rooms cost about SFr60 (£23 or $36). There are about 100 motels in Switzerland — their prices range from SFr25-100 per person. All prices include continental breakfast, service and taxes. All hotel accommodation is licensed, apart from the hotels belonging to the Blue Cross Federation (the league against alcohol).

Camping. Numerous sites throughout Switzerland, with charges starting at around SFr3 per person, tent or car. A list is available from *Verband Schweizerischer Campings* (VSC), Im Sydefadeli 40, 8037 Zurich. Free camping on uncultivated land is allowed in most cantons.

Sleeping out. Not illegal, but it can get very cold up in the mountains. Usually acceptable in city parks.

Youth Hostels. A highly detailed map and list is available from tourist offices or *Schweizer Bund fur Jugendherbergen* (SJH), Wildhainweg 19, 3001 Bern (Tel: 24 55 03). Rates vary from SFr6-SFr15. The Zurich Youth Hostel offers hostellers who stay for two nights or more a free book of discount vouchers for use in the city.

Mountain Huts. Accommodation in these refuges is intended for genuine hikers or climbers. Details from *Schweizer Alpen-Club* (SAC), Helvetiaplatz 4, 3005 Bern (Tel: 43 36 11).

Finding and Booking Accommodation. It's always advisable to book in advance, or at least don't leave it till too late in the day. There always seems to be a conference or fair which makes accommodation scarce, and, in the main cities almost non-existent, particularly during the summer.

The Swiss National Tourist Office can give you lists of hotels and motels, with all facilities and prices. The list of hotels is also available from the Swiss Hotels Association, Monbijoustr. 130, 3001 Bern (Tel: 50 71 11 for enquiries or complaints). These lists give the telephone numbers of local tourist offices, which can handle last minute bookings. Some tourist offices set up seasonal accommodation offices, often, as in Geneva (Tel: 732 53 40), in the main railway station. If ever you're really stranded in a town, head for the station and look for the Travellers' Aid personnel, who wear yellow, white and red armbands.

Communications

General information on telephones and English language newspapers and radio broadcasts is given in the introduction.

Post. In towns, post offices are open from 7.30am-noon and 1.45-6pm Monday-Friday. On Saturdays, offices close at 11am. The head post office in Zurich, at Kasernenstrasse 95/99 (Tel: 245 41 11), is open from 6.30am-10.30pm Monday-Friday, 6.30am-8pm on Saturday, and from 11am-10.30pm on Sundays. Main post offices have a free poste restante service. Mail boxes are yellow.

Philatelists can arrange an annual subscription to receive all the new issues of Swiss and United Nations (Geneva) stamps. Contact the General Directorate of PTT, Philatelic Agency, Parkterrasse 10, 3000 Bern (Tel: 62 27 28) for Swiss stamps; or the United Nations Postal Administration, Palais des Nations, 1211 Geneva 10 (Tel: 34 60 11).

The correct way to address mail is: name, street (name, then number); town, preceded by a four-figure code, and, if writing from abroad, the country code CH-.

Telephone. The system is all automatic, and area codes are listed in all call boxes and in front of directories. Zurich = 01; Bern = 031; Basel = 061; Geneva = 022. Long distance and international calls can also be made through the operator (dial 114) or from telegraph offices in main post offices.

Public phones booths are aluminium and glass; in most of them, coin boxes have slots for SFr 5, SFr 1, and 10c, 20c and 50c coins. Lift the receiver, insert at least 40c and dial. Unused coins are returned when you replace the receiver. The international prefix is 00 and international calls can be made from all payphones.

Credit cards are accepted by some phones. All payphones have instructions in English. The operator code is 114 for collect (reverse charge) calls.

All public phones have directories, with information in French, German and Italian. The country is covered by 18 multi-coloured volumes. Blue pages give services and useful numbers; green pages — information on international calls; pink pages — tables of postal rates, lists of post codes and telephone area codes; yellow pages — commercial directory; white pages — alphabetical list of subscribers, first sub-divided alphabetically into communities within the area.

Useful numbers: 111 — Directory Enquiries; 112 — Number Unobtainable/Out of Order; 114 — International; 117 — Police; 118 — Fire; 120 — Tourist Information and (winter only) Snow and Avalanche Report; 150 — Early Morning Alarm; 160 — Exchange Rates; 161 — Time; 162 — Weather Report; 163 — Road Conditions; 164 — Sports Information; 167 — News in German; 168 — News in French; 169 — News in Italian.

Telegrams. Can be sent from post offices or by phone — dial 110.

Broadcasting. The Swiss Broadcasting Company's wire broadcasting network produces some English language programmes, notably a news and weather bulletin at 12.15 pm and *Dateline* at 2.45 pm and 7.15 pm. These can be heard on Channel 1 of the wire broadcasting network in hotels throughout Switzerland.

Health and Hygiene

For general information on hygiene, first aid, insurance and medical treatment, see the introduction.

Hygiene. In spite of the terrible pollution of the lakes, which in many cases has killed off all natural life, Switzerland must still be counted as one of Europe's cleanest countries. All tap water is drinkable, and there are, of course, many brands of mineral water on the market. There is little chance of food poisoning or disease and, when you're up in the mountains, all ailments, real and imaginary, tend to disappear. Sufferers from rheumatism (gout was a favourite among the Victorians) can profitably visit one of the many spas. A free guide to the spas — *A Short Climatic Guide to Switzerland* — is available from the *Schweizerische Vereinigung der Klimakurorte,* Montreux.

Treatment. Switzerland has no National Health Service, but the local authorities take good care of their inhabitants and insurance is compulsory for most of the population. There are no reciprocal agreements covering foreign tourists, so private insurance is necessary. Doctors' fees and hospital costs are high, but good treatment is assured.

Emergencies. As in other countries, chemists have their duty rota — lists on any chemist's door. The emergency number is 117, but the large towns have special numbers for medical emergencies (47 47 00 in Zurich), given at the foot of the directory. All hospitals have emergency wards, with doctors on 24-hour duty. The major rail stations also have permanent medical teams on duty.

Insurance. Most insurance policies don't automatically cover skiing accidents and loss or breakage of ski equipment, so you have to pay extra premiums. If you're going mountaineering, you'd do well to enrol with the *Schweizerische Rettungsflugwacht* (Swiss Air Rescue), Dufourstrasse 43, 8008 Zurich (Tel: 47 22 30). Subscriptions are around SFr 150 per family for a year. In exchange you have free use of their ambulance-helicopters, and, if necessary, free emergency repatriation flights to any point in Europe (and to points outside Europe if you're prepared to pay the extra costs). The emergency 24-hour number is 01-47 47 47.

Entertainment

Sport. Switzerland is most famous for skiing, and offers some of the best slopes in Europe. There are over 130 ski schools, and 2,000 instructors, teaching courses from infant beginners through to ultra-advanced. The winter season runs from November to April, but around Christmas the accommodation is booked up well in advance, and the lifts and slopes are crowded. Things calm down a lot during January. Twelve of the higher ski resorts also stay open during the summer. Snow reports from larger resorts are published from January-March in British newspapers, and are also available on *Prestel* 34 427.

The Alps also offer opportunities for hiking and mountaineering. Set routes for hikes are marked by yellow signs and painted marks on strategic rocks. To appreciate the flowers, May and June are the best months. If you're a more serious climber you'd be advised to join the Swiss Alpine Club, Obergrundstrasse 42, 6003 Lucerne (Tel: 041-22 62 23).

Eating out. Restaurants are open from 8 or 9 am till about 10 pm, but you may find that many of them only serve hot food at rather limited hours, like 12-2 pm and 7-9 pm. A simple continental breakfast of coffee, butter and jam costs around SFr 5 in a restaurant. Typical prices are about SFr 15-25 for *fondue* or *raclette* or any other main course (at least £6 or $9). Set meals are cheapest but not always on offer. Restaurant prices for Swiss wine start around SFr 20 a bottle; other European wines may be cheaper. You can have cheaper meals at station buffets and at *Mövenpick* restaurants, both of which serve hot meals all day and stay open late at night, at least by Swiss standards. The snack bars of supermarkets and department stores offer basic self-service meals for around SFr 10. The *Migros* chain is recommended.

Serious drinking is done at the inns, which are also the scenes of serious card-playing. The national game is called *Jass* — rather likes whist. Never order your drinks at the bar — waiter service is the rule, since it's illegal to drink standing up. As a concession to the principle of licensing hours, spirits may not be served before 9 am. The minimum age for drinking is 18.

Police. The police are very polite and civilised, and even if you get on the wrong side of them, they'll treat you as a human being, not as a convict. The emergency number for contacting them is 117. The police headquarters in Zurich is at Bahnhofquai 3 (Tel: 216 71 11).

Laws. With the great Swiss respect for all things clean and tidy, bear in mind that the laws most likely to catch you out are those that protect the natural order — drunkenness is the obvious one, and penalties for littering are very severe. Niggly things like crossing the road against the red light are likely to bring you a warning — plead ignorance in English. Another aspect of the Swiss character is the way laws tend to be actually enforced — as opposed to just having warnings posted.

Driving Offences. The police can fine you on the spot for most offences: up to SFr 40 for parking or not using headlights in poor visibility; SFr 60 or more for speeding. Drunken driving goes through the courts and may result in prison and confiscation of your licence.

Nude Bathing. There are no official nudist lakeside beaches open to the general public, but there are a number of naturist clubs where you can bare all. For details contact the Swiss Naturist Organisation, Postfach 12, 2075 Thielle.

Drugs. Fine and up to two years medical treatment or imprisonment for possession; up to five years in prison for selling.

Legal Aid. Embassies can be very helpful and influential, but free legal aid is hard to come by. Some of the contact addresses in the *Help and Information* section might come in useful.

For general information on useful contacts and complaints procedures, see the introduction.

Embassies and Consulates.

British Embassy, Thunstr. 50, 3005 Bern (Tel: 44 50 21).
British Consulate General, 37-39 rue Vermont, 1211 Geneva (Tel: 734 38 00).
British Consulate General, Dufourstr. 56, 8008 Zurich (Tel: 47 15 20).
  There are also British honorary consulates in Lugano and Montreux.

  American Embassy, Jubiläumstr. 93-95, 3005 Bern (Tel: 799 02 11).
  American Consulate General, Zollickerstr. 141, 8008 Zurich (Tel: 81 68 30).

  Canadian Embassy, Kirchenfeldstr. 88, 3005 Bern (Tel: 44 63 81).

Lost Property. The central office (*Fundbüro*) in Zurich is at Werdenühlestrasse 10, 8001 Zurich (Tel: 216 25 50) for all lost property including that mislaid on Zurich city transport.

Baby-sitting. There are agencies in the larger towns, but not so many in the Italian area. Look up *Baby-sitting* in the directory. Or try looking around at university notice-boards.

Information. The Swiss National Tourist Office has its headquarters at Bellariastrasse 38, 8027 Zurich (Tel: 288 11 11). Every town has its own tourist office for local information and hotel bookings — the terms are *Office de Tourism* in French, *Verkehrsverein* or *Verkehrsbüro* in German, *Ente Turistico* in Italian. Often, as in Zurich (Tel: 211 12 56), these offices are located in the railway stations; in Basel it's at Blumenrain 2 (Tel: 25 50 50); in Geneva at Gare de Cornavin (Tel: 738 52 00); in Bern in the station (Tel: 22 12 12). A daily tourist information bulletin is available by dialling 120.

Free Maps. From National Tourist Offices, banks and local tourist offices, generally of a high standard. The larger towns also supply transport maps.

Help. Drop-in, Dufourstrasse 181, 8008 Zurich (Tel: 55 53 11; emergency night number 47 47 00) is run by the university psychiatric department, and deals with drug problems and any other emotional problems or traumas. For sympathy, dial 143 for the *Dargebotene Hand* (or *la main tendue*) service.

Disabled Travellers. The *Schweizerische Invalidenverband,* Froburgstrasse 4, 4600 Olten (Tel: 062 32 12 62) issues a hotel guide (*Hotelführer*) and holiday guide (*Ferienführer*) for the disabled. Town guides to Basel, Bern, Lausanne, Lucerne, St. Gallen, Zurich are available from Mobility International Schweiz, Riesbachstrasse 58, Postfach, 8034 Zurich (Tel: 383 0497).

Student Travel. *Schweizerischer Studentenreisedienst Reisen* (SSR), Bäckestr. 52, 8026 Zurich (Tel: 242 30 00); also offices at Schmiedenhof, Basel 12 (Tel: 25 71 71), 3 rue Vignier, Geneva (Tel: 29 97 33); and in Bern, Lausanne, Neuchâtel, St. Gallen, Biel, Chur, Fribourg, Lucerne, Winterthur.

English Language Churches. St. Andrew's (Anglican), Promenadengasse, Zurich (Tel: 34 60 24); Holy Trinity (Anglican), rue du Mont Blanc, Geneva (Tel: 31 51 55); Calvin Auditoire (Scottish Presbyterian), Place Taconnerie, Geneva (Tel: 98 29 09).

American Express. Bahnhofstrasse 20, Zurich (Tel: 211 83 70); 7 rue du Mont Blanc, Geneva (Tel: 31 76 00); and offices in Basel, Bern, Lausanne, Locarno, Lucerne, Lugano, Montreux and St. Gallen.

Liechtenstein

Area. 61 square miles   **Population.** 26,500

Capital. Vaduz (population 5,000)

Liechtenstein is an independent principality ruled by Prince Hans-Adam II. However, the eleven communities which comprise Liechtenstein are effectively part of Switzerland in many respects. There are no frontier formalities along the Swiss border; and the Austrian border is manned by Swiss officials, with the same entry procedures as Switzerland. Liechtenstein is part of the Swiss telephone system: area code 075. Swiss currency is used. Postal rates are the same as in Switzerland but Liechtenstein stamps must be used.

Getting Around. Liechtenstein is traversed by the main Zurich-Vienna line (and forms part of the Orient Express route to Venice). There are three stations: Schaan, Nendeln and Schaanwald. The capital and other communities are connected by *Postauto* (post bus). A monthly pass valid on all buses within the country, and those to neighbouring Swiss and Austrian towns, costs SFr 100 from post offices. Taxis can be requested by dialling 22443 or 23336. Ring 21753 for details of horse-drawn coaches.

Accommodation. As well as the usual collection of hotels and inns, there is a youth hostel between Schaan and Vaduz (Tel: 25022) and two alpine huts: Gafadurahütte and Pfälzer-Hutte.

Entertainment. Skiing and hiking are the main attraction. For the more sedentary, Vaduz has a postal museum, a music school and the National Gallery. The gallery is on the first floor of the Engländer building in the town centre. Wines produced in Liechtenstein can be sampled at wholesale prices at the Hofkellerei, Feldastrasse 4, Vaduz (Tel: 21018).

Help and Information. The National Tourist Office is on the ground floor of the Engländer building at Städle 37-38 in Vaduz (Tel: 21443). There is permanent branch at Malbun, and one at Schaanwald open May-October. For consular assistance, contact the relevant Consul in Zurich, Innsbruck or Salzburg, or telephone the Irish Consul in Vaduz on 21623.

Calendar of Events

Public Holidays are shown in **bold**. Those marked * are not observed in all cantons.

January 1	**New Year**
January 2	***Berchtoldstag****
February	Carnivals: the most spectacular in Basel, Lötschental, Schwyz, Zug, Luzern, Einsiedeln, Unterengstringen and Ellikon
March/April	**Good Friday, Easter Monday:** Egg races in the cantons of Basel and Berne
April	*Sechseläuten* Festival at Zurich
April-May	Golden Rose of Montreux International TV Festival
May/June	**Whit Monday**
May/June	**Ascension Day:** riding the parish bounds in Beromünster, Sempach and Hitzkirch
May/June	**Corpus Christi***
June 1	Napoleonic processions in Geneva
late June	Cow fights and cattle processions to the High pastures in the canton of Valais
late June/July	Children's Festival at St Gallen
mid July	Alpine Festivals in many mountain villages
July-August	William Tell celebrations in Interlaken
August 1	**Independence Day**
mid August	Geneva Festival
August 15	**Assumption**
September	International Music Festival at Luzern
mid September	International Jazz Festival at Zurich
late September	Grape harvest festivals at Sierre, Neuchâtel, Lugano and Lutry
mid October	Opera Festival at Lausane
late October	*Alplerkilbi* (Alpine Festivals) in Obwalden and Nidwalden
November 1	**All Saints' Day**
December 8	**Conception***
December 25, 26	**Christmas**

Turkey

SULTAN AHMET MOSQUE   W.S.

Area. 300,930 square miles   **Population.** 53,000,000

Capital. Ankara (population: 3,460,000)

Weather. There are enormous climatic variations between the coasts and the mountainous interior of Turkey. When it is quite warm on the Aegean coast in April, the snow has not yet melted from the mountain passes in the Anatolian hinterland. Severe Siberian winters are experienced in the central, northern and eastern regions forcing roads to close and making travel difficult between November and April. Temperatures along the Black Sea coast are milder, though not as warm as on the south coast. Although the Mediterranean coast (Antakya to Marmaris) enjoys balmy winters with temperatures in the 50s, surprisingly few charter flights or package holidays operate over the winter (though this may change as the tidal wave of tourism advances). Winters in Istanbul are very cold with occasional snowfalls.

The average high for the summer months in Istanbul is a pleasant 28°C/82°F so the heat is rarely unbearable even if it is a little too humid. The southern coastal regions, on the other hand, are semi-tropical and the summer heat can be debilitating here as in the baked interior of the country. Few buildings are equipped with fans.

The annual rainfall varies from 10 inches in Central Turkey to 10 times as much on the Black Sea coast, so if the dust of the interior becomes oppressive, head north to the lush tea gardens along the Black Sea. The bulk of Istanbul's rain falls in the spring and again in autumn, creating muddy conditions over the winter. Smog is becoming a serious problem in the large cities, especially Ankara between

221

September and April. Water shortages are also a recurring problem in cities and villages alike.

THE PEOPLE

Although Turkey will strike you as racially homogeneous, in fact only 85% of the population of 53 million are ethnic Turks. Estimates vary on the breakdown of the other 15%, but a high proportion are Kurds, almost all of them living in southeast Turkey.

The Turkish record on race relations is far from impressive. Having forcibly "repatriated" after World War I all the Greeks who had been living in Turkey for generations and having reputedly massacred between 600,000 and 1.5 million Armenians in 1915 (all references to Armenia are banned to this day), the Turkish authorities continue to maltreat the Kurdish people, for example prohibiting them from speaking their language in public. Frequent reports of torture and even murder of Kurds are a blot on the copybook of a nation aspiring to join the European Community. Even Saatchi and Saatchi, whom the Turkish government has hired to improve its image, may have trouble explaining away such reports. These tensions should not affect tourists, unless they travel close to the Syrian border in areas of Kurdish insurgency. In contrast to their mistreatment of minorities, the government has welcomed huge numbers of ethnic Turks who have been driven out of Bulgaria.

Politics. The Turkish Republic came into existence in 1923 and was modernised primarily by Mustafa Kemal, who was later given the name Ataturk, which means father of the Turks. His reforms include the creation of the secular state with religious tolerance for all, westernisation of dress, and the substitution of the Roman alphabet for Arabic script.

Turkey is once again run on democratic lines after a period of martial law following the military coup in 1980. Executive power lies in the hands of the Prime Minister and his ministers, although the President has the power of veto. The majority of seats in the National Assembly are held by the Motherland Party. For some time Turkey has been seeking to become a full member of the European Community; the Community has put off even considering its application until 1993.

Religion. All but a tiny number of Turkey's people are Sunni Muslim, though only half the population are practising. Turkey is not immune to the tendency towards Islamic fundamentalism, and a few city councils are defying Ataturk's legacy of a secular state, by passing laws such as enforced segregation of male and female students on buses. So far these have been isolated cases, and there is little chance of a sudden and sweeping shift, but do not be too surprised if a local asks you (whether you are male or female) to cover bare limbs.

Language. Although it has been speculated that Turkish belongs to the language group which includes Finnish and Hungarian, mastering a little of the vocabulary is easier than in those languages. English is increasingly being taught in schools and many people, especially young men in the carpet trade, are eager to practise. Trying out one or two Turkish phrases on these friendly interlocutors is always rewarding; "çok guzel" is probably the most handy when asked how you like their country. This is one country where a phrase book can be an asset, when you meet monolingual Turks who wish to carry on a conversation by pointing at phrases. A pocket dictionary is perhaps more helpful for interpreting menus, signs, etc. and for ease of looking up single words, e.g. "afternoon" or "receipt".

German is the most widely understood second language because of the number of Turkish migrant workers who have lived in Germany and also because of the annual invasion of German tourists.

The change to the Roman alphabet from Arabic script in 1928 has made life much easier for the English-speaking traveller, though the sentence structure of Turkish is completely alien.

Making Friends. It is the overwhelming friendliness of the Turkish people which fills so many travellers with enthusiasm for the country. The incessant invitations to drink tea in cafes or private homes, the spontaneous offers of assistance in crowded bus stations, the smiles and greetings on all sides produce in most visitors a warm appreciation for the Turks. Occasionally there may be an ulterior motive behind gestures of friendship (usually a desire to lead you to a carpet shop). Nevertheless contact with the natives is almost always a great pleasure.

Although many of the traditions of hospitality arise from their Islamic culture, the social distortions found in stricter Islamic countries like Pakistan are absent in Turkey. Lone women travellers will not escape overtures which may be unwelcome, but they are rarely pestered and harassed as they are in, say, Arab countries. Men and women travellers are equally susceptible to harassment by carpet salesmen and shoe cleaners. A favourite ploy of the latter is to ask meekly for a cigarette. With false gratitude, they insist on cleaning your shoes. They then demand payment for the polish used, and will follow you halfway across a city if you refuse.

Exposure to western ways has been sufficient for most Turks not to be too shocked by most tourists' behaviour, and serious misunderstandings are few. Naturally women should be sensitive, especially when travelling in the east, and refrain from looking boldly into the eyes of strangers and from wearing revealing clothing. Women on their own who take the time to wander around the back streets of towns and villages during the daytime are often invited in by women or school children.

A supply of duty-free cigarettes, preferably Marlboros, might go some way to repaying kindness from men. Take a few foreign coins or low denomination notes to give to children all of whom seem to collect foreign money. You can also while away companionable hours in village cafes if you know how to play backgammon, Turkey's national game.

Red Tape

Visas. Until November 1989 Turkey had one of the most laid-back immigration policies outside the European Community. But in retaliation for Britain's decision to impose a visa requirement on Turks visiting Britain, UK citizens must now obtain a visa at a cost of £5 at a port of entry. Visas are still not required for Australian, American, Canadian, Irish or New Zealand passport holders for visits of up to 3 months. If you want to stay longer than 3 months, you are supposed to obtain a residence permit *(ikamet vesikasi)* which costs 15,000 Turkish lira (£4.50) and lasts up to 6 months. If you fail to do so before the initial 3 months expire, you will be charged triple that sum upon departure. An alternative to getting a residence permit is to cross over to Greece every 3 months and get a fresh visa. Official travel agents' manuals warn that people arriving with insufficient funds and a disreputable appearance may be turned back. In fact the incidence of this happening is very rare.

Customs. Usually a verbal declaration is enough on entry and luggage is not searched. Valuable items may be registered in your passport to ensure that they are taken out of the country. The duty-free allowance is 400 cigarettes (twice the usual limit), 50 cigars, 200gr tobacco, a generous 5 litres of spirits and 1½kg of instant coffee. Since both tobacco and drink are so cheap in Turkey, you may not want to bother with duty frees.

Be very careful about buying old artefacts since the export of antiques is strictly forbidden unless you obtain a licence. The "Statistical Form for Foreigner Arrivals & Departures" which you must fill out at either end of your visit warns, "It is forbidden to take any plant, wildlife, archaeological or historical relics out of Turkey." This is hypocritical in view of recent scandals involving the wholesale denuding of hillsides by Turks who profit from the sale of wildflower bulbs abroad.

Border Formalities. Formalities at entry points in Western Turkey are quick and straightforward whether you arrive by charter fight, ferry or car. Because of strained relations between Greece and Turkey, there can be a frustrating amount of form filling involved on boat crossings to and from Greek islands, even for day trips, mostly on account of Greek bureaucracy. If crossing from Greece by land, you should be in a vehicle rather than on foot. Try to hitch a lift, since taxis capitalize on this rule and charge over the odds.

Partly as an outcome of glasnost, a new border point has opened between Turkey and the USSR at the Sarp Gate on the Black Sea beyond Hopa. Although it has not yet been used by Western travellers, this may come in time. You may cross into the USSR only if you have obtained a Soviet visa in advance. The main rail crossing into the Soviet republic of Armenia is east of Kars at the city of Leninakhan (Gümrü in Turkish). Transport links have now been repaired following the devastating earthquake which wrecked the Soviet city in 1988. Further south, road travellers may be allowed to cross from Tasburun to the Armenian capital of Yerevan (Erivan in Turkish) once ethnic unrest ceases.

Internal Travel Restrictions. Certain areas of Turkey are restricted for visitors, for example military zones, some areas bordering the USSR, and Kurdish areas where there is unrest, for instance the mountainous district of Hakkari in the south-east corner of Turkey. If you do try to approach an off-limits zone, you will probably encounter roadblocks and be turned back. If you wish to visit a site which is in a military zone (e.g. Ani near Kars and Toprakkale near Van), the local tourist office can advise on obtaining permission to visit.

Agri Dagi, better known as Mount Ararat and famous as the resting place of Noah's Ark, is strictly out of bounds. Mountaineering parties must apply to the Ministry of Foreign Affairs in Ankara (Tel: 134 29 20) for permission months in advance.

As in Eastern European countries it is forbidden to photograph airfields, railway lines or anything in sensitive border areas. Look for signs "Yasak bolge" or "Yabancilara yasaktir," which indicate restricted areas.

Student Cards. Because of the widespread forging of International Student Cards in Turkey, many places are becoming reluctant to honour genuine ones. If you encounter this problem, try to produce some other document which indicates your student status. A British Rail Young Person's Rail card has been known to work when an ISIC card has failed. Several travel agencies in Sultanahmet (Istanbul) issue student cards on skimpy evidence.

£1 = TL3,350   TL1,000 = £0.30
$1 = TL2,100   TL1,000 = $0.50

Currency. The unit of currency is the Turkish lira (TL) sometimes represented by a symbol resembling a pound sign. The lira was once divided into 100 kurus, but due to the high annual rate of inflation (at present 75%), kurus are now extinct. Even the small coins (TL10 and TL25) are seldom seen.

Coins. TL10, TL25, TL50, TL100, TL500.

The TL100 coin can be either a silver coin the size of a 10 pence piece or a small gold coin.

Notes. TL100, TL500, TL1,000, TL5,000, TL10,000, TL20,000, TL50,000.

All notes bear a picture of Ataturk and are of indeterminate hue; the TL1,000 and TL10,000 notes are especially easy to confuse. Since the TL100 and TL500 coins were introduced, the mauve TL100 and the blue TL500 notes are becoming rare. Hoard TL1,000 notes which are by far the most useful denomination. Some old notes of different (though still indeterminate) colours are still in circulation. If a merchant refuses to accept them, take them to a bank.

Import and Export. There is no limit to the amount of foreign currency that may be taken into or out or Turkey, though there is an export limit of $1,000 worth of Turkish lira. Exchange slips showing conversion of foreign currency should be kept, though it is unlikely you will need them. You may reconvert $100 worth of lira on departure without showing exchange receipts.

Changing Money. The exchange rate doesn't vary much from one bank to another; even hotels use a rate which usually tallies with the official rate. As a rule, the rate is more favourable in Turkey than in the UK so avoid stocking up on lira before you leave home, unless you plan to arrive at a small airport at a weekend. The İş Bankasi, which has branches throughout the country, can be relied on to carry out exchange transactions, though they may charge a commission when the other major banks (like the Esbank and Töbank) do not. Mobile banks have begun to appear in resorts and near important tourist sites. These are convenient, especially since they tend to stay open on weekends and evenings, but you can't expect the courteous treatment (including proffered cups of tea) which you often receive in permanent banks away from the tourist trail. It is also a good idea to count your change more carefully at tourist banks where the temptation to offload obsolete notes or shortchange naive customers might be too great for some staff.

Some banks which display the "Kambiyo/Change/Wechsel" sign change only notes, not travellers' cheques, so it might be worth carrying a few notes to prevent the frustration of having to search for another bank. Also it may be necessary to resort to your cash supplies in the remote places of Eastern Turkey where travellers' cheque transactions are comparatively rare. Eurocheque cards can be used at most banks (on the beaten track) to support cheques drawn on British banks.

The official literature advises tourists to keep all their exchange Turkish money receipts, though these are unlikely to be needed unless you try to reconvert a large number of lira on departure. Exchange counters at Istanbul airport willingly exchange Turkish money (including coins) with no fuss and no commission (though they may not have £1 coins in stock). Bureaux de change at smaller ports of departure may not be so obliging.

Credit Cards. More and more establishments are accepting credit cards, though it is still possible to encounter a resort restaurant which assumes Visa cards are cheque guarantee cards. The cost of meals and overnight accommodation is so low that credit cards are not really necessary unless you intend to hire a car or take a domestic flight. Visa has recently installed some cash dispensers in Istanbul and the major resorts which permit withdrawals of up to £100 in Turkish currency.

The Black Market. The black market is a risky proposition, more because the people in the business are often con artists than because it is against the law.

In Istanbul the majority of transactions take place in Tahtakale Caddesi near the Misir Carsisi (Spice Bazaar); avoid asking a policeman for directions to this street. If you do intend to use the black market which may give you a gain of about 20%, familiarise yourself with the appearance of Turkish currency first and try to work with a partner. Jewellery shops and other tourist outlets are often willing to exchange money at black market rates and are less likely to try to cheat you. Newspapers, including the English language *Daily News*, publish an official rate against the US dollar and a "free market" rate though this is usually well below street rates.

Emergency Cash. A few years ago, the only way to raise emergency cash in Turkey was the same as in India, by selling whisky and Western cigarettes. But lately, opportunities for earning wages have been increasing and many travellers extend their time in Turkey by teaching English or working in the tourist industry. "Help Wanted" signs can be seen in the windows of bars and carpet shops early in the season (March/April) in the main resorts. The more usual way to fix up employment is to be approached by the proprietor of a pension where you are staying and whom you have got to know slightly. Obviously this only happens in places frequented by tourists, such as Göreme and major yachting centres like Kusadaşi, Bodrum and Marmaris. The latter often have quayside notice boards where advertisements for crew, hostesses and maintenance staff are posted.

Another way of earning money which has become common over the past couple of years is to teach English, though this generally requires a longer commitment, unless you happen to be able to fill a vacancy at the end of the academic year (May/June). Language institutes in Istanbul in particular often recruit teachers by posting notices in the budget hotels of Sultanahmet. Although the wages are reasonable by local standards — as much as a million lira (£300) a month — many teachers have reported that it can be a struggle extracting earned wages from their employers.

It is most unusual for foreigners undertaking work of this kind to be granted a work permit. Therefore you will have to leave the country every 3 months as mentioned above (see *Red Tape)*.

Opening Hours. Banks and most offices are open Monday to Friday from 08.30am to noon and from 1.30pm till 5pm. The same hours apply to shops Monday to Saturday, though many stay open till 7pm. The fact that Friday is the Muslim holy day does not affect commerce. Along the Aegean and Mediterranean coasts during the summer, some shops and banks observe the afternoon siesta and open again for the evening.

Getting Around

The information in this section is complementary to that given in the corresponding section in the introduction.

CAR

Rules and Requirements. National driving licences in English, French or German are accepted in Turkey, but an International Driving Permit is required if you wish to drive a vehicle with Turkish registration, e.g. a rental car. You may drive your own vehicle in Turkey for up to 3 months without a *carnet de passage,* but particulars of the vehicle will be entered in your passport. If your vehicle is severely damaged or completely wrecked while inside Turkey, and you have to abandon it, the customs office *(Gümrük Müdürlügü)* must see or take delivery of it, so that your passport can be suitably endorsed. If your vehicle is stolen, you will have to obtain a special certificate from the Governor of the province (*vali*). For stays exceeding 3 months, a *tryptique* must be obtained from the Turkish Touring and Automobile Club (address below).

Third party insurance is obligatory. As in the United States many Turkish drivers are under-insured and it is therefore essential that foreign drivers have full cover. The best solution is to get an international green card from a specialist insurer in your own country (see *Introduction*). Make sure you specify that you want it endorsed for the Asian as well as the European part of Turkey. You can buy Turkish third party insurance from the *Dogan Sigorta* office at the frontier or from TTOK (Turkish Touring and Automobile Club, Halaskärgazi Cad. 364, Sisli, Istanbul; tel: 131 46 31). This costs TL10,000-TL15,000 per month, but is arguably less than adequate.

Road System. The quality of roads continues to improve and, except on the approach roads to big cities, traffic is relatively light. The best roads are the heavily used E5 between Istanbul and Ankara, the E80 through Erzurum to Iran (though there are still sections of gravel) and the E90 along the south through Adana and Urfa. The government plans to complete a 4-lane motorway from Edirne to Iskenderun by 1993 and all roads are to be paved. You may encounter the occasional toll, not only on the bridge over the Bosphorus in Istanbul but on certain stretches of E roads.

In winter certain passes, such as the Tahir Pass (between Erzurum and Agri) and the Kopdagi Pass (between Trabzon and Askale) are closed due to heavy snowfalls. Problems also occur on the main route to Syria which crosses the Taurus Mountains, on which a toll is charged.

Signposting is generally adequate. Yellow signs can usually be counted on to appear near places of touristic interest.

Rules of the Road. Turkish road signs conform to international standards and driving is on the right. The maximum speed is 90km/h outside built-up areas (whether or not you are on a dual carriageway) and 50km/h in urban areas. All motorists are supposed to carry a first aid kit and two warning triangles, though the police are much more likely to check for seatbelts (something the locals are still very slap-happy about). You can be given an on-the-spot fine for minor infringements and there are stories of tourists being falsely accused of speeding. The best policy here is to feign bewilderment at the policeman's Turkish and hope he abandons his illicit quest.

Highway Hazards. Cautious driving is essential to avoid an accident. Public transport tends to stop suddenly and without warning, and pedestrians, especially children, often dart out into the road without looking. All of these problems are accentuated at night when you might encounter donkey carts, etc. with no lights.

Although Turkish drivers rely on their horns far less than is the custom further east, do not hesitate to alert the locals of your approach by an occasional blast.

Travelling motorists occasionally report that they encounter hostility, mostly from stone-throwing children in remote areas. Try to pass through these areas as quickly and unobtrusively as possible. Also exercise extreme caution when driving in winter when road conditions can be treacherous.

Turkey has one of the highest accident rates in the world and involvement in an accident can be both financially and psychologically (as well as physically) damaging. It is not unknown for foreigners to be imprisoned while police reports and other paperwork are completed. Foreign drivers who are in an accident involving a pedestrian can expect to be taken into custody. Don't sign anything you don't understand and insist that an English-speaking policeman or interpreter be provided. Even for trivial accidents, you should be sure to obtain a police report. An alcohol test is standard, so do not drive after drinking.

The standards of Turkish driving are rising, partly due to government safety campaigns; ten years ago macho Turks tended to view foreign male drivers in a purely competitive light, while going to elaborate lengths to be polite to female drivers. This is no longer so noticeable.

TTOK, the official motoring organization, operates road rescue services but only on the main routes. Ring 146 70 90 or 521 65 88 for assistance. Otherwise you must seek help from local mechanics most of whom are skilled and whose services are very cheap by European standards. Garages are often grouped together in one street. There are agents for most foreign makes of car in Ankara, Istanbul and Izmir; Renault is the most widespread.

Fuel. Because of ready oil supplies from Iraq, petrol is cheaper than in other Mediterranean counties, i.e. TL850-900 (around £1.30 per UK gallon or $1.80 per US gallon) per litre. Petrol stations are numerous along main routes. Unleaded petrol is virtually non-existent.

Car Rental. If you are hiring a car through one of the major multi-nationals like Hertz, Avis or Budget, it is normally about 20% cheaper to arrange it from your home country. A week's rental including unlimited mileage and all extras should work out to be about £200 ($320) which is about the sixth most expensive in Europe. On the spot car hire will cost about £50 a day. Once you are in Turkey, you can rent a vehicle from any number of local operators in most resorts, though you may have trouble finding self-drive hire cars east of Göreme. One of the cheapest deals being advertised at the time of writing was from Blue Car Rentals located across from the Ankara Hilton; their all-inclusive price for one week's rental was US$224. Check the adverts in the *Daily News* for other possibilities. In view of how reliable, extensive and cheap public transport is, and how nerve-racking driving in Turkey can be, many prefer to stick to the buses.

TRAIN

Travelling second class on the trains is even cheaper than buses: on longer journeys not much more than half the price. Both first and second class seats are bookable in advance. But because the purpose of Turkish trains is primarily to haul freight, the services can be very slow and often arrive late. *Ekspres* trains can be slower than their name indicates, but still considerably faster than ordinary trains, so it is usually worth paying the surcharge. Couchettes are comfortable and will be provided with linen (though no blankets) if another small surcharge is paid. All trains have a dining car (labelled "Lokanta") where the food is unexciting, but the old-fashioned decor creates an interesting atmosphere. They are also not air-conditioned. There are student discounts of 10%, and 20% is deducted if you purchase a return ticket.

There are two railway stations in Istanbul. The European trains depart from Sirkeci in the old city (tel: 527 00 50/1); trains to the rest of Turkey and on to Asia depart from Haydarpasa (tel: 336 20 63), a magnificent temple to the train, across the Bosphorus on the Asian side.

Devotees of steam trains may want to take one of the steam services which Turkish State Railways have retained for the benefit of tourists. One of the most scenic sections is between Isparta and Egridir north of Antalya. Holidays based on steam travel can be arranged through World Steam Tours in the UK (tel: 0602 334714).

BUS

The efficiency and comfort of Turkey's bus network puts the coach services of most other countries to shame. Between major cities, services are fast, frequent and cheap. There are a great many private bus companies competing with one another which will be very clear as soon as you enter any city bus station (*otogar*), especially the enormous bustling ones in Istanbul and Ankara. Prices vary between different companies. For example, 100 miles of travel can vary between TL3,500 and TL5,000 (£1 and £1.50 or $1.60 and $2.40) depending on the various luxuries offered by the company.

Despite price variations, most travellers choose their company according to the most convenient departure time, something you can't do if you follow the first helpful Turk to the ticket desk in which he probably has a vested interest. By law, the companies should post their fares as well as their range of destinations and departure times, so the prospect of choosing a service is not as daunting as it may seem at first sight. If you buy a ticket in advance (which is possible though usually not necessary except in high summer), make sure that you get on a bus belonging to the company which issued the ticket. It is also possible to flag down a long distance bus on the open road, provided there are seats.

For more comfort and slightly higher prices look for the Varan Bus Company which offers air-conditioning, hostess service and video entertainment on some routes such as the $7\frac{1}{2}$ hour Istanbul to Ankara run on double-decker coaches. But even without any frills, bus travel is convenient and pleasant. All buses carry supplies of chilled mineral water and splash around a refreshing lemon cologne every so often (a habit of hospitality practised in Turkish homes as well). There are frequent rest and refreshment stops, so even long journeys are not too gruelling, except possibly for people who suffer from cigarette smoke.

DOLMUŞ

A dolmuş is a minibus or transit van which connects even remote villages with the larger centres and also operates in cities (see *City Transport* below). It is often described as a collective taxi which is misleading since it operates along a prescribed route, though it will collect and deposit passengers at any point along that route. The word dolmuş is related to *dolma* the word for stuffed vine leaves; both are from the root for "stuffed". Some dolmuşes wait until they are (over) full before leaving, others keep to a vague schedule. Often the country services are alarmingly oversubscribed, though the local people usually defer politely to foreigners and leave the seats vacant. If you are early enough, claim the back corner as far from the crush and jostling as possible.

Fares for local journeys (e.g. a mile or two from the bus station to town) are usually TL250-350 (8p or 13c) while longer country journeys usually work out at TL350 (10p or 16c) for 10km/6 miles of travel. During the journey, watch for the amount the locals are proffering, though it is rare for a dolmuş driver to overcharge tourists. The only thing to watch out for is if he sets off with an almost empty vehicle; you and your companions may discover you have unwittingly chartered the dolmuş at taxi prices.

When trying to find the dolmuş you want, start by enquiring at the otogar, mentioning your destination, since dolmuşes to different destinations leave from different ranks or *garaji*.

AIR

The THY office in London (11/12 Hanover St, W1R 9HE; 071-499 9240) will send you the complete timetable which will help you to plan an itinerary, though it does not include fares. If you are short of time it is worth considering taking an internal flight between two of the 13 airports in the country, since flights are relatively cheap and can usually be booked at short notice. Virtually all flights are routed through Istanbul or Ankara and connections are not always immediate. There are no subtle gradations in the fares; for example the fare Ankara to Van (750 miles) is the same as Ankara to Trabzon (460 miles), i.e. TL 105,000 (£33 or $53).

Travellers under 24 who book within 24 hours of departure pay only TL69,000 (£21.50 or $35) for *any* domestic flight with the exception of Istanbul to Antalya and Istanbul to Dalaman.

Be prepared for laborious security checks including body searches and the necessity of re-identifying your luggage on the tarmac after you have checked it in the terminal. Also, hang on to your boarding card which occasionally is requested at your destination. Since 1988, smoking has been prohibited on all domestic flights.

HITCH-HIKING

The prospects for the hitch-hiker in Turkey are very good. Because of the hospitable nature of the people and because young hitching travellers are a relative novelty, there is no trouble in getting lifts. All manner of vehicles, including carts and tractors, taxis and police cars, are likely to stop. It is highly recommended for travelling between the archaeological sites between Kuşadasi and Bodrum, and in Cappadocia. It is a good idea to insist (politely) on wearing a seatbelt. Many Turkish drivers assume a sticker saying "Allah Korusun" (Allah protect me) is an adequate substitute.

Especially in the east of the country, you may be asked to share costs with the driver. Many hitch-hikers have recommended Londra Mocamp, a truck stop on the outskirts of Istanbul, for getting long distance lifts in both directions. It is sometimes possible to chat up the drivers and arrange a lift.

BOAT

Turkish Maritime Lines offer an affordable alternative to land travel. The British agent for TML is Sunquest Holidays, Aldine House, 9-15 Aldine Street, London W12 8AW (Tel: 081-749 9933). Ferries sail from Istanbul south along the Aegean coast to Izmir and east along the Black Sea to Trabzon. During the summer, the Aegean trip departs early afternoon on Monday, Wednesday and Friday and arrives 18 or 19 hours later. The cheapest fare (for a seat only) is about TL35,000 (£10 or $16). There may be other south coast services between Marmaris and Antalya, though these operate like expensive cruises rather than public transport. Another popular sea-going option is to charter a traditional wooden schooner known as a *gulet* to explore the coast. These are available from places like Bodrum for about £200 or $320 a day (4-berth) whether bareboat or crewed. If interested, enquire at Bodrumtur (Tel: 6141 3376).

There are two possible car ferry services along the Black Sea coast, one between Istanbul and Giresun via Sinop and Samsun, the other direct to Trabzon. Both operate only once or twice a week so advance booking is usually necessary. Neither trip is very speedy: the ferry which departs from Istanbul at 6 pm on Wednesday arrives in Sinop 5 pm Thursday, Samsun 6.30 pm Friday and Giresun 6 pm that evening. The Trabzon service departs Istanbul 7 pm on Monday and 9 am on Friday arriving about 36 hours later. If you can manage such a long journey without a berth, you can do the trip cheaply, again for £10 or $16 one way.

The booking office in Istanbul is clearly labelled "Danizcilik Bankasi TAO" (Tel: 43 35 00) and is located just east of the Galata Bridge on the Galata side. Student discounts are available. Services are reduced in the winter months.

CITY TRANSPORT

In the big cities, you will find red municipally operated buses (marked IETT in Istanbul, EGO in Ankara) running alongside private buses, usually blue, which makes life a little complicated for the newcomer. Tickets for the municipal service should be bought at special kiosks for TL350 (10p or 16c); you can deposit a cash fare on the private buses. If you haven't managed to obtain a ticket in advance, locals in the queue or on the bus may offer to sell you one from their stock.

Taxis are numerous in all towns and are marked with black and white/yellow checked markings. The majority now have functioning meters (which start at TL800/25p) though it is as well to ascertain this before departure and agree a price if necessary. Most inner city trips will be less than TL2,000 (60p/96c) except in resorts where rip-offs are common. Taxi drivers don't always switch off their illuminated sign once they pick up a passenger.

City dolmuşes can usually be distinguished from taxis by the fact that their destination is written on the front and by their solid yellow band instead of checkered marking. Dolmuş fares are fixed by the city council so there is little chance of being diddled. They follow a set route but will pick you up and set you down at any point on the route; you pay for the distance travelled.

Accommodation

The government plans to increase the number of hotel beds to nearly a quarter of a million by 1990, which is 5 times more than there were in 1983. Although most of these are intended for package tourists, inevitably the number of rooms available to independent travellers will increase, so there is little chance of being turned away from a town or resort for lack of accommodation.

The tourist office accommodation brochure has only a selection of hotels, mostly in the posher category starting from $10 single (prices are quoted in dollars).

Outside resorts there is a large gulf in price and comfort between Turkish-style hotels which are very numerous in towns and cities, and more luxurious hotels, which are often booked out by tour groups and where a single room will probably cost at least TL50,000 (£15 or $24). Whether or not you will enjoy or even tolerate staying at the very basic, very cheap local hotels is entirely a matter of personal standards. You can't expect a single room costing TL5,000 (£1.50 or $0.90) to have much character; with luck it will have a bed with clean sheets, a functioning lock and key and a sink. The supply of water is far from reliable in many places, so canny travellers have a shower whenever the supply is on. Bedbugs (*Tahtakurusu*) can also be a problem; ask the management for some insecticide. Another disadvantage of these local hotels is that fellow guests tend to be very noisy (especially during Ramazan).

Standards are higher in tourist centres like Göreme where there is fierce competition for the tourist dollar, and prices are higher in the big cities. *Pansiyons* are often pleasant family-run establishments which may offer meals. Some advertise themselves as hostels though this is usually a ruse to catch the eye of the budget traveller. Rooms in private homes are not common but they do exist; look for the sign *Oda Var*. Hotel touts will often meet you at bus stations; try bargaining for a lower price if there is competition.

Camping. A selection of campsites is listed in the annually updated hotel brochure. The well known chain of BP Mocamps quote their rates in US dollars: $3 per person, $1.50 per car plus a 20% surcharge in July/August. Some campers maintain that this does not represent good value. Tourist hotels with a garden may allow camping on their property. If you are reluctant to camp in the wilds, which is usually quite acceptable, ask petrol stations for permission to pitch your tent or park your campervan nearby. In exchange for a packet of cigarettes they may invite you to use their loos. Asking permission of locals to camp in any spot that takes your fancy is especially recommended in eastern Turkey where there is a shortage of serviced campsites and where you might inadvertently end up camping in a military zone.

Communications

Telephone. Public telephones take tokens called *jetons*, available from any post office and most tobacconists. They come in 3 sizes: small *(kucuk)*, medium *(normal)* and large *(büyük)*, costing TL100 (3p/5c), TL500 (15p/24c) and TL1,000 (30p/48c) respectively. The *jeton* is dropped into the machine after you have satisfied yourself that the telephone is in working order and before dialling. The cost of a call to Britain is TL4,500 (£1.35/$2.16) per minute if operator-controlled and TL2,750 (82p/$1.32) if dialled direct. The international operators (who speak English) can be reached by dialling 528 23 03. For direct dialling of international calls, dial 99, then the country code and number.

The easiest way to make a long distance call is from a booth in a post office, where you simply pay at the counter. (You can also buy a phone card, though phones which accept them are hard to find outside airports and tourist areas.) You can make direct dial calls between most cities within Turkey; dial 9, then the city code and the number. Some city codes are: Istanbul 1, Ankara 4, Kusadasi 6361, Erzurum 011. It can sometimes be difficult to get a line. If it is urgent you can book a "flash call" or *yildirim*. The telephone system is less erratic than it used to be, though you may still have to dial several times or wait for the lines to clear.

Telegrams to Britain cost TL1,000 (30p/48c) a word (minimum 7 words) and are likely to arrive in a mangled form, due to difficulty in transmitting English. Faxes can also be sent from many post offices at exorbitant cost, e.g. TL22,500 (£6.75/$10.80) for one page to the UK.

Post. Post offices are recognisable by their yellow PTT signs, meaning Post, Telegraph and Telephone. The major ones are open 8am till midnight, Monday to Saturday or even 24 hours a day. A poste retante service is available from the central post office in all towns. You may be asked for your passport when collecting mail, but this is usually just so there will be no doubt as to the spelling of your name. There may be a small fee for each piece of mail collected. Poste restante letters should be sent to you at the Merkez Postanesi (i.e. Central Post Office).

Air mail letters should be marked "Ucak Ile," in the absence of an air mail sticker. When enquiring about the up-to-date postal charges, do not be surprised to find an utter lack of consensus. Take the average and stick to it! At the time of writing a post card to Europe cost TL500 (15p/24c) and to the rest of the world TL600 (18p/28c), while letters to Europe cost TL600 and to the rest of the world TL900 (30p/48c). From big city post offices mail to Britain takes 4-6 days; from smaller places 7-10 days.

Newspapers. The *Daily News*, published in Ankara, is the only English language daily. It is sold at a few outlets in most cities and in the tourist areas of Istanbul (e.g. Sultanahmet and Istiklal Caddesi). At TL700 (21p/33c) it costs about a fifth of the price of a 2-day old *International Herald Tribune* and provides some interesting insights into Turkish politics as well as reasonable coverage of world events, mostly provided by Reuters and the other major news agencies. The *Daily News* is aimed more at expatriates than tourists, and focuses more on Ankara than Istanbul.

Broadcasting. Although much of the television programming is imported from America, all of it is dubbed into Turkish. The *Daily News* gives the programme schedule for the two channels. A news bulletin is read in English every night at 11pm on channel 2. Televisions are often left on in cafes and restaurants so you may have no choice but to enjoy the stagey videos favoured by Turkish television of heroes of folklore singing and dancing on mountain top or at sea. The original soundtrack of imported films and series is often broadcast simultaneously on FM radio, which is useful if you have a walkman with radio.

There is a meteorological bulletin in English broadcast daily on the short wave band (16m.) from 3.30-4pm and on 31m. between 11pm and midnight. It may be easier to catch the television weather report at 8.40pm with charts covering the whole country which are easily understood.

The BBC World Service can be picked up in Turkey on the following wavelengths: MHz 15.070, 12.095, 9.660, 6.180.

Health and Hygiene

The World Health Organisation reports that potential malaria risk exists from March to the end of November in the provinces of Adana, Hatai, Icel, Hakkari and Siirt. There is no chloroquine resistance as yet. On the other hand, the risk is so small that most travellers and expatriates do not take malaria prophylaxis, and there have been no reported cases of the disease for some time. Mosquitoes can be a nuisance along the south coast so be sure to take a good repellent or coils.

Treatment is free or cheap in government-run hospitals, though the standards of care are not consistently high. Most foreigners patronise private hospitals and clinics (addresses under city headings) or Red Crescent facilities.

Water and Hygiene. According to a recent survey, nearly half of those surveyed were affected by some illness when they went to Turkey. Only in major cities is the water chlorinated, thereby reducing the risk of "Ataturk's revenge". Drink the very cheap bottled water (*su*) and carry purifying tablets for the water in which you wash fruit. Restaurants sometimes use bottles instead of pitchers for tap water, so make sure your bottle of water has a foil cap.

Travellers who find the eastern style of toilet distressing will be glad to learn that Turkey has a Foundation for Clean Toilets but disappointed to hear that in 1989, it found only 12 winners in the whole country. Avoid putting loo paper down the toilet since it is foreigners' habits which are often responsible for clogging up the plumbing. The words for Ladies and Gents are similar so be careful: Ladies is *Bayon* Gents is *Bay*.

Items from chemists such as tampons and deodorant are very expensive.

Nightlife. In tourist resorts you should find sufficient discos, cocktail bars, etc. to while away your nights and your money if you are so inclined. A special warning about the "Turkish Evenings" you will probably see advertised for about £10 ($16) each. These may include perfectly adequate Turkish food and traditional entertainment, such as belly dancers and folk music; but the package is likely to also include "sophisticated international entertainment" consisting of invitations to join in a rendition of "Y Viva Espana" and "The Birdy Song".

Museums and Archaeological Sites. Most museums and archaeological sites are open daily except Mondays. Entrance fees vary enormously from around TL2,000 (60p/$1) to TL10,000 (£3/$4.80). Museums may charge photographers up to twice the cost of an entrance ticket for the right to take photographs.

Eating Out. There is a great tradition among Turkish men of eating out, both for lunch and dinner, so there is never a shortage of eating places, though there may be a shortage of variety on the menu. Even when there is a long printed menu, the restaurant may have only the core dishes available. More downmarket places will have no menu and therefore no way for you to ascertain the prices ahead of time, though you can be fairly confident that you will not be overcharged. Restaurants in tourist resorts often post a large blackboard with prices outside to lure in passers-by.

The most popular establishments are *kebapçis* and *köftecis* where the standard meal consists of soup (*çorba* usually made from lentils), followed by kebab and salad and eaten with a great deal of white bread. All of this costs about TL4,000 (just over £1/$1.60). There are of course fancier places which may feature fish, tripe soup or mixed grills. Much of Turkish cuisine overlaps with Greek, especially a preference for bland stewed dishes of meat and aubergine, as does the habit of inviting the customer into the kitchen to choose dishes by pointing.

A typical Turkish breakfast as served in many hotels for about £1/$1.60 consists of tea, bread, tomato, cucumber, olives, white cheese and sometimes a boiled egg. If you crave something sweeter for breakfast, look for a *pastane* (pastry shop) where a large helping of *baklava* or *kadayif* will cost about TL1,000 (30p/48c). These are open throughout the day and evening for you to indulge your sweet tooth.

Below is a basic vocabulary for eating out:

balik	— fish (varies from place to place; *çinakop* is a variety of seabass; also look for *kiliç* or swordfish)
piliç	— chicken
et	— meat (usually lamb, served stewed with vegetables)
et yemez kimse	— vegetarian
köfte	— spiced ground meat rissoles
arnavut cigeri	— spiced lamb's liver fried with onions
iskembe çorbasi	— mutton tripe soup with garlic and lemon (eaten by the locals to cure hangovers)
dolma	— vegetables (e.g. vine leaves, peppers, tomatoes) stuffed with rice and nuts.
imam bayildi	— cold dish of aubergines, onions and tomatoes in olive oil (means "the priest swooned")
pilav	— dish with rice or (occasionally) cracked wheat
zeytinyagli	— cold vegetables in olive oil
cacik	— cucumber in yoghurt with garlic and olive oil
börek	— flaky pastry filled with cheese, spinach or meat
ekmek	— bread
sütlaç	— cold rice pudding
baklava	— filo pastry with nuts and syrup
kadayif	— shredded wheat with nuts and syrup
süt	— hot, sweet milk
seker	— sugar
tuz	— salt
ayran	— salty yoghurt drink like buttermilk
bira	— beer (Danish lager type)
sarap	— wine (sek-dry; tatli-Sweet)
raki	— the national drink: aniseed liqueur like ouzo, drunk with meals

Drinking. Tea (*çay*) is the universal drink. It is grown in abundance on the shores of the Black Sea around Rize, is very cheap (TL100 or 3p/5c in local haunts) and is drunk in small glasses with two sugar lumps and no milk. You can tell when you're in tourist territory when you are offered a choice of apple or lemon tea. The former is artificially flavoured (brand name: *Lezzo*). Coffee is less commonly available, probably because it is 5 times more expensive than tea. Whereas tea is often drunk in family settings in tea gardens (*çay bahçesi*), coffee is drunk in male-dominated *kahves*.

Beer is more common than wine, especially in the east. One theory to account for this preference is that the *Koran* prohibits wine but does not mention beer. The most common brand of beer is the palatable Efes Pilsen, which costs about 50p for a half-litre bottle in a restaurant, considerably less from shops. Turkish-produced wines can be quite good. Try Doluca (especially Villa Doluca), Kavaklidere or Buzbağ, which again cost about £1 from shops. Raki, the Turkish version of ouzo, is the national spirit; beware of mixing it with anything other than water.

Ayran, whether commercially produced or freshly mixed, is a very refreshing summer drink as is the pure fruit juice (*meyva su*) which Turkey produces. The cherry one (e.g. brand name *Tamek*) is particularly good and can cost anything from TL500 to TL1,500 (15p-45p/22c-66c) depending on the popularity of the establishment with tourists. The most unusual way to buy a cold drink is from an itinerant şerbet seller who carries a chilled tank of an odd-tasting refreshment on his back and hoses some into a glass for TL100 (3p/5c).

Shopping. It is not only wealthy Germans on tour buses who buy carpets in Turkey. A surprisingly large number of backpackers find themselves cashing in a few of their higher denomination travellers' cheques to buy a carpet or *kilim*. (The latter is a flat woven floor covering which is cheaper than a carpet.) After a week or two of travelling around Turkey, you may conclude that you are the only foreigner not to have succumbed to temptation and that 95% of all Turkish men are in the carpet trade, a false impression created by the fact that carpet salesmen are more likely to speak English and to befriend tourists. Some have learned to use sophisticated soft-sell techniques, for example they may tell you that anyone who claims that only natural dyes have been used is lying, since chemical dyes are now in universal use.

The main centres of carpet weaving and selling are Kayseri and Van. Although carpets and kilims for sale in Turkey are somewhat cheaper that they are in the West, the quality may be inferior, as determined by the number of knots per square centimetre, the permanence of the dyes and the materials used. Specialist dealers abroad cannot be deceived as easily as tourists. For example some carpets described as silk are in fact silk on cotton known as floss silk, which good carpet shops will not stock. Given that you are not a carpet expert nor are you buying for investment, the only rule is to spend a long-time bargaining and buy only one you are sure you like and can afford. Leather is also a good buy in Turkey.

If you are not prepared to part with £80/$130 or more, pre-recorded tapes constitute a bargain souvenir. In addition to the ubiquitous Euro-disco, larger record shops and kiosks in tourist areas stock a wide range of well recorded rock music for TL5,000 (£1.50). This is your chance to add to your collection of Dire Straits, Prince, George Michael, etc.

Smokers who want to go native will smoke a local brand such as Maltepe which costs TL600 (18p/28c). Turks with aspirations prefer Marlboros, which cost TL2,400 (72p/$1.15) even when bought from shoeless children who have access to contraband sources.

Most prices in Turkey are not negotiable, but if you shop for souvenirs in a bazaar you must be prepared to bargain for the best price. As a rough guide to bargaining cut the price first quoted by half, then start haggling. Never lose your temper; be firm and definite over the amount you are prepared to pay. You may even have to walk away and thereby run the risk of not being implored to come back. Local bargainers spin elaborate yarns about why they can afford only a certain amount for the item in question as much to amuse and entertain the merchant as anything else. On the other hand, don't enter into lengthy and serious negotiations unless you're serious about buying the object.

Drugs. There is only one word of advice on the subject of drugs and smuggling in Turkey; DON'T. If you find yourself tempted, try to find a rerun cinema showing the harrowing film *Midnight Express*. The sentence for simple possession can be 30 years. (There is no legal distinction between soft and hard drugs and also you can be considered guilty by association if you are caught in the company of drug-users). Even if you are innocent, it will take a long time for your case to be heard, and you will be held in a prison where conditions may not be quite as dreadful as they are in *Midnight Express* but will by no means be luxurious. The prosecution has the right of appeal against any sentence thought to be too lenient.

There are a number of British nationals detained in Turkish prisons, all of them held in Izmir. If you seriously want to take them books or food or just visit them, contact Prisoners Abroad (071-833 3467) who, after an interview, can supply a letter of introduction to the British Consul in Izmir, who can in turn arrange a visit.

Crime. There is a special branch of the police for tourists, but they are not as widespread as the tourist police in Greece. In Istanbul they are based in Sultanahmet: Tel: 528 53 69. In general crime levels are low, so you are unlikely to need their help. There were however reports in 1989 of a gang in Istanbul who were drugging and robbing foreigners by offering them spiked fruit drinks. There are also accounts of male travellers being invited into bars by strangers and subsequently being charged £100 for one drink and the unwanted company of a woman, so beware.

Nude Bathing. Nude bathing is not permitted. Even topless sunbathing is against the law, but is tolerated in some resorts.

Help and Information

General information is also given in the introduction.

Embassies and Consulates.

British Embassy, Sehit Ersan Caddesi 46 /A, Cankaya, Ankara (Tel: 127 43 10).
British Consulate-General, Mesrutiyet Caddesi No 34, Tepebasi, Beyoglu, PK33, Istanbul (Tel: 144 75 40)
British Vice Consulate, 1442 Sokak No 49/51, Alsancak, Izmir PK300 (Tel: 211759). There are honorary British Consulates in Antalya, Bodrum, Iskenderun and Marmaris.

American Embassy, 110 Ataturk Boulevard, Ankara (Tel: 126 54 70).
American Consulate General, 104-108 Mesrutiyet Caddesi, Tepebasi, Istanbul (Tel: 151 36 02).
American Consulate-General, 92 Ataturk Caddesi, Izmir (Tel: 14 94 26).
There is also an American consulate in Adana.

Canadian Embassy, Nenehatun Caddesi No 75, Gaziosmanpasa, Ankara (Tel: 136 12 75).
Canadian Consulate, Buyuksdere Caddesi Bengun Han 107 Kat 3 Gayrettepe, Istanbul, Turkey (Tel: 172 51 74).

Information. There are nearly 100 tourism information offices throughout the country. These are not uniformly useful; when asked about times and frequency of buses, ferries, etc. some are likely to refer you to the private travel agency or bus station down the road. But offices may have printed information in English or maps which are worth picking up; they should also be able to advise on the procedures for visiting sites in or near military zones. The central office in Istanbul is at Mesrutiyet Cad. No: 57/6-7, Galatasaray (Tel: 145 65 93), and the central office in Ankara is at Istanbul Cad. 4, Ulus (Tel: 311 22 47). In Izmir the office is at GOP Bulv. Buyuk Efes Oteli Alti, 1/C (Tel: 142127).

Student Travel. Genctur Youth Tourism, Yerebatan Caddesi 15/3, Sultanahmet (POB 1263 Sirkeci, Istanbul) (Tel: 526 54 09). Silatur (Youth and Student Travel Centre) Emek Ishani (Gokdelen), Kat 11 No.1109, Kizilay, Ankara (Tel: 118 13 226).

Calendar of Events

January 1	New Year's Day
April 23	National Independence Day and Children's Day
May 19	Youth and Sports Day
August 30	Victory Day (to commemorate the final rout of invading forces 1922)
October 29	Republic Day

There are also two religious festivals each year: Seker Bayrami, the Sugar Festival, which lasts for three days at the end of Ramazan, the month of daytime fasting in the spring. The other one is Kurban Bayrami, The Festival of Sacrifices, lasting four days in the summer.

Yugoslavia

MOSTAR

Area. 98,766 square miles   **Population.** 23,600,000

Capital. Belgrade (population 1,250,000)

Weather. The Adriatic coast has hot summers and mild winters. Although there is a fair amount of rain throughout the year one hotel on the Adriatic island of Hvar is sufficiently confident of good summer weather that it gives free accommodation in the event of rain. Inland, the climate is Alpine: drier, but colder in the winter.

THE PEOPLE

As increasing numbers of tourists will testify, the Yugoslavs are becoming progressively more westernised in their outlook. The federation has moved so far away from its Eastern bloc neighbours in recent year that it is appropriate now to treat the country as a Western European nation.

Most Yugoslavs take great pride in their society, which they regard as independent and egalitarian. Although individually they may appear aloof at first, most are extremely friendly and hospitable. The Serbs (39%) comprise the largest ethnic group, followed by the Croats (20%), Bosnians (9%), Slovenes (8%) and Macedonian (6%); Albanian (8%) and Hungarian (2%) minorities reside in the respective border regions.

Politics. A "socialist federal republic" consisting of Bosnia-Herzegovina, Croatia,

239

Macedonia, Montenegro, Serbia and Slovenia; the "autonomous provinces" of Kosovo and Voyvodina are part of Serbia. Since President Tito died in May 1980, the Presidency and leadership of the League of Communists has rotated among party members representing each republic and autonomous province. The key to the prevailing ideology is "self-management", a phrase that both describes the economic system and emphasizes Yugoslav independence from Soviet influence. True democracy does not as yet exist at a national level, although at local level factories are managed by workers' councils. Various ethnic tensions in Yugoslavia, particularly among the Albanian population of Kosovo, have delayed the development of a single main opposition to the Communist Party.

Religion. Half the population is Eastern Orthodox (mainly in Serbia, Macedonia and Montenegro); 10% is Muslim (predominantly in Bosnia and Kosovo); and 30% Catholic (elsewhere). Although the constitution guarantees complete freedom of religion, in practice authorities try to clamp down on foreigners actively promoting religion. The state seems happy, however, for pilgrims of any nationality to visit the village of Medjurgorje (between Mostar and the Adriatic), where the Virgin Mary reputedly appears every evening to a group of young people.

Languages. There are three official languages: the one most widely spoken is Serbo Croat; Slovene (in the north) and Macedonian (in the south) are also widespread. The Roman alphabet is used in Slovenia and on the Adriatic coast (Croatia and coastal areas of Montenegro and Bosnia-Herzegovina); elsewhere, the Cyrillic alphabet is used. Albanian is spoken by a sizeable proportion of residents in Kosivo. English is the first foreign language taught in schools, followed by German. Italian is widely spoken in the Italian frontier area.

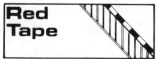

Red Tape

See the introduction for details of passports, customs regulations, duty free allowances, vaccinations and importing pets.

Passports and Visas. British visitors with a full passport are allowed to stay up to 90 days without a visa; applications for extensions must be made through the police within the first seven days. British travellers with Visitor's Passports will be issued on arrival with a special pass for use as an identity card for up to 30 days. A small fee is payable. Americans and people from most other countries outside Europe must obtain visas.

Customs. In addition to a reasonable amount of items for personal use as gifts, travellers may import free of duty: 200 cigarettes or 50 cigars or 250 grams tobacco; 1 litre wine; $\frac{1}{4}$ litre spirits; $\frac{1}{4}$ litre eau de cologne; and 25 grams perfume.

Money

100 paras = 1 new dinar(D)
£1 = 20 D   1 D = £0.05
$1 = 12.50 D   1 D = $0.08

For general information on handling, exchanging and raising money, see the introduction. The inflation rate in Yugoslavia has been so great in recent years that the dinar was revalued in January 1990 to make transactions more manageable. It remains to be seen whether the new currency and other measures taken by the government to reduce inflation will stabilise prices, but it is to be expected that dinar prices will rise. But exchange rates should also alter in the tourist's favour, and so the sterling and dollar equivalents of prices quoted in this chapter should remain fairly constant. Many tourist services are priced in US$ or German DM to avoid frequent price changes. You are advised to take money in small denomination dollar or sterling travellers cheques so that you do not have to change too much money at once if rates are changing fast.

Currency. At the time of writing only the 50 dinar note in the new currency is in circulation, alongside the old notes which are worth one ten thousandth of their previous value. Thus the 1,000,000 D note is worth 100 new dinar, the 100,000 note is worth 10 new dinar, the 20,000 dinar note is worth 2 new dinar, the 5,000 dinar note is worth 0.50 dinar (or 50 paras), etc. The old notes are to remain valid throughout 1990 while the new notes are issued, along with a new coinage. The old coins are no longer valid.

Banking Hours. Most open 7am-noon and 3pm-7 or 8pm, Monday to Saturday. Some large branches remain open at lunchtime. Money may only be exchanged at banks, registered travel bureaux and official exchange offices, such as are located in airports and many hotels. These latter keep longer hours than banks. Exchange receipts should be kept until you leave Yugoslavia, as they will be needed if you want to reconvert hard currency.

Shopping Hours. About 8am-7 or 8pm, Monday-Friday; 8am-3pm Saturday; many shops still shut for the traditional siesta (noon-4pm). Some food shops also open on Sundays, 7-11 or 12am.

Import and Export. For the first visit in any calendar year, imports and exports of Yugoslav currency are limited to 1,200 D. For subsequent visits (as will be shown in your passport) the limit is 500 D. Note that foreign currency exchanged into dinars cannot be reconverted, unless you buy *dinar-cheques*. These are effectively travellers cheques which can be used virtually as cash, and additionally entitle the holder to a 10% discount in hotels and restaurants.

Emergency Cash. A very few intrepid travellers have found work in the tourist industry on the Adriatic coast, or picking fruit on the banks of the Danube, but these opportunities should definitely not be relied upon. Your best plan is to sell whatever possessions you can and head for Italy.

The information below is complementary to information given in the introduction.

CAR

The Green Card or frontier insurance is compulsory. Upon entry to Yugoslavia, any visible damage to a vehicle must be certified, and the certificate produced upon departure. Failing this, any uncertified damaged will result in the detention of both car and owner until the circumstances of the damage are ascertained. A first aid kit and full set of replacement bulbs must be carried at all times.

A warning triangle must be carried at all times; motorists towing a trailer or caravan require two.

Parking. Parking is by meters. Parking offenders are fined on the spot or towed away.

Petrol. Two grades: *normal* (86 octane) and *super* (98 octane). Super costs 6.70 D per litre (£1.50 per imperial gallon, $2 per US gallon). Unleaded petrol (95 octane) is slightly more expensive at 8.10 D per litre. It is currently available from 120 garages on main roads. Petrol coupons can be bought abroad or at the frontier in units of 10 litres; these give what amounts to a bonus of 5% extra petrol. Unused coupons can be refunded upon departure. Any petrol carried in spare cans is subject to duty when crossing the frontier.

Tolls. A number of stretches of genuine motorway (as opposed to the spinal *autoput*) — plus the Učka tunnel and the bridge to the island of Krk — charge tolls. Regional offices of the RAC in Britain have up to date information about charges.

Touring Club. The *Auto-Moto Savez Jugoslavijc* (AMSJ) has its head office at Ruzveltova 18, 11000 Belgrade (Tel: 401 699) and offices in all major towns. They run a motoring help and information service (SPI) in most towns, with a universal telephone number: 987. Most offices open 8am-8pm daily.

Accidents and Breakdowns. For breakdowns contact the SPI (see above). In cases of accident, all drivers are legally obliged to stop and help, even if not directly involved. If anyone is injured, the police (dial 92) must be informed, but take care: if you're found to be at fault, you could end up in prison. Hence, the average injured party will make an offer you can't refuse, although it may be outside the limits of your bank account. If you know the local language, you might find a means of dissuasion, or even threaten him with police action for his carelessness. If you turn and run, you might find you are on the wanted list. If your car is damaged in an accident you should obtain a certificate from the police before leaving the scene, otherwise you may face difficulties when you try to leave the country. Should your vehicle be too badly damaged, you must place it in the hands of the authorities.

TRAIN

Rail services are run by *Zajedmoca Jugoslavenskih Zeljeznica* (JZ). The network does not extend very far, although a building programme is continuing. Services off the main inter-city routes are slow due to steep gradients and less-than-modern equipment. A journey of 100km would cost 110 Dinar (equivalent to £5.50 or $8.80 for a journey of 60 miles).

There are five classes of train: *ekspresni* (express), *poslovni* (rapid), *brzi* (semi fast), *putnicki* (slow) and *sinobus* (small diesel train). A supplement is payable for travel within Yugoslavia on expresses, except for holders of tickets issued outside the country.

Cheap Deals. Children under four travel free; 4-12 at half fare.

BUS

In the absence of a comprehensive rail network, coach services are very popular and efficiently run. Rather than a single national enterprise, each town of any size has its own company which runs long-distance services. Arrivals and departures at important towns are co-ordinated to permit easy transfers. Compared with rail travel, coaches are very fast and comfortable. Fares are slightly more than for the comparable distance by train, but do not vary significantly from one company to another.

AIR

Internal flights are run by JAT, Birčaninova 1, Belgrade (Tel: 131 392); Air Yugoslavia, Mose Pijade 1, Belgrade (Tel: 325 635); Aviogenex, Milentija Popovica 9, Belgrade (Tel: 603 198). and Adria Airways Kuzmeiceva 7, Ljubljana (Tel: 313 366). Transport from Belgrade to the airport is by bus from the JAT terminal every 20 minutes, fare 20 D. A departure tax of US$7 is charged to passengers on international flights.

HITCH-HIKING

Technically illegal on parts of the main *autoput* through the centre of the country, but the main problem on this route is likely to be competing hitch-hikers rather than police. The alternative main route along the Adriatic coast is easier to hitch going north than south, since there are more lay-bys and service stations on the inland side than the seaward. Off the main routes, progress is likely to be slow but pleasurable.

BOAT

Most of the Adriatic hydrofoil and ferry services are run by *Jadrolinija,* Obala Jugoslavenske Mornarice 16, Rijeka (Tel: 22-356). Tickets for the hydrofoil cruises on the Danube are available from travel agents such as Derdapturist and Yugotours.

CITY TRANSPORT

Taxis. Official taxis, which are all metered, may carry a sign with the word *Taxi*. Other vehicles plying for hire are not official and not metered, therefore may charge what they want. Fares vary from town to town, but expect to pay around 60p/$1.00 per mile.

Bus/Tram/Trolleybus. Tickets for buses, trams and trolley buses can be bought either from the driver or in advance from tobacconists. Destination boards in Belgrade appear in Cyrillic script. Tram no.2 covers most places of interest on its circular route.

Accommodation

See the introduction for information on youth hostels, other hostels and advance booking of accommodation.

Hotels, Pensions and Inns. Hotels are classified as L (de luxe), A, B, C and D. A double room with breakfast in an L-class hotel (which includes many tourist hotels on the Adriatic coast) could set you back £100 ($160) in peak season, but half that off-season. Pensions are graded from 1 down to 3. Note that if you stay in a hotel or pension for more than three days, full board can be imposed. Establishments below the minimum standards for hotels and pensions are classed as inns. A double room plus breakfast costs as little as £9 ($15) in an inn.

Motels. About 160 motels are marked on the standard tourist map of Yugoslavia (free from tourist offices). These are, by and large, purely functional and fairly expensive; £20 ($32) for a room without breakfast is typical.

Bed and Breakfast. Rooms in private households are available in many resorts.

Breakfast is not always provided, but in some all meals are included in the price. In summer, you might pay £20 ($32) for a top-grade double room with full board, dropping off-season to £6 ($10) for a lower category bed-only arrangement.

Youth and Student Accommodation. Yugotours-Narom, Duce Dakoviča 31, 11000 Belgrade (Tel: 339030) operates International Centres in Dubrovnik, Rovinj, Becici and Koapaonik. In addition, the Yugoslav Youth School Organisation (*Ferijalni Savez Jugoslavije*, at the same address) has student hotels in larger cities and runs 35 youth hostels which charge 150D-500D per night.

Camping. Tourist offices issue an annual list of sites. Prices vary according to standards; the range per person, tent or car is £1-£4 ($1.60-$6) per night. Camping away from official sites is frowned upon unless a permit is obtained in advance from the local tourist office or municipal authority.

Sleeping Out. In keeping with the belief that most foreigners are rich enough to pay for accommodation, sleeping rough is frowned upon, particularly on the Adriatic beaches and in city parks.

Finding and Booking Accommodation. Travel agencies in Yougoslavia will book accommodation for a fee, but usually only in the more expensive hotels. Local tourist offices or Tourist Associations can sometimes provide details of inns and pensions.

Tax. A small nightly tax (depending on area and season) is levied on all kinds of accommodation.

Communications

General information on telephones and English language newspapers and radio broadcasts is given in the introduction.

Post. Post offices keep normal shop hours, but large ones will waive the siesta, staying open from 7 am-8 pm. Stamps can be bought at tobacconists' shops or kiosks (look for the sign *Trafika*), or from most hotel reception desks. Poste restante letters should be addressed *Glavna Posta,* followed by the name of the town.

The correct way to address mail is: name; town (preceded by a five-figure code, the first two figures of which are related to the town's telephone area code); street (name then number). When writing from abroad, the town code is preceded by the country code YU-.

Telephone. Coin-operated public telephones are being gradually superseded by cardphones. This is because of the high inflation rate (which means that coin systems can barely cope). Telephones are rarely found on the streets, but tend to hide away in post offices, cafes, restaurants, hotels, and public buildings like stations, airports and hospitals. Most calls can be dialled direct: insert your card or cash, dial and you will be connected automatically. If there is no reply, replace the receiver to return your money or card. Area codes include: Belgrade — 011; Novi Sad — 021; Zagreb — 041; Dubrovnik — 050; Rijeka — 051; Ljubljana — 061; Sarajevo — 071; Titograd — 081; Skopje — 091. The international prefix is 99.

For International Direct Dial calls to UK, insert a phonecard and dial 9944. Dial UK area code (minus initial 0) and local number insert more coins on signal check for refunded coins.

Collect and BT Chargecard calls are available through overseas operator, check locally for code to access operator.

The numbers for telephone and emergency services vary slightly from place to place, but the following number apply to Belgrade and many other towns; operator and directory enquiries (in English) — 988; Police — 92; fire brigade — 93; ambulance — 94.

Telegrams. Can be sent at main post offices; or dial 96.

Radio. Most Yugoslav stations regularly broadcast tourist information in English during the summer. In particular, Radio Ljubljana (918 kHz AM) carries news and information at 9.35 am, Monday-Friday. The shipping forecast in English is broadcast on the same station at 6.35 am and 9.55 am daily.

Health and Hygiene

For general information on hygiene, first aid, insurance and medical treatment, see the introduction.

Hygiene. Water is safe to drink from mains supplies anywhere, but other sources such as public fountains in rural villages should be treated with suspicion.

Reciprocal Agreement. British citizens, on production of their passports, are entitled to free medical treatment, either as out-patients or in-patients, and some dental treatment. A Charge is made for prescribed medicines.

Entertainment

Sport. Yugoslavs are very keen on their football. Red Star Belgrade and Hadjuk Split are consistently good. Water sports are popular along the Adriatic, particularly on the islands. In winter, the Alps of Slovenia in the north west of Yugoslavia and in the east, Kopavnik in Serbia have become very popular with skiers seeking cheap holidays; prices for hotels, lift passes and ski hire are considerably lower than in neighbouring Austria and Italy.

Fishing. Hotels, municipal authorities and angling clubs issue permits for freshwater fishing. On the Adriatic coast, a permit is not required for ordinary angling, but underwater fishing requires a locally issued permit and restricts the daily catch to 5 kg. Sub aqua diving requires a permit from the Secretariat for Internal Affairs.

Eating and Drinking. Catering standards have improved significantly with the increase of tourism. Restaurant menus now bear a reasonably close relationship to dishes actually available, and bars and cafes carry a good selection of drinks. Meals are basic: cold meats, pickles and bread are staple foods. A simple meal in an unpretentious restaurant should cost around 70 D (£3.50 or $5.50). More exotic foods are available at higher prices, including dried bear ham. Beers are predominantly Pilsner-type lagers, tasty and cheap at around 8 D (40p/60c) a glass. White Riesling wine is as popular in Yugoslavia as it is abroad (in Britain, the best-selling white wine is Yugoslav *Laski Riesling*), but locally-produced wines — red or white — are generally cheaper. Yugoslavia claims to have invented the spritzer (white wine and soda), known locally as *spricer*. Imported drinks are extremely expensive; *slivovitz,* the national drink distilled from plums, is a taste well worth acquiring if you're on a low budget. For soft drinks, try the dense fruit juice known as *marelica kruska*.

Nightlife. By western European standards, fairly unsophisticated. However resorts on the Adriatic coast and winter sports venues have their fair share of discos and live music. There are many casinos along the Adriatic Coast.

Police. The militia are used to the normal excesses of foreigners on holiday, but take a very dim view of any activity which could be construed as against the interests of the state. The more serious offences in the broad category include distributing political or religious literature and infringing the strict rules on photography.

Driving Offences. On-the-spot fines are the norm for minor offences, including speeding. There is a fine for not wearing a seat belt. For alcohol-related offences, or those which cause injury to other parties, penalties are strict.

Nude Bathing. Yugoslavia is Europe's leading proponent of the all-over tan. Many Adriatic beaches are officially designated for nude bathing, and many bathers disrobe entirely even on those beaches which are not.

Restricted Areas. A number of sensitive military and border zones are designated out-of-bounds to foreign travellers. Full details are obtainable from Yugoslav Consulates, and can be found in the booklet *Notes for Travellers to Communist Countries,* published by the Foreign and Commonwealth Office, Clive House, Petty France, London SW1H 9HD.

General information is also given in the introduction.

Embassies and Consulates.
British Embassy, Generala Zdanova 46, 11000 Belgrade (Tel: 645-055).
British Consulate, Ilica 12, 41000 Zagreb (Tel: 424-888).
British Consulate, Obala Marsala Titova 10, 58000 Split (Tel: 41-464).
British Consulate, Atlas, Pileone, 50 000 Dubrovnik (Tel: 27 333).

American Embassy, Kneza Milosa 50, Belgrade (Tel: 645-655).
American Consulate General, Braće Kavurića 2, Zagreb (Tel: 444-800).

Canadian Embassy, Kneza Miloša 75, Belgrade (Tel: 644-666).

Information. Information to distinguish between tourist information bureaux, Tourist Associations and commercial travel agencies. The first are municipal offices which offer advice and (sometimes) free maps. Tourist Associations are effectively Chambers of Commerce (comparable to French *Syndicats d'Initiative*) which give away maps and usually impartial advice. Travel agencies — such as *Atlas, Kompas, Inex, Yugotours* and *Putnik* — are money-making concerns which sell maps and provide advice which normally directs you towards their services. In Belgrade, the Tourist Information Office is in the subway next to the Albania building on Terazije Street (Tel: 635-343).

Youth and Student Travel. Yugotours-Narom, Takovska 12, 11000 Belgrade (Tel: 333 055).

American Express. Atlas, Mose Pijade 11, Belgrade (341-471). Also at Atlas offices in Dubrovnik, Pula, Slit, Zagreb and elsewhere.

Calendar of Events

Public Holidays are shown in **bold.** Those marked * are celebrated only in the republics named.

January 1-2	**New Year**
May 1-2	**Labour Day**
May-Sept (Thursdays)	Korčula: *Moresta* Sword Dance — symbolic dance
May-December	Belgrade: *Skadarlija* evenings — musical and theatrical events
late May	Plitvice: 'Plitvice wedding' — marriage of ten couples from different countries by the highest waterfall in Plitvice
late May	Belgrade Youth Day celebration
late June	Sibenek: Yugoslav Festival of Children
late June-mid Sept	Zagreb Summer Festival
July 4	**Veteran's Day**
July 7*	**National Day in Serbia**
July 10-August 25	Dubrovnik Summer Festival
July 13*	**National Day in Montengro**
mid July-mid August	Split Summer Festival
late July	Pula: Yugoslav Film Festival
late July	Zagreb: International Review of Original Floklore — Competition held in city streets
July 22*	**National Day in Slovenia**
July 27*	**National Day in Croatia and Bosnia-Herzegovina**
August 2*	**National Day in Macedonia**
late August	Ohrid: Festival of songs from Macedonia
mid September	Belgrade: International Theatre Festival
October 11*	**National Day in Macedonia**
November 29-30	**Republic Day**

Scandinavia

OLD TOWN, AARHUS, DENMARK   W.S.

Scandinavia is made up of western Europe's five most northerly countries — Denmark, Finland, Iceland, Norway and Sweden. Because these countries have many features in common, they have been included together in one chapter, with a separate section for each country covering particular aspects such as Money, Communications, Health and Getting Around. The first few pages of the chapter treat subjects common to all five countries. This general information is complementary to the information given under the separate countries, and readers will get a complete picture only by taking the two sections together.

Weather. Summers are long and warm, but not without rain, so don't go without a raincoat or jacket. The midnight sun can be seen north of the Arctic Circle around midsummer; and, even as far south as Stockholm and Oslo, there's a midnight twilight. Winters are long and cold, with lots of snow, long nights, and several weeks or months of complete darkness in the north. During the winter, Scandinavians tend to go into a sort of hibernation, going to bed about 8pm; they make up for it in the long summer evenings.

The largest single factor affecting climatic variations is the Gulf Stream, which warms up the north-western coast of Norway. Thus temperatures in Bergen are higher than in many of the more southerly towns inland or on the Baltic coast. the Gulf Stream affects the southern coast of Iceland, but not Greenland, which may be entirely surrounded by pack ice during a heavy winter.

THE PEOPLE

The people are very polite and helpful. Some older people are also extremely reserved, so it's often difficult to make contact with them, but young people are usually open and friendly. Scandinavia has undergone a social revolution, most noticeable in Sweden, which has resulted in a very free society, with the order maintained by unwritten codes of behaviour rather than by a system of policing. The whole of Scandinavia can be seen as a social experiment, the results of which have not yet been fully determined, although the standard of living has risen dramatically, as has the cost of living. Unwanted side effects are reflected in the higher than average figures for alcoholism.

Politics. All five Scandinavian countries are extremely stable parliamentary democracies. Norway, Sweden and Denmark are also constitutional monarchies; Finland and Iceland are republics.

Religion. There is complete freedom of religion, but the vast majority of Scandinavians are Lutheran (Protestant). All churches are open to visitors, and many double as community centres.

Language. Danish, Icelandic, Swedish and Norwegian are all Germanic languages, and very closely related to each other. Finnish belongs to the Finno-Ugrian group of languages, related only to Hungarian, and very difficult to learn. However, English is widely spoken throughout Scandinavia, with German as the second foreign language taught in most schools. In Finland, Swedish is the second official language, and the native language along the western coast. The Lapps also have their own language, which is gradually becoming obsolete.

Making Friends. Although the social structures are liberal, the Scandinavians themselves can be very reserved, and a deep and meaningful conversation might be considered as an invasion of privacy. If you get to know anyone well enough to be invited into a Scandinavian home, it's customary to take a present for the host or hostess — flowers are quite usual for either. Another common custom when entering someone's home (except in Denmark) is to take your shoes off, and proceed in stockinged feet. This is not for religious reasons, but through the bitter experience of getting mud or snow on the carpets.

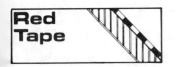
Red Tape

See the introduction for details of passports, customs regulations, vaccinations and importing pets. Customs requirements are discussed separately under each of the Scandinavian countries.

Passports and Visas. As far as passports are concerned, the five Scandinavian countries count as one zone; there are normally no passport checks when crossing from one country to another. Holders of British, American or Canadian passports may stay up to three months in the whole zone. Requests for extensions are handled by the police. Holders of British Visitors' Passports may only stay a total of three months in any nine, and may not apply for an extension.

Getting Around

See the introduction and the individual countries for further information.

CAR

Scandinavian roads are comparatively traffic-free except in the southern cities, but road conditions get worse the further north you travel. Greenland has no roads outside the settlements; Iceland's road network is limited to coastal areas, and was only extended all the way round the island in 1974. The west coast of Norway is also slow going, and you have to rely a lot on the ferries to cross fjords. There is a small charge for these ferries, but there are no toll roads. There is a motorway network in Denmark, around the Finnish, Norwegian and Swedish capitals, and in the southern parts of Sweden. Many of the mountain passes, particularly in Norway, are blocked from November till May.

Rules and Requirements. The green card is no longer required for British vehicles, except in Iceland. The red reflecting warning triangle is obligatory. In towns, trams are normally overtaken only on the right, except in one-way streets or where there is insufficient room on the right. Seat belts must be worn by front seat passengers; in Sweden and Denmark, children under 12 are banned from the front seat. Smoking is universally forbidden at petrol stations, and within urban areas in Norway. The minimum driving age is 18.

TRAIN/BUS

Only the four mainland countries have railways. In Iceland and in the north of Norway and Finland, long-distance land travel is by bus only, including the four day stretch from Bodø to Kirkenes in Norway. Bus services also complement and overlap the rail services in other parts of mainland Scandinavia. Tickets are bought from the driver (or in advance from railway stations) and cost about the same as rail tickets.

Trains are divided into two classes, first being about 50% more expensive than second. Second class fares are highest in Norway and Sweden — a journey of 100 km (62 miles) work out at around £8.80 ($14) and £7.80 ($12.50) respectively. The same journey would cost around £5 ($8) in Finland and Denmark. The further you travel, the less it costs per mile.

Cheap Deals. The *Nordturist* ticket gives unlimited travel on Scandinavian railways and DSB ferries. Second class costs around £135/$216 for 21 days, first costs £181/$290. It is obtainable from Scandinavian railway offices abroad.

Children under 4 (under 6 in Sweden) travel free; half fare up to age 12 (16 in Norway and Sweden).

See also under the individual countries.

AIR

Considering the slowness of ground transport throughout Scandinavia, air travel is a valuable time-saver, and it's also cheap compared to other countries. The three main airlines — SAS, Finnair and Icelandair — offer reductions for families, groups, youths, students and people over 65.

BOAT

Ferries and coastal steamers play a major role in Scandinavian transport. For car ferries, you should always book in advance whenever possible. Timetables and fares are available from National Tourist Offices.

Students, or those who were once students, can usually get 50% discount on boat fares with the flimsiest of evidence, such as an out of date student card.

See the introduction for information on youth hostels, other hostels, and advance booking of accommodation.

Hotels/Motels. There is no official system of categorisation, although an establishment must conform to certain standards before it can be called a hotel. Prices don't normally include breakfast, but all-inclusive terms can usually be arranged. A double room generally costs about 50% more than a single. A cheap single room might cost around £15 ($24) in Finland or Iceland, slightly more in Denmark, Norway and Sweden. The *Bonus Pass* scheme allows 15%-50% discount on Inter Scan and Point hotels throughout Scandinavia. The card costs £14 and is valid from June 1st -September 1st and on weekends between September 2nd and May 31st. Details from National Tourist Offices.

Pensions and Hopits. These are cheaper than hotels, but the standard isn't necessarily lower than the cheapest hotels. *Hospits* come closest to large scale boarding houses or high class hostels.

Inns. The inn is still the centre of village life in Denmark, where it is recognised by the sign *Kro*. Price for full board is about 350kr (£30 or $50).

Farms/Private Houses. This type of accommodation is catching on in a big way (except in Norway) and prices are about the same as the cheapest hotels. The best sources of information are the local tourist offices.

Chalets/Summer Cottages/Holiday Villages. These are rented by the week or month, and are best booked in advance, either as part of a package holiday or independently. Local tourist offices can supply lists of addresses and make reservations.

Mountain Lodges/Tourist Huts. These two types of accommodation are found in the remoter areas, particularly in Norway and Iceland. Electricity and running water are rare, and tourist huts, with dormitory accommodation, are not always accessible by road, but useful for hikers.

Camping. There are camp sites throughout Scandinavia, but you are allowed to pitch your tent anywhere, so long as crops or property are not damaged. In Finland, the tendency is now towards camping only on official camp sites; but in Sweden you can camp on private property for one night without even asking permission. All four countries are heavy on litter and the risk of forest fires. In Denmark you need either an international camping carnet or a Danish camping pass (24kr from any camp site).

Sleeping out. Illegal in Denmark. It's not illegal in the other countries, but the nights are cold, even in summer.

Hygiene. All Scandinavian countries are extremely clean, and all tap water is drinkable. Iceland is possibly the cleanest place in Europe; it is free of pollution due to the exploitation of natural local geological thermal resources as the principle source of heating, and because it is away from the path of acid rain which affects much of northern Europe. Nor is there much internal pollution; smoking regulations are the strictest in Europe.

Medical and Dental Treatment. All health care is extremely good and phenomenally expensive. Emergency treatment for those not covered by insurance of reciprocal agreements is usually given free. Details are given under *Health* in each country section.

Sport. The emphasis, as far as the tourist trade is concerned, is on winter sports. The season runs from December to March or April. Denmark is too flat for Alpine skiing, as is most of Finland, but Norway and Sweden have some excellent slopes. All four mainland countries offer good territory for cross-country skiing. On the first Sunday in March each year, a 53-mile cross-country ski race is held at Mora in Sweden. If you want to enter, write to Vasaloppet, S-792 00 Mora (Tel:0250-1 08 78 or 1 04 55). Applications must be in by the end of January.

Nightlife. The most noticeable uniquely Scandinavian aspect, at least in Denmark and Sweden, is the absence of sex censorship in films and live stage shows. Scandinavia makes a lot of films, both arty and blue, but the cinemas are dominated by English and American movies, which are always shown with the original soundtrack. Cinemas and theatres are very strict with latecomers, so arrive on time or you'll risk being turned away, whether you've made a reservation or not.

Music. Jazz fans are well catered for in summer: many festivals are staged, including those at Skeppsholmen (Stockholm, mid June), Kongsberg (Norway, early July), Copenhagen (mid July), Pori (Finland, mid July) and Molde (Norway, late July).

Museums and Galleries. The normal opening hours are about 10am-5pm. Most state museums and galleries are free in Norway and Denmark, but admission charges are made in Sweden and Finland. However, many Finnish museums offer free admission one day a week, so check it out beforehand.

Breweries. In Copenhagen, the two breweries (*Carlsberg*, Ny Carlsbergvej 140 and *Tuborg*, at Strandvej 54) run conducted tours on Mondays to Fridays, ending with free beer. *Tuborg* tours run continuously from 8.30am-12.30pm and at 2.30pm. *Carlsberg* have tours at 9am, 11am and 2.30pm.

Saunas. Finland is the real home of the sauna, but you'll find them all over Scandinavia, either attached to hotels, or as separate institutions. The ritual sounds quite gruesome — alternating extreme heat with ultra-cold treatment, either in the snow, the sea, a lake or a cold shower, and gently stimulating the blood flow with birch twigs. In fact, it's supposed to be one of the best forms of relaxation. An interesting experience, anyway.

Eating Habits. The Scandinavians start their day with a large breakfast of coffee and rolls or bread with cheese, eggs, cold meat and jam. You can economise by taking advantage of hotel buffet breakfasts, which give you the chance of filling yourself up so you only need a light lunch. Lunch is usually a minor affair of sandwiches and coffee — workers take a very short lunch break, preferring to eat on the job, so they can knock off earlier in the afternoon. The evening meal might be taken as early as 4pm, and not usually later than 7 or 8pm. It's generally the more expensive kind of restaurants that stay open later, but the larger cities are open until 2 or 3am in winter, and even later in summer. Lunch-only restaurants (*frokostrestaurants*) in Denmark are usually good value.

Specialities. The most well known speciality is the cold table — a buffet arrangement of various kinds of cold meat, fish and cheeses, and as many varieties of bread (including the Scandinavian crispbreads) to go with it. In restaurants, you're allowed as much as you can eat for a fixed price, but the way to do it is to take a little at a time, and go back for more as often as you like. You're also allowed to change your plate, for instance between the fish and meat courses. This is known as *smørgasbord* in Sweden, *kolde bord* in Denmark, *koldtbord* in Norway, and *voileipapoyta* in Finland (*smørgasbord* is also understood). In Denmark, *Smørrebrød* refers to the famous open sandwiches, a snack-version of the full buffet.

Eating out. Restaurants tend to be expensive, and the best deals, where available, are the set menus for three course meals. The cheapest restaurants are those run by department stores, where the set meal costs around £5 ($8). Station cafeterias are known for their filling breakfasts — eat as much as you can for about £4 ($6.50).

For cheap, quick snacks, you'll find hamburger stands, grills, bars (*baari* in Finnish) and self-service cafeterias in most towns. There are McDonalds and BurgerKings in many towns where you can get a hamburger and chips for around £2.50 ($4.00).

Drinking. Licensing laws are very strict throughout Scandinavia, as are the laws regarding drinking and driving. Normal strength beer was actually illegal in Iceland between 1915 and 1989. Most restaurants are licensed to serve beers, wines and spirits, but the less expensive the restaurant, the less of a licence it usually has. Establishments that serve only drinks are confined to the large towns; they often call themselves *pubs* and charge very high prices. The term *bar* usually refers to a snack bar or a coffee bar. However, most licensed restaurants are allowed to serve drinks without making you buy a meal.

The most common and popular drink is beer, which comes in three strengths: *Export* is the strongest, and *Pils* (or *Pilsner*) is the medium strength; weak beer is pretty tasteless. Wines are all imported. In restaurants, it's usually cheapest to buy a carafe (usually $\frac{3}{4}$ litre). The most common type of spirits is *aquavit* (schnaps). Finland has some exotic liqueurs, made from cloudberries (*Lakka*) and whortleberries (*Mesimarja*), as well as home produced vodka. Prices for all spirits are high in Scandinavia, due to outrageous taxes; in Sweden a bottle of whisky will cost at least £25. The native brands always work out cheapest.

Because of strict drink-driving regulations, most Scandinavians do their drinking at home, and when they do go out to parties, it's customary for the drivers to stay stone sober. If you're at a social function and don't wish to drink, the recognised sign is to turn your glass upside down. No one will be offended. The practice of *skal* — whereby guests do not drink until the host has proposed their health is widespread.

Even for off-sales, Finland, Iceland and Sweden are very strict. While the weakest beers can be bought in supermarkets, anything more potent is rigorously controlled. The Finnish state liquor organisation (which has a monopoly on off-sales) is known as *Alko*. Its Swedish counterpart, *Systembolaget,* displays only non-alcoholic wines in its shop windows. However, a typical Scandinavian attitude to alcohol is that if a drink is there, it needs to be drunk. The average Finn spends two or three occasions during his life drying out. In any large Scandinavian city, it is not uncommon to see grown men literally crawling home after an alcoholic binge; the usual police haul on a midweek night in Helsinki is 100 drunks.

For more details of licensing laws and restrictions on off-sales, see the section on *The Law* under the separate countries.

Smoking. Cigarettes and even cigarette papers are expensive in Scandinavia: for example, in Norway 20 cigarettes will cost around 30kr (£2.80 or $4.50). Smokers are advised to take full advantage of their duty free entitlement.

For detailed information on the law, see the sections on the individual countries.

Laws. Alcoholism is Scandinavia's worst social problem, and the law does its best to fight it. So you're likely to be taken in if you're drunk on the streets, and likely to spend some time in jail if you're found driving under the influence. Illicit drugs are even more unpopular — solitary confinement is usual prior to trial, which can easily be for two months or more.

Throughout the sparsely populated areas of Iceland and the north Scandinavian mainland, the law tries to protect wildlife and the natural order: don't break branches off trees, dispose of your rubbish in fields or woods, disturb birds' nests, drop lighted cigarettes, etc. In Lappland certain seasons are set aside in which only native Lapps have the right to pick cloudberries and whortleberries. So even picking these may be illegal. Drivers who kill or injure reindeer or elks will not be popular — all such accidents must be reported to the police.

Denmark

Area. 16,633 square miles   **Population.** 5,200,000

Capital. Copenhagen (population: 650,000)

The information given below is complementary to information given in the section on *Scandinavia*, above.

For details of passports, see the section on *Scandinavia*. See also the introduction for general information.

Customs. Because of prior agreements among the Nordic countries, Danish duty free allowances do not entirely coincide with the EC allowance shown in the introduction. The two-tier system is based not upon whether goods were bought and taxed in the Community, but on their immediate origin prior to being imported.

Variation from the quantities given in the introduction include an increased tobacco allowance from non-European residents; tea and coffee allowances as given under *Belgium;* and a minimum age of 17 for tobacco and alcohol, 15 for the coffee allowances. European residents staying less than 24 hours in Denmark may not import any alcohol, and are only entitled to reduced tobacco allowances. Apart from used items for personal use and re-export, other goods (including beer) are restricted to 2,750 kr. if arriving from another EC country otherwise 600 kr.

100 øre = 1 krone (kr)
£1 = 11.3 kr   1 kr = £0.09
$1 = 7 kr   1 kr = $0.14

For general information on handling, exchanging and raising money, see the introduction.

Coins. 25 øre, 50 øre, 1 kr, 10 kr.

Notes. 20 kr (multi-coloured), 50 kr (blue and grey), 100 kr (multi-coloured), 500 kr (blue/yellow), 1,000 kr (brown/grey).

Banking Hours. Monday-Friday, 9.30 am-4 pm (6 pm on Thursdays). In provincial towns, hours vary widely; many banks close for lunch, say 12-2 pm. In Copenhagen, the exchange bureau at Central Station (where the air terminal is situated) stays open 7 am-10 pm. At Kastrup Airport you can change money from 6.30 am-10 pm.

Shopping Hours. Opening times are 9/10 am-5.30/6 pm, Monday-Friday, with late opening (7 or 8 pm) on Fridays; 9 am-noon or 2 pm on Saturdays. On the first Saturday of the month shops are allowed to open from 9 am to 5 pm. You can buy groceries until midnight each at the City Market, Central Station in Copenhagen and at the railway in Odense, Aarhus and Aalborg.

Import and Export. No restrictions for tourists on importing currency, but you can take amounts exceeding 25,000 kr (in Danish notes) out of the country only if you can prove that this is not more than you brought in.

Tipping. Hotels and restaurants — include 15% service charge in their bills. Taxis — included on the meter in most places, but 10% or so still expected in some smaller towns. Station porters, where they can be found, charge fixed rates of about 5 kr per item. Otherwise hire a trolley for kr 10. Give 1 or 2 kr for the use of a wash basin in public toilets.

Emergency Cash. One of the prerequisites for entering Denmark is that you should have enough money to make you way home. Once in Denmark, EC citizens are allowed to look for work without a permit. Use-it, Rådhusstraede 13, 1466 Copenhagen K issue entitled *Working in Denmark* which gives information for citizens of Common Market countries seeking employment. The best opportunities for short term casual work are in hotels and fast food restaurants. Busking, hawking and street selling are generally illegal; except in the pedestrian area of central Copenhagen, where busking is permitted in summer from 1-5 pm on Saturday afternoons.

Taxes. There is a 22% value added tax (MOMS) on most goods and services. Some shops offer exemptions on single expensive items that are shipped directly out of the country or taken as travellers' luggage. Participating shops display a red and white "Danish Tax-Free Shopping Sign", which looks rather like the British Rail symbol.

Getting Around

For additional information, see the introduction and the section on *Scandinavia*, above.

CAR

Rules. Dipped headlights should be used at all times even in broad daylight by motorcyclists.

Place Names. Copenhagen is København.

Parking. Parking is controlled by discs, available from police stations, post offices, banks and petrol stations. In Copenhagen, the time limit is shown on signs. Meters (limit: 3 hours) are also in operation in Copenhagen and some other towns, and take 1, 5 and 10 kr coins. The sign *Stopforbud* means no waiting; *Parkering Forbudt* = no parking. The alternate day system (see the introduction) is signposted *Datostop* or *Dataparkering*.

Petrol. Leaded petrol is now only available in a super grade (98 octane) at around 7.17 kr a litre (£2.85 per UK gallon, $3.85 per US gallon). Unleaded petrol is slightly cheaper. Fill up before joining the motorway, as there are no petrol stations. Many stations are unattended and accept 20 kr notes.

Touring Club. *Forende Danske Motoreje* Firskovvej 32, Postboks 500, 5800 Lyngby (Tel: 45 93 08 00).

Accidents and Breakdowns. There are emergency road patrols on all the main highways. An emergency towing service (run by the *Falck Organisation*) is available in all towns; in Copenhagen, dial 15 18 08. In cases of accident involving injury of material damage, the police must be called (dial 0 0 0).

TRAIN/BUS

Train and bus services are run by DSB (Danish State Railways), who have information points at all major rail stations (in Copenhagen, dial 33 14 88 00). Supplements are payable for Inner City and *Lyntog* (lightning) trains, on which reservations are compulsory.

Cheap Deals. In addition to the cheap deals given under *Scandinavia*, DSB also offer "The Denmark Card" which grants unlimited travel on all trains and Danish Railway Ferries for one month: the card costs 2,050 kr.

BICYCLE

Cycles can be hired from main railway stations for about 30 kr a day. The most entral rental agency in Copenhagen is *Københavns Cyklebørs* near the Central tation (Tel: 33 14 07 17). Organised tours are run by various tourist offices, ffiliated to the *Dansk Cyklist Forbund,* Kjeld Langesgade 14, Copenhagen (Tel: 3 32 31 21), a helpful organisation that can answer any particular queries about 'cling in Denmark. The Danish Tourist Office produces a useful leaflet entitled On a Bike in Denmark".

IR

us connections for the SAS Terminal in Copenhagen Central Station to Kastrup irport cost 25 kr and take 25 minutes. There are also direct land/sea connections etween Kastrup Airport and Malmö in Sweden. Regular taxi flights to the smaller lands are operated by Copenhagen Airtaxi.

EA

openhagen is linked to Malmö in Sweden by hydrofoil, (hourly from 6 am to idnight: 33 12 80 88 for information) and ship (three daily; 32 53 15 85). Prices art at around 35 kr one-way by ship, double by hydrofoil. The main link from enmark to Sweden is the ferry from Helsingør (Elsinor) to Helsingborg, which ns every 15 minutes from 5 am-2 am for around 20 kr each way. To Germany, e Rødbyhavn — Puttgarten ferry costs the same and runs hourly. There are merous other ferries linking the islands of Denmark to each other and to Norway, land and East Germany.

TCH-HIKING

enmark is probably the fastest of the Scandinavian countries, if only because the short distances and relatively high density of traffic. If you prefer some nning to your trip, the notice boards at Use It, Rådhusstraede 13, Cope3nhagen ry a number of advertised rides.

When leaving Copenhagen for Elsinore (Helsingør) plus Norway and Sweden the E47, take bus no. 1 or 187 to Hans Knudsens Plads or Ryuparken Station, take the S-Bahn to Ryuparken Station and stand on Lyngbyvej.

Going south (to Rødbyhavn and Germany) take the S-Bahn to Ellebjerg Station, n walk along Folehaven (A2) to Gammel Koge Landevej. Going west to Funen 1 Jutland you want Roskildevej (A2): take the S-Bahn to Tastrup.

TY TRANSPORT

xis. Can be hailed (look for the green *fri* sign), telephoned (dial 31 35 35 35 Copenhagen) or found at taxi ranks outside stations large hotels, etc. In penhagen and other large towns, the tip is included on the meter. The initial nge is 12 kr; thereafter 7 kr per km (£0.70 or $1 a mile).

s/S-Bahn. Copenhagen is divided into zones, the first three being designated inner city area. Bus tickets cost 8 kr each for travel in 2 zones with one hour all buses and the S-Bahn. Other tickets vary in price from 12 kr for travel in ones to 32 kr for travel in 8 zones. Buses are one-man operated; board at the

front and buy tickets from the driver. You can buy a discount card worth ten :
zone fares for 70 kr. Tickets are stamped with the date and time of issue. Smokin
is not allowed on any buses. S-Bahn tickets are only valid if stamped in the machine
on station platforms. The S-Bahn is covered by Eurailpass and Inter-Rail ticke

The set fine (called as "surcharge") for travelling without a valid and tim
stamped ticket is 150 kr on buses and 250 kr on trains. Buses and trains run fron
5 am (6 am on Sundays) to around midnight, with a reduced bus service continuin
until 2.30 am.

For bus information in Copenhagen dial 31 54 51 91: for S-Bahn informatio
call 33 14 17 01.

The *Copenhagen Card* offers unlimited free travel throughout the capital an
North Sealand, plus discounts on travel to Sweden and free admission to museun
and other attractions. Prices (children 5-11 half-price): one day 90 kr; two da
— 140 kr; three days 180 kr. The card is sold at hotels, travel agencies, touri
offices and rail stations.

For details of the type of accommodatio
available, see the *Accommodation* sectic
under *Scandinavia,* above.

Finding and Booking Accommodation. Tl
Danish Tourist Board publishes an annual list of hotels, pensions (minimum sta
— one week), inns and motels. Local tourist offices can provide details of can
sites, youth hostels and rooms in private houses.

There is no official hotel classification system, but cleanliness and comfort ca
be relied upon. Prices outside Copenhagen start at around 200 kr (£17.50 or $28.5
per night for a double room, including breakfast, but without a bathroom. Pric
in Copenhagen can be 75% higher. The cheapest hostels are often *Missionhotel*
where no alcohol is permitted.

A scheme known as "Inn Checks" that allows for prepayment for rooms in e
Danish inns is operated. The cost for a double room for one night, includi
breakfast and a private bathroom, is 396 kr. "Inn Checks" can be bought fro
tourist offices and travel agents inside Denmark or for further details contact *Dar
Kroferie,* Sondergade 31, 8700 Horsens (Tel: 75 62 35 44).

Campers can buy a complete camping guide, price 75 kr in bookshops, kios
or by post (20 kr extra) from *Campingrådet,* Olof Palmes Gade 10, 2i
Copenhagen Ø. Camping carnets are compulsory in camping sites, but can
bought upon arrival.

Copenhagen has a room booking service at Kiosk P, Central Station; alternative
you can call 33 12 28 80 from 9am-5pm, Monday to Friday. Outside Copenhage
you must either write direct to the hotels, or to the local tourist offices, whe
addresses are given in the National Tourist Office's hotel list. To reserve a summ
cottage, write to the local tourist bureaus or Dancenter, Falkoner Allé 2C
Frederiksberg (Tel: 31 19 09 00). For information on Youth Hostels, cont
Denmarks Vandrerhjem, Vesterbrogade 39, 1620 Copenhagen V (Tel: 31 31
12); their cost for a one night stay is from 35kr-65kr. For information on che
accommodation in Copenhagen including "sleep-ins" (65kr per night, includ
breakfast) which are run from the end of June to the end of August. Contact ł
It, Rådhusstraede 13, 1466 Copenhagen K (Tel: 33 15 65 18). *Use It* will also h
if you're planning to study in Copenhagen for any length of time.

land Camps. *O-lejr* arose "because of a need for meaningful holidays". Most mps involve groups living in tents on remote Danish islands in a commune and orking together on manual tasks, or discussing political or cultural questions. r further details, contact O-lejr-kontoret, Vendersgade 8, DK-1363K (33 11 55 81).

Communications

General information on telephones and English language newspapers and radio broadcasts is given in the introduction.

Post. Post offices are open 9 or 10am-5 or 30pm, Monday-Friday, and 9-12am Saturdays. The central post office in openhagen (where Poste Restante letters should turn up) is at Tietgensgade 37. e post office at Central Station opens at 7am until 9pm daily. There is a free ste restante service at all main post offices.
The correct way to address mail is; name; street (name, then number); town, eceded by a four-figure code (which is in turn preceded by the country code K-if writing from abroad). Copenhagen is followed by a letter indicating the stal zone in the city.

lephones. The whole of Denmark is covered by an automatic system. Telephone des in Copenhagen changed on January 1st, 1990. Numbers that used to begin th 01 now begin with a number between 31 and 39; numbers that began with now begin with a number between 42 and 49. These prefixes must be used n if you are dialling inside Copenhagen. Other codes are listed in all directories. e international prefix is 009. For the UK dial 009 44 followed by UK area code inus initial 0) and the local number.
Public phones take 25 øre, 1kr, 5kr and 10kr coins. A local call costs 1kr. You t the money in before dialling, but no coins are returned even if you fail to make ur connection, so start with a minimum. On the other hand, you're allowed re than one call for your money, if the time hasn't run out. All public telephones rmit international calls. For Collect (reverse charge) and BT Chargecard calls l 0015 for operator. From some payphones you may need to insert 2x25øre 1kr first. An experimental cardphone system is in use, initially in Roskilde. one 0030 for help, 0034 for information. The emergency number to call the brigade, police or an ambulance is 000.
All public telephones should have a directory, which comes in the usual two ts — personal and commercial. The letters AE, Ø and Å come at the end of alphabet. The Copenhagen personal directory is in two parts: A-K and L-Å. ere is some information in English and German.

egrams. Are sent from telegram office and post offices, or dial 0022 for nestic, 0023 for Europe, 0024 for intercontinental. In Copenhagen, the office Kobmagergade 37 (Tel: 33 12 09 03) is open 24 hours.

oadcasting. The news is broadcast in English on Danish Radio 3 (1060 kHz 1042 kHz AM) at 8.30am, Monday to Saturday. Short reports on summer ekend traffic are included in these bulletins on Thursdays, Fridays and Saturdays summer.

Health and Hygiene

For general information on health, hygiene, medical treatment and insurance, see the introduction.

Reciprocal Agreements. All foreign visitors can get free emergency treatment in casualty wards, provided they are too ill to return home. British residents can also claim free medical care and considerable refunds on prescribed medicines and dental treatment on production of their passport (Form E111 is not necessary). The scheme is run by the health department of local councils (known as *Borger representationen* in Copenhagen and Frederiksburg, otherwise *amtskommune*). Some doctors and dentists make no charge and claim costs direct from the council; others will charge the full fee so take the receipt to the council for full reimbursement. Free hospital treatment will be arranged either by a doctor or by the hospital authorities on production of your passport. Enquiries and complaints to *Socialstyrelsen* (the National Board of Social Welfare) 6, Kristinebery, 2100 Copenhagen O.

Emergencies. Chemists are known as *apoteker;* the duty rota is posted on each chemist's door. The larger cities have a number of 24-hour chemists, the most central in Copenhagen being Steno Apotek at Vesterbrogade 6c, 1620 Copenhagen V (Tel: 33 14 82 66).

In dire emergencies, dial 000 or go to the emergency ward at any hospital. The following hotels in the Copenhagen area have casualty wards; Rigshospitalet Frederik den V's vej 9, 2100 Ø (Tel: 31 39 66 33); Bispebjerg Hospital, Bispebjer Bakke, 2400 NV (Tel: 31 81 12 50); Sundby Hospital, Italiensvej 1, 2300 S (Tel 31 55 15 55); Hvidovre Hospital, Kettegard Allé 30, 2650 Hvidovre (Tel: 31 4 14 11); and Frederiksberg Hospital, Nordre Fasanvej 57, 2000F (Tel: 31 34 7 11). For emergency dental treatment in Copenhagen, try the Tandlaegevagton, Osl Plads 14, 2100 0 from 8pm to 9.30pm daily plus from 10am to noon at weekends You will have to pay cash for your treatment. For VD treatment try the Bispebjer Hospitals (for address see above).

The Law

For general information see the section o *Scandinavia,* above.

Police. Polite and helpful. In Copenhagen the police headquarters is at Polititorve 1567 Copenhagen V (Tel: 33 14 14 48).

Driving Offences. You're liable to imprisonment for drunken driving even if damage has been caused. Drivers may be faced with heavy on-the-spot fines eve minor offences; your car may be impounded if you can't pay.

Nude Bathing. Officially only allowed on private naturist beaches, but unofficial tolerated on other beaches.

Drugs. The legal distinction between possession and supply is hazy, so offende are likely to be charged instead with conspiracy, and face up to six yea imprisonment.

Licensing Laws. Denmark is the slackest of the Scandinavian countries, with restrictions on licensing hours; but a minimum age limit of 18 for purchasi alcohol.

Legal Aid. If you're broke, the state will appoint a lawyer for you. The student organisation Kobenhavns Retshjaelp 1704 Copenhagen V (Tel: 33 11 06 78), offers free legal aid, but the service is mainly intended for Danes.

For information on useful contacts and complaints procedures, see the introduction.

Embassies and Consulates.
British Embassy, Kastelsvej 36, 2100 Copenhagen Ø (31 26 46 00).
There are also honourary consulates in Aabenraa, Aalborg, Aarhus, Esbjerg, Fredericia, Odense and Ronne.

American Embassy, Dag Hammarskjølds Allé 24, 2100 Copenhagen Ø (31 42 31 44).

Canadian Embassy, Kristen Bernikowsgade 1, 1105 Copenhagen (33 12 22 99).

Lost Property. The Copenhagen *Hittegodskontoret* is at Carl Jacobsensvej 20, 2500 Valby (Tel: 31 16 14 06). It is open Monday-Friday 10 am-2 pm (5 pm on Thursdays).

Baby-sitting. Scandinavia's oldest and largest agency is *Minerva,* Smallegade 52A, 2000 Copenhagen F (Tel: 31 19 00 90). Multi-lingual babysitters will even take your children sightseeing.

Guides. Supplied by local tourist offices. In Copenhagen, dial 33 11 13 25.

Information. The Danish Tourist Board has offices (*turist bureauet*) throughout the country. The head office in Copenhagen is opposite the Town Hall at H. C. Andersen Boulevard 22, 1555 Copenhagen V (Tel: 33 11 13 25).

Free Maps. From the National Tourist Board offices.

Help. For suicide or emotional problems, the Nikolaj Kirke in Copenhagen has a organisation, similar to the Samaritans, called *Sankt Nikolaj Tjenesten,* open 10 am-3 pm weekdays, 1-3 pm Sunday (Tel: 33 12 14 00).

Disabled Travellers. For help, advice and information, contact the Danish National Association for the Disabled, Hans Knudsens Plads 1A, 2100 Copenhagen Ø; or the Society and Home for the Disabled, Borgervaenget 5-7, 2100 Copenhagen (Tel: 31 18 26 11), who publish a *Hotel Guide for the Handicapped* costing 25 kr.

Student Travel. Dis Rejser, Skindergade 28, 1159 Copenhagen K (Tel: 33 11 00 44); Green Tours/DVL Rejser, Kultorvet 7, 1175 Copenhagen (Tel: 33 13 27 27).

Youth Information Centre. *Use It* (from *Huset* = the house), Rådhusstraede 13, 1466 Copenhagen K (Tel: 33 15 65 18) — government funded, but no less effective for that. Their notice boards tell of cheap accommodation and restaurants, pre-arranged petrol-sharing rides, weekly events, discos and concerts (including free outdoor concerts in summer). They also hand out free maps of Copenhagen and an alternative guide (*Playtime*), and run a free left luggage service. Opening hours vary but are from 9 am to 7 pm daily between June 15th and September 14th.

English Language Church. St. Alban's (Anglican), Langelinie, Copenhagen.

American Express. Amager Torv, 18-20, Copenhagen (Tel: 33 12 23 01).

Greenland

Although geographically closer to Canada than to Europe, Greenland is still politically part of Denmark despite the introduction of home rule in 1979. The world's largest island (840,000 square miles) is mostly covered in ice; the climate is affected by the Polar Current (rather than the Gulf Stream) which keeps temperatures down: 70° is exceptionally high for the south in summer, minus 60° F is not unknown in winter. Warm, windproof clothes and solid footwear are essential throughout the year.

The island's 50,000 Eskimo and European (mainly of Danish descent) inhabitant live in settlements dotted along the coastal plains and on offshore islands. The native language, Greenlandic, is of Eskimo origin, but Danish is also very common Most of the younger generation speak English.

Passports and Visas. Documents required are the same as for Denmark, but special approval is needed for stays in the American military zones at Thule and Søndre Strømfjord. Paperwork is obtainable from the nearest Danish Embassy; approval is not necessary for transit journeys via Søndre Strømfjord.

Customs. The duty free allowances are a miserly 750 ml of spirits (for those aged 18 or over) plus 200 cigarettes (15 years or over).

Money. Danish currency is used. Nuuk, the largest town, has two banks. Financial business in other towns is handled by branches of the two banks or by KNI (Greenland Trade) who change foreign money, travellers cheques and Eurocheques.

Place Names. Danish names are gradually being replaced by Greenlandic versions Nuuk (Greenlandic) = Godthab (Danish); Ilulissat = Jakobshavn.

Getting Around. Normally, entry to Greenland is by air; from Copenhagen to Søndre Stømfjord and Narsarsuaq all year; from Reykjavik to Kulusuk and Narsarsuaq in summer; or from Frobisher Bay in Canada to Nuuk.

Internal transport is also primarily by air: the network is covered by Greenlandair who operate DASH-7s and a helicopter service. Delays must always be anticipated especially due to weather, and extra costs thus incurred are normally the traveller responsibility. West coast towns are also connected, in summer, by KNI vessels whose fares are similar to the corresponding air fares. Enquiries about all domestic traffic should be addressed to KNI offices, or, in Denmark, to KNI Strandgade 100, Copenhagen K (Tel: 54 6001).

Dog sleds can be hired at most towns in northern & east Greenland for around 750 kr a day. You can also hire a fur coat for the journey. Don't be too friendly with the dogs — they're not completely tame.

Tourism and Activities. Not terribly well developed, although there are hotels in most towns. In the southern tip of the island a project is under way to encourage hikers: several mountain huts are already open and cost around 50 kr a night. But you may only use them if you buy a permit from the DVL-Rejser, Kultorvet 7, 1175 Copenhagen K. Camping is permitted almost anywhere, but if you are keen to avoid having to camp, you are strongly advised to book accommodation before you go.

For tourist offices, look for the *Turistforening* signs in larger towns.

Cross country expeditions, mountaineering and similar activities must first receive the approval of the Commission for Scientific Research in Greenland, Øster Voldgade 10, 1350 Copenhagen K. Send off detailed plans with itinerary, duration, names of all participants, purpose of the expedition, etc. Plan well in advance. If you find a meteorite, you must hand it in to the "pertinent scientific institution" in Denmark.

Public Holidays. January 1, January 6, Maundy Thursday, Good Friday, Easter Monday, Whit Monday, Ascension Day, Common Prayer Day, December 24-26 and December 31.

Faroe Islands

The Faroe Islands, despite being closer to Scotland and Norway than to Denmark, are a self-governing community under the Danish Crown. All but one of the 18 islands are inhabited, by a total of 48,000 people. Törshaven, the largest town can be reached by boat from Scotland, Norway, Denmark and Iceland. The airport at Vagar has regular services with Copenhagen and Reykavik. There is a Faroe currency in circulation, a Faroe krone being equivalent to a Danish krone. The islands have some of the strictest restrictions on alcohol in the world: wine and spirits are not generally available, and you can only obtain low alcohol beer in shops and restaurants: but you can order normal beer direct from Faroe breweries, and it will be delivered the next day. The islands are connected to the international telephone network: dial the international prefix then 298. Further information from the Tourist Board, Reyngota 17, FR-100 Törshavn (Tel: 1 22 77). Britain has a honourary consulate at Yviri vid Strond 19, FR-100 Törshavn (Tel: 1 35 10).

Finland

Area. 130,100 square miles

Population. 4,900,000

Capital. Helsinki (population 500,000)

The information given below is complementary to the general information given in the section on *Scandinavia*, above.

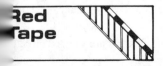
Red Tape

For details of passport requirements, see the section on *Scandinavia*, above. See also the introduction for general information.

Customs. For visits of over 24 hours, foreign

travellers may import a reasonable amount of goods for personal use; and other goods to a value of 500 FIM (250 FIM for under 16's.) For European residents these goods may include 200 cigarettes or 250 grams tobacco; 15kg foodstuffs; 2 litres beer; and either two litres of wine or one litre of wine and one litre of spirits. Residents outside Europe are entitled to 400 cigarettes or 500 grams of tobacco. Age limits are 15 for tobacco goods; 18 for alcohol under 18° (ie beers and most wines); 20 for alcohol 18° and over (ie spirits and some wines). Controlled or prohibited items include livestock, plants, medicines, narcotics, firearms and ammunition.

Frontier Areas. There are restrictions on movements in frontier areas (land and water); if you intend to travel near a frontier, contact the local police or coastguards for clearance, or write to the Ministry of the Interior, Frontier Guard Headquarters, Korkeavuourenkatu 21, 00131 Helsinki 13. Frontiers with the Soviet Union close 8pm-8am.

100 penni (p) = 1 Finnmarkka (FIM)
£1 = 6.80 FIM   1 FIM = £0.15
$1 = 4.25 FIM   1 FIM = $0.23

For general information on handling, exchanging and raising money, see the introduction.

Coins. 5p., 10p., 20p., 50p., 1 FIM, 5 FIM.

Notes. 5 FIM (blue/green), 10 FIM (green), 50 FIM (brown), 100 FIM (violet), 500 FIM (blue).

Banking hours. Monday-Friday, 9.30am-4pm. Exchange offices at Helsinki Rail Station and airport, and major tourist offices and border posts keep longer hours particularly in summer. Hotels and restaurants are likely to give a lower rate of exchange.

Shopping Hours. Shops open around 8.30am, Monday-Friday, and close at 5pm Tuesday-Thursday, 8pm on Mondays and Fridays, (summer), 4pm (winter) or Saturdays. The underground shopping complex in Helsinki Railway Station is open daily until 10pm.

Import and Export. No import limits; export of Finnish currency restricted to 10,000 FIM in notes and travellers' cheques, unless you declared more upon arrival.

Tipping. In hotels add 15% to the bill to cover service (if the management has not already done so for you); restaurants — included in the bill (14%; 15% on Sundays and holidays). Taxis — no tip necessary. Station porters — small fixed charge per item, no additional tip necessary.

Emergency Cash. Prospects are not good, since you aren't allowed to work without a work permit. Even the chances of illegal seasonal work in hotels and restaurants are slim, since the tourist industry is not highly developed. Busking, begging and street-selling are illegal; nor is there anywhere to sell blood — you can give blood but you only get a cup of coffee in exchange. There is a weekly lottery — known as *Lotto* — with results in the Sunday papers.

Taxes. Purchase tax (up to 20%) is deducted from articles that are shipped directly out of the country by the shop.

Getting Around

For additional information, see the introduction and general section on *Scandinavia,* above.

CAR

Rules and Requirements. When driving outside towns lights must be used day and night.

Road Signs. Road works — *Tietyo;* Slow — *Aja Hitaasti;* Frost damage — *Kelirikko;* Slippery surface — *Liukasta;* Loose stones — *Irtokiviä;* Ferry — *Lossi; Räjäytystyö, sulje radiolähetin* — Danger, explosives, switch off your radio!

Place Names. Many town in the west of Finland have a second name in Swedish: Helsinki is Helsingfors: Turku is Åbo; Pietersaari is Jakobstad. Both versions should be shown on road signs. In Helsinki, street names are given in both Finnish and Swedish; the Finnish versions are used here.

Parking. Lights must be used. In Helsinki, parking is controlled by meters, which take 50p. and 1 FIM coins, and operate from 8am-5pm, Monday-Saturday. No Parking = *Pysäköiminen kielletty.*

Petrol. In the South, 2-star *regular* costs 3.27 FIM a litre (£2.16 per UK gallon, $2.88 per US gallon); 4-star around 3.60 FIM a litre. Unleaded petrol costs the same as 2-star. The further north you go, the more expensive it is, and the fewer petrol stations there are.

Insurance. Claims are dealt with by the Finnish Motor Insurance Bureau *(Liikennevakuutusyhdistys),* Bulevardi 28, 00120 Helsinki 12 (Tel: 19251).

Touring Club.*Autoliitto,* Kansakoulukatu 10 Helsinki 10 (Tel: 694 0022).

Accidents and Breakdowns. The universal emergency number for police and ambulance is 000.

TRAIN

Railway services are run by Finnish State Railways *(Valtionrautatiet),* PB 488, SF00101 Helsinki (information — 659 411). Seat reservations are obligatory on EP trains at an additional cost of 15 FIM and on IC trains at 25 FIM second class and 50 FIM firstclass.

Cheap Deals. Reductions for groups of at least three people and children under 2 years.

The Finnrail Pass offers unlimited rail travel for 1 week (400 FIM), 2 weeks (600 FIM) or 3 weeks (750 FIM).

BUS

The monopoly for long distance coach travel is in the hands of *Oy Matkahuolto Ab,* Pohjoinen Rautatiekatu 119 C, PL 709 00100 Helsinki 100 (Tel: 602 122 for inquiries; 642 744 for complaints and lost property). Bus fares are cheaper than second class rail fares. The Helsinki coach station is at Simonkatu (Tel: 602 122). For information on coach timetables, dial 046. Rural areas are often served by post buses.

AIR

Internal flights are run by Finnair, whose head office is at Mannerheimintie 102, 00250 Helsinki (Tel: 818 81). Surprisingly, domestic fares are among the cheapest in Europe. There are discounts on certain routes at weekends. The Finnair Holiday Ticket gives unlimited travel on internal air routes for 15 days. The ticket is only obtainable outside Finland and costs around £155($250) or £125 ($200) for a youth ticket.

Buses to Helsinki-Vantaa Airport take 35 minutes and cost 15 FIM from the rail stations and the Finnair Terminal in the Intercontinental Hotel at Toolonkatu 21. Bus tickets can be bought from the driver. For airport and flight information dial 821 122.

HITCH-HIKING

Dismally slow in the north, but good in the south. Leaving Helsinki for Turku (E3), take tram 4 to near the start of the motorway. For Tampere (E79), take bus 10 to its terminus. For Lahti and the east take bus 1 or 6 to the Hameentie/Sturenkatu junction.

CITY TRANSPORT

Taxis. All taxis have a yellow sign *Taksi* which is illuminated when the taxi is free. In Helsinki, the basic charge is 10 FIM (3 FIM extra from 6pm-6am and after 2pm on Saturdays, and all day Sunday) then 3.50 FIM per km (£0.85 or $1.36 per mile). Taxis can be hailed, hunted out at taxi ranks, or telephoned (look up *autoasemat*).

Bus/Tram. Helsinki public transport is run by HKL, Toinenlinja 7, 00530 (Tel: 765966 for information); there are sales and information offices at Simonkatu 1 and Rautatentoria and Hakaniemi metro stations. Tickets (6.50 FIM flat rate, ten tickets for 58 FIM) can also be bought at the City Tourist Office and about 300 shops and kiosks displaying the black and yellow HKL emblem (two arrows forming a circle). Buses and trams are one-man operated: board at the front and buy your ticket from the driver. Helsinki also has a metro line which connects the city centre with the eastern suburbs.

A single bus or tram ticket costs 6.50 FIM, or you can buy a 10-ride ticket for 58 FIM. Tourist tickets giving unlimited travel cost 48 FIM for 1 day 96 FIM for 2 days, and 144 FIM for 3 days. Monthly and yearly tickets are available to Helsinki residents only. Tram route 3T is a circular tourist route, with sightseeing commentary in four languages in summer. With single or ten trip tickets you are allowed to make transfers within one hour of commencing your journey.

Unlimited travel on buses, trams, trains and the metro in Helsinki, Espoo and Vanta is also provided by the Helsinki Card, which confers various additional benefits on the holder including a free 1½ hour coach tour (daily in summer, on Tuesdays, Thursdays and Sundays in May and September, and on Sundays in winter), free admittance to over 50 museums and sights, reductions on car and bike hire, and many other bonuses including a free daily paper, a free shoe polish and a free half hour game of billiards. The card costs 65 FIM for 1 day, 90 FIM for 2 days and 110 FIM for 3 days and is available from tourist offices and various hotels. Childrens' cards are just over half the price of the adult card.

For details of the types of accommodation available, see the *Accommodation* section under *Scandinavia*, above.

Finding and Booking Accommodation. In Helsinki, the central reservations office is the *Hotellikeskus* at the Central Station (Tel: 171 133): reservation fee of about 10 FIM. Reservations can also be made (similar fee) through the 24-hour *Ageba* service — offices at Helsinki-Vantaa airport and the South Harbour. Outside Helsinki, try local tourist offices. The *Finncheque* scheme allows travellers to use prepaid hotel vouchers costing around 155 FIM per person in payment for double rooms (for a single room there is a 75 FIM surcharge) in many chain hotels — you must buy the cheques (and book only the first night's accommodation) in advance.

For reservations in holiday cottages, farms and holiday villages, contact Holiday Chain — *Lomarengas,* Malminkaari 23, 00700 Helsinki (Tel: 351 613 21), or *Suomen 4-H-Liitto,* Undenmaankatu 24, 00120 Helsinki 12 (Tel: 642 233). The Youth Hostels head office is *Suomen Retkeilymajajärjestö (SRM),* Yrjönkatu 38 B, 00100 Helsinki 10 (Tel: 694 0377).

General information on telephones and English language newspapers and radio broadcasts is given in the introduction.

Post. Post offices are open 9 am-5 pm Monday-Friday. The office in Helsinki Rail Station is open until 9 pm. The yellow stamp machines outside post offices take 1 and 5 FIM coins. Stamps can also be bought at bookstores, newsagents, stations and hotels but a small surcharge may be added. Mail boxes are yellow. The main office in Helsinki, and the Helsinki poste restante office, is at Mannerheimintie 11, by the Central Station. For postal information, dial 195 5117.

The correct way to address mail is: name; street (name, then number); town, preceded by a five-figure code and followed by a two-figure code. The five-figure code is preceded by the country code SF- if you're writing from abroad.

Telephone. Most call boxes take 1 and 5 FIM coins, Put the coin in before dialling; if you aren't connected, it will be returned when you replace the receiver. Most public phones can now dial long distance and international calls direct. For an International Direct Dial call to UK, dial 990 44 followed by UK area code (minus initial 0) and number you wish to dial. Calls are cheaper after 6 pm.

Area codes begin with 9, not the customary 0: Helsinki's code is 90; the international prefix is 990. Otherwise call the operator — the number varies from place to place but is 09 in Helsinki (92024 for calls to Sweden, 92022 for other international calls). For enquiries, dial 020 for price enquiries, dial 023 (92023 for international). For international operator calls eg collect (reverse charge) and BT Chargecard dial 92022 for operator. For UK Direct calls dial 9800 10440 from all phones.

Directories come in the usual two parts — personal (alphabetical) and commercial. The letters Ä and Ö come at the end of the alphabet. Information contained in the Helsinki directories includes explanations of the services available (in Swedish as well as Finnish), emergency and information numbers, street plans of Helsinki, and one long paragraph in English on how to use the telephone. Outside

Helsinki the personal subscriber section is first divided into communities.

Numbers for information and emergency services vary from place to place; useful numbers in Helsinki (elsewhere, check the directory) include; 03 — crime police; 005 — fire; 018 — news in English; 058 — tourist information in English; 0066 — ambulance; 008 — duty doctor; 000 — general emergency number.

Telegrams. Can be sent from post offices, or dial 021 (not from public phones). There is a 24-hour telegraph service at Mannerheimintie 11 B.

Newspapers. In summer, several of the large dailies, including *Hufvudstadsbladet,* print a column of news in English. There is also a multi-lingual monthly *Helsinki Today,* put out free by the Helsinki Tourist Office.

Broadcasting. The Radio Finland Network One broadcasts early morning news in English during the summer on FM and 558, 963 and 1254 kHz AM. If you need to broadcast an emergency message on Finnish radio, hunt out the local *Yleisradio* representative in the telephone directory.

For general information on hygiene, first aid, insurance and medical treatment, see the introduction.

Medical Treatment. Medical costs will normally be high, as elsewhere, but emergency hospital treatment is offered free to all uninsured foreigners at the Helsinki University Central Hospital, Meilahti Hospital, Haartmaninkatu 4 (Tel; 47 11 — open 24 hours). British passport holders should be able to secure reductions for other medical and dental care.

Emergencies. Pharmacies (*apteekki*) have a duty rota covering nights and weekends — the list is posted in all pharmacy windows. Helsinki has a 24-hour pharmacy at Mannerheimintie 96 (Tel: 415 778). The pharmacies at Mannerheimintie 5 (Tel: 179 092) and Siltasaarenkatu 18 (Tel: 753 7496) are open daily from 7 am to midnight. In Helsinki, doctors also have a duty rota (*lääkärinvälitys*) — dial 008; as do hospital casualty departments — dial 735 001 for information. Permanent 24 hour service is offered for dental treatment (dial 736 166); casualties (at Töölö Hospital, Töölönkatu 40; dial 40261); and for the ambulance service (dial 0066 or the general emergency number 000).

For general information, see the section on *Scandinavia,* above.

Police. The Helsinki police headquarters is at Pasilanraitio 13, 00240 Helsinki. Call 002; or 003 for the crime police; or 000 for the general emergency number.

Driving Offences. Driving doesn't mix with even the slightest drop of alcohol. With just the smallest fraction of the legal limit in your veins, you could end up in prison, convicted, possibly, for dangerous driving if they can't technically do you for drunken driving.

Drugs. Two years for possession; up to ten years for supplying.

Licensing Laws. The minimum age for purchase or consumption of alcohol is 18. Because of the strict liquor laws, moonshining is a profitable business in the backwoods, where the popular illegal beverage is known as *pontikka*. Beer up to 3.6° is not restricted; but anything stronger needs a licence and is only available at licensed bars or restaurants or at official liquor stores (known as *Alkoliliike*, or *Alko* for short). These open 10 am-5 pm, (9 am-2 pm on Saturday, but are closed on Saturdays between May 1st and September 30th, Sundays and holidays). Spirits (over 18°) may not be sold or served before noon. Restaurants may serve beer from 11 am.

Legal Aid. There is a state system for appointing free lawyers if you're broke.

For information on useful contacts and complaints procedures, see the introduction.

Embassies.
British Embassy, Uudenmaankatu 16-20, 00120 Helsinki 12 (Tel: 647 922).

There are Honorary Consulates in Kotka, Kuopio, Oulu, Pori, Tampere, Turku, and Vassa.

American Embassy, Itäinen Puistotie 14A, 00140 Helsinki (Tel: 171 931).

Canadian Embassy, Pohjois Esplanadi 25B, 00100 Helsinki (Tel: 171 141).

Lost Property. The central police lost property office in Helsinki is at Päijänteenkatu 12A, 7th Floor, 00510 Helsinki (Tel: 189 3180). For things lost on Helsinki public transport, go to Eino Leinon katu 8, 1st floor (Tel: 472 2290).

Information. The Finnish Tourist Board has its head office at Töölönkatu 11, PO Box 625, SF-00101 Helsinki (Tel: 403011), and another office at Unionkatu 26, 00130 Helsinki. The office for northern Finland is at Maakuntakatu 10, PO Box 8154, 96101 Rovaniemi (Tel: 60 17201). All towns also have their own local and city tourist office (Matkailutoimisto); in Helsinki this is at Pohjoisesplanadi 19, 00100 Helsinki (Tel: 1693757). For a summary of the day's events in English dial 058.

Free Maps. From national and local tourist offices, Free city transport maps from HKL offices.

Help. Samaritans — 601 066; Alcoholics Anonymous — 170 006.

Student Travel. *Travela* — FSTS, Mannerheimintie 5c, 00100 Helsinki (Tel: 624 101).

English Language Church. Tuomiokirkon (Anglican), Senaatintori, Helsinki 17 (Tel: 467 530).

American Express. Travek, Alekasanterinkatn 21, City Passage, 00100 Helsinki (Tel: 661 453); and offices in Turku and Hanko.

Public Holidays

January 1 New Year	Good Friday
Easter Monday	May 1 May Day
Ascension Day	Whit Monday
Midsummer's Day	November 1 All Saints
December 6 Independence Day	December 24-26 Christmas

Iceland

Area. 39,769 square miles   **Population.** 247,000

Capital. Reykjavik (population) 93,300)

The information given below is complementary to information given in the section on *Scandinavia,* above.

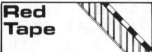

For details of passports, see the section on *Scandinavia.* See also the introduction for general information.

Customs. Duty free allowances include personal effects and items intended as gifts (no maximum value is specified). Travellers aged 16 or over may bring 200 cigarettes or 250 grams of other tobacco products; travellers aged 20 or over may also import one bottle spirits (up to 47°) and one litre of wine or other alcohol up to 21° or 6 litres of imported beer or 8 litres of domestic beer. The duty-free shop at Keflavik Airport is open to *arriving* passengers. This avoids lugging vast quantities of spirits and cigarettes on and off aircraft, making the journey much easier (and safer). Prohibited or restricted goods include livestock; raw meat and poultry products; butter; medicines, narcotics and poisons; firearms and ammunition.

Exit Permit. Anyone staying in Iceland for more than a month requires a valid Income Tax Clearance or Tax Exemption Certificate before being allowed to leave.

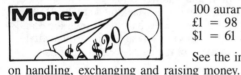

100 aurar (a) = 1 króna (kr), plural krónur.
£1 = 98 kr.   10kr = £0.10
$1 = 61 kr.   10kr = $0.16

See the introduction for general information on handling, exchanging and raising money.

Coins. 10a., 50a., 1kr, 5kr, 10kr, 50kr.

Notes. 100kr (green), 500kr (red), 1,000kr (purple), 5,000kr (blue)

Banking Hours. 9.15am-4pm, Monday-Friday; 5-6pm on Thursdays; large branches have an exchange service open 10-12am on Saturdays.

Shopping Hours. 9am-6pm, Monday-Thursday, 9am-10pm, Friday. Most of the shops that open on Saturdays will close by noon.

Import and Export. Icelandic currency is restricted to 8,000 kr.

Tipping. Service charges are always included. No need to tip.

Emergency Cash. Job prospects are reasonable in the fishing (and fish-processing) industry, although officially work permits must be obtained before entering Iceland. There is a national lottery, run by the University of Iceland and drawn monthly.

Taxes. Sales tax of 2% on most goods and services, usually included in quoted prices except for car hire and other rental agreements. Employees' sickness benefit of 2.5% on hotel charges. Visitors can claim an eventual refund of sales tax on purchases over 3,000 kr in value if they complete a refund voucher at the time of purchase. Look for participating shops with window stickers saying "Tax Free".

Getting Around

See also the introduction and the section on *Scandinavia,* above. Never assume that buses, planes or boats operate daily — outside summer many services cease altogether.

CAR

Rules and Regulations. Headlights must be used at all times.

Parking. Meters cost up to 50kr for 30 minutes.

Petrol. Only one grade of leaded petrol — 92 octane — is available; this costs about 45kr for a litre (£2.06 per UK gallon, $2.77 per US gallon). Unleaded petrol (92 octane) is slightly cheaper at 43kr per litre.

Touring Club. FIB, Borgatun 33, Reykjavik (Tel: 29 999) operate special road patrols at weekends in June, July and August.

BUS

In the absence of a rail network, long distance public transport is by bus, air or occasionally boat. Buses are cheaper, but not always by a great amount; on some routes, only 5% cheaper than air. In addition, poor road surfaces make travel by bus slower than in most countries. However, bus drivers will stop anywhere upon request.

Bus travel is run by the member companies of the BSI (Icelandic Bus Routes Union). They all use the same terminal in Reykjavik: *Umferdamidstödin* on Hringbraut (Tel: 2.23.00).

Cheap Deals. Unlimited bus travel for periods from one week ($200, around £125) to one month ($365, about £230) when you buy a *Timamidi*. Or a *Hringmidi* — a circumnavigation of Iceland by bus, in your own time, with unlimited stopovers but no backtracking — for $170 (about £106).

AIR

Internal flights are operated by Icelandair and Eagle Air (who also run sightseeing tours by air). Bus connections from Hotel Loftleider, at the town airport in Reykjavik, take 45 minutes to international airport at Keflavik and cost 310kr one-way. A tax of around 900kr is payable when buying a ticket for an international flight; internal flights (including those to the Faroe Islands and Greenland) charge a tax of about 120kr.

HITCH-HIKING

Legal, but not widely practised. Since buses stop anywhere upon request and constitute a large part of long-distance traffic, you may attract curiosity if you refuse to catch them. The only certainty when hitch-hiking is that you won't have to walk far to get out of towns.

CITY TRANSPORT

Taxis. Can be hailed or telephoned. All cabs are metered. The basic rate is about 25kr per km in daytime (£0.40 or $0.65 per mile).

Bus. Reykjavik's city bus service is run by Straetisvagnar Reykjavikur, Borgartun 35, 105 Reykjavik (Tel: 1.27.00). To cut costs you can buy books of 26 tickets at Laekjartorg and Hlemmur terminals for 1,000kr, or from bus drivers you can buy 6 tickets for 300kr; otherwise fares work at a flat rate of 55kr (with one transfer per ticket). When entering the bus, you must deposit either your ticket or the exact fare in the cyliner, and obtain a ticket if you need a transfer.

For details of the types of accommodation available, see the *Accommodation* section under *Scandinavia,* above.

Finding and Booking Accommodation. Reservations can be made by local tourist offices. The national chain of Edda summer hotels (mostly converted boarding schools) is run by the Iceland Tourist Bureau, Skogarhlid 6, Reykjavik (Tel: 2.58.55). Some Edda hotels include dormitories offering cheap accommodation if you use your own sleeping bags. Rooms in private houses, guest houses and farm houses are available but not cheap. The 18 youth hostels are run by the *Bandalag Islenskra Farfugla,* Laufasvegur 41, 101 Reykjavik (Tel: 2.49.50); their brochure also lists campsites, mountain huts owned by the Touring Club of Iceland (Öldugata 3, Reykjavik. Tel: 1.96.33), and cheap accommodation requiring travellers to bring their own sleeping bags. There are over 70 campsites; in addition, campers are allowed to pitch tents anywhere provided the landowner's permission is first obtained. You may encounter rescue huts erected by the life saving association *Slysavarnfeleg Islands.* These are for use in dire emergencies only.

General information on telephones and English language newspapers and radio broadcasts is given in the introduction.

Post. Post offices are open 8am-5pm, Mondays; 9am-5pm, Tuesday-Friday. In Reykjavik, the main post office is at the junction of Loekjangata and Hverfisg. The post office in the Central Bus Station is open from 8.30am-7.30pm, Mondays-Fridays, and from 9am-3pm on Saturdays.

The correct way to address mail is: name; street (name then number); town. Town or area codes are listed in the telephone directory; when writing from abroad, prefix the town code with the country code IS.

Telephone. Calls to all parts of Iceland and most foreign countries can be dialled direct; the international prefix is 90. For International Direct Dial calls back to the UK dial 9044. For the international operator, dial 09. Collect or BT chargecard calls can not be made from payphones. International Direct Dial calls can be made from all telephones and payphones which accept 1, 5 and 10kr coins. For the operator for local calls dial 03; long distance — 02; complaints — 05; The area code for Reykjavik is 91.

Long distance and international calls can also be made at telegraph *(Simstödin)* and telephone offices. The opening hours for the central office at Austurvöll Square in Reykjavik are 9am-7pm, Monday-Saturday, 11am-6pm, Sundays.

Outside Reykjavik, directories are first sub-divided alphabetically into localities. General information is included on postal and telecommunications services, information in English on pages 10-12. In the Icelandic alphabet, the letter đ comes after d;ø, æ and ö come after z. Names are listed alphabetically by *first* name; Icelander's surnames are simply their father's name suffixed *-son* (for sons) or — *dottir* (for daughters); women retain this surname after marriage. Fortunately, the telephone directory lists each persons occupation alongside their name.

Useful numbers in Reykjavik include: police — 1.11.66; fire, ambulance — 1.11.00; time — 04; weather — 1.70.00; road information — 2.10.00; tourist information — 2.58.55.

Telegrams. Can be placed at telegraph offices (see above), or by phone: dial 06; or 1.64.11 after 9pm.

Newspapers. Two periodical glossies in English: *Iceland Review* (quarterly) and *News from Iceland* (monthly). There is monthly publication entitled *What's On in Reykavik* published in English.

Broadcasting. Radio Reykavik Programme 1 has a daily news programme in English at 7..30am from June to August. Other English programmes are those transmitted by the NATO base at Keflavik for the benefit of base personnel.

For general information on health, hygiene, medical treatment and insurance, see the introduction.

Reciprocal Agreements. British subjects are entitled to free in-patient treatment upon production of NHS cards. British children aged 6-15 years qualify for free emergency dental treatment.

Emergencies. The first aid/casualty/poisons clinic in Reykjavik is at the Borgarspitali, Fossvogi; for the emergency ambulance service, dial 1.11.00. The chemist at Storholt 1 is open 24 hours a day. The following duty rotas exist: chemists — listed in newspapers, or dial 1.88.88; doctors — dial 1.15.10 on weekdays, 8am-5pm otherwise dial 1.88.88; dentists — weekends only at Reykjavik Health Clinic, dial 2.24.11.

For information on useful contacts and complaints procedures, see the introduction.

Embassies and Consulates.
British Embassy, Laufasvegur 49, PO Box 230, 101 Reykjavik (Tel: 1.58.83); plus an honorary Vice-Consulate at Akureyri. American Embassy, Laufasvegur 21, Reykjavik (Tel: 2.91.00). Canadian Consulate General, Suourlandsbraut 10, Reykavik. (Tel: 68 08 20).

Information. Iceland Tourist Board, Laugavegur 3, IS-101 Reykjavik (Tel: 27488) supplies information in reply to written enquiries. When in Iceland contact: Tourist Information Center, Ingólfsstraeti 5, IS-101 Reykjavik (Tel: 623045).

A number of travel agencies in downtown Reykjavik will also provide information and sell tours and excursions.

American Express. Utsyn Travel Agency, Alfabakki 16, IS-109 Reykjavik (Tel: 603022).

Disabled Travellers. The Organisation of the Handicapped in Iceland (Sjalfsbjorg — Landssamband fatlaora), Hatun 12, IS-105 Reykjavik will supply general information.

Police. The central police station in Reykjavik is at Hverfesgata 113, IS-105 Reykjavik (Tel: 11166). The downtown police ward is at Customs Building, Tryggvagata. Lost property and Immigration Police are at Hverfisgata 115, IS-105 Reykjavik (Tel: 0200).

Photography. You need a special permit to approach the nests and/or take pictures of eagles, falcons, snowy owls and little auks.

Public Holidays

January 1 New Year	Maundy Thursday
Good Friday	Easter Monday
First Day of Summer	May 1 Labour Day
Ascension Day	Whit Monday
June 17 National Day	First Monday of August
December 24-26 Christmas	December 31
New Year's Eve	

Norway

Area. 125,057 square miles.   **Population.** 4,200,000

Capital. Oslo (population: 460,000).

The information given below is complementary to information in the section on *Scandinavia,* above.

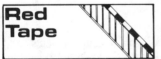
Red Tape

For details of passports, see the section on *Scandinavia,* above. See also the introduction for general information.

Customs. Duty free allowances include personal effects (which must be re-exported); 2 litres beer; either 2 litres wine or 1 litre wine and 1 litre spirits; 200 cigarettes or 250 grams other tobacco products; 200 cigarette papers; 11 kg sweets and chocolate; other items to a value of 350 kr (700 kr for European residents in transit; 3,500 kr for non-European residents in transit). Travellers under 15 are not entitled to tobacco allowances; travellers under 20 are not entitled to alcohol allowances. The following items are restricted or prohibited: eggs, potatoes, narcotics, medicines, poisons, birds, animals and animal products, plants, firearms and ammunition, spirits over 60° proof. You cannot import more than 25 roses and/or carnations without prior permission from the Norwegian Ministry of Agriculture.

100 øre — 1 krone (kr), plural Kroner.
£1 = 11 kr   1 kr = £0.09
$1 = 6.90 kr   1 kr = $0.14

For general information on handling, exchanging and raising money, see the introduction.

Coins. 10 øre, 50 øre, 1 kr, 5 kr, 10 kr, 50 kr.

Notes. 5 kr (blue/brown), 10 kr (blue), 50 kr (green), 100 kr (brown), 500 kr (green), 1,000 kr (brown).

Banking Hours. 8.15 am-4 pm in winter, to 3 pm in summer, Monday-Friday (optional late opening until 5 pm, Thursdays). Outside banking hours, try main railway stations, tourist offices and customs posts; hotels and restaurants will give a lower rate of exchange. Credit cards are not accepted at petrol stations.

Shopping Hours. 9 am-5 pm, Monday-Friday in winter, 9 am-4 pm in summer; 9 am-1 pm, Saturdays. Some shops stay open until 7 pm on Thursdays.

Import and Export. No import limits; export limit of 5,000 kr in Norwegian notes. Notes of more than 100 kr may not be imported or exported, and are difficult to exchange outside Norway.

Tipping. Hotels, restaurants — nearly always included in the bill (*service inkludert*), otherwise 10-15%. Taxis — 5%. Station porters are non-existent, so you don't need to tip them.

Emergency Cash. The best chances of picking up casual work are in hotels and fish processing plants. Norwegian Youth Hostels also have a steady demand for unskilled domestic staff. Employment agencies are forbidden by law. Work permits should be obtained before entering Norway, but foreigners may seek work each summer between 15 May and 30 September without formality. There is a lottery — drawn monthly — for which tickets cost 20 kr.

For additional information, see the introduction and the section on *Scandinavia,* above.

CAR

Rules and Regulations. Front and rear seat belts must be warn. Dipped headlights must be used at all times, day and night. In early 1990 a toll of around £1/$1.60 was imposed on drivers entering the centre of Oslo.

Road Signs. Slow — *Kjør Sakte;* Soft verges — *Svake Kanter;* Cattle grid — *Ferist;* One way — *Envegskøring;* Diversion — *Omkjøring;* Road works — *Veiarbeide;* Loose gravel — *Løs Grus.*

Parking. No Parking = *Parkering/Stopp Forbudt*. In Oslo, parking is controlled largely by meters which take 1 kr and 5 kr coins. During the day (8 am-5 pm, Monday-Friday: 8 am-3 pm on Saturdays), meters operate. The charges begin at 10 kr for the first hour; the second hours costs 12 kr and the third hour costs 15 kr.

On non-metered and otherwise unrestricted streets in cental Oslo, you may park free for up to 30 minutes between 8 am and 5 pm, Monday-Friday, 8 am-3 pm Saturdays. Outside these hours, there is no time limit except on streets with bus or tram routes, where there is a two-hour limit. To facilitate street cleaning operations, the alternate day system (see the introduction), based on odd and even house numbers, operates between midnight and 7 am each night.

A leaflet entitled *Tourist Map and How to Park in Oslo* is obtainable free at petrol stations, hotels and tourist information offices.

Petrol. Unleaded petrol costs 5.50 kr a week: superleaded (98 octane) costs 5.88 kr a litre (£2.40 per imperial gallon, $3.20 per US gallon). Petrol stations are few and far between in the north. Many stations are now fitted with automatic self-service machines that take 10 kr and 50 kr bills: petrol from these is slightly cheaper.

Touring Clubs. KNA, Drammensveien 20C, Oslo 2 (Tel: 56 19 00); NAF (*Norges Automobil-Forbund*), Storgata 2, Oslo 1 (Tel: 42 94 00).

Tolls. Tolls of between 4 kr and 42 kr are payable on some roads and bridges.

Accidents and Breakdowns. There are 24-hour NAF patrols on the major mountain roads and some other main roads from June to August. NAF Emergency Centre in Oslo has a 24-hour breakdown service (Tel: 33 41 10), and a nation-wide 24-hour service. In cases of accident involving physical injury, the police must be informed — dial 11 00 11 in Oslo.

Trailers. Many Norwegian roads present problems to cars towing caravans, boats or trailers, so anyone thinking of doing so should obtain a copy of the map *Caravanning in Norway* from the National Tourist Office.

TRAIN

The rail network is run by Norwegian State Railways (NSB), Storgata 33, PO Box 9115 Vaterland, Oslo 1. The main sales and information office is at Stortingsgate 28, Oslo 1 (Tel: 42 94 60). The cost per km falls steeply for journeys of over 600 km. Reservations are compulsory for express trains (*Ekspresstog*).

Children under 4 travel free; 4-15 at half fare.

BUS

The terminal in Oslo is at Grønlandstorg (dial 41 28 90 for information on timetables and fares). Much of Norway is covered by routes operated by the *Bussekspress* consortium: for information contact them at Jernbanetorget Z, Oslo 1 (Tel: 33 08 62). They offer a *Buss Pass* that gives a 33.3% reduction of fares.

BICYCLE

The Norwegian Tourist Board produces a free cycling map to Norway: send a stamped addressed envelope. The national cycling association is Syklistenes Lands-forening Nedregt 5, Oslo 5. Bicycles may be taken on all trains except expresses, and buses in rural districts. Local tourist information offices can give information on hiring bikes.

AIR

Fornebu airport (Tel: 12 01 20 for information) is reached from Oslo by airport coach from the Central Rail Station (20 kr) or city bus 31 from Wessels plass (10 kr).

HITCH-HIKING

Legal, but not easy. If you want a definition of the word "bleak", stand on the Bergen-Trondheim road in the middle of winter. For heading south or east out of Oslo (E6 or E18 to Stockholm or Gothenburg) try Bispegata; west to Bergen (E18), take the underground to Skøyen and stand on Drammensveien; north to Trondheim (E6) — underground to Carl Berners Plass and hitch along Trondheimsveien.

CITY TRANSPORT

Taxis. You can find them cruising the streets and outside the railway station, or you can telephone for one (dial 38 80 90 in Oslo or look up *Drosjer*). For advance reservations, dial 38 80 80 (only between 09.00-15.00). Rates are 16 kr fixed charge then 4 kr per km (£0.60 or $0.93 per mile). Complaints and lost property are handled by the Oslo Taxisentral, Trondheimsveien 100.

Underground. Oslo has two underground lines: one runs east and the other runs west from Stortinget station.

Bus/Tram. Single tickets on bus or tram in Oslo cost 13 kr. Pocket timetables are available from conductors and at "Trafikanten" (by the Central station), for timetables and fare enquiries, dial 17 70 30.

Boat. For information on Oslo's ferry services and timetables, dial 17 70 30. Single tickets cost 13 kr.

Accommodation

For details of the types of accommodation available, see the *Accommodation* section under *Scandinavia,* above.

Finding and Booking Accommodation. National Tourist Offices supply lists of hotels, motels, youth hostels, camp sites and farms offering accommodation. They also give the telephone numbers of the local tourist offices, which can make reservations in their respective areas. In Oslo, *Oslo Promotion* runs an advance booking service by mail (write to Oslo Pro, Innkvartering, Radhusgt. 23, N-0158 Oslo or telephone 33 43 86), requiring a 100 kr deposit, 30 kr of which is retained as a booking fee. *Oslo Pro* also runs a last-minute booking service in the Central station and at the City Hall (booking fee 15 kr).

For information on youth hostels, contact Norske Vandrerhjem, Dronningensgate 26, 0154 Oslo (Tel: 42 14 10). They have 82 hostels around the country with prices around 70 or 80 per night. To reserve a chalet, write to*Den Norske Hyutteformidling,* Kierschowsgate 7, Boks 3207, Oslo 4 (Tel: 37 19 00); or, for chalets in the southern fjord area, contact *Fjordhytter,* Jon Smørsgt 11, 5011 Bergen (Tel: 23 20 80). Mountain huts in the remoter areas are available for hire to members of the Norwegian Mountain Touring Association (DNT), Stortingsgate 28, Oslo 1.

Fisherman's huts (used during the winter cod season) are rented out to tourists in summer. Details from Norske Vandrerhjen (address above).

Camping. Norway has 1,300 campsites, graded from one to three stars. On average one night costs around 35 kr for one adult and a tent. You may camp on uncultivated land for up to two days without consulting the owner unless it is less than 150 metres from a dwelling. The Norwegian Campsite Association (*Norges Campingplass forbund*) is based at Dronningensgt 10-12, Oslo 1 (Tel: 42 12 03).

Communications

General information on telephones and English language newspapers and radio broadcasts is given in the introduction.

Post. Post offices are open 9am-5pm, Monday-Friday and 9am-1pm on Saturdays. The head post office in Oslo is at Dronningensgate 15 (open 8am-8pm Monday-Friday, 9am-1pm Saturday, closed Sundays and holidays); counter 24 is for poste restante mail. Stamps can also be bought at newspaper kiosls. For postal information, dial 40 90 50. There is a philatelic service *(Postens Frimerket jeneste)* at Schweigaards gate 33 BII: the postal address is POB 3770 Gamlebyen, 0135 Oslo I.

The correct way to address mail is: name; street (name, then number); town, preceded by a four-figure postal code (which is preceded by the country code N-if writing from abroad). Oslo is also followed by a single-figure zone number.

Telephone. Public phones take 1 kr and 5 kr coins; the minimum charge is 2 kr. Telephone offices are usually open between 9am and 4pm Monday-Friday and 9am-1pm on Saturdays. In Oslo, the central telephone office at Kongensgate 12 is open 24 hours a day. The international prefix is 095.

To use public phones, lift the receiver, insert the money (minimum 1 kr), then dial. If there is no reply the money is returned by placing the receiver. Area codes include: Oslo — 02, Bergen — 05; the international prefix is 095.

For IDD calls to UK, insert at least 5 kr, dial 09544. Dial the UK area code (minus initial 0) and local number; insert more coins when signal sounds. Payphones accept 1,5 & 10 kr coins.

Collect and BT Chargecard calls can be made from all phones. The operator access code is 0115.

Directories come in the usual two parts — personal (alphabetical) and commercial — and there should be one in each public telephone. Useful and emergency numbers are listed at the front of the personal section, along with instructions and explanations of services available. The letters Æ, Ø and Å come at the end of the alphabet.

Useful numbers in Oslo include: fire and general emergency — 42 99 00; police — 11 00 11.

Telegrams. Can be sent from telegraph stations (see above); or by telephone: dial 013. Dial 090 for information.

Broadcasting. During the summer, at 9.45am daily, Norwegian Radio broadcasts the news and weather forecast in English, French and German. The wavelength varies in different parts of the country — in Oslo it's 218 kHz LF, in Bergen 890 kHz AM.

Health and Hygiene

For general information on hygiene, first aid, medical treatment and insurance, see the introduction.

Reciprocal Agreement. British subjects can obtain free hospital in-patient treatment simply by producing their passport. For out-patient treatment, and visits to a doctor or a dentist the fee must first be paid in full, then take the receipt, along with your British passport, to the local health insurance office (*Trygdekontor*) for partial reimbursement (80%). You must claim before leaving Norway. The scheme only extends to public hospitals (out-patient treatments at polyclinics) and doctors and dentists on the public roll. Prescription charges must be paid in full.

Emergencies. Chemists (*apoteken*) keep a duty rota to cover nights and weekends — the list is posted in all chemists' windows. Other 24-hour services in Oslo include the ambulance and casualty service at the City Polyclinic, Storgata 40 (Tel: 20 10 90) and the Dental Polyclinic at Töyensenter, Kolstadgate 18 (Tel: 67 48 46).

The Law

For general information, see the section on *Scandinavia*, above.

Police. In Oslo, the police headquarters is at Grønlandsleivet 44 (Tel: 66 90 50).

Driving Offences. The fine for over-parking at a meter is 200 kr, increased by 100 kr if it's not paid within 14 days. Sometimes, in Oslo, cars are towed away — if this happens to you, call the police on 66 90 50. The maximum alcohol limit for driving is 0.05%: the statutory penalty for drunken driving is 21 days in jail, plus loss of licence for a year — expect worse if you cause any damage.

Drugs. Normal penalties are a fine and/or up to three years; up to 15 years for cases of, for instance, large scale dealing or importation.

Licensing Laws. Off sales of wines and spirits are restricted to the state run *Vinmonopolet* stores, which are closed on Sundays and holidays. The sale of beer is less restricted. In bars and restaurants, spirits may not be served before 3 pm (1 pm in resort hotels), and not at all on Sundays and holidays. Many of the smaller hotels can only afford licences for beer and wine. The minimum age for the purchase and consumption of alcohol is 18 (20 for spirits). Because of the strict laws, and high taxes on alcohol, moonshining is widespread in the backwoods.

Legal Aid. If you have no money, the court will appoint a lawyer for you, but he may not be as effective as one you pay.

Nude Bathing. Officially, special areas are designated for nudism, but the practice is widespread and unofficially condoned. For further information, write to *Norsk Naturist Forbund,* Box 189, Senturm, Oslo 1.

Smoking. A law has been passed prohibiting smoking in all public buildings — including Oslo Central Station.

For information on useful contacts and complaints procedures, see the introduction.

Embassies and Consulates.
British Embassy, Thomas Heftyesgate 8, 0264 Oslo 2 (Tel: 55 24 00).
British Consulate, Sluppenveien 10, 7001 Trondheim (Tel: 96 82 11).
British Consulate, Sorhauggt 139, 5501 Haugesund (Tel: 23033).

There are Honorary Consulates at Alesund, Bergen, Kristiansund, Harstad, Stavanger and Tromso.

American Embassy, Drammensveien 18, Oslo 2 (Tel: 44 85 50).

Canadian Embassy, Oscarsgate 20, Oslo 3 (Tel: 46 69 55).

Lost Property. The central police lost property office in Oslo is at Schwensengate (open 10 am-2 pm, Monday-Friday, 10 am-1.30 pm on Saturday).

Guides/Secretaries/Interpreters. In Oslo, *Contact Service* can provide all types of assistance at very short notice, including trained secretaries and interpreters. Their address is Linstowgate 6 (Tel: 69 54 31). Specially trained guides, including ski guides, are provided by the Oslo Guide Service, at the City Hall (Tel: 41 48 63).

Information. The Norwegian Tourist Board (NTB) has its head office at Langkaia 1, Oslo 1 (Tel: 42 70 44).
For specific information on hiking and mountaineering, and detailed trail maps, contact the DNT, Stortingsgate 28, Oslo. Membership (which costs 200 kr, or 130 kr if you're under 21) entitles you to use the DNT mountain huts.
The Oslo Promotion; Turistinformation is at the City Hall; postal enquiries to the Oslo Pro, Rådhusgaten 23, 0158 Oslo 1 (Tel: 33 43 86). They issue three useful free leaflets; an Oslo map; the yearly *Oslo Guide,* and the monthly *Whats On.*

Free Maps. From local tourist offices.

Disabled Travellers. The Norwegian Association for the Handicapped has published a travel guide for the disabled; it is available free from the Norwegian Tourist Board in London (but send £1 to cover postage) or direct from Norges HandiKapforbund, PO Box 9217, Vaterland, N-0134 (send an international money order for 25 kr).

Student Travel. Terra Nova Travel, Dronningensgate 26, Oslo 1 (Tel: 42 14 10).

English Language Church. St. Edmund's (Anglican), Mødollergata 30, Oslo (Tel: 55 24 00).

American Express. Karl Johans Gate 33, Oslo 1 (Tel: 42 91 50); also offices in Bergen, Stravanger, Tromso and Trondheim, all under the auspices of the Winge Travel Bureau.

Public Holidays

January 1 New Year
Good Friday
May 1 Labour Day
May 17 National Day

Maundy Thursday
Easter Monday
Ascension Day
Whit Monday

December 25-26 Christmas

Spitzbergen

This group of islands, known in Norwegian as Svalbard, is 1,000 miles north of the Arctic Circle and close to the true north pole. Under the 1920 treaty it is technically part of Norway, although there is a considerable Soviet presence. There are only three settlements of any size on Spitzbergen. The Norwegian settlement, Longyearbyen, is the most important, and it is also the capital of the group of islands. The other ones are the Soviet settlements Pyramiden and Barentsburg. Pyramiden is the northernmost town.

It is possible to stay over night in hotels or guest houses in all three settlements. Entry is normally by sea or air from Norway to Longyearbyen. Travel inside Spitzbergen is daily by boat or snow scooters, which are widely available for hire. For further information, contact: Spitzbergen Travel A/S (SpiTra) 9170 Longyearbyen or the Governor's Office, 9170 Longyearbyen.

Sweden

Area. 174,000 square miles

Population. 8,400,000

Capital. Stockholm (population: 1,410,000).

The information given below is complementary to information given in the section on *Scandinavia, above.*

Red Tape

For details of passports, see the section on the *Scandinavia, above.* See also the introduction for general information.

Customs. Duty free allowances include a reasonable amount of articles for personal use; 200 cigarettes or 100 cigarillos or 50 cigars or 250 grams tobacco (double for residents outside Europe); 200 cigarette papers (which attract tax of about 2,000% in Sweden); 1 litre spirits and 1 litre wine (2 litres of spirits or wine for non-European residents); 2 litres beer; 15 kg foodstuffs (but no more than 5 kg animal fats; no more than $2\frac{1}{2}$ kg butter); and other goods to a value of 275 kr. The minimum age is 15 for tobacco, 20 for alcohol.

Money

100 öre = 1 krona (kr) — plural kronor
£1 = 10.25 kr   1 kr = £0.10
$1 = 6.40   1 kr = $0.16

See the introduction for general information on handling, exchanging and raising money.

Coins. 5 öre, 10 öre, 25 öre, 1 kr, 10 kr, 50 kr, 100 kr, 200 kr.

Notes. 5 kr (brown or mauve), 10 kr (blue), 50 kr (beige-brown), 100 kr (grey-blue), 1,000 kr, 10,000 kr (both multicoloured).

Banking Hours. Monday-Friday, 9.30 am-3 pm (hours may be shorter in rural areas). In many cities, they reopen 4.30-6 pm. Longer hours at exchange bureaux at airports, ports, frontier posts and international railway stations.

Shopping Hours. Monday to Friday, 9 am-6 pm; on Saturdays shops close any time between 1 and 4 pm. In Stockholm, several department stores open all day on Saturday and for a few hours on Sundays. Also open on Sundays are the shops at the underground stations Hötorget, T-Centralen and Ostermalms Torg.

Import and Export. No restrictions on import: only up to 6,000 krona may be exported, in notes of 1000 kr or less.

Tipping. Hotels — 15%, almost always included in the bill (*service inkluderat*). Restaurants — 13%, likewise. Taxis — *12-15%*, not included on the meter. Porters — fixed charges of 2 kr per item. Cloakroom attendants — 4 or 5 kr.

Emergency Cash. Official work permit requirements are extremely strict, but jobs in hotels and restaurants can sometimes be found in the south and west, and picking fruit in the south. Picking wild berries in forests in summer and selling the produce on the streets has been known to work. Otherwise, sell your mascara (which, like cigarette papers, is very highly taxed).

Taxes. There is VAT of 19% on just about every except medicines, postal and telephone charges and public transport. As a foreigner, you're entitled to exemption of tax on certain more expensive items; have them sent directly to your home by the shop, or take them via the airports at Stockholm, Malmö or Gothenburg, where (if you have the right paperwork) you get an immediate cash refund of sales tax. Look for a sign saying *Taxfree* in shops.

Getting Around

For additional information, see the introduction and the section on *Scandinavia*, above.

CAR

Rules and Requirements. Dipped headlights must be must used at all times, even in broad daylight.

Road Signs. Slow — *Sakta;* Single line — *En fil;* Danger — *Fara.*

Parking. Stockholm has some of the most complex parking rules in Europe, and other Swedish towns and cities are not far behind the capital in confusing the motorist. Meters (which take 25 öre, 50 öre, 1 kr and 5 kr coins) come in five colours, indicating the maximum length of stay: Red (30 minutes), Yellow (1 hour), Grey (2 hours), Green (4 hours) and Blue (12 hours). The central islands of Gamlastan and Riddarholmen are continuous no-parking zones. Elsewhere in the city, signs designate the maximum parking time within certain hours, with regulations additionally for street cleaning (usually on one night per week, when parking is banned). In the suburbs the odd/even dates system is widely used. The fine for overstaying or illegal parking ranges from 150-500 kr. If your vehicle is towed away, phone 54 21 20.

You may wish to play it safe by leaving your car at one of the 23 official car parks. Details are given on the *Parkering i Stockholm* map, available from tourist offices.

Petrol. Leaded 96 octane (*regular*) costs 4.54 kr a litre; 98 octane (*super*) costs 4.62 kr a litre (£2.03 per Imperial gallon, $2.70 per US gallon). Unleaded petrol (95 octane) costs 4.42 kr a litre. Petrol stations are few and far between in the north, so fill up whenever you get the chance, and carry a can of spare fuel. Self service is quite common and some pumps are operated by the insertion of 10 and 100 kr notes. Look for signs saying *Nattöpet Sedel Automat*.

Touring club. *Motormännens Riksförbund*, Sturegatan 32, 102 48 Stockholm (Tel: 782 38 00).

Accidents and Breakdowns. In cases of emergency, accident or insurance problems, contact the *Larmtjänst*, whose toll free number is 020 91 00 40. In cases of accident, the police must be called (90 000). Beware of elks; one-fifth of all Swedish road accidents involve collision with elks.

TRAIN/BUS

The rail network is run by Swedish State Railways (SJ), whose information office (*Resebyrå*) is at Vasagatan 22, 111 20 Stockholm (Tel: 762 5815). Reservations (15 kr) are compulsory on express trains. SJ also runs a long distance bus network that overlaps and complements their rail service. Local and long distance bus services are also run by several private companies, the largest being *Linjebuss,* Box 23038, 10435 Stockholm (Tel: 729 13 00); or go in person to Sveavägen 145. Smoking is not allowed on any buses.

BICYCLE

Cycles can be hired from various outlets, including some rail stations. For details of inclusive cycling tours, contact the Swedish Touring Club, Box 25, 10120 Stockholm.

AIR

Connections from Stockholm to Arlanda airport (26 miles) take 45 minutes and cost 30 kr by bus from the SAS Terminal, Vasagatan 6-14, calling at Hagaterminalen and Järva Krog; for bus times, dial 23 60 00. Buses also leve from Uppsala; for information dial 018-12 01 15. Most domestic flights are run by SAS and its subsidiary LIN. Malmö has a direct land-sea connection by hovercraft with Kastrup airport across the water in Copenhagen for SAS passengers.

HITCH-HIKING

A general reluctance among Swedish motorists to up hitchers can be alleviated by a smart appearance and a national flag. For the E3 and E4 south from Stockholm, take the underground to Hornstull; west of Oslo (E18), underground to Hallonbergen; north to Norrtalje (E3), underground to University.

CITY TRANSPORT

Taxis. Taxis can be found cruising, or at taxi ranks, or you can telephone for one. The sign *ledig* means For Hire. Fares are high, with a minimum charge of 14 kr; a two mile journey will cost around 60 kr (£5.85 or $9.37) for one passenger, with extra charges for more passengers and luggage. Waiting time is charged at 2 kr per minute. Rates are about 15% higher from 7 pm-6 am and at the weekends. Taxis can be telephoned 24 hours a day by dialling 15 00 00 in Stockholm; 17 03 40 in Gothenburg; 70 000 in Malmö; an extra 30 kr is charged for taxis ordered by phone. In Stockholm, you can request an English speaking driver by dialling 15 04 00.

Bus/Underground/Tram. All cities have bus services, most of which run 24 hours. Gothenburg also has a tram service. Stockholm has the country's only underground railway: the *tunnelbana*, centred on T-Centralen station. Buses are one-man operated: enter at the front and pay the driver. Smoking is not allowed on any city transport.

Transport is Stockholm is run by *Storstockholms Lokaltrafik* (SL) at Tegnérgatan 2A (Tel: 23 60 00). A zone system operates; each ticket costs around 4 kr and the lowest fare (for travel within one zone) is two tickets. Tickets are valid for one hour, permit return journeys during that hour, and are interchangeable between bus and underground.

Cheap Deals in Stockholm. You can buy a book of 20 tickets (*förkopshäfte*) for 45 kr. A 24-hour unlimited travel card costs 40 kr (inner city only) or 22 kr (the entire SL network); the 72-hour card, price 76 kr, covers the whole network and includes free admission to selected attractions. Any of these travel cards entitles you to free admission to the Tram Museum. Or for 70 kr you can buy the 24 hour *Key to Stockholm* card, which gives free admission to 55 attractions as well as free travel.

All these cheap deals must be bought in advance from *Pressbyrån* kiosks, SL offices and tourist bureaux.

For details of the types of accommodation available, see the *Accommodation* section under *Scandinavia*.

Finding and Booking Accommodation.

Many Swedish hotels offer lower rates at weekends and in the summer when their usual guests are on holiday. Both normal and reduced rates are described in the annual free booklet *Hotels in Sweden* available from Tourist Offices. This booklet also contains details of the inclusive package deals marketed by several towns (including Stockholm) which include reductions on accommodation, travel and sightseeing. In addition it describes the package deals offered by some of the hotel chains, including the "SARA Hotels Scandinavian Bonus Pass", the "Scandic Hotel Cheque Scheme" and the "Sweden Hotels Pass". One of the most reasonable is the "Hotel Passport" scheme operated by Biltur-Logi, which offers bed and breakfast for around 160 kr per person at 200 hotels, guesthouses and inns throughout Sweden; for information contact Biltur-Logi, 793 03 Tallberg (Tel: 247 509 25). Some of these deals must be booked before you enter Sweden.

In exchange for a commission fee of 10-40 kr., local tourist offices will book you a room up to the last minute. In Stockholm, postal reservations should be requested of the Stockholm Tourist Association, Box 7542, 103 93 Stockholm. Personal applications to either Hamngatan 27, Stockholm (Tel: 789 2000); or to the *Hotellcentralen*, which is open from 8 am-9 pm daily from May 1st-September 30th and from 8.30 am-5 pm Mondays-Fridays at other times of year, on the lower floor of Central Station (Tel: 24 08 80). A booking fee of about 20 kr will be charged.

For information on the summer availability of rooms in student hostels in Stockholm, contact *SFS-Serviceverksamhet,* Drottninggatan 89, 113 60 Stockholm (Tel: 34 01 80).

Youth Hostels (*Vandrarhem*) are run by STF, Drottninggatan 31-33, Box 25, 101 20 Stockholm (Tel: 08 790 3100). They cost 60-105 kr. per night, according to grade and season.

An ancient law known as *Allemannsrätt* allows one night's camping on any unfenced land without permission from the landowner. It involves responsibilities as well as privileges; no rubbish or dangerous fires. There are a fair sprinkling of official camp sites — the one in Stockholm is at Sätra.

Communications

General information on telephones and English language newspapers and radio broadcasts is given in the introduction.

Post. Letter boxes are yellow. Post office hours are generally Monday-Friday, 9 am-6 pm; 9 am-1 pm on Saturdays. Stamps are also sold at newspaper kiosks and newsagents. There is a free poste restante service at main post offices: in Stockholm, at Vasagatan 28-34 (normally open 8 am-8 pm Monday to Friday, 9 am-3 pm Saturdays and 9 am-11 am Sundays but currently only open from 8 am-6.30 pm Mondays-Fridays while rebuilding work is being carried out). The philatelic service has a shop at the Postal Museum at Lilla Nygatan 6. For postal information, dial 781 20 05 in Stockholm (elsewhere look up *Postens Upplysning*).

The correct way to address mail is: name, street (name, then number); town preceded by a five-figure postal code (which in turn is preceded by the country code S- if writing from abroad). Where you have both a box number and street address, the postal code may be different for each; give the box number and its code, and omit the street address altogether.

Any Swedish post office will be able to offer you the post code list (*postnummer katalog*).

Telephone. The telephone system is completely automatic, and instructions are printed in English, both in call-boxes and in the directories. Public telephones are found at telegraph offices, not post offices. The coin boxes are of three types: those which take only 1kr coins; others which have only one slot but which accept 50 øre, 1kr and 5kr coins; and some with three slots for 25 øre, 50 øre and 1kr coins. You put the coins in before you dial; if you don't get connected, replace the receiver to have your money returned. Most calls are cheaper from 6 pm to 8 am and at weekends. Area codes include: Stockholm — 08; Gothenburg — 031; Malmo — 040; Uppsala — 018. The international prefix is 009. You must dial this plus the country code, then pause until you hear a second tone before continuing. To dial the UK dial 009 44 wait for second dial tone, dial the UK area code (minus initial 0) and local number. A cardphone network is spreading from its origin in Uppsala. For calls via the operator, dial 000 (inland) or 0081 (the UK, Eire, Canada and the USA). For BT chargecard or collect (reverse charge) calls dial 0081. For UK Direct calls dial 020 795 144 from any Telephone. Payphones require a 2kr coin.

All public telephones should have local directories; they come in two parts — alphabetical (first subdivided into communities) and commercial. The letters Å, Ä and Ö come at the end of the alphabet. Names beginning with C (eg Carlsson) are listed together under K (Karlsson); similarly, W and V are regarded as the same.

Information given at the front of the alphabetical section includes a breakdown of postal and telecommunications services, street plans of the area covered, and instructions on using the telephone; this last is also given in English. At the end of the directory, under the heading *Om kriget kommer,* are plans of action in case of sudden outbreak of war or invasion — including evacuation diagrams, information on alarm signals, how to protect yourself, etc.

Numbers for emergency and special services vary, but are given at the front of all directories. The numbers below refer to Stockholm. Elsewhere, look up the words given in parentheses:

News *(nyheter)* — 07 10; weather *(fröken väder)* — 23 95 00; time *(fröken ur)* — 905 10; tourist information *(frida)* — 22 18 40.

Numbers for the operator (000) and emergencies (90 000) are the same everywhere. For directory enquiries, when calling from Stockholm, dial 901 40 for Stockholm and area; 901 60 for the rest of Scandinavia; 0019 for other countries.

Telegrams. Can be sent from telegraph offices (in Stockholm at Skeppsbron 2) or from a private telephone — dial 0020.

Newspaper. In summer, *Dagens Nyheter,* one of the leading Swedish newspapers, has an English section on the back page; the Friday edition gives a complete run-down of the week's events and entertainments in Stockholm. Stockholm also has a weekly (*This Week in Stockholm*), available from hotels and travel agencies. In Gothenburg, *Veckan i Göteborg* has a big English section.

Broadcasting. In summer, Swedish Radio broadcasts the news in English daily at 6 pm, on 92 MHz VHF.

Health and Hygiene

For general information on hygiene, first aid, medical treatment and insurance, see the introduction.

Reciprocal Agreement. On production of their passports, British travellers are entitled to free hospital treatment. Out-patient treatment and visits to doctors must be paid in full (fee 65kr), plus medicines at 75kr. British children qualify for free dental treatment; adults must pay half the normal charge.

Pharmacies. Keep normal shop hours. Any pharmacy (*apotek*) can give you the free book *Läkare och Tandläkare,* giving details of all medical and dental services available locally. Pharmacies keep a duty rota for nights and weekends — lists in any pharmacy window. In Stockholm the pharmacy C W Scheele (Klarabergsgatan 64, 111 12 Stockholm) is open 24 hours a day.

Emergencies. Apart from the chemist rota, 24-hour services in Stockholm include accident and casualty services at hospital polyclinics; anti-poison service (*Giftinformationscentralen*) — dial 33 12 31; nurses, or questions on medical care 44 92 00. Other 24-hour services throughout Sweden respond to the general emergency number; dial 90 000 and ask for *ambulans* (ambulance), *flygambulans* (air ambulance), *flygräddning* (air rescue), *sjöräddning* (sea rescue), *brandlarm* (fire), *läkare* (duty doctor) or *tandläkare* (dentist).

For general information, see the section on *Scandinavia,* above.

Police. The police headquarters in Stockholm is ag Agnegatan 33-37 (Tel: 769 30 00). They provide an information service on almost any subject. In emergencies, dial 90 000 and ask for *Polislarm.*

Nude Bathing. In keeping with the Swedish attitude towards censorship and naked bodies, nude bathing is tolerated and widely practised.

Driving Offences. The police can levy on-the-spot fines for speeding and other offences. Anyone with over 50mg alcohol per 100ml blood is breaking the law; the police make random spot checks. The penalty for drunken driving is imprisonment and loss of licence.

Drugs. Up to three years for possession; for importation or dealing, a minimum of three years and a maximum of ten.

Licensing Laws. Age limits are 20 for spirits, otherwise 18. Off sales are available only in the official *Systembolaget* stores. Spirits are not served or sold before noon.

Legal Aid. There is an official system, consisting of public lawyers, whom you pay according to your means. Look up *Allmänna Advokatbyråer* in the telephone directory.

For information on useful contacts and complaints procedures, see the introduction.

Embassies and Consulates.
British Embassy, Skarpögatan 8, 115 27 Stockholm (Tel: 67 01 40); plus Honorary Consuls in Malmö and Gävle.

American Embassy, Strandvägen 101, 115 27 Stockholm (Tel: 63 05 20).

Canadian Embassy, Tegelbacken, 4, 103 25 Stockholm (Tel: 23 79 20).

Lost Property. Daily storage charges are made on lost property, which is normally not kept more than three months. The term for lost property office is *Hittegodsexpedition.* The central office in Stockholm is at Tjärhovsgatan 21 (Tel:

769 30 75). They provide an information service on almost any subject. In emergencies, dial 90 000 and ask for *Polislarm* (free from call boxes).

Baby-sitting. Ask at local tourist offices. Baby care is very advanced — you can leave your child at the babysitting section of several large department stores, while you shop in peace. Or leave them at one of the supervised playgrounds at Humlegården or Vasaparken in Stockholm.

Information. The Swedish Tourist Board, Box 7473, 10392 Stockholm, shares the same accommodation (Hamngatan 27) and telephone number (789 2000) as the Stockholm Tourist Association (postal address: Box 7542, 103 93 Stockholm), and the Swedish Institute. The building is known as *Sverigehuset*. For tourist information phone "Miss Tourist" on (08) 22 18 40.

There is a nationwide network of tourist offices (*Turistbyråer*), marked by the international *i* sign (blue on white), for local information and room reservations. They also run a "Sweden at Home" scheme, if you want to meet Swedes in their own homes.

For information on cultural activities, contact *Kulturhuset*, Sergels Torg, Box 16414, 10327 Stockholm.

For a summary of the day's events, dial 22 18 40.

Free Maps. Free road maps of any quality are very hard to come by. Free town plans from local tourist offices. Note that the Stockholm public transport map, available at news kiosks, is not free.

Disabled Travellers. Town guides for the disabled are available from the local councils (social services or architects' departments) of Halmstad, Kristianstad, Linköping, Lund, Malmö, Norrköping, Örebro, Örnsköldsvik, Oxelösund, Skövde, Sollefteå, Tranåas and Trelleborg. The Swedish Tourist Board publishes a *Guide for Disabled Travellers to Sweden*. For more information and help in Stockholm, contact the *Socialförvaltingen*, Bondegatan 37-39, 116 33 Stockholm (Tel: 58 80 00).

Student Travel. *SFS-Resor,* Drottninggatan 89, 113 60 Stockholm (Tel: 34 01 80); also arrange summer accommodation in student hostels. STF, Drottninggatan 31, Bot 25, 101 20 Stockholm (Tel: 790 32 00).

Student Organisations. Stockholm Student Reception Service, Körsbärsvägen 2, 114 23 Stockholm, serves mainly students from overseas, dealing with all kinds of problems. Similar offices (open only in the summer) are at Götabergsgatan 17, Gothenburg (Tel: 031-81 29 06); and Sandgatan 2, Lund (Tel: 046-13 52 00).

English Language Church. Sts. Peter and Sigfrid (Anglican), Strandvägen 76, Stockholm (Tel: 61 22 23).

American Express. Sturegatan 8, 114 35 Stockholm (Tel: 23 83 00); Ostra Hamngatan 39, Gothenburg (Tel: 17 40 20).

Public Holidays

January 1 New Year's Day	January 6 Epiphany
Good Friday	Easter Monday
Ascension Day	Whit Monday
June 6 Flag Day	Midsummer's Day
November 1 All Saints	December 24-26 Christmas